# PILOT'S
# HANDBOOK
# of Aeronautical
# Knowledge

## FEDERAL AVIATION ADMINISTRATION

**Flight Standards Service**

ARCO PUBLISHING, INC.
219 Park Avenue South, New York, N.Y. 10003

# Foreword

The *Pilot's Handbook of Aeronautical Knowledge* contains essential, authoritative information used in training and guiding pilots. Applicants for pilot certification, flight instructors, and flying school staffs have often suggested that the Federal Aviation Administration issue this type of material under one cover. This handbook responds to those requests.

Also, this revised handbook tells the pilot for the first time how to use to his best advantage: (a) *Airman's Information Manual*, (b) data in FAA-approved Airplane Flight Manuals, and (c) basic instruments required for airplane attitude control.

Except for Federal Aviation Regulations pertinent to civil aviation, those subject areas in which an applicant for private pilot certification may be tested are covered in this handbook. Not all topics which appear herein are discussed in depth, however. The handbook is intended to assist the applicant for private certification as well as the applicant for advanced pilot certification and should be useful as a basic reference text to student pilots and instructors.

Comments regarding this publication should be directed to the Department of Transportation, Federal Aviation Administration, Flight Standards Technical Division, P. O. Box 25082, Oklahoma City, Oklahoma 73125.

Fourth Printing, 1980
Published by ARCO PUBLISHING, Inc.
219 Park Avenue South, New York, N.Y. 10003

ISBN 0-668-03479-3
Printed in the United States of America

# CONTENTS

## I. Principles of Flight

## II. Weather

## III. Navigation

## IV. Aircraft and Engine Operation

## V. Flight Instruments

## VI. Aircraft Performance

# SECTION I—PRINCIPLES OF FLIGHT

## 1.  Forces Acting on the Airplane

The airplane in straight-and-level unaccelerated flight is acted on by four forces—*lift*, the upward acting force; *weight*, or gravity, the downward acting force; *thrust*, the forward acting force; and *drag*, the backward acting, or retarding force of wind resistance. Lift opposes weight and thrust opposes drag (fig. 1). These four forces act on an airplane in any attitude of flight, but for the purposes of our discussions in this handbook we will deal *only with their relationships during straight and level unaccelerated flight*. Although these four forces are acting on the airplane in any attitude of flight, only their relationship during straight-and-level flight will be discussed. (Straight-and-level flight is coordinated flight at a constant altitude and heading.)

Drag and weight are forces inherent in anything lifted from the earth and moved through the air. Thrust and lift are artificially created

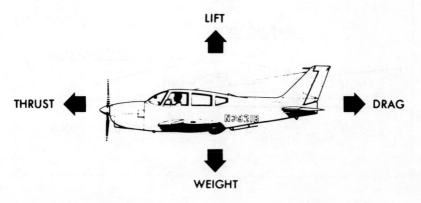

Figure 1. *Relationship of forces in flight.*

1

forces used to overcome the forces of nature and enable an airplane to fly. The engine-propeller combination is designed to produce thrust to overcome drag. The wing is designed to produce lift to overcome the weight (or gravity).

In straight-and-level, unaccelerated flight, lift equals weight and thrust equals drag, though lift and weight will not equal thrust and drag. Any inequality between lift and weight will result in the airplane entering a climb or descent. Any inequality between thrust and drag while maintaining straight-and-level flight will result in acceleration or deceleration until the two forces become balanced.

Before discussing these four forces further, let us examine some of the terms used extensively in this section.

*Airfoils*  An airfoil is a device which gets a useful reaction from air moving over its surface. In our discussion we will consider an airfoil a device which, when moved through the air, is capable of producing lift. Wings, horizontal tail surfaces, vertical tails surfaces, and propellers are all examples of airfoils.

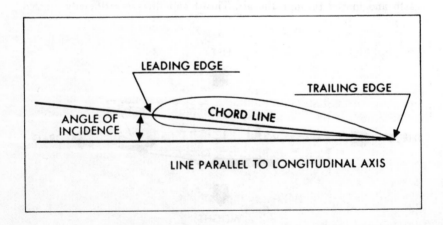

Figure 2. *Cross-sectional view of an airfoil.*

For convenience, we will use a cross-sectional view of a wing in our discussion. Generally the wing of the type of aircraft the private pilot will fly looks in cross-section like the one in figure 2. The forward part of an airfoil is rounded and is called the *leading edge*. The aft part is narrow and tapered and is called the *trailing edge*. A reference line often used in discussing airfoils is the *chord*, an imaginary straight line joining the extremities of the leading and trailing edges.

**Angle of Incidence**   The angle of incidence is the angle formed by the *longitudinal axis* of the airplane and the chord of the wing. The longitudinal axis is an imaginary line that extends lengthwise through the fuselage from nose to tail. The angle of incidence is measured by the angle at which the wing is attached to the fuselage. The angle of incidence is fixed —it normally cannot be changed by the pilot.

**Relative Wind**   The relative wind is the direction of the air flow with respect to the wing. If a wing is moving forward and downward, the relative wind moves backward and upward (fig. 3). If a wing is moving forward horizontally, the relative wind moves backward horizontally. If a wing is moving forward and upward, the relative wind moves backward and downward. Thus, the flight path and relative wind are parallel but travel in opposite directions.

Relative wind is created by the motion of the airplane through the air. It is also created by the motion of air past a stationary body. An airplane parked on the ramp with a mass of air (the wind) flowing over its surfaces is subject to relative wind.

Relative wind can likewise be created by a combination of the motions of the body and the air. An airplane on the takeoff roll is subject to the relative wind created by its motion along the ground and also by the moving mass of air (the wind). For this reason, takeoffs should be made into the wind.

It is important, however, to remember that during flight *only the motion of the airplane produces a relative wind—the direction and speed of the wind have no effect on the relative wind*. Wind direction and speed only affect the movement of the airplane over the ground. During flight, the actual flight path of the airplane determines the direction of the relative wind, the relative wind flowing parallel and opposite the flight path.

**Angle of Attack**   The angle of attack is the angle between the wing chord line and the direction of the relative wind (or between the chord

3

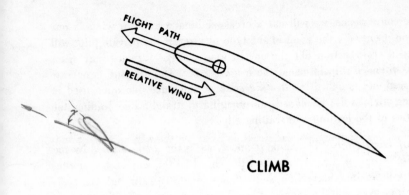

**CLIMB**

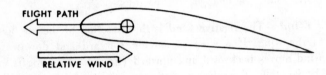

**LEVEL FLIGHT**

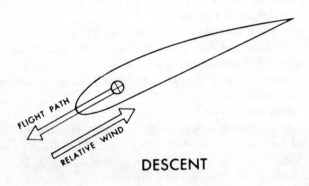

**DESCENT**

Figure 3. *Relationship between flight path and relative wind.*

line and the flight path) (fig. 4). The angle of attack should not be confused with the angle of incidence. The angle of incidence is determined when the airfoil is designed and is that specific angle of attack at which the ratio between lift and drag is the highest. For example, if the angle of incidence is 2°, the wing would be mounted on the fuselage so that the angle between the longitudinal axis of the airplane and the chord line of the airfoil is 2°.

Remember, the angle of incidence is fixed but the angle of attack may be changed by the pilot and is based on the flight path (fig. 5).

**Bernoulli's Principle** To understand how lift is produced, we must examine a phenomenon discovered many years ago by the scientist Bernoulli and later called Bernoulli's Principle: *The pressure of a fluid (liquid or gas) decreases at points where the speed of the fluid increases.* In other words, Bernoulli found that within the same fluid, in this case air, high speed flow is associated with low pressure, and low speed flow with high pressure. This principle was first used to explain changes in the pressure of fluid flowing within a pipe whose cross-sectional area varied. In the wide section of the gradually narrowing pipe, the fluid moves at low speed, producing high pressure. As the pipe narrows it must contain the same amount of fluid. In this narrow section, the fluid moves at high speed, producing low pressure. (See fig. 6.)

An important application of this phenomenon is made in giving lift to the wing of an airplane, an airfoil. The airfoil is designed to *increase the velocity of the airflow above* its surface, thereby *decreasing pressure above* the airfoil. Simultaneously, the impact of the air on the lower surface of the airfoil increases the pressure below. This combination of pressure decrease above and increase below produces lift. (See figs. 7 and 8.)

**Lift** Probably you have held your flattened hand out of the window of a moving automobile. As you inclined your hand to the wind, the force of air pushed against it forcing your hand to rise. The airfoil (in this case, your hand) was deflecting the wind which, in turn, created an equal and opposite dynamic pressure on the lower surface of the airfoil, forcing it up and back. The upward component of this force is lift; the backward component is drag (see fig. 9).

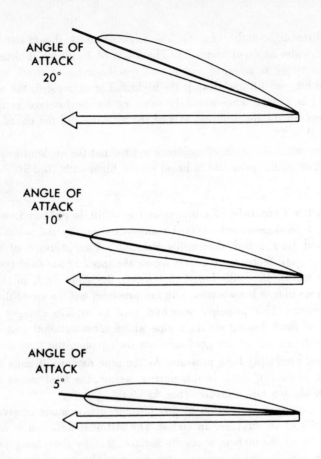

Figure 4. *The angle of attack is the angle between
the wing chord and the flight path.*

**Relationship Between Angle of Attack and Lift** As noted previously, the angle of attack is the acute angle formed by the relative wind and
the chord line of the wing. At a zero angle of attack, the pressure below
the wing would be equal to the atmospheric pressure. In this case, all of
the lift would be produced by the decrease in pressure (less than atmospheric pressure) along the upper surface of the wing. At small angles of
attack, the impact or positive pressure (above atmospheric pressure)
below the wing would be almost negligible, most of the lift still being
produced by the decreased pressure above the wing.

6

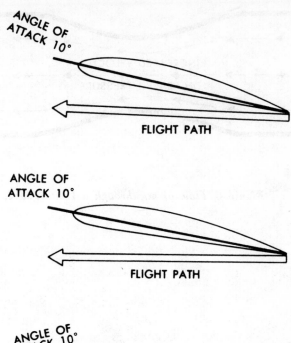

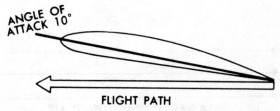

Figure 5. *The angle of attack is always based on the*
*flight path, not the ground.*

As the angle of attack is increased, the impact, or positive pressure
on the lower surface of the wing will increase. Also, the pressure above the
wing will continue to decrease (so long as the air continues to follow the
curvature of the wing) because the effective camber (curvature) of the
airfoil is increased, requiring the air to travel a greater distance in the
same period of time. According to Bernoulli's Principle, it must, therefore,
travel faster, producing a greater decrease in pressure. The combination of
inceasing positive pressure below the wing and decreasing negative pressure above the wing results in a greater pressure differential between the

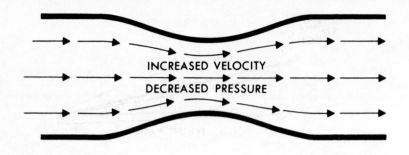

Figure 6. *Flow of air through a Venturi tube.*

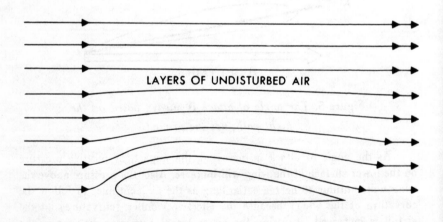

Figure 7. *Curvature of airfoil and layer of undisturbed air act as the constriction in a Venturi tube.*

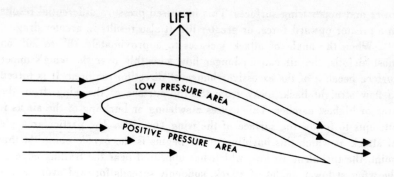

Figure 8. *Difference in pressure between upper and lower wing surfaces produces lift.*

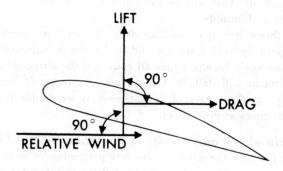

Figure 9. *Relationship between relative wind, lift, and drag.*

9

lower and upper wing surfaces. This increased pressure differential results in a greater upward force, or greater lift. It also results in greater drag.

When the angle of attack inceases to approximately 18° to 20° on most airfoils, the air can no longer flow smoothly over the wing's upper surface because of the excessive change of direction required. It is forced to flow straight back, away from the top surface of the wing, from the area of highest camber. This causes a swirling or burbling of the air as it attempts to follow the surface of the wing (fig. 10). The particular angle of attack at which this burbling of air begins is the *burble point*. At this point, the turbulent airflow, which has appeared near the trailing edge of the wing at lower angles of attack, suddenly spreads forward over the entire upper wing surface. This results in a sudden increase in pressure on the upper wing surface which, in turn causes a sudden and large loss of lift with a sudden increase in resistance (drag).

### Relationship of Thrust and Drag in Straight-and-Level Flight

During straight-and-level flight at a constant airspeed, thrust and drag are equal in magnitude. When the thrust output of the propeller is increased, thrust momentarily exceeds drag and the airspeed will increase (provided straight-and-level flight is maintained). However, the increase in airspeed will also cause an increase in drag. At some new and higher airspeed, thrust and drag forces again become equalized, and speed again becomes constant.

At some point, the thrust output will reach its maximum. The airspeed will increase accordingly until drag equals thrust, when a constant airspeed will prevail. This will be the top speed for that airplane in that configuration and attitude.

When thrust becomes less than drag, the airplane decelerates to a slower airspeed (provided straight-and-level flight is maintained), where the two forces again become equal. Of course, if the airspeed becomes too slow, the airplane will stall. With an increase in airspeed, drag increases very rapidly—as the square of the airspeed. If we double the airspeed, we have four times as much drag.

### Relationship of Lift and Gravity in Straight-and-Level Flight

Lift, the upward force on the wing, always acts perpendicular to the direction of the relative wind. In straight-and-level flight, lift counteracts the airplane weight. When lift is in equilibrium with weight, the airplane neither gains nor loses altitude. If lift becomes less than weight, the airplane will enter a descent; if lift becomes greater than weight, the airplane will

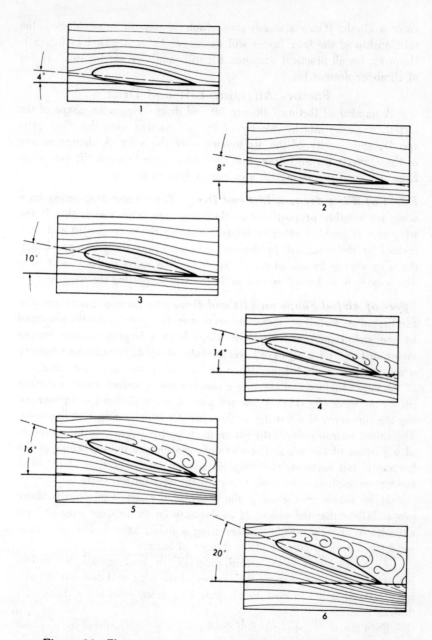

Figure 10. *Flow of air over a wing at various angles of attack.*

11

enter a climb. (Once a steady-state climb or descent is established, the relationship of the four forces will no longer be as depicted in figure 1. However, for all practical purposes, lift still equals weight for small angles of climb or descent.)

## Factors Affecting Lift and Drag

A number of factors influence lift and drag—wing area, shape of the airfoil, angle of attack, velocity of the air passing over the wing (airspeed), and density of the air moving over the wing. A change in any of these affects lift and drag, and the relationship between lift and drag. Each means of increasing lift also causes drag to increase.

*Effect of Wing Area on Lift and Drag*   The lift and drag acting on a wing are roughly proportional to the wing area. This means that if the wing area is doubled, other variables remaining the same, the lift and drag created by the wing will be doubled. The only way the pilot can change the wing area is by use of certain types of flaps, such as the Fowler flap, which extends backward as well as downward, increasing the wing area.

*Effect of Airfoil Shape on Lift and Drag*   As the upper curvature, or camber, of an airfoil is increased (up to a certain point), the lift produced by the airfoil increases. High-lift wings have a large curvature on the upper surface and a concave lower surface. Wing flaps cause an ordinary wing to approximate this condition by increasing the curvature (camber) of the upper surface and creating a concave lower surface, thus increasing lift on the wing (fig. 11). A lowered aileron accomplishes this by increasing the curvature of a portion of the wing. Of course, drag also increases. The raised aileron reduces the lift on the wing by decreasing the curvature of a portion of the wing. The elevators can change the curvature of the horizontal tail surfaces, changing the amount and direction of lift. The rudder accomplishes the same thing for the vertical tail surfaces.

If ice forms on the wing, the shape of the airfoil is altered. Many people believe that the weight of ice forming on an airplane wing at high altitudes or in cold weather makes icing a flying hazard. This increased weight is only a small part of the danger of icing.

As the ice forms on the airfoil, especially the leading edge, the airflow is disrupted. The ice changes the camber of the wing and destroys the airfoil shape, designed to give the airplane its greatest efficiency (highest lift to drag ratio).

Even the slightest coating of frost on a wing can prevent an airplane from taking off. The smooth flow of air over the surface of the airfoil is

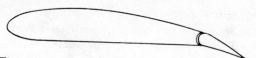

Figure 11. *Use of flaps increases lift and drag.*

disrupted and the lift capability of the wing is destroyed. This is why it is extremely important that *all frost, snow, and ice be removed from the airplane before takeoff.*

**Effect of Angle of Attack on Lift and Drag**   The effects of the angle of attack on lift have already been discussed. As the angle of attack is increased, both the lift and drag are increased, up to a certain point (fig. 12).

**Effect of Airspeed on Lift and Drag**   An increase in the velocity of the air passing over the wing (airspeed) increases lift and drag. Lift is increased because (1) the impact of the increased relative wind on the lower surface of the wing creates a higher or greater positive pressure; (2) the increased speed of the relative wind over the upper surface means

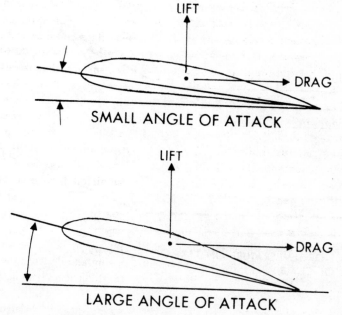

Figure 12. *Lift and drag increase with an increase in angle of attack.*

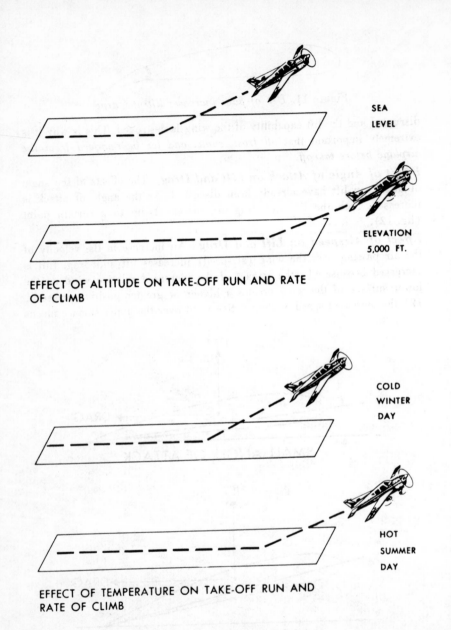

SEA
LEVEL

ELEVATION
5,000 FT.

**EFFECT OF ALTITUDE ON TAKE-OFF RUN AND RATE OF CLIMB**

COLD
WINTER
DAY

HOT
SUMMER
DAY

**EFFECT OF TEMPERATURE ON TAKE-OFF RUN AND RATE OF CLIMB**

Figure 13. *Effect of altitude, temperature,*

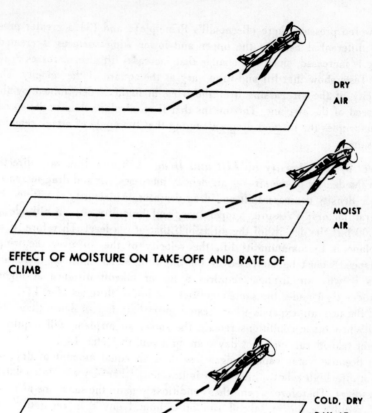

**EFFECT OF MOISTURE ON TAKE-OFF AND RATE OF CLIMB**

DRY AIR

MOIST AIR

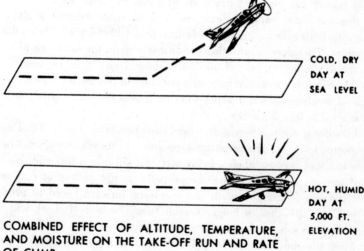

COLD, DRY DAY AT SEA LEVEL

HOT, HUMID DAY AT 5,000 FT. ELEVATION

**COMBINED EFFECT OF ALTITUDE, TEMPERATURE, AND MOISTURE ON THE TAKE-OFF RUN AND RATE OF CLIMB**

*and humidity on takeoff run and rate of climb.*

15

a lowered pressure there (Bernoulli's Principle); and (3) a greater pressure differential between the upper and lower wing surfaces is created. Drag is increased, since any change that increases lift also increases drag.

Tests show that lift and drag vary as the square of the velocity. The velocity of the air passing over the wing in flight is determined by the airspeed of the airplane. This means that if an airplane doubles its speed, it quadruples the lift and drag (assuming that the angle of attack remains the same).

**Effect of Air Density on Lift and Drag**  Lift and drag vary directly with the density of the air—as air density increases, lift and drag increase; as air density decreases, lift and drag decrease. Air density is affected by several factors: Pressure, temperature, and humidity. At an altitude of 18,000 feet the density of the air is half that at sea level. Therefore, if an airplane is to maintain its lift, the velocity of the air over the wings (airspeed) must be increased or the angle of attack must be increased. This is why an airplane requires a longer takeoff distance at higher altitudes than under the same conditions at lower altitudes (fig. 13).

Because air expands when heated, warm air is less dense than cool air. When other conditions remain the same, an airplane will require a longer takeoff run on a hot day than on a cool day (fig. 13).

Because water vapor weighs less than an equal amount of dry air, moist air (high relative humidity) is less dense than dry air (low relative humidity). Therefore, when other conditions remain the same, the airplane will require a longer takeoff run on a humid day than on a dry day (fig. 13). This is especially true on a hot, humid day because then the air can hold much more water vapor than on a cool day. The more moisture in the air, the less dense the air.

Less dense air also produces other losses beside the loss of lift. Engine horsepower falls off. The propeller loses some of its efficiency, because of power loss and because blades, being airfoils, will take a less effective bite out of the less dense air. Since the propeller is not pulling at maximum force, it takes longer to obtain the necessary forward speed to produce the required lift—thus, a longer takeoff run. The rate of climb will also be less for the same reasons.

From the above discussion, it is obvious that *a pilot should beware of high, hot, and humid conditions*—high altitudes, hot temperatures, and high moisture content (high relative humidity). A combination of these three conditions could be disastrous (fig. 13), especially when combined with a short runway or other takeoff-limiting conditions.

# 2. Function of the Controls

***Axes of an Airplane in Flight*** An airplane may turn about three axes. Whenever the attitude of the airplane changes in flight (with respect to the ground or other fixed object), it will rotate about one or more of these axes.

Think of these axes as imaginary axles around which the airplane turns like a wheel. The three axes intersect at the center of gravity and each one is perpendicular to the other two (fig. 14).

***Longitudinal Axis*** The imaginary line that extends lengthwise through the fuselage, from nose to tail, is the *longitudinal axis*. Motion about the

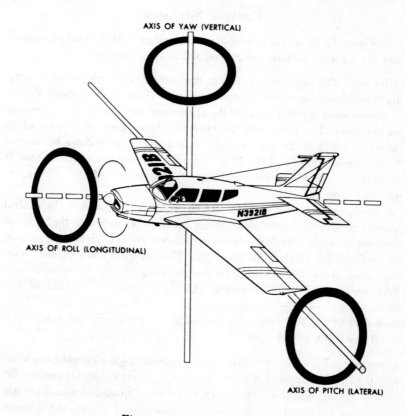

AXIS OF YAW (VERTICAL)

AXIS OF ROLL (LONGITUDINAL)

AXIS OF PITCH (LATERAL)

Figure 14. *Axes of rotation.*

longitudinal axis is *roll* and is produced by movement of the ailerons located at the trailing edges of the wings.

***Lateral Axis*** The imaginary line which extends crosswise, wing tip to wing tip, is the *lateral axis*. Motion about the lateral axis is *pitch* and is produced by movement of the elevators at the rear of the horizontal tail assembly.

***Vertical Axis*** The imaginary line which passes vertically through the center of gravity is the *vertical axis*. Motion about the vertical axis is *yaw* and is produced by movement of the rudder located at the rear of the vertical tail assembly.

## Control Surfaces

Figure 15 shows the conventional arrangement of the cockpit controls and the airplane surfaces which respond to these controls.

***Ailerons*** The two ailerons, one at the outer trailing edge of each wing, are movable surfaces that control movement about the longitudinal axis. The movement is *roll*. Lowering the aileron on one wing raises the aileron on the other. The wing with the lowered aileron goes up because of its increased lift, and the wing with the raised aileron goes down because of its decreased lift (fig. 16). Thus, the effect of moving either aileron is aided by the simultaneous and opposite movement of the aileron on the other wing.

Rods or cables connect the ailerons to each other and to the control wheel (or stick) in the cockpit. When pressure is applied to the right on the control wheel, the left aileron goes down and the right aileron goes up, rolling the airplane to the right. This happens because the down movement of the left aileron increases the wing camber (curvature) and thus increases the angle of attack. The right aileron moves upward and decreases the camber, resulting in a decreased angle of attack. Thus, decreased lift on the right wing and increased lift on the left wing cause a roll and bank to the right.

***Elevators*** The elevators control the movement of the airplane about its *lateral* axis. This motion is *pitch*. The elevators form the rear part of the horizontal tail assembly and are free to swing up and down. They are hinged to a fixed surface—the horizontal stabilizer. Together, the horizontal stabilizer and the elevators form a single airfoil. A change in position

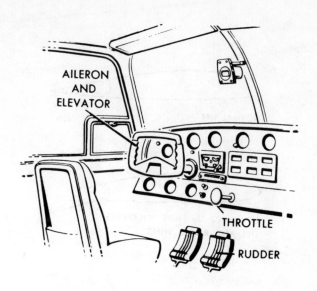

Figure 15. *Conventional arrangement of controls is shown above.*
*The airplane surfaces that respond to the controls are shown below.*

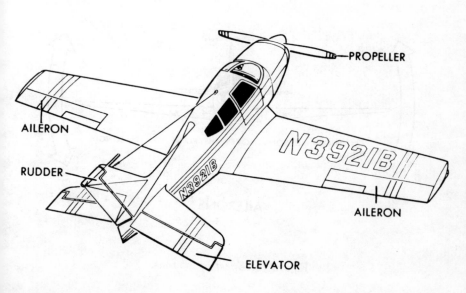

19

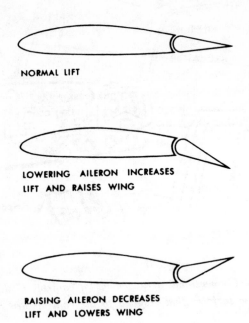

NORMAL LIFT

LOWERING AILERON INCREASES
LIFT AND RAISES WING

RAISING AILERON DECREASES
LIFT AND LOWERS WING

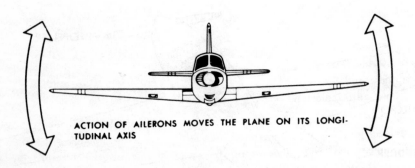

ACTION OF AILERONS MOVES THE PLANE ON ITS LONGI-
TUDINAL AXIS

## AILERONS

Figure 16. *Effect of ailerons.*

of the elevators modifies the camber of the airfoil, which increases or decreases lift.

Like the ailerons, the elevators are connected to the control wheel (or stick) by control cables. When forward pressure is applied on the wheel, the elevators move downward. This increases the lift produced by the horizontal tail surfaces. The increased lift forces the tail upward, causing the nose to drop (fig. 17). Conversely, when back pressure is applied on the wheel, the elevators move upward, decreasing the lift produced by the horizontal tail surfaces, or maybe even producing a downward force. The tail is forced downward and the nose up.

The elevators control the angle of attack of the wings. When back pressure is applied on the control wheel, the tail lowers and the nose raises, increasing the angle of attack. Conversely, when forward pressure is applied, the tail raises and the nose lowers, decreasing the angle of attack.

**Rudder** The rudder controls movement of the airplane about its vertical axis. This motion is *yaw*. Like the other primary control surfaces, the rudder is a movable surface hinged to a fixed surface which, in this case, is the vertical stabilizer, or fin. Its action is very much like that of the elevators, except that it swings in a different plane—from side to side instead of up and down (fig. 18). Control cables connect the rudder to the rudder pedals.

**Trim Tabs** A trim tab is a small, adjustable hinged surface on the trailing edge of the aileron, rudder, or elevator control surfaces. Trim tabs are laborsaving devices that enable the pilot to release manual pressure on the primary controls.

Some airplanes have trim tabs on all three control surfaces that are adjustable from the cockpit; others have them only on the elevator and rudder; and some have them only on the elevator. Some trim tabs are the ground-adjustable type only.

The tab is moved in the direction opposite that of the primary control surface, to relieve pressure on the control wheel or rudder control. For example, consider the situation in which we wish to adjust the elevator trim for level flight. ("Level flight" is the attitude of the airplane that will maintain a constant altitude.) Assume that back pressure is required on the control wheel to maintain level flight and that we wish to adjust the elevator trim tab to relieve this pressure. Since we are holding back pressure, the elevator will be in the "up" position (fig. 19). The trim tab must then be adjusted downward so that the airflow striking the tab will hold the elevators in the desired position. Conversely, if forward pressure is being held, the elevators will be in the down position, so the tab must be moved upward to relieve this pressure. In this example, we are talking about the tab itself and not the cockpit control.

Rudder and aileron trim tabs operate on the same principle as the elevator trim tab to relieve pressure on the rudder pedals and sideward pressure on the control wheel, respectively.

# 3. Loads and Load Factors

Airplane strength is measured basically by the total load the wings are capable of supporting without permanent damage. The load imposed upon the wings depends very largely upon the type of flight. The wings must support not only the weight of the airplane but also the additional loads imposed during maneuvers.

In straight-and-level flight the wings support a weight equal to the airplane and its contents. So long as the airplane is moving at a constant airspeed in a straight line, the load supported by the wings remains constant. When the airplane assumes a curved flight path—all types of turns, pullouts from dives, or when abrupt or excessive back pressure is used on the elevator control—the actual load supported by the wings will be much greater because of the centrifugal force produced by the curved flight. This additional load results in the development of much greater stresses in the wing structure.

**Load Factor**   The *load factor* is the ratio of the load supported by the wings of the airplane to the actual weight of the airplane and its contents, *i.e.*, it is the actual load supported by the wings at any given time, divided by the weight of the airplane and its contents.

At a load factor of 2, the wings support twice the weight of the airplane and its contents; at a load factor of 4, they support four times the weight of the airplane and its contents.

Each airplane has a maximum permissible load factor (limit load factor) which should not be exceeded. As a pilot, you should have the basic information necessary to fly your airplane safely within its structural limitations. Be familiar with the situations in which the load factor may approach maximum, and avoid them. If you meet such situations inadvertently—in dives and steep descending spirals—you need to know the right recovery technique.

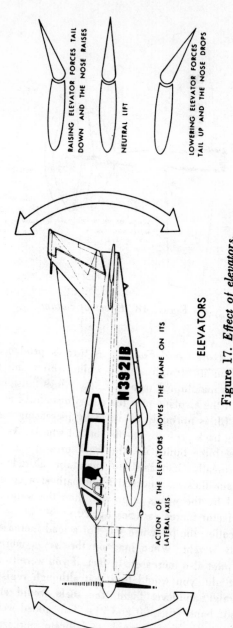

RAISING ELEVATOR FORCES TAIL DOWN AND THE NOSE RAISES

NEUTRAL LIFT

LOWERING ELEVATOR FORCES TAIL UP AND THE NOSE DROPS

ELEVATORS

ACTION OF THE ELEVATORS MOVES THE PLANE ON ITS LATERAL AXIS

Figure 17. *Effect of elevators.*

23

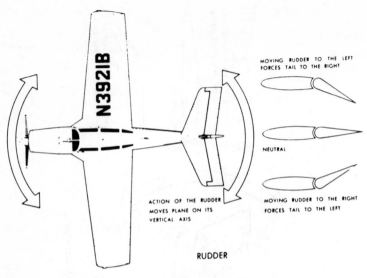

MOVING RUDDER TO THE LEFT
FORCES TAIL TO THE RIGHT

NEUTRAL

ACTION OF THE RUDDER
MOVES PLANE ON ITS
VERTICAL AXIS

MOVING RUDDER TO THE RIGHT
FORCES TAIL TO THE LEFT

RUDDER

Figure 18. *Effect of rudder.*

***Effect of Turn on Load Factor*** A turn is produced by lift pulling the airplane from its straight course while overcoming gravity. Thus, if altitude is to be maintained in a turn, the wings must produce lift equal to the weight of the airplane plus the centrifugal force caused by the turn. The increased lift is normally obtained by increasing the angle of attack (*i.e.*, increasing back pressure on the control wheel). As the bank steepens and centrifugal force builds up, this back pressure on the control wheel must be continually increased to maintain altitude. Therefore, any time the airplane flies in a curved flight path at a constant altitude, the load supported by the wings is greater than the weight of the airplane, thus the load factor increases. (See fig. 20.)

One indication the pilot will have of a load increase is the feeling of increased body weight. When load on the wings increase, the effective weight of the pilot also increases. In fact, if you were to sit on a bathroom scale during flight, you would find that although registering your exact weight in straight-and-level flight, the scale would show double your weight in a 60° bank (figs. 20 and 21). This added weight can be easily sensed and is a fairly reliable guide to indicate increases up to twice the

Elevators in the neutral position

Up position of the elevators is required to hold the

nose in the level flight attitude

Trim tab must be adjusted downward to hold ele-

vators in this position to relieve the pressure on the

control wheel

Figure 19. *Effect of trim tabs.*

normal load. As the load approaches three times normal, you will notice a sensation of blood draining from your head and a tendency of your cheeks to sag. A considerably greater increase in load may cause you to "grey out" or "black out," or temporarily lose your vision.

**Effect of Turbulance on Load Factor** One additional cause of large load factors is severe vertical gusts. These gusts cause a sudden increase in the angle of attack, resulting in large wing loads which are resisted by the inertia of the airplane. If you encounter severe turbulence, immediately slow the airspeed to the *maneuvering speed* (discussed in Chapter 19), since the airplane is built to withstand such disturbance at this speed.

**Effect of Speed on Load Factor** The amount of excess load that can be imposed on the wing depends on how fast the airplane is flying. At slow speeds, the available lifting force of the wing is only slightly greater than the amount necessary to support the weight of the airplane. Consequently, the load factor cannot become excessive even if the controls are moved abruptly or the airplane encounters severe gusts. The reason for this is that the airplane will stall before the load can become excessive. At high speeds, the lifting capacity of the wing is so great that a sudden movement of the controls or a strong gust may increase the load factor beyond safe limits. Because of this relationship between speed and safety, certain "maximum" speeds have been established. Each airplane is restricted in the speed at which it can safely execute maneuvers, withstand abrupt application of the controls, or fly in rough air. This speed is referred to as the maneuvering speed and will be considered in our discussion of the airspeed indicator (Chapter 19).

Summarizing, at speeds below maneuvering speed, the airplane will stall before the load factor can become excessive. At speeds above maneuvering speed, the limit load factor for which an airplane is stressed can be exceeded by abrupt or excessive application of the controls or by strong turbulence.

**Effect of Load Factor on Stall Speed** As load factor increases, stalling speed increases. We have already stated that load factor increases when an airplane follows a curved flight path—turns, pullouts from dives or sudden or excessive application of back pressure on the control wheel. Consequently, the stalling speed also increases in these same maneuvers.

Figure 22 shows that in a 60° bank, the stall speed increases by more than 40 percent. In a 75° bank, the load factor is approximately 4 and the stall speed is doubled (increased by 100 percent).

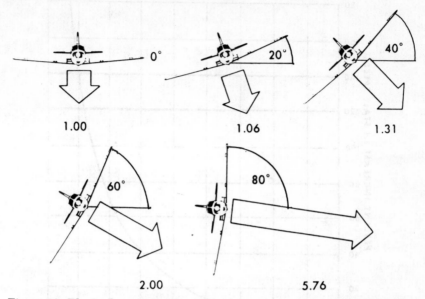

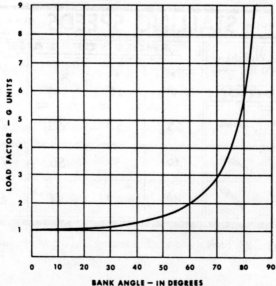

Figure 20. *The load supported by the wings increases as the angle of bank increases. The increase is shown by the relative lengths of the white arrows. Figures below the arrows indicate the increase in load factor. For example, the load factor during a 60-degree bank is 2.00 and the load supported by the wings is twice the weight of the plane in level flight.*

Figure 21. *Load factor chart.*

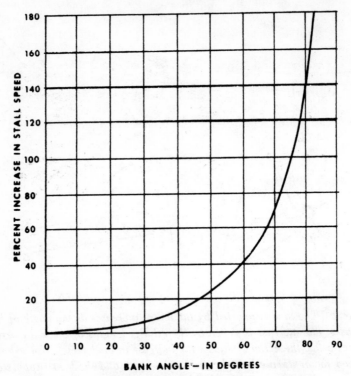

Figure 22. *Stall speed chart.*

| =Power Off= **STALLING SPEEDS** MPH = CAS | | | | |
|---|---|---|---|---|
| **ANGLE OF BANK** | | | | |
| Gross Weight 1600 lbs. CONDITION | 0° | 20° | 40° | 60° |
| Flaps UP | 55 | 57 | 63 | 78 |
| Flaps 20° | 49 | 51 | 56 | 70 |
| Flaps 40° | 48 | 49 | 54 | 67 |

Figure 23. *Stall speed vs. flap setting and angle of bank.*

The minimum limit load factor for normal category airplanes weighing less than 4,000 pounds is 3.8. This value is exceeded in a 75° bank. There are two reasons then why excessively steep banks should be avoided —the airplane will stall at a much higher airspeed and the limit load factor can be exceeded.

*Effect of Turns on Stall Speed*   As the angle of bank increases during a constant altitude turn, the stall speed increases. Actually, we have already stated this previously in relation to load factor but wish to re-emphasize it here because a pilot most likely can relate an increase in stall speed to an increase in angle of bank easier than he can relate the increase in stall speed to an increase in load factor. Why? Because he can *see* the increase in angle of bank but cannot see the increase in load factor.

Figure 23, which is an excerpt from an owners manual, shows graphically how the stall speed increases with increases in angle of bank in an airplane under various flap settings. When progressing from straight-and-level flight with flaps up, stalling speed increases from 55 m.p.h. to 78 m.p.h.; with flaps down 40°, stalling speed increases from 48 m.p.h. to 67 m.p.h. In each case, the stall speed increases approximately 40 percent. This rate of increase is predicted by the stall speed chart in figure 22.

You will note that the number of miles-per-hour increase in stall speed (fig. 23) is not the same for each 20° increase in bank. The amount of increase is greater for each successive 20° bank increase. For example, with flaps up, the stall speed increases 2 m.p.h. for the first 20° increase in bank; 6 m.p.h. for the second 20° increment; and 15 m.p.h. for the third 20° increment.

Between 60° and 80°, the increase would be approximately 54 m.p.h. These rates of increase are also predicted by the chart in figure 22 since the curve steepens more rapidly as the bank increases.

You will also note from figure 23 that the stall speed decreases as more flaps are used. From flaps up to the 40° down position, stall speed decreases 7 m.p.h., 8 m.p.h., 9 m.p.h., and 11 m.p.h., respectively, for banks 0°, 20°, 40°, and 60°.

From the interpretations we have just made relative to figure 23, you should realize the importance of relating the airspeed used in the traffic pattern (or during any low altitude maneuver) to the angle of bank and flap setting used. The steeper the bank and the less the flaps, the greater the airspeed should be. This is especially true in the turn to base leg and base leg turn to final approach, since the airspeed is generally reduced during this sequence of events. Follow the manufacturers recommendations on airspeeds to use.

# SECTION II — WEATHER

## 4. Weather Information for the Pilot

What does a pilot need to know about weather? Despite the development of many ingenious devices, improvements in aircraft design, powerplants, radio aids, and navigation techniques, safety in flight is still subject to conditions of limited visibility, turbulence, and icing.

To avoid hazardous flight conditions, pilots must have a fundamental knowledge of the atmosphere and weather behavior.

The uninitiated may wonder why the pilot needs more than the general information available to him from the predictions of the "weather man." The answer is well known to the experienced pilot. Meteorologist's predictions are based upon movements of large air masses and upon local conditions at specific points where weather stations are located. Air masses do not always perform as predicted, and weather stations are sometimes spaced rather widely apart; therefore, the pilot must understand weather conditions occurring between the stations as well as the conditions different from those indicated by weather reports.

Moreover, the meteorologist can only predict the weather conditions; the pilot must decide whether his particular flight may be hazardous, considering his type of aircraft and equipment, his own flying ability, experience, and physical limitations.

This section is necessarily brief. It is not intended for a meteorologist, but is designed to help the pilot by giving him a general background of weather knowledge plus the following basic information:

1. Aids provided by the National Weather Service and FAA to give the pilot weather information.
2. Sources of weather information available to the pilot.
3. Special knowledge the pilot needs in order to understand the weather terms commonly used.
4. Interpretation of weather maps, teletypewriter sequences, flying-weather forecasts, and other data.

5. Conditions of clouds, wind, and weather that are merely inconvenient, those that are dangerous, and those that the pilot can use to advantage.
6. Methods for avoiding dangerous conditions.
7. Significance of the cloud formations and precipitation the pilot encounters in flight, and safety procedures advisable.

Although no amount of information will take the place of actual experience, this discussion of weather characteristics will give the pilot practical suggestions for avoiding trouble while he is learning, and will provide a basis upon which he may build sound judgment as he gains experience.

**Aids to the Pilot**   Throughout the conterminous United States a network of some 520 airport weather stations determine and report current weather.

At most of these stations, trained personnel are on duty 24 hours a day, making observations and sending hourly reports to central points.

Because weather near the earth's surface often results from conditions at high altitudes, about 160 of the National Weather Service's stations release and track balloons every 6 hours to determine wind direction and speed at the upper levels. The National Weather Service also operates approximately 70 radiosonde stations. From each station a radio transmitting device attached to a balloon ascends every 12 hours to altitudes above 10 miles, providing a complete record of temperature, pressure, and humidity at the higher levels. Many of these stations also observe weather by specially designed weather radar.

Periodically, this material is collected by radio, telephone, and teletypewriter and plotted on weather maps. From these maps, meteorologists make their weather predictions.

Four times daily, the National Weather Service issues scheduled forecasts especially designed to indicate anticipated flying conditions. At other times as necessary, they amend these forecasts and issue warnings of especially hazardous flying weather. Scheduled forecasts are valid for 12 hours. *Area forecasts* are prepared for areas covering all 50 states. *Terminal forecasts* are prepared for more than 380 terminals in the conterminous 48 states and for many more in Alaska, Hawaii, and Puerto Rico.

This service is available to pilots at airports and weather stations, as well as by radio broadcast. In addition, trained meteorologists are on duty day and night at more than 200 air terminals to chart and analyze weather reports and discuss weather conditions with pilots.

You should visit the National Weather Service or FAA Flight Service Station (FSS) in person to obtain the weather information appropriate to your flight. However, as a further aid, you can get this preflight weather service by telephone. To take full advantage of the special service, use the following procedure when telephoning for weather information, because it will help the briefer serve you:

1. Identify yourself as a pilot. (Many callers want information for purposes other than flying.)
2. State your aircraft number, your intended route, destination, intended time of takeoff, and approximate time enroute.
3. Advise if you intend to fly only VFR.

A number of locations with high aviation activity have available a Pilots' Automatic Telephone Weather Answering Service (PATWAS). This service provides unlisted telephone numbers (*i.e.*, not in the local telephone directory) over which transcribed aviation weather information can be obtained. Forecasts are prepared by the National Weather Service; Flight Service Stations record the National Weather Service script along with other information for dissemination. There are also unlisted numbers that will reach weather briefing offices so that you can obtain information directly from a weather briefer and talk to a forecaster if necessary. These restricted numbers are listed in the *Airman's Information Manual* and should be used by any pilot wanting the latest weather information and forecasts.

Intelligent use of these aids, and a fundamental knowledge of weather characteristics, will enable the pilot to understand the present weather, be aware of changes likely to occur, and to plan and make a safe flight.

# 5. Nature of the Atmosphere

We live at the bottom of an ocean of air called the atmosphere. This ocean extends upward from the earth's surface for a great many miles, gradually thinning as it nears the top. The exact upper limit has never been determined. Near the earth's surface, the air is relatively warm from contact with the earth. (The temperature in the United States averages about 59° F. the year round.) As altitude increases, the temperature decreases by about 3.5° F. for every 1,000 ft. (normal lapse rate) until air temperature reaches about 67° F. below zero at 7 miles above the earth.

For flight purposes, the atmosphere is divided into two layers: the upper layer, where temperature remains practically constant, is the "stratosphere"; the lower layer, where the temperature changes, is the "troposphere" (see fig. 24). Although jets may routinely fly in the stratosphere, the private pilot usually has no occasion to go that high; his interest centers in the lower layer—the troposphere. It is this region that all weather occurs and practically all our flying is done. The top of the troposphere lies 5 to 10 miles above the earth's surface.

Obviously a body of air as deep as the atmosphere has tremendous weight. It is hard to realize that the normal sea-level pressure upon our bodies is about 15 pounds per square inch, or a total of 20 tons upon the average man. The reason we do not collapse is that this pressure is equalized by an equal pressure within the body. In fact, if the pressure were suddenly released, the human body would explode like a toy balloon. As we fly upward in the atmosphere, we not only become colder (it is usually freezing above 18,000 ft.) but we also find that the air is thinner. At first, pressure is rapidly reduced and at 18,000 ft. is only half as great as at sea level.

**Oxygen and the Human Body** The atmosphere is composed of gases —about four-fifths nitrogen and one-fifth oxygen, with approximately 1 percent of various other gases mixed in. Oxygen is essential to human life. At 18,000 ft, with only half the normal atmospheric pressure, we would be breathing only half the normal amount of oxygen. Our reactions would be definitely below normal, and many of us would become unconscious. In fact, the average person's reactions become affected at 10,000 ft.

To overcome these unfavorable conditions at high altitudes, pilots who fly in this upper atmosphere use oxygen-breathing equipment and wear heavy clothes, often electrically heated; or they fly in sealed cabins in which temperature, pressure, and oxygen content of the air can be maintained within proper range.

# 6. Significance of Atmospheric Pressure

In Chapter 5 we mentioned that the average pressure exerted by the atmosphere is approximately 15 pounds per square inch at sea level.

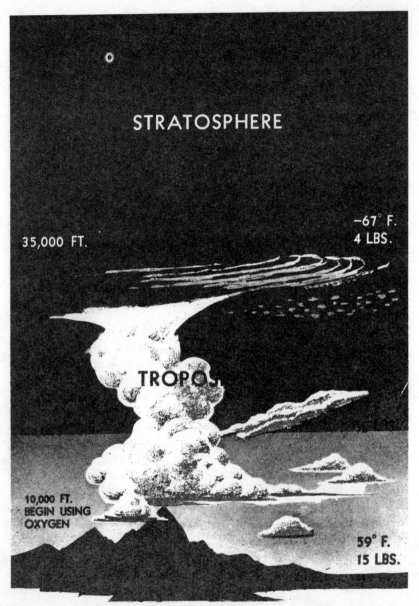

STRATOSPHERE

35,000 FT.

−67° F.
4 LBS.

TROPO...

10,000 FT.
BEGIN USING
OXYGEN

59° F.
15 LBS.

Figure 24. *The troposphere and stratosphere are the realm of flight.*

This means that a column of air 1 inch square extending from sea level to the top of the atmosphere would weigh about 15 pounds. The actual pressure at a given place and time, however, depends upon several factors—altitude, temperature, and density of the air column. These conditions very definitely affect flight.

**Measurement of Atmospheric Pressure**   How is pressure measured, recorded, and reported by the National Weather Service? A barometer is generally used which measures the height of a column of mercury in a glass tube, sealed at one end and calibrated in inches. An increase in pressure forces the mercury higher in the tube; a decrease allows some of the mercury to drain out, reducing the height of the column. In this way, changes of pressure are registered in terms of inches of mercury. The standard sea-level pressure expressed in these terms is 29.92 inches at a standard temperature of 59° F.

The mercurial barometer is cumbersome to move and difficult to read. A more compact, more easily read, and more mobile barometer is the aneroid; although it is not as accurate as the mercurial. The aneroid barometer is a partially-evacuated cell sensitive to pressure changes. The cell is linked to an indicator which moves across a scale graduated in pressure units.

If all weather stations were at sea level, the barometer readings would give a correct record of the distribution of atmospheric pressure at a common level. To achieve this result, each station translates its barometer reading into terms of sea-level pressure A difference of 1,000 ft. of elevation makes a difference of about 1 inch in the barometer reading. Thus, if a station located 5,000 ft. above sea level found the mercury to be 25 inches high in the barometer tube, it would translate and report this reading as 30 inches (fig. 25). Actually, the reduction of pressure to sea level is not so simple, but in this way a uniform measurement can be established which will show only the variations in pressure caused by conditions other than altitude.

Since the rate of decrease in atmospheric pressure is fairly constant in the lower layers of the atmosphere, the approximate altitude can be determined by finding the difference between pressure at sea level and pressure at the given altitude. In fact, the aircraft altimeter is an aneroid barometer with its scale in units of altitude instead of pressure.

**Effect of Altitude on Atmospheric Pressure**   You have probably concluded that atmospheric pressure decreases as altitude increases. This

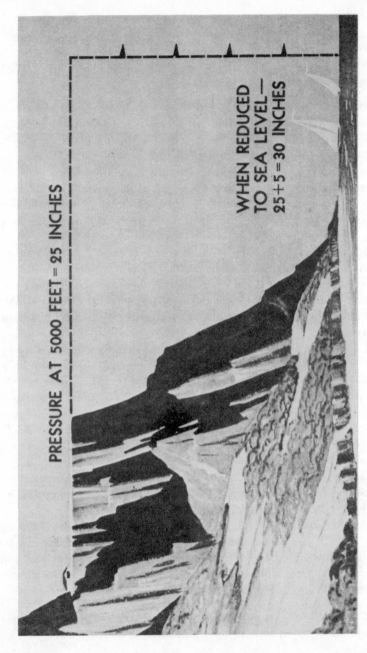

PRESSURE AT 5000 FEET = 25 INCHES

WHEN REDUCED TO SEA LEVEL— 25 + 5 = 30 INCHES

Figure 25. *Barometric pressure at a weather station is expressed as pressure at sea level.*

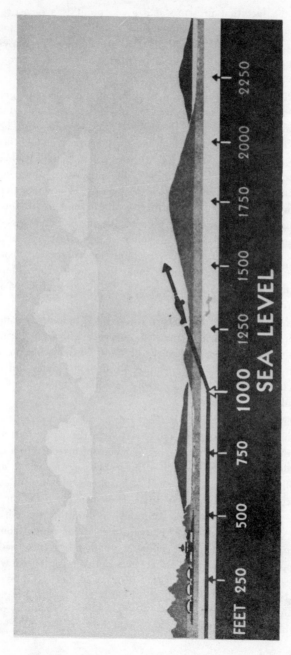

Figure 26. *Atmospheric density at sea level enables a plane to take off in a relatively short distance.*

follows from the fact that pressure at a given point is a measure of the weight of the column of air above that point. As altitude increases, pressure diminishes as the weight of the air column decreases. This decrease in pressure (increase in density altitude) has a pronounced effect on flight.

***Effect of Altitude on Flight*** For ordinary flights, the most noticeable effect of a decrease in pressure (increase in density altitude) due to an altitude increase becomes evident in takeoffs, rates of climb, and landings. An airplane that requires a 1,000-foot run for takeoff at a sea-level airport will require a run almost twice as long to take off at Denver, Colo., which is approximately 5,000 ft. above sea level. The purpose of the takeoff run is to gain enough speed to get lift from the passage of air over the wings. If the air is thin, more speed is required to obtain enough lift for takeoff —hence, a longer ground run. It is also true that the engine is less efficient in thin air, and the thrust of the propeller is less effective. The rate of climb, too, is much slower at Denver, requiring a greater distance to gain the altitude to clear any obstructions. In landing, the difference is not so noticeable except that the plane has greater ground speed when it touches the ground (figs. 26 and 27).

***Effect of Differences in Density*** Differences in density caused by changes in temperature cause changes in pressure which, in turn, create motion in the atmosphere, both vertically and horizontally, producing winds and, in conjunction with moisture, producing clouds and precipitation—in fact, all the phenomena called "weather." These items will be taken up in subsequent chapters.

***Pressure Recorded in "Millibars"*** The mercury barometer reading at the individual weather stations is converted to the equivalent sea-level pressure and then translated from terms of inches of mercury to a measure of pressure called millibars. One inch of mercury is equivalent to approximately 34 millibars; hence, the normal atmospheric pressure at sea level (29.92), expressed in millibars, is 1,013.2 or roughly 1,000 millibars. For economy of space, the entry is shortened by omitting the initial 9 or 10 and the decimal point. The usual pressure readings range from 950.0 to 1,040.0. On the hourly weather report, a number beginning with 5 or higher presupposes an initial "9," whereas a number beginning with a 4 or lower presupposes an initial "10." For example: 653 = 965.3; 346 = 1034.6; 999 = 999.9; 001 = 1,000.1, etc. In fig. 54, you will note the fourth element in the aviation weather report is sea-level pressure coded 132; this is decoded 1013.2 millibars.

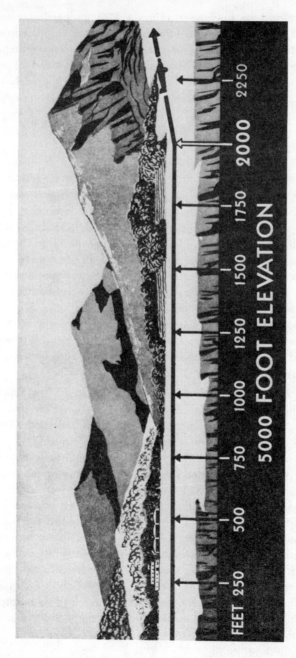

Figure 27. The distance required for take-off increases with the altitude of the field.

Individually these pressure readings are of no particular value to the pilot; but when pressures at different stations are compared or when pressures at the same station show changes in successive readings, it is possible to determine many symptoms indicating the trend of weather conditions. In general, a marked fall indicates the approach of bad weather and a marked rise indicates a clearing of the weather.

# 7. Wind

The pressure and temperature changes discussed in the previous chapter produce two kinds of motion in the atmosphere—vertical movement of ascending and descending currents, and horizontal flow known as "wind." Both of these motions are of primary interest to the pilot because they affect the flight of aircraft in takeoff, landing, climbing, speed, and direction; they also bring about changes in weather, which may make the difference between a safe flight or disastrous one.

Conditions of wind and weather occurring at any specific place and time are the result of the general circulation in the atmosphere, which will be discussed briefly in the following pages.

The atmosphere tends to maintain an equal pressure over the entire earth, just as the ocean tends to maintain a constant level. Whenever the equilibrium is disturbed, air begins to flow from areas of higher pressure to areas of lower pressure.

***The Cause of Atmospheric Circulation*** The factor that upsets the normal equilibrium is the uneven heating of the earth. At the equator, the earth receives more heat than in areas to the north and south. This heat is transferred to the atmosphere, warming the air and causing it to expand and become less dense. Colder air to the north and south, being more dense, moves toward the equator forcing the less dense air upward. This air in turn becomes warmer and less dense and is forced upward, thus establishing a constant circulation that might consist of two circular paths; the air rising at the equator, traveling aloft toward the poles, and returning along the earth's surface to the equator, as shown in figure 28.

This theoretical pattern, however, is greatly modified by many forces, a very important one being the rotation of the earth. In the Northern Hemisphere, this rotation causes air to flow to the right of its normal path. In the Southern Hemisphere, air flows to the left of its normal path. For simplicity we shall confine our discussion to the motion of air in the Northern Hemisphere (fig. 29).

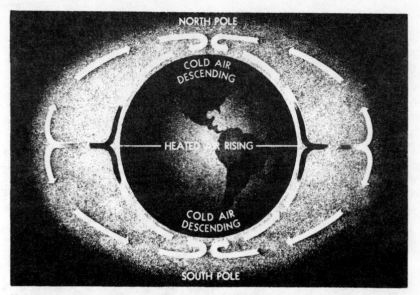

Figure 28. *Heat at the equator would cause the air to circulate uniformly, as shown, if the earth did not rotate.*

As the air rises and moves northward from the equator, it is deflected toward the east, and by the time it has traveled about a third of the distance to the pole, it is no longer moving northward, but eastward. This causes the air to accumulate in a belt at about latitude 30°, creating an area of high pressure. Some of this air is then forced down to the earth's surface, where part flows southwestward, returning to the equator, and part flows northeastward along the surface.

A portion of the air aloft continues its journey northward, being cooled en route, and finally settles down near the pole, where it begins a return trip toward the equator. Before it has progressed very far southward, it comes into conflict with the warmer surface air flowing northward from latitude 30°. The warmer air moves up over a wedge of the colder air, and continues northward, producing an accumulation of air in the upper latitudes.

Further complications in the general circulation of the air are brought about by the irregular distribution of oceans and continents, the relative effectiveness of different surfaces in transferring heat to the atmosphere, the daily variation in temperature, the seasonal changes, and many other factors.

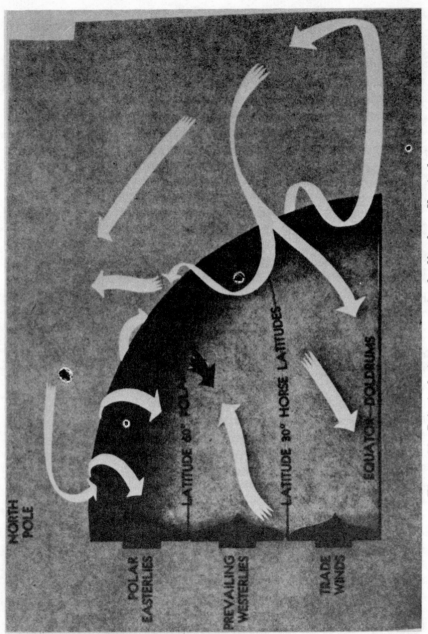

NORTH POLE

POLAR EASTERLIES

LATITUDE 60° POLA

PREVAILING WESTERLIES

LATITUDE 30° HORSE LATITUDES

TRADE WINDS

EQUATOR DOLDRUMS

Figure 29. *Principal air currents in the Northern Hemisphere.*

42

Regions of low pressure, called "lows," develop where air lies over land or water surfaces that are warmer than the surrounding areas. In India, for example, a low forms over the hot land during the summer months, but moves out over the warmer ocean when the land cools in winter. Lows of this type are semipermanent, however, and are less significant to the pilot than the "migratory cyclones" or "cyclonic depressions" that form when unlike air masses meet. These lows will be discussed in detail under "occlusions" in Chapter 10.

*Wind Patterns*   At present, we are concerned with the wind patterns associated with areas of high and low pressure. In the Northern Hemisphere, wind is deflected to the right of its course. Air moving outward from a "high" flows in a clockwise spiral, and air moving toward a "low" flows in a counterclockwise spiral. A knowledge of these patterns frequently enables a pilot to plan his course to take advantage of favorable winds, particularly during long flights. In flying from east to west, for example, he would find favorable winds to the south of a high, or to the north of a low (figs. 30 and 31).

We have now discussed the theory of general circulation in the atmosphere, and the wind patterns formed within areas of high pressure and low pressure. These concepts account for the large-scale movements of the wind, but do not take into consideration the effects of local conditions that frequently cause drastic modifications in wind direction and speed close to the earth's surface.

*Convection Currents*   Certain kinds of surfaces are more effective than others in heating the air directly above them. Plowed ground, sand, rocks, and barren land give off a great deal of heat, whereas water and vegetation tend to absorb and retain heat. The uneven heating of the air causes small local circulations called "convection currents," which are similar to the general circulation just described.

This is particularly noticeable over land adjacent to a body of water. During the day, air over land becomes heated and less dense; colder air over water moves in to replace it forcing the warm air aloft and causing an on-shore wind. At night the land cools, and the water is relatively warmer. The cool air over the land, being heavier, then moves toward the water as an off-shore wind, lifting the warmer air and reversing the circulation (figs. 32 and 33).

Convection currents cause the bumpiness experienced by pilots flying at low altitudes in warmer weather. On a low flight over varying surfaces,

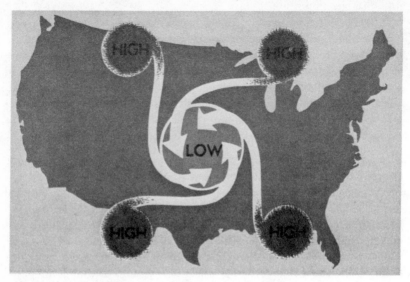

Figure 30. *Circulation of wind within a "low."*

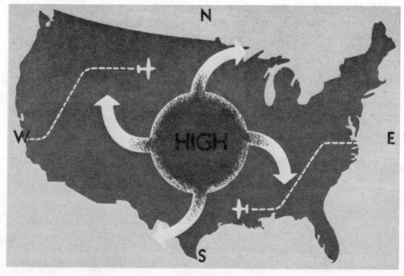

Figure 31. *Use of favorable winds in flight.*

44

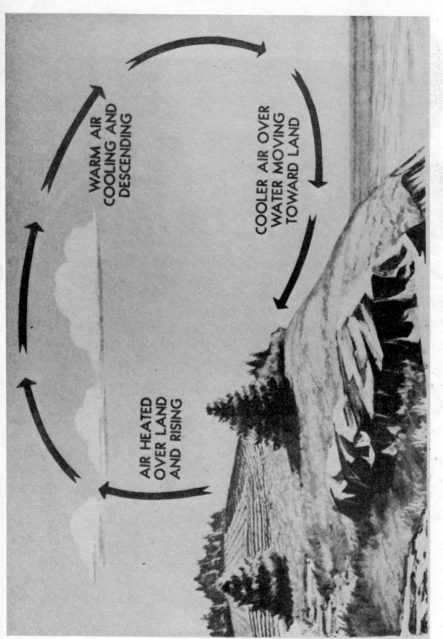

WARM AIR COOLING AND DESCENDING

COOLER AIR OVER WATER MOVING TOWARD LAND

AIR HEATED OVER LAND AND RISING

Figure 32. *Convection currents form on-shore winds in daytime.*

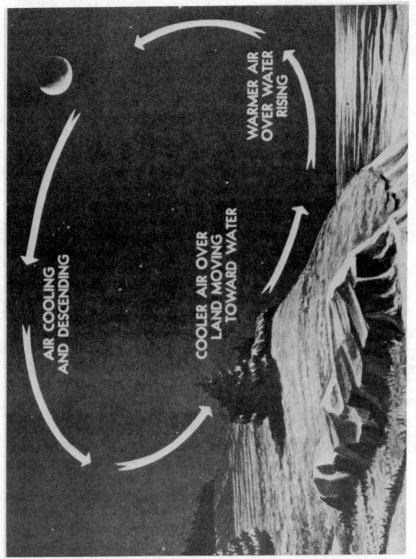

AIR COOLING
AND DESCENDING

COOLER AIR OVER
LAND MOVING
TOWARD WATER

WARMER AIR
OVER WATER
RISING

Figure 33. *Convection currents form off-shore winds at night.*

the pilot will encounter updrafts over pavement or barren places and downdrafts over vegetation or water. Ordinarily, this can be avoided by flight at higher altitudes. When the larger convection currents form cumulus clouds, the pilot will invariably find smooth air above the cloud level (fig. 34).

Convection currents also cause difficulty in making landings, since they affect the rate of descent. For example, a pilot making a constant glide frequently tends to land short of or overshoot his spot, depending upon the presence and severity of convection currents (figs. 35 and 36).

These effects of local convection, however, are less dangerous than the turbulence caused when wind is forced to flow around or over obstructions. The only way for the pilot to avoid this invisible hazard is to be forewarned, and to know where to expect unusual conditions.

**Effect of Obstructions on Wind** When the wind flows around an obstruction, it breaks into eddies—gusts with sudden changes in speed and direction—which may be carried along some distance from the obstruction. A pilot flying through such turbulence should anticipate the bumpy and unsteady flight that may be encountered. This turbulence—the intensity of which depends, of course, upon the size of the obstacle and the velocity of the wind—can present a serious hazard during takeoffs and landings. For example, during landings it can cause a pilot to "drop in"; during takeoffs it could cause the aircraft to fail to gain enough altitude to clear low objects in its path. Any landings or takeoffs attempted under gusty conditions should be made at higher speeds, to maintain adequate control during such conditions (fig. 37).

This same condition is more noticeable where larger obstructions such as bluffs or mountains are involved. As shown in figure 38, the wind blowing up the slope on the windward side is relatively smooth and its upward current helps to carry the aircraft over the peak. The wind on the leeward side, following the terrain contour, flows definitely downward with considerable turbulence and tends to force the aircraft into the mountain side. The stronger the wind, the greater the downward pressure and the accompanying turbulence. Consequently, in approaching a hill or mountain from the leeward side, a pilot should gain enough altitude well in advance. *Because of these downdrafts, it is recommended that mountain ridges and peaks be cleared by at least 2,000 ft.* If there is any doubt about having adequate clearance, the pilot should turn away at once and gain more altitude. Between hills or mountains, where there is

47

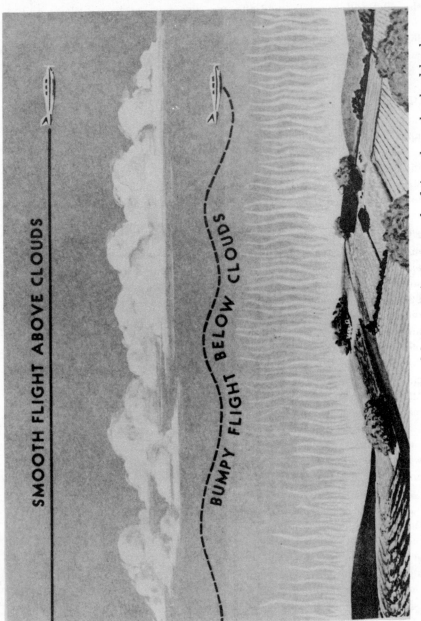

Figure 34. *Avoiding turbulence caused by convection currents by flying above the cloud level.*

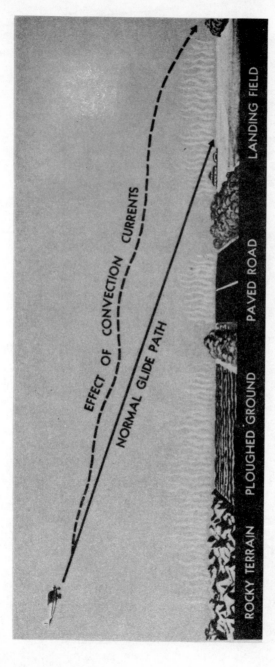

Figure 35. *Varying surfaces affect the normal glide path. Some surfaces create rising currents which tend to make the pilot overshoot the field.*

49

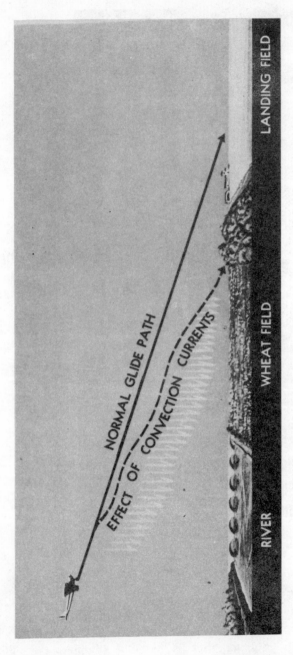

Figure 36. *Descending currents prevail above some surfaces and tend to make the pilot land short of the field.*

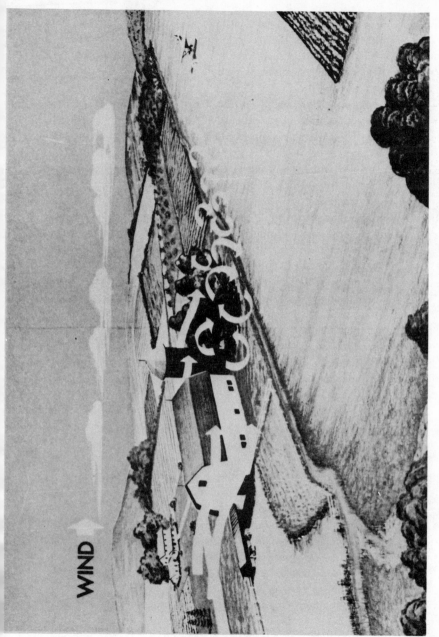

WIND

Figure 37. Turbulence caused by obstructions to normal flow of air.

51

a canyon or narrow valley, the wind will generally veer from its normal course and flow through the passage with increased velocity and turbulence. A pilot flying over such terrain needs to be alert for wind shifts, and particularly cautious if he is making a landing.

***Wind Representation on Weather Map*** The excerpted portion of a surface weather map (fig. 39) provides information about winds at the surface. The wind direction at each station is shown by an arrow. The arrowhead is represented by the station circle and points in the direction toward which the wind is blowing. Winds are given the name of the direction *from which* they blow; a northwest wind is a wind blowing *from* the northwest.

Wind speed is shown by "feathers" or "pennants" placed on the end of the arrow. The speed is indicated by the number of half feathers, full feathers, or pennants. Each half feather represents approximately 5 knots, each full feather indicates approximately 10 knots, and each flag 50 knots. Thus 2½ feathers indicates a wind speed of approximately 25 knots; a flag and 2½ feathers indicates a wind speed of approximately 75 knots, etc. The pilot can thus tell at a glance the wind conditions prevailing at maptime at any weather station.

Observations of the winds at upper levels are made every 6 hours at about 160 stations. Pilots can obtain this information and forecasts of expected winds through all weather reporting stations.

***Isobars*** The pressure at each station is recorded on the weather map, and lines, *isobars*, are drawn to connect points of equal pressure. Many of the lines make complete circles to surround areas marked H (high) or L (low).

Isobars are quite similar to the contour lines appearing on aeronautical charts. However, instead of indicating altitude of terrain and steepness of slopes, isobars indicate the amount of pressure and steepness of pressure gradients. If the gradient (slope) is steep, the isobars will be close together, and the wind will be strong. If the gradient is gradual, the isobars will be far apart, and the wind gentle (fig. 40).

Isobars furnish valuable information about winds in the first few thousand feet above the surface. Close to the earth, wind direction is modified by the contours over which it passes, and wind speed is reduced by friction with the surface. At levels two or three thousand feet above the surface, however, the speed is greater and the direction is usually

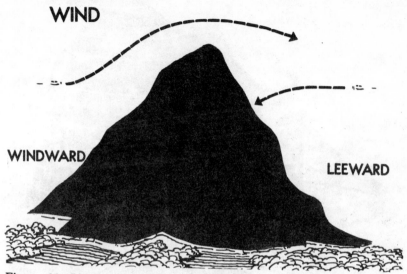

WIND

WINDWARD

LEEWARD

Figure 38. *Planes approaching hills or mountains from windward are helped by rising currents. Those approaching from leeward encounter descending currents.*

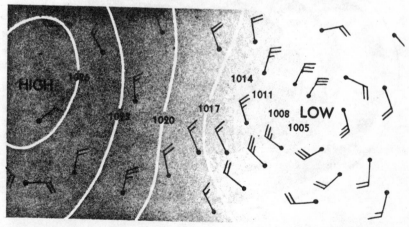

HIGH   1026

1023   1020

1017   1014

1011

1008   LOW
1005

Figure 39. *Speed and direction of wind are shown on weather map by wind arrows and isobars.*

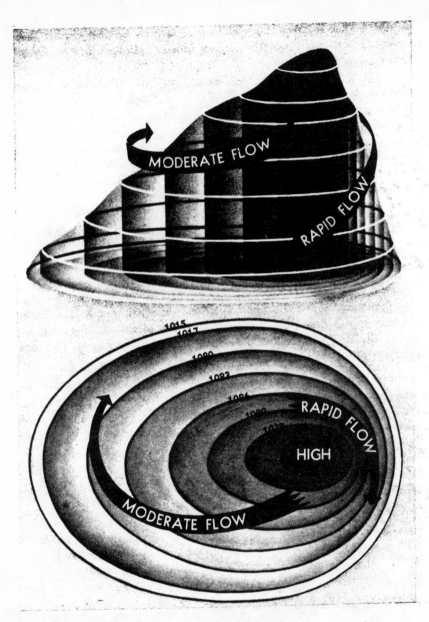

Figure 40. *Above: Flow of air around a "high." Below: Isobars on a weather map indicate various degrees of pressure within a high.*

parallel to the isobars. Thus, while wind arrows on the weather map excerpt indicate wind near the surface, isobars indicate winds at slightly higher levels (fig. 39).

In the absence of specific information on upper wind conditions, the pilot can often make a fairly reasonable estimate of the wind conditions in the lower few thousand feet on the basis of the observed surface wind. He generally will find that the wind at an altitude of 2,000 ft. above the surface will veer about 20° — 40° to the right and almost double in speed. The veering will be greatest over rough terrain and least over flat surfaces. Thus, a north wind of 20 knots at the airport would be likely to change to a northeast wind of 40 knots at 2,000 ft.

# 8. Moisture and Temperature

The atmosphere always contains a certain amount of foreign matter —smoke, dust, salt particles, and particularly moisture in the form of invisible water vapor. The amount of moisture that can be present in the atmosphere depends upon the temperature of the air. For each increase of 20° F. the capacity is about doubled; conversely, for each decrease of 20° F. the capacity becomes only half as much.

**Relative Humidity** We often speak of "the humidity," by which we mean the apparent dampness in the air. A similar term used by the National Weather Service is *relative humidity*, a ratio of the amount of moisture present in any given volume of air to the amount of moisture possible in that volume of air at prevailing temperature and pressure. For instance, "75 percent relative humidity", means that the air contains three-fourths of the water vapor which it is capable of holding at the existing temperature and pressure.

**Temperature-Dew Point Relationship** For the pilot, the relationship discussed under relative humidity is expressed in a slightly different way— as "temperature and dew point." It is apparent from the foregoing discussion that if a mass of air at 80° F. has a relative humidity of 50 percent and the temperature is reduced 20°, to 60° F., the air will then be saturated (100 percent relative humidity). In this case, the original relationship will be stated as "temperature 80—dew point 60." In other words, dew point is the temperature to which air must be cooled to become saturated.

Dew point is of tremendous significance to the pilot because it represents a critical condition of the air. When temperature reaches the dew point, water vapor can no longer remain invisible, but is forced to condense, becoming visible on the ground as dew or frost, appearing in the air as fog or clouds, or falling to the earth as rain, snow, or hail. (NOTE: *This is how water can get into the fuel tanks when the tanks are left partially filled overnight.* The temperature cools to the dew point and the water vapor contained in the fuel tank air space condenses. This condensed moisture then sinks to the bottom of the fuel tank, since water is heavier than gasoline. This topic will be discussed in more detail later in this handbook.)

***Methods by Which Air Reaches the Saturation Point*** It is interesting to note the various ways by which air can reach the saturation point. We have already shown how this is brought about by a lowering of temperature such as might occur under the following conditions: when warm air moves over a cold surface; when cold air mixes with warm air; when air is cooled during the night by contact with the cold ground; or when air is forced upward. Only the fourth method needs any special comment.

When air rises, it uses heat energy in expanding. Consequently, the rising air loses heat rapidly. If the air is unsaturated, the loss will be approximately 5.5° F. for every 1,000 ft. of altitude.

Warm air can be lifted aloft by three methods; by becoming heated through contact with the earth's surface (convection currents discussed in Chap. 7); by moving up a sloping terrain (as wind blowing up a mountainside); and by being forced to flow over another body of air (when air masses of different temperatures and densities meet). Under the last condition, the warmer, lighter air tends to flow over the cooler, denser air. This will be discussed in "Fronts," Chapter 10.

Air can also become saturated if it is subjected to precipitation.

Whatever the cause, the pilot knows that when temperature and dew point at the ground are close together, he must be alert for low clouds and fog. Temperature and dew point are reported in degrees Fahrenheit and are shown as the fifth element in the aviation weather report, fig. 54. (Note: The chart in figure 41 may be used to convert degrees Fahrenheit to degrees Centigrade, and vice vesa. The example 0° C. equals 32° F.)

***Effect of Temperature on Air Density*** Atmospheric pressure not only varies with altitude it also varies with temperature. When air is

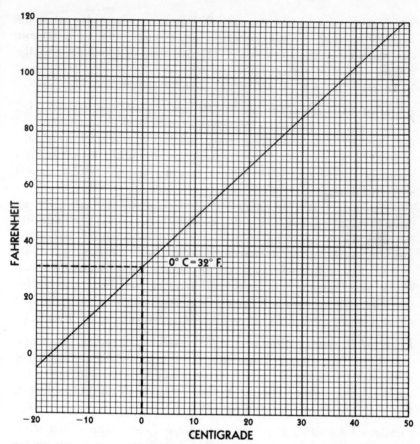

Figure 41. *A chart used for converting degrees Centigrade to degrees Fahrenheit and vice versa.*

heated, it expands and therefore has less density. A cubic foot of warm air is less dense than a cubic foot of cold air. This decrease in air density (increase in density altitude), brought about by an increase in temperature, has a pronounced effect on flight.

**Effect of Temperature on Flight** Since an increase in temperature makes the air less dense (*increases* density altitude), the takeoff run will be longer, the rate of climb slower, and the landing speed (ground speed) faster on a hot day than on a cold day. Thus, an increase in temperature has the same effect as an increase in altitude. An airplane which requires a ground run of 1,000 ft. on a winter day when the temperature is 0° F. will require a much longer run on a summer day when the temperature is 100° F. An airplane which requires the greater portion of a short runway to take off on a cold winter day may be unable to make it off this runway on a hot summer day (fig. 13).

**Effect of High Humidity on Air Density**  A common misconception of many people is that water vapor weighs more than an equal volume of dry air. *This is not true.* Water vapor weighs approximately five-eighths as much as an equal volume of perfectly dry air. When the air contains moisture in the form of water vapor, it is not as heavy as dry air and so is less dense.

Assuming that temperature and pressure remain the same, the air density varies inversely with the humidity—that is, as the humidity increases, the air density decreases (density altitude *increases*) ; and, as the humidity decreases, the air density increases (density altitude *decreases*).

The higher the temperature, the greater the moisture-carrying ability of the air. Therefore, air at a temperature of 100° F. and a relative humidity of 80 percent will contain a greater amount of moisture than air at a temperature of 60° F. and a relative humidity of 80 percent.

**Effect of High Humidity on Flight**  As discussed earlier, the thinner (less dense) the air, the longer the takeoff roll, the slower the rate of climb, and the higher the landing speed. Since high humidity makes the air less dense (increases density altitude), the takeoff roll will be longer, rate of climb slower, and landing speed higher (fig. 13).

**Combined Effect of High Altitude, High Temperature, and High Humidity on Flight**  As indicated earlier in this section, each of the foregoing conditions can seriously affect flight characteristics. When all three condtions are present, the problem is aggravated. Therefore, beware of "high, hot, and humid" conditions (high-density altitudes), and by using performance charts, take the necessary precautions, to make sure the runway is long enough for a takeoff (fig. 13). (See Exam-O-Gram No. 33, appendix 1.)

# 9. Results of Condensation

In Chapter 8 we noted that when temperature and dew point are close together, the moisture in the air condenses and becomes visible in the form of fog or clouds, and that any further reduction in temperature will cause the moisture to be "squeezed out" in the form of dew, frost, or precipitation—rain, snow, hail, or sleet.

**Dew and Frost**   When the ground cools at night, the temperature of the air immediately adjacent to the ground is frequently lowered to the saturation point, causing condensation. This condensation takes place directly upon objects on the ground as dew if the temperature is above freezing, or as frost if the temperature is below freezing.

Dew is of no importance to aircraft, but a frost deposit creates friction which can interfere with the smooth flow of air over the wing surfaces, preventing takeoff. Therefore, frost should always be removed before flight.

**Fog**   When the air near the ground is within a few degrees of the dew point, the water vapor condenses and becomes visible as fog. There are many types of fog, varying in degree of intensity and classified according to the particular phenomena which cause them. One type, "ground fog," which frequently forms at night in low places, is limited to a few feet in height, and is usually dissipated by the heat of the sun shortly after sunrise. Other types, which can form any time conditions are favorable, may extend to greater heights and persist for days or even weeks. Along seacoasts, fog often forms over the ocean and is blown inland. All fogs produce low visibilities and therefore constitute a serious hazard to aircraft.

**Clouds**   There are two fundamental types of clouds. First, those formed by vertical currents carrying moist air upward to its condensation point are lumpy or billowy and are called "cumulus" (fig. 42), which means an "accumulation" or a "pile." Second, those which develop horizontally and lie in sheets or formless layers like fog are called "stratus" (fig. 43), which means "spread out."

When clouds are near the earth's surface they are generally designated as "cumulus" or "stratus" unless they are producing precipitation, in which case the word "nimbus" (meaning "rain cloud") is added— as "nimbostratus" or "cumulonimbus" (fig. 44).

If the clouds are ragged and broken, the word "fracto" (meaning "broken") is added—as "fractostratus" or "fractocumulus."

The word "alto" (meaning "high") is generally added to designate clouds at intermediate heights, usually appearing at levels of 5,000 to 20,000 ft.—as "altostratus" or "altocumulus."

Clouds formed in the upper levels of the troposphere (commonly between 20,000 and 50,000 ft.) are composed of ice crystals and generally have a delicate, curly appearance, somewhat similar to frost on a window pane. For these clouds the word "cirro" (meaning "curly") is added— as "cirrocumulus" or "cirrostratus." At these high altitudes there is also a fibrous type of cloud appearing as curly wisps, bearing the single name "cirrus."

In Chapter 10 the relationship will be shown between the various types of clouds and the kind of weather expected. At present we are chiefly concerned with the flying conditions directly associated with the different cloud formations.

The ice-crystal clouds (cirrus group) are well above ordinary flight levels of light aircraft and normally do not concern the pilots of these aircraft, except as indications of approaching changes in weather.

The clouds in the "alto" group are not normally encountered in flights of smaller planes, but they sometimes contain icing conditions important for commercial and military planes. Altostratus clouds usually indicate that unfavorable flying weather is near.

The low clouds are of great importance to the pilot because they create low ceilings and low visibilities. They change rapidly, and frequently drop to the ground, forming a complete blanket over landmarks and landing fields. In temperatures near freezing, they are a constant threat because of the probability of icing. The pilot should be constantly alert to any changes in conditions, and be prepared to land before visibility is suddenly obscured.

Cumulus clouds vary in size from light "scud" or fluffy powder puffs to towering masses rising thousands of feet in the sky. Usually they are somewhat scattered, and the pilot can fly around them without difficulty. Under some conditions, particularly in the late afternoon, they are likely to multiply, flatten out, and close in. This may leave the pilot with no alternatives except to reverse his course or find a safe landing field before the clouds close in completely or high winds, squalls, and rain or hail begin.

Cumulonimbus clouds are very dangerous. When they appear individually or in small groups, they are usually of the type called "air-mass thunderstorms" (caused by heating of the air at the earth's surface) or "orographic thunderstorms" (caused by the up-slope motion of air in mountainous regions). On the other hand, when these clouds take the form of a continuous or almost continuous line, they are usually caused by a front or squall line. The most common position for a squall line is

CUMULUS     ALTOCUMULUS     CIRROCUMULUS

Figure 42. *Cumulus clouds at they appear at low, intermediate, and high levels.*

Figure 43. *Stratus-type clouds at various altitudes.*

FOG

STRATUS

ALTOSTRATUS

CIRROSTRATUS

Figure 44. *Various types of bad weather clouds.*

63

in advance of a moving front, but one can form in air far removed from a front.

Since the cumulonimbus clouds are formed by rising air currents, they are extremely turbulent; moreover, it is possible for an airplane flying near by to be sucked into the cloud. Once inside, an airplane may encounter updrafts and downdrafts with velocities as great as 3,000 feet per minute. Airplanes have been torn apart by the violence of these currents. In addition, the clouds frequently contain large hailstones capable of severely damaging aircraft, lightning, and great quantities of water at temperatures conducive to heavy icing. Many "unexplained" crashes have probably been caused by the disabling effect of cumulonimbus clouds upon airplanes which have been accidentally or intentionally flown into them. The only practical procedure for a pilot caught within a thunderstorm is to reduce airspeed. This lessens the strain on the aircraft structure, just as slow driving over rough roads lessens the strain on an automobile. A safe speed for an airplane flying through turbulence is an airspeed not greater than the maneuvering speed for the particular airplane (to be discussed in Chap. 19).

Figure 45 shows the important characteristics of a typical cumulonimbus cloud. The top of the cloud flattens into an anvil shape, which points in the direction the cloud is moving, generally with the prevailing wind. Near the base, however, the winds blow directly toward the cloud and increase in speed, becoming violent updrafts as they reach the low rolls at the forward edge.

Within the cloud and directly beneath it are updrafts and downdrafts; in the rear portion is a strong downdraft which becomes a wind blowing away from the cloud.

The cloud itself is a storm factory. The updrafts quickly lift the moist air to its saturation point, whereupon it condenses and raindrops begin to fall. Before these have reached the bottom of the cloud, updrafts pick them up and carry them aloft, where they may freeze and again start downward, only to repeat the process many times until they have become heavy enough to break through the updrafts and reach the ground as hail or very large raindrops. As the storm develops, more and more drops fall through the turbulence, until the rain becomes fairly steady. The lightning that accompanies such a storm is probably due to the break-up of raindrops, which produces static electricity that discharges spasmodically as lightning. This causes a sudden expansion of the air in its path, resulting in thunder.

It is impossible for a small plane to fly over these clouds (they frequently extend to 50,000 ft.). Usually they are too low to fly under. When they are close together the clear space between them is an area of violent turbulence. If the clouds are isolated, indicating local thunderstorms, it usually is possible to fly around them; but they should be given a wide berth *since they may travel rapidly*. If, however, they are "frontal" or squall line storms, they may extend for hundreds of miles, and the only safe procedure is to land immediately and wait until the cumulonimbus cloud formation has passed.

*Ceiling*  The height above ground of the lowest layer of clouds reported as broken or overcast and not classified as "thin" is the ceiling. Clouds are reported as broken when they cover six-tenths to nine-tenths of the sky and as overcast when they cover more than nine-tenths. The ceiling is *unlimited* if the sky is cloudless or less than six-tenths covered as seen from the ground. Pilots should obtain the latest information on ceilings from the hourly sequence reports. Forecasts of expected changes in ceilings and other conditions also are available at weather stations.

*Visibility*  Closely related to ceiling and cloud cover is "visibility"— the greatest horizontal distance at which prominent objects can be distinguished with the naked eye. Visibility, like ceiling, is included in hourly weather reports and in aviation forecasts.

*Precipitation*  The various forms of precipitation do not require lengthy discussion. In addition to possible damage by hail and the danger of icing, precipitation may be accompanied by low ceilings, and in heavy precipitation, visibilities may suddenly be reduced to zero.

It should be obvious that aircraft which may have accumulated snow while on the ground should never be flown until all traces of snow have been removed, including the hard crust that frequently adheres to the surfaces. An aircraft which has been exposed to rain followed by freezing temperatures should be carefully cleared of ice and checked before takeoff to ascertain that the controls operate freely.

# 10.  Air Masses and Fronts

Large, high pressure systems frequently stagnate over large areas of land or water with relatively homogenious surface conditions. They take on characteristics of these "source regions"—the coldness of polar

Figure 45. *Cross-section of a cumulonimbus cloud (thunderhead).*

WIND

regions, the heat of the tropics, the moisture of oceans, or the dryness of continents.

As they move away from their source regions and pass over land and sea, the air masses are constantly being modified through heating or cooling from below, lifting or subsiding, absorbing or losing moisture. Actual temperature of the air mass is less important than its temperature in relation to the land or water surface over which it is passing. For example, an air mass moving from polar regions usually is colder than the land and sea surfaces over which it passes. On the other hand, an air mass moving from the Gulf of Mexico in winter usually is warmer than the territory over which it passes.

If the air is colder than the surface, it will be warmed from below and convection currents will be set up, causing turbulence. Dust, smoke, and atmospheric pollution near the ground will be carried upward by these currents and dissipated at higher levels, improving surface visibility. Such air is called "unstable."

Conversely, if the air is warmer than the surface, there is no tendency for convection currents to form, and the air is smooth. Smoke, dust, etc., are concentrated in lower levels with resulting poor visibility. Such air is called "stable."

From the combination of the source characteristics and the temperature relationship just described, we can categorically associate air masses with certain types of weather.

### Characteristics of a Cold (Unstable) Air Mass

Type of clouds _____cumulus and cumulonimbus.
Ceilings _____generally unlimited (except during precipitation).
Visibilities _____excellent (except during precipitation).
Unstable air _____pronounced turbulence in lower levels (because of convection currents).
Type of precipitation __occasional local thunderstorms or showers—hail, sleet, snow flurries.

### Characteristics of a Warm (Stable) Air Mass

Type of clouds _____ stratus and stratocumulus (fog, haze).
Ceilings _____generally low.
Visibilities _____ poor (smoke and dust held in lower levels).
Stable air _____ smooth, with little or no turbulence.
Type of precipitation __ drizzle.

When two air masses meet, they do not mix readily unless their temperatures, pressures, and relative humidities are very similar. Instead, they set up boundaries called frontal zones, or "fronts," the colder air mass projecting under the warmer air mass in the form of a wedge. This condition is termed a "stationary front" if the boundary is not moving.

Usually, however, the boundary moves along the earth's surface, and as one air mass withdraws from a given area it is replaced by another air mass. This action creates a moving front. If warmer air is replacing colder air, the front is called "warm"; if colder air is replacing warmer air, the front is called "cold."

## Warm Front

When a warm front moves forward, the warm air slides up over the wedge of colder air lying ahead of it.

Warm air usually has high humidity. As this warm air is lifted, its temperature is lowered. As the lifting process continues, condensation occurs, low nimbostratus and stratus clouds form and drizzle or rain develop. The rain falls through the colder air below, increasing its moisture content so that it also becomes saturated. Any reduction of temperature in the colder air, which might be caused by upslope motion or cooling of the ground after sunset, may result in extensive fog.

As the warm air progresses up the slope, with constantly falling temperature, clouds appear at increasing heights in the form of altostratus and cirrostratus, if the warm air is stable. If the warm air is unstable, cumulonimbus clouds and altocumulus clouds will form and frequently produce thunderstorms. Finally, the air is forced up near the stratosphere, and in the freezing temperatures at that level, the condensation appears as thin wisps of cirrus clouds. The upslope movement is very gradual, rising about 1,000 ft. every 20 miles. Thus, the cirrus clouds, forming at perhaps 25,000 ft. altitude, may appear as far as 500 miles in advance of the point on the ground which marks the position of the front (fig. 46).

*Flight Toward an Approaching Warm Front*   Although no two fronts are exactly alike, we may gain a clearer understanding of the general pattern if we consider the atmospheric conditions which might exist when a warm front is moving eastward from St. Louis, Mo. (Refer to fig. 46 during this discussion.)

At St. Louis, the weather would be very unpleasant, with drizzle and probably fog.

At Indianapolis, Ind., 200 miles in advance of the warm front, the sky would be overcast with nimbostratus clouds, and continuous rain.

At Columbus, Ohio, 400 miles in advance, the sky would be overcast with stratus and altostratus clouds predominating. A steady rain would be about to begin.

At Pittsburgh, Pa., 600 miles ahead of the front, there would probably be high cirrus and cirrostratus clouds.

If we flew from Pittsburgh to St. Louis, ceiling and visibility would decrease steadily. Starting under bright skies, with unlimited ceilings and visibilities, we would note lowering stratus-type clouds as we neared Columbus and soon afterward we would encounter precipitation. After arriving at Indianapolis, we would find the ceiling too low for further flight. Precipitation would reduce visibilities to practically zero.

Thus, we would be forced to remain in Indianapolis until the warm front had passed, which might require a day or two.

If we wished to return to Pittsburgh, we would have to wait until the front had passed beyond Pittsburgh, which might require 3 or 4 days. Warm fronts generally move at the rate of 10 to 25 miles an hour.

On our trip to Indianapolis we probably would have noticed a gradual increase in temperature and a much faster increase in dew point, until the two coincided.

We would also have found the atmospheric pressure gradually lessening because the warmer air aloft would have less weight than the colder air it was replacing. This condition illustrates the general principle that a falling barometer indicates the approach of stormy weather.

## Cold Front

Consider now the weather conditions accompanying a cold front. When the cold front moves forward, it acts like a snow plow, sliding under the warmer air and tossing it aloft. This causes sudden cooling of the warm air and forms cloud types that depend on the stability of the warm air.

*Fast-Moving Cold Fronts*   In fast-moving cold fronts, friction retards the front near the ground, which brings about a steeper frontal surface. This steep frontal surface results in a narrower band of weather concentrated along the forward edge of the front. If the warm air is stable,

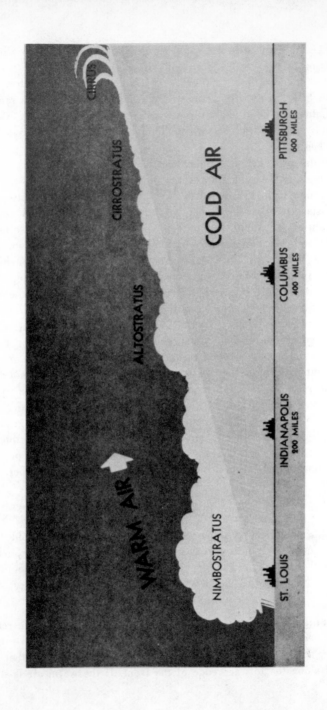

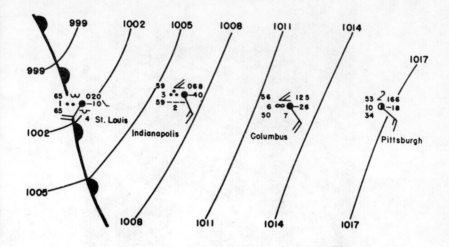

STL M10⊕1R- 020/65/65/2218/960
IND M4⊕50⊕3R 068/59/59/1612/973
CMH E60⊕6H 125/56/50/1318/990
PIT 150-① 166/53/34/1312/002

Figure 46. *A warm front: (left) cross-section; ( top ) as shown on weather map; ( above ) as reported by teletype sequences.*

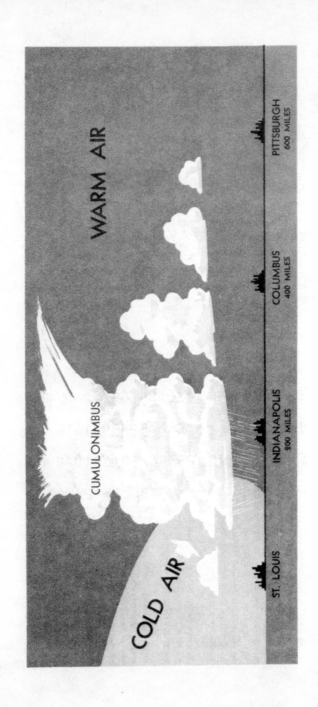

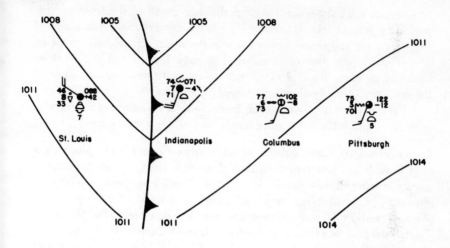

STL       3Ø①1Ø  Ø88/46/33/3Ø18/979

IND      M1Ø⊕3TRW  Ø71/74/71/2Ø24/974

CMH    M25①6H  1Ø2/77/73/2Ø12/983

PIT      35①3K  122/75/7Ø/2Ø12/989

Figure 47. *A cold front: ( left ) cross-section; ( top ) as shown on a weather map; ( above ) as reported by teletype sequences.*

an overcast sky may occur for some distance ahead of the front, accompanied by general rain. If the warm air is conditionally unstable, scattered thunderstorms and showers may form in the warm air. In some cases, an almost continuous line of thunderstorms may form along the front or ahead of it. These lines of thunderstorms (squall lines) contain some of the most turbulent weather experienced by pilots.

Behind the fast-moving cold front there is usually rapid clearing, with gusty and turbulent surface winds, and colder temperatures.

*Comparison of Cold Fronts With Warm Fronts*  The slope of a cold front is much steeper than that of a warm front and the progress is generally more rapid—usually from 20 to 35 miles per hour, although in extreme cases, cold fronts have been known to move at 60 miles per hour. Weather activity is more violent and usually takes place directly at the front instead of in advance of the front. However, especially in late afternoon during the warm season, a squall line will frequently develop as much as 50 to 200 miles in advance of the actual cold front. Whereas warm front dangers lie in low ceilings and visibilities, cold front dangers lie chiefly in sudden storms, high and gusty winds, and turbulence.

Unlike the warm front, the cold front rushes in almost unannounced, makes a complete change in the weather within the space of a few hours, and passes on. The squall line is ordinarily quite narrow in width, but is likely to extend for hundreds of miles in length. Altostratus clouds sometimes form slightly ahead of the front, but these are seldom more than 100 miles in advance. After the front has passed, the weather often clears rapidly and we have cooler, drier air and usually unlimited ceilings and visibilities—almost perfect flying conditions.

*Flight Toward an Approaching Cold Front*  If we were to make the flight from Pittsburgh toward St. Louis (fig. 47) when a cold front was approaching from St. Louis, we would experience conditions quite different from those associated with a warm front. The sky in Pittsburgh would probably be somewhat overcast with stratocumulus clouds typical of a warm air mass, the air smooth, and the ceilings and visibilities relatively low although suitable for flight.

As the flight proceeded, these conditions would prevail until we reached Indianapolis. At this point, if we were wise, we would check the position of the cold front by consulting a recent weather map and teletype sequences, or the meteorologist. We should probably find that the front was now about 75 miles west of Indianapolis. A pilot with sound judgment based on knowledge of frontal conditions, would remain in Indianapolis until the front had passed—a matter of a few hours—and then continue to his destination under near perfect flying conditions.

If, however, we were foolhardy enough to continue our flight toward the approaching cold front, we would soon notice a few altostratus clouds and a dark layer of nimbostratus lying low on the horizon, with perhaps cumulonimbus in the background. Two courses would now be open to us: (1) Either to turn around and outdistance the storm, or (2) to make an immediate landing which might be extremely dangerous because of gustiness and sudden wind shifts.

If we were to continue farther, we would be trapped in a line of squalls and cumulonimbus clouds, the dangers of which have already been described. It may be disastrous to fly beneath these clouds; impossible, in a small plane, to fly above them. At low altitudes, there are no safe passages through them. Usually there is no possibility of flying around them because they often extend in a line for 300 to 500 miles.

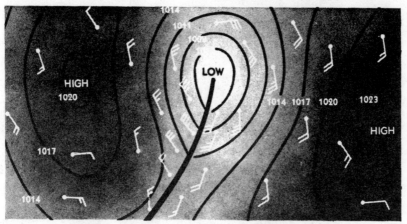

Figure 48. *Weather map indication of wind shift line (center line leading to low).*

*Wind Shifts* Wind shifts perhaps require further explanation. The wind in a "high" blows in a clockwise spiral. When two highs are adjacent, the winds are in almost direct opposition at the point of contact as illustrated in figure 48. Since fronts normally lie between two areas of higher pressure, wind shifts occur in all types of fronts, but they usually are more pronounced in cold fronts.

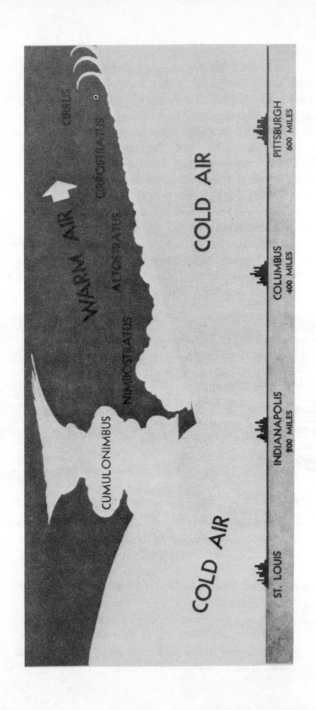

76

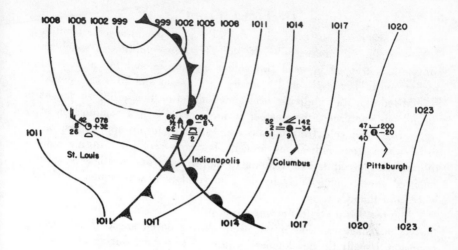

| STL | 35①8 | Ø78/42/26/3123G4Ø/976 |
| IND | W5X½ TRW-A | Ø58/66/62/2928G45/97Ø |
| CMH | B8Ø⊕2F | 142/52/51/1617/995 |
| PIT | E13Ø①7 | 2ØØ/47/4Ø/1312/Ø12 |

Figure 49. *An occluded front: (left) cross-section; (top) as shown on a weather map; (above) at reported by teletype sequences.*

# Occluded Front

One other form of front with which the pilot should become familiar is the "exclusion" or "occluded front." This is a condition in which an air mass is trapped between two colder air masses and forced aloft to higher and higher levels until it finally spreads out and loses its identity.

Meteorologists subdivide occlusions into two types, but so far as the pilot is concerned, the weather in any occlusion is a combination of warm front and cold front conditions. As the occlusion approaches, the usual warm front indications prevail—lowering ceilings, lowering visibilities, and precipitation. Generally, the warm front weather is then followed almost immediately by the cold front type, with squalls, turbulence, and thunderstorms.

Figure 49 is a vertical cross section of an occlusion. Figure 50 shows the various stages as they might occur during development of a typical occlusion. Usually the development requires 3 or 4 days, during which the air masses may progess as indicated on the map.

The first stage (A) represents a boundary between two air masses, the cold and warm air moving in opposite directions along a front. Soon, however, the cooler air, being more aggressive, thrusts a wedge under the warm air, breaking the continuity of the boundary, as shown in (B). Once begun, the process continues rapidly to the complete occlusion as shown in (C). As the warmer air is forced aloft, it cools quickly and its moisture condenses, often causing heavy precipitation. The air becomes extremely turbulent, with sudden changes in pressure and temperature.

Figure 51 shows the development of the occluded front in greater detail.

Figure 52 is an enlarged view of (C) in figure 50, showing the cloud formations and the areas of precipitation.

In figures 46, 47, and 49, a panel representing a surface weather map is placed below each cross-sectional view. These panels represent a bird's-eye or plan view, and show how the weather conditions are recorded. A warm front is indicated by a red line, a cold front by a blue line, an occluded front by a purple line, and a stationary front by alternating red and blue dashes. The rounded and pointed projections are generally omitted from manuscript maps, but are placed on facsimile, printed, or duplicated maps to distinguish the different fronts.

Remember that a frontal line on the weather map represents the position of the frontal surface *on the earth's surface*. A pilot flying west

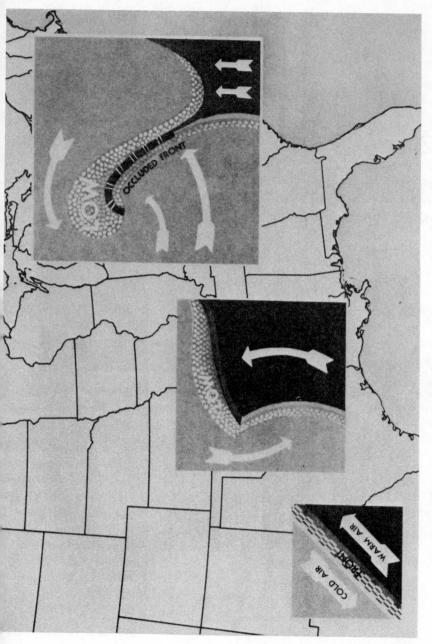

Figure 50. Three stages in the development of a typical occlusion moving northeastward.

*(A) Air flowing along a front in equilibrium.*

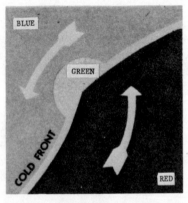

*(B) Increased cold-air pressure causes "bend."*

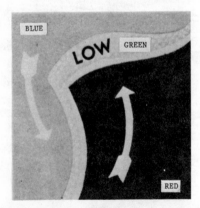

*(C) Cold air begins to surround warm air.*

Figure 51. *Development of an occlusion. If warm air were red and cold air aloft looking toward the*

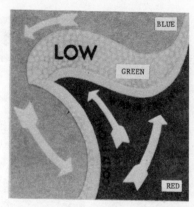

*(D) Precipitation becomes heavier.*

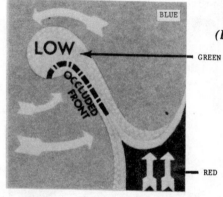

*(E) Warm air completely surrounded.*

*(F) Warm-air sector ends in mild whirl.*

were blue, this is how various stages of an occlusion would appear to a person
earth. *(Precipitation is green.)*

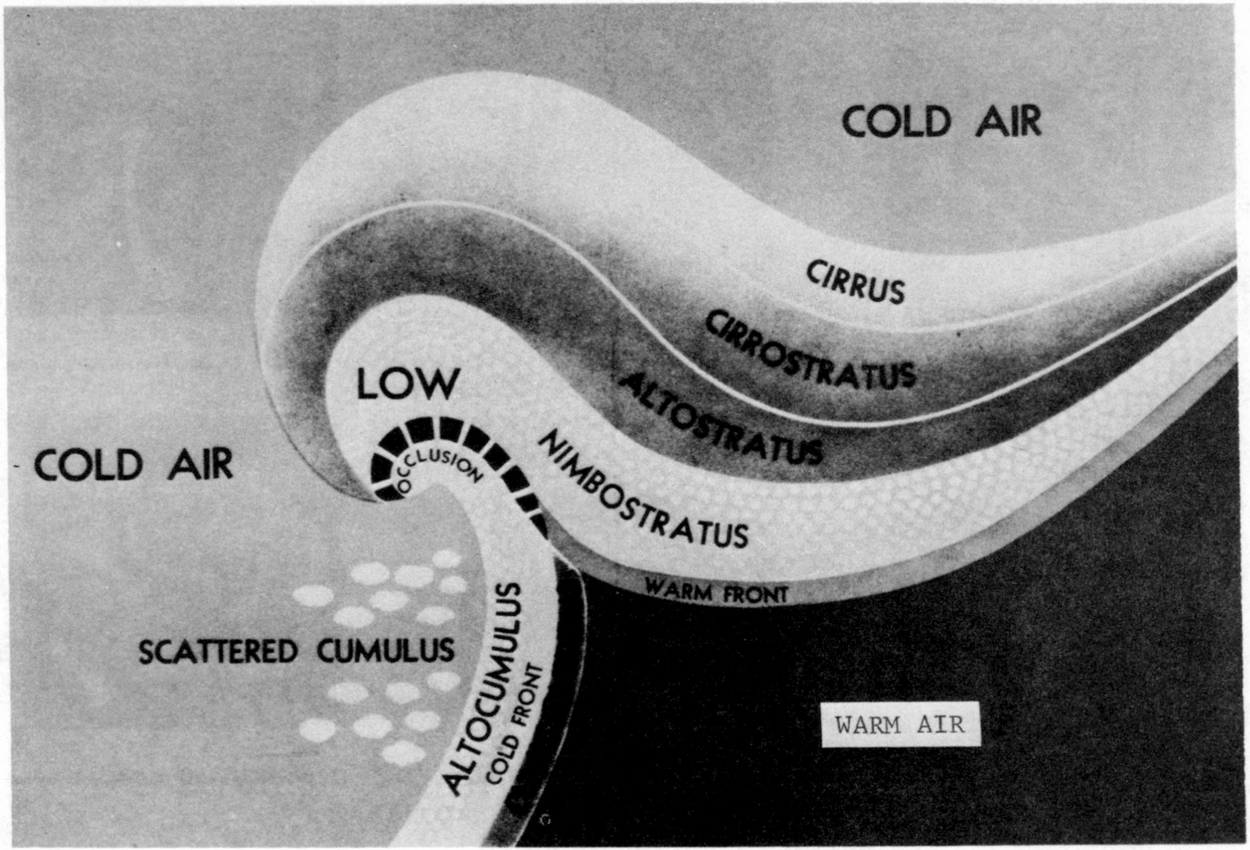

**Figure 52.** *Cloud formations and precipitation accompanying a typical occlusion. (Details of the third stage of development series shown in figure 50.)*

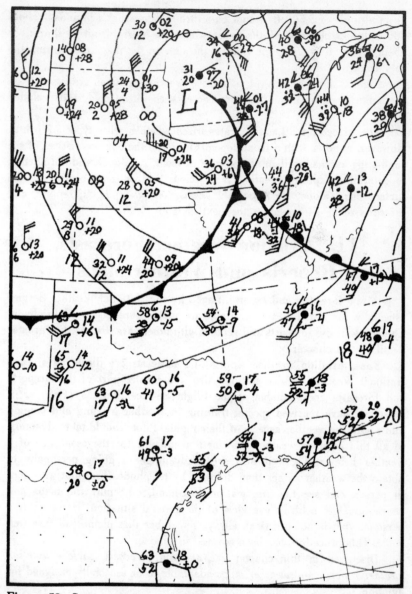

Figure 53. *Section of typical weather map showing methods indicating weather facts important to pilots.*

at an altitude of 5,500 ft. would pass through the frontal boundary about 100 miles in advance of the point where the warm front is shown, or about 25 to 50 miles to the rear of the line on the map representing the cold front.

Fig. 53 is a section of a surface weather map as transmitted on facsimile. It shows a low pressure center with warm, cold, and occluded fronts.

The preceding discussion catagorizes weather with types of fronts. However, weather with a front depends more on the characteristices of the conflicting air masses than on the type of front. A pilot should not attempt to determine expected weather from fronts and pressure centers on the surface chart alone. *He must rely heavily on other charts, reports, and forecasts* to be discussed in the next chapter.

# 11. Aviation Weather Forecasts, Reports, and Weather Maps

A few forecasts and reports, issued by the National Weather Service especially for aviation and available to pilots, were discussed briefly in Chapter 4. These forecasts and reports with others are discussed in greater detail in this chapter.

These aviation weather reports and forecasts are displayed at each National Weather Service station. Also, the greater part of these reports and forecasts are available at the Flight Service Stations (FSS). FSS personnel have received special training in weather briefing and helping pilots with the weather aspects of their flights. Pilots should take advantage of all this aviation weather information and ask for the assistance of a weather briefer. There is also every advantage in going personally to obtain the weather rather than doing it by telephone. The pilot who goes in person can see the information first-hand, especially the maps and charts, and get a bird's eye view of the general situation. However, if a personal visit is not practical, always remember that phone calls are welcome. This procedure has been covered in Chapter 4.

Discussed in this chapter are *aviation forecasts, surface aviation weather reports,* and *weather maps* adaptable to or especially designed for aviation.

### Aviation Forecasts

Forecasts especially prepared for aviation include Area Forecasts

(FA), Terminal Forecasts (FT), In-Flight Weather Advisories (SIGMET and AIRMET), and Winds and Temperatures Aloft Forecasts (FD).

*Area Forecast* Area forecasts are issued every 6 hours by several forecast offices covering the 50 states. Each area comprises several states or portions of states. The forecast includes expected weather for a 12-hour period in detail and a more general outlook for an additional 12 or 18 hours. It describes areas of clouds and significant weather, ceilings, height of cloud bases and tops, surface visibilities, and the movements of major weather disturbances such as thunderstorms and squall lines. It also gives heights of the freezing level and zones of expected icing and turbulence. Figure 54, Key to Aviation Weather Reports and Forecasts, includes a brief explanation of this forecast. (The Key to Aviation Weather Reports and Forecasts is revised from time to time. Current copies may be obtained from Flight Service Stations or from the Superintendent of Documents, U.S. Government Printing Office.)

### *Example of an Area Forecast*
FA GSW Ø81845
19Z TUE-Ø7Z WED

OKLA TEXAS
HGTS ASL UNLESS NOTED

SYNOPSIS. FLOW OF MOIST UNSTBL AIR WL CONT OVR MUCH OF AREA FM ERN SLPS OF DAVIS-GUADALUPE MTNS EWD.
CLDS AND WX. SCTD TO WIDLY SCTD SHWRS AND TSTMS CSTL SECS AND INLAND FOR ABT 75-1ØØ MI WITH CONDS LCLY C8X1TRW TOPS 4ØØ. TOPS OF SHWRS TO 2ØØ. ELSW IN MOIST AIR SCTD TO ISOLD SHWR AND TSTMS WITH TSTMS ACTVTY INCRG DURG AFTN. MOST SHWRS AND TSTMS DSIPIG CSTL SECS BY Ø2Z AND OVR INTR SECS BQ Ø3Z BUT SOME PSBL CONTG THRUT PD.

OTRW OVR AREA FM ERN SLPS OF DAVIS-GUADALUPE MTNS EWD 15-25①V①60-1ØØ AGL WITH FEW PATCHES OF C7-12⊕V①. VSBYS LCLY 2-5 MI IN HAZE INDUS SMK AND PCPN AREAS. SOME PATCHES OF HIR 12Ø①V①14Ø AND 3ØØ-①V-① ABV LOW CLDS. CLD LYRS WL BE MULTI AND VRBL IN AND NEAR SHWRS AND TSTMS. MOST LOW CLDS DSIPTG BY Ø2Z. LTLCG TIL PATCHY LOW ST C7-14⊕V①4Ø DVLPG OVR PARTS OF INTR SECS OF S CNTRL SERN TEX ARND Ø4Z INCRG AND SPRDG N

# KEY TO AVIATION WEATHER REPORTS.....

| LOCATION IDENTIFIER AND TYPE OF REPORT* | SKY AND CEILING | VISIBILITY WEATHER AND OBSTRUCTION TO VISION | SEA-LEVEL PRESSURE | TEMPERATURE AND DEW POINT | WIND | ALTIMETER SETTING | RUNWAY VISUAL RANGE | CODED PIREPS |
|---|---|---|---|---|---|---|---|---|
| MKC | 150M25⊕ | 1R-K | 132 | 58/56 | 18Ø7 | /993/ | RØ4LVR2ØV4Ø | /Ø55 |

**SKY AND CEILING**
Sky cover symbols are in ascending order. Figures preceding symbols are heights in hundreds of feet above station.

Sky cover symbols are:

Ø   Clear: Less than 0.1 sky cover

⊖   Scattered: 0.1 to less than 0.6 sky cover

⊕   Broken: 0.6 to less than 0.9 sky cover

⊕   Overcast: More than 0.9 sky cover

-   Thin (When prefixed to the above symbols.)

-X   Partial obscuration: 0.1 to less than 1.0 sky hidden by precipitation or obstruction to vision (bases at surface.)

X   Obscuration: 1.0 sky hidden by precipitation or obstruction to vision (bases at surface.)

Letter preceding height of layer identifies ceiling layer and indicates how ceiling height was obtained. Thus:

A   Aircraft          R   Radar

B   Balloon           W   Indefinite

E   Estimated         V   Immediately following numerical value indicates a varying ceiling

M   Measured

**VISIBILITY**
Reported in Statute Miles and Fraction. (V Variable)

**WEATHER AND OBSTRUCTION TO VISION SYMBOLS**

| | | | |
|---|---|---|---|
| A   Hail | IC  Ice Crystals | RW  Rain Showers |
| BD  Blowing Dust | IF  Ice Fog | S   Snow |
| BN  Blowing Sand | IP  Ice Pellets | SG  Snow Grains |
| BS  Blowing Snow | IPW Ice Pellet Showers | SP  Snow Pellets |
| D   Dust | | SW  Snow Showers |
| F   Fog | K   Smoke | T   Thunderstorm |
| GF  Ground Fog | L   Drizzle | T+  Severe Thunderstorm |
| H   Haze | R   Rain | ZL  Freezing Drizzle |
| | | ZR  Freezing Rain |

Precipitation intensities are indicated thus:
-- Very Light  - Light  (no sign) Moderate  + Heavy

**WIND**
Direction in tens of degrees from true north, speed in knots. 0000 indicates calm. G indicates gusty. Peak speed follows G or Q when gusts or squalls are reported. The contraction WSHFT followed by local time group in remarks indicates windshift and its time of occurrence. (Knots X 1.15 = statute mi/hr.)

EXAMPLES: 3627 360 Degrees, 27 Knots.
3627G40 360 Degrees, 27 Knots peak speed in gust to 40 knots.

**ALTIMETER SETTING**
The first figure of the actual altimeter setting is always omitted from the report.

**RUNWAY VISUAL RANGE (RVR)**
RVR is reported from some stations. Extreme values for 10 minutes prior to observation are given in hundreds of feet. Runway identification precedes RVR report.

**CODED PIREPS**
Pilot reports of clouds not visible from ground are coded with MSL height data preceding and/or following sky cover symbol to indicate cloud bases and/or tops respectively.

**DECODED REPORT**
Kansas City Record observation. 1500 feet scattered clouds, measured ceiling 2500 feet overcast, visibility 1 mile, light rain, smoke, sea level pressure 1013.2 millibars, temperature 58°F, dewpoint 56°F, wind 180° 7 knots, altimeter setting 29.93 inches. Runway 04 left, visual range 2000 ft variable to 4000. Pilot reports top of overcast 5500 feet (MSL).

**\*TYPE OF REPORT**
The omission of type-of-report data identifies a scheduled record observation for the hour specified in the sequence heading, the time of an out-of-sequence special observation is given as "S" followed by a time group (24-hour clock GMT), e.g. "PIT S 0715 XM". A special indicates a significant change in one or more elements. Local reports are identified by "LCL" and a time group. Locals are transmitted on local teletypewriter circuits only.

TERMINAL FORECASTS contain information for specific airports on ceiling, cloud heights, cloud amounts, visibility, weather condition and surface wind. They are written in a form similar to the AVIATION WEATHER REPORT.

CEILING Identified by the letter "C".
CLOUD HEIGHTS In hundreds of feet above the station (ground)
CLOUD LAYERS Stated in ascending order of height
VISIBILITY In statute miles, but omitted if over 8 miles
SURFACE WIND In tens of degrees and knots, omitted when less than 10.

EXAMPLE OF TERMINAL FORECASTS

C15⊕ Ceiling 1500', broken clouds

O11/2GF Clear, visibility one and one-half miles, ground fog.

201C70⊕6K 3230G Scattered clouds at 2000' ceiling 7000 overcast visibility 6 miles, smoke, surface wind 320 degrees 30 knots, gusty

C5X1/4S+ Sky obscured, vertical visibility 500 ft, visibility one-fourth mile, heavy snow.

AREA FORECASTS are 12-hour forecasts plus 12-hour OUTLOOKS (18 hour outlook in FA valid at 1300Z) of cloud, weather and frontal conditions for an area the size of several states. Heights of cloud tops, icing, and turbulence are ABOVE SEA LEVEL (ASL), ceiling heights, ABOVE GROUND LEVEL (AGL), bases of cloud layers are ASL unless indicated. Area Forecasts are amended by SIGMET's or AIRMET's.

SIGMET or AIRMET warn airmen in flight of potentially hazardous weather such as squall lines, thunderstorms, fog, icing, and turbulence. SIGMET concerns severe and extreme conditions of importance to all aircraft. AIRMET concerns less severe conditions which may be hazardous to some aircraft or to relatively inexperienced pilots. Both are broadcast by FAA on NAVAID voice channels.

WINDS AND TEMPERATURES ALOFT (FD) FORECASTS are computer prepared forecasts of wind direction (nearest 10° true N) and speed (knots) for selected flight levels. Temperatures aloft (°C) are included for all levels (±2500 ft above station elevation) except the 3000-foot level.

EXAMPLES OF WINDS AND TEMPERATURES ALOFT (FD) FORECASTS.

FD WBC 121745
BASED ON 121200Z DATA
VALID 130000Z FOR USE 1800-0300Z TEMPS NEG ABV 24000

| FT | 3000 | 6000 | 9000 | 12000 | 18000 | 24000 | 30000 | 34000 | 39000 |
|---|---|---|---|---|---|---|---|---|---|
| BOS | 3127 | 3425-07 | 3420-11 | 3516-27 | 3512-38 | 311649 | 292451 | 283451 | |
| JFK | 3026 | 3327-08 | 3324-12 | 3322-16 | 3120-27 | 2923-38 | 284248 | 285150 | 285749 |

At 6000 feet ASL over JFK wind from 330° at 27 knots and temperature minus 8° C.

PILOTS report in-flight weather to nearest FSS

**Figure 54. Key to aviation weather reports.**

AND WWD AND LWRG LCLY TO C4-6⊕2-4R-F BY Ø7Z.

ICG. MDT TO HVY MXD ICGICIP AB V FRZG LVL OF 135-15Ø.

TURBC. MDT TO SVR ALL LVLS IN AND NEAR SHWRS AND
TSTM BLDUPS.

OTLK Ø7Z-19Z WED. CDFNT WL MOV INTO EXTRM NRN PTN
OF SWRN TEX AFT 12Z WITH SCTD SHWRS AND TSTMS ALG
AND NEAR FNT. LOW ST INCRG AND CONT TO LWR DURG
NGT AND SPREADG TO MOST OF AREA FM ERN SLPS OF
GUADALUPE-DAVIS MTNS EWD EXCP FOR IMDT CST. EXTSV
AREAS OF C4-7⊕2-5FHK DVLPG BY 12Z WITH PSBL SOME AREAS
OF NEAR ZERO-ZERO. CIGS AND VSBYS WL IPV RPDLY AFT
15Z AND BCM 15-25①V① BY 18Z. WDLY SCTD SHWRS AND
TSTMS DVLPG OVR CSTL WTRS AFT Ø9Z AND OVR PARTS OF
INTR SECS OF S CNTRL SERN TEX BY DABRK. INCRG SHWR
AND TSTMS ACTVTY OVR INTR SECS DURG AFTN AND ALG
AND ABT 1ØØ-15Ø MI AHD OF FNT.

*Plain Language Interpretation* In the first line of the area forecast,
FA indicates it is an area forecast; SAT identifies the originating station
which, in this example, is San Antonio, Texas; and "08" indicates that
the forecast was made on the eighth day of the month with "1845"
being the time in Greenwich Mean Time (GMT) at which the forecast
was made.

The second line covers the valid period of the forecast which, in this
example, is from 1900 Greenwich Mean Time on Tuesday to 0700 Greenwich Mean Time on Wednesday. This would be from 1300 Central Standard Time (CST) Tuesday to 0100 CST Wednesday or from 1400 Central
Daylight Time (CDT) Tuesday to 0200 CDT on Wednesday.

The plain language interpretation of this area forecast is as follows:
Area forecast for the period 1 p.m. CST Tuesday to 1 a.m. CST
Wednesday for Southwestern, South Central, and Southern Texas.
Cloud heights are above sea level unless otherwise noted.

*Synopsis* Flow of moist, unstable air will continue over much of
the area from the eastern slopes of the Davis-Guadalupe Mountains eastward.

*Clouds and Weather* Scattered to widely scattered showers and
thunderstorms in the coastal sections and inland for about 75 to 100

miles with conditions locally, ceiling 800 ft. obscured, visibility 1 mile in thunderstorms and rainshowers with tops at 40,000 ft. Tops of showers to 20,000 ft. Elsewhere in the moist air, scattered to isolated showers and thunderstorms dissipating in the coastal sections by 8 p.m. and over interior sections by 9 p.m. but some possibly continuing throughout the forecast period.

Otherwise, over area from the eastern slopes of the Davis-Guadalupe Mountains eastward, scattered clouds at 1,500 to 2,500 ft. above ground level variable to broken at 6,000 to 10,000 ft. above ground level with a few patches where the ceilings will range from 700 to 1,200 ft. overcast variable to broken.

Visibilities locally will be 2 to 5 miles because of haze, industrial smoke, and precipitation areas. There will be some higher clouds at 12,000 ft. scattered, variable to broken, with tops 14,000 ft. and thin scattered variable to thin broken clouds at 30,000 ft. Cloud layers will be multiple and variable in and near showers and thunderstorms. Most low clouds should be dissipating by 0200 GMT. Little change until patchy low stratus with ceilings 700 to 1,400 ft. overcast variable to broken with tops 4,000 ft. developing over parts of interior sections of south central and southeastern Texas around 10 p.m., increasing and spreading northward and westward and lowering locally by 1 a.m. to ceilings 400 to 600 ft. overcast and visibilities 2 to 4 miles in light rain and fog.

*Icing* Moderate to heavy mixed icing in clouds and in precipitation above the freezing level of 13,500 to 15,000 ft.

*Turbulence* Moderate to severe at all levels in and near showers and thunderstorm buildups.

*Outlook 1 a.m. to 1 p.m. CST Wednesday* A cold front will move into the extreme northern portion of southwestern Texas after 6 p.m. with scattered showers and thunderstorms along and near the front. Low stratus clouds will increase and continue to lower during the night, spreading to most of the area from the eastern slopes of Guadalupe-Davis Mountains eastward except for the immediate coast. Extensive areas with overcast ceilings 400 to 700 ft. and visibilities 2 to 5 miles in fog, haze, and smoke will develop by 6 a.m. with the possibility that some areas will be near zero-zero. Ceilings and visibilities will improve rapidly after 9 a.m. with clouds becoming scattered variable to broken at 1,500 to 2,500 ft. by 12 noon. Widely scattered showers and thunderstorms will develop over coastal waters after 3 a.m. and over parts of interior sections of south central and southeastern Texas by daybreak. Shower and thunderstorm activity will increase over interior sections during the afternoon and along and about 100 to 150 miles ahead of the front.

**Terminal Forecasts** Terminal forecasts are issued every 6 hours generally for a 12-hour period for more than 380 terminals with high aviation activity. They state specifically expected ceiling and clouds, visibility, weather and obstructions to vision, and surface wind conditions at each terminal. If a change is expected during the forecast period, this change and the expected time of the change are given. If the surface wind is expected to be less than 10 knots, it is omitted from the forecast. If visibility is expected to be greater than 8 miles, it also is omitted.

The terminal forecast is very similar in format to the surface weather report (hourly sequence). Pilots who can read and interpet sequence reports should experience no difficulty in reading terminal forecasts. Figure 54 also briefly describes the terminal forecast.

**Example of a Terminal Forecast**
FT1 Ø81645
17Z TUE-Ø5Z WED

AUS C15①12Ø① 1412 FEW RW AND TRW. 19Z C3Ø①3ØØ① 1412 WDLY SCTD C1Ø⊕2TRW. Ø2Z 3ØØ-① OCNL 2Ø①. Ø4Z C1Ø⊕7 161Ø . .

SJT C3Ø⊕ 1815G ⊕V①. 2ØZ 45①12Ø①C3ØØ① 1715G WDLY SCTD C15⊕2TRW. Ø3Z 12Ø①3ØØ-① 1812 . .

SAT C25① 1612 ①V① WDLY SCTD RW AND TRW. 19Z 35①2ØØ-① 1612 WDLY SCTD C1Ø⊕2TRW. Ø2Z 3ØØ-① 161Ø OCNL 2Ø① Ø4Z C1Ø⊕7 161Ø . .

**Plain Language Interpretation** In this terminal forecast FT indicates terminal forecasts; the "1" indicates that the forecasts will be for a 12-hour period (FT 2 would indicate that the forecasts are for a 24-hour period); "08" indicates that the forecasts were made on the eighth day of the month; and "1645" indicates the time of the forecast in Greenwich Mean Time (GMT). The valid period of the forecast (second line) is from 1700 GMT Tuesday to 0500 GMT Wednesday. This would be from 1100 Central Standard Time (CST) to 2300 CST Tuesday or from 1200 Central Daylight Time (CDT) Tuesday to 0000 CDT Wednesday.

The plain language interpretation of the terminal forecast for AUS (Austin, Texas) is:

At 11 a.m. CST Tuesday: Ceiling 1,500 ft., broken clouds with a higher layer of broken clouds with bases at 12,000 ft. AGL (above ground level); surface wind from 140° (true) at 12 knots; and a few rainshowers and thunderstorms with rain showers. By 1 p.m.: Ceiling 3,000 ft., broken clouds with higher broken clouds with bases at 30,000 ft. AGL; surface wind from 140° (true) at 12 knots; and widely scattered thunderstorms and rainshowers with ceiling 1,000 ft., overcast, and visibilities of 2 miles. By 8 p.m.: Thin broken clouds at 30,000 ft. AGL with occasional scattered clouds at 2,000 ft. AGL. By 10 p.m.: Ceiling 1,000 ft. overcast, visibility 7 miles, and surface wind from 160° (true) at 10 knots.

The plain language interpretation of the terminal forecast for SJT (San Angelo, Texas) is:

At 11 a.m. CST Tuesday: Ceiling 3,000 ft. overcast with the overcast variable to broken clouds; surface wind from 180° (true) at 15 knots, gusty. By 2 p.m.: Scattered clouds at 4,500 and 12,000 ft. AGL with ceiling at 30,000 ft., broken clouds; surface wind from 170° (true) at 15 knots and gusty; widely scattered areas with ceilings of 1,500 ft. overcast and visibilities of 2 miles in thunderstorms and rainshowers. By 9 p.m.: Scattered clouds at 12,000 ft. with thin broken clouds at 30,000 ft.; surface wind from 180° (true) at 12 knots.

***In-Flight Weather Advisories*** When weather is not adequately covered by the latest forecasts, the National Weather Service issues short-term forecasts of potentially hazardous weather by means of unscheduled IN-FLIGHT WEATHER ADVISORIES. These warning forecasts are in two categories—SIGMETs and AIRMETs.

***SIGMET*** A SIGMET identifies weather phenomena of particular significance to the safety of transport category and other aircraft. This advisory covers tornadoes, lines of thunderstorms (squall lines), embedded thunderstorms, hail of three-quarters inch or more, severe and extreme turbulence, severe icing, and widespread duststorms or sandstorms lowering visibilities to less than 2 miles.

***AIRMET*** An AIRMET identifies weather phenomena less severe than those covered by a SIGMET but still important to light aircraft safety. This advisory covers moderate icing; moderate turbulence; extensive areas of visibilities less than 2 miles and/or ceilings less than 1,000 ft., including mountain ridges and passes; and winds of 40 knots or more within 2,000 ft. of the surface.

Each FSS broadcasts any advisory which affects an area within 150 nautical miles of the station or within 150 nautical miles of a remote facility controlled by the station. They broadcast the advisory for the first hour after issuance; during the remainder of its valid period, they broadcast only the advisory number and state that it is current. An AIRMET is broadcast at 15 and 45 minutes past the hour; and a SIGMET, on the hour and at 15, 30, and 45 minutes past the hour. Advisory broadcasts at 15 minutes past the hour are part of the scheduled broadcast.

During preflight briefing, the FSS or National Weather Service briefer will advise you of any SIGMET or AIRMET for an area and valid time that may affect your proposed flight. In flight you will receive these advisories during radio contacts with FSS stations.

## Example of a SIGMET
FL SAT Ø81830
Ø81830-Ø82300
SIGMET CHARLIE 1. OVR SRN TEX WITHIN AN AREA BNDD BY SAN ANTONIO-PALACIOS-4Ø S OF CORPUS CHRISTI-COTULLA SCTD TO LCLY NMRS SHWRS AND TSTMS FQTLY IN BRKN LNS WITH TOPS TO 45Ø. CONDS CONTG BYD 23Z.

*Plain Language Interpretation* "FL" indicates an in-flight advisory; SAT (San Antonio, Texas, the originating station); "08" the eighth day of the month, and 1830 GMT (12:30 p.m. CST) the time at which the advisory was made and it is valid from 12:30 p.m. to 5 p.m. on the eighth day of the month.

*SIGMET Charlie 1* Over Southern Texas, within an area bounded by the four points of San Antonio, Palacios, 40 miles south of Corpus Christi and Cotulla, there will be scattered to locally numerous showers and thunderstorms frequently in broken lines with tops to 45,000 ft. Conditions will continue beyond 5 p.m.

## Example of AIRMETS
FL ELP Ø8171Ø
Ø8171Ø-Ø82200

AIRMET ALPHA 1. IN SRN ARIZ SRN NM AND EXTRM SWRN TEX MDT TURBC OCNLY SVR FOR LGT ACFT BLO 13∅ MSL AFT 18∅∅.

FL SAT ∅816∅5
∅816∅5-∅818∅∅

AIRMET BRAVO 1. OVR SWRN TEX 5∅ MI EITHER SIDE OF A LN FM 4∅ E OF EAGLE PASS TO 3∅ NNE OF FORT STOCKTON CIGS FQTLY BLO 1 THSD WITH VSBYS OCNL LESS THAN 2 MI IN PCPN AND FOG. HIR TRNN AND HILLS OCNL OBSCD. CONDS CONTG TIL 18Z.

*Plain Language Interpretation*

AIRMET ALPHA 1 is valid on the eighth day of the month from 1710 Greenwich Mean Time (10:10 a.m., Mountain Standard Time) to 2200 GMT (3 p.m. MST). In southern Arizona, southern New Mexico, and extreme southwestern Texas, moderate turbulence will occur and occasionally become severe for light aircraft below 13,000 ft. mean sea level after 11 a.m. MST.

AIRMET BRAVO 1 is valid on the eighth day of the month from 1605 GMT (10:05 a.m. CST) to 1800 GMT (12 noon CST). Over southwestern Texas, 50 miles to either side of a line from 40 miles east of Eagle Pass to 30 miles north-northeast of Fort Stockton, ceilings frequently will be below 1,000 ft. with visibilities occasionally less than 2 miles in precipitation and fog. Higher terrain and hills occasionally will be obscured. Conditions will continue until 12 noon.

*Winds and Temperatures Aloft Forecast*  Charted winds aloft observations are available at most briefing outlets equipped with facsimile. However, these reports are several hours old when received and do not necessarily represent wind that will be encountered during subsequent flights.

The private pilot is most interested in the *winds- and temperatures-aloft forecast* which forecasts the winds and temperatures at selected altitudes and is issued every 6 hours. Depending upon station elevation, wind direction and speed are normally forecast for mean sea level (MSL) altitudes of 3,000 ft., 6,000 ft., 9,000 ft., and 12,000 ft., and for pressure altitudes of 18,000 ft., 24,000 ft., 30,000 ft., 34,000 ft., and 39,000 ft. (Pressure altitude is the altitude shown on a pressure altimeter set at the standard altimeter setting of 29.92 inches.) Because of terrain effect, no forecasts will be made for levels less than 1,500 ft. above station elevation. For example, if station elevation is more than 1,500 ft. (mean sea level), no forecast will be given for the 3,000-foot level. If station elevation is more than 4,500 ft., no forecast will be given for the 6,000-foot level, and so on.

Temperatures are forecast for all wind forecast levels except the 3,000-foot level or the lowest level when this level is less than 2,500 ft. above station elevation. The 3,000-foot level will not have a forecast temperature at any time. If the first forecast wind level for a given station is 6,000 ft. but the station elevation is greater than 3,500 ft., then there will be no forecast temperature for the 6,000-foot level because the first reported wind level is less than 2,500 ft. above the station elevation.

Wind direction is forecast in *true* direction from which it is blowing and speed is forecast in knots (nautical miles per hour).

Temperature is forecast in degrees Celsius (Centigrade). Temperatures are preceded by a plus $(+)$ or minus $(-)$ sign up through the 24,000-foot level, depending upon whether the temperature is above or below $0°C$. Above this forecast level, the minus $(-)$ sign is omitted.

Weather briefing stations equipped with facsimile will display charted FDs, and some stations not so equipped may plot the charts locally. Figure 55 is a section of a facsimile chart for one level of the FD. Note the station model on the lower part of the chart. On this model, the wind arrow with a single barb graphically shows direction from which the wind is forecast to blow. "DD" is coded direction in tens of degrees and must agree with the arrow (example: 26 means 260 degrees. "TT" is forecast temperature in degrees Celsius. "FFF" is wind speed in knots).

The complete facsimile transmission includes wind and temperatures for eight forecast levels. If charted winds are not available, you can extract the information directly from teletypewriter copy, although this method is slower.

## Examples of Winds-Aloft Forecasts (to 24,000 ft.)

FD WBC 190545
BASED ON 190000Z DATA
VALID 191200Z FOR USE 0600-1500Z. TEMPS NEG ABV 24000

| FT | 3000 | 6000 | 9000 | 12000 | 18000 | 24000 |
|----|------|------|------|-------|-------|-------|
| DAL | 1625 | 1827+10 | 2133+06 | 2339−02 | 2345−12 | 2357−23 |
| ABI | | 1826+08 | 2033+05 | 2242−03 | 2349−14 | 2359−24 |
| ABQ | | | 2227+08 | 2235−01 | 2352−13 | 2363−25 |
| HOU | 9900 | 9900+14 | 2310+08 | 2415+01 | 2427−10 | 2442−21 |

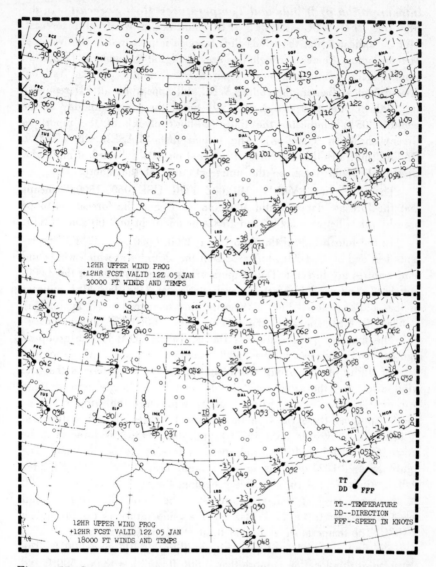

Figure 55. *Section of a forecast winds and temperatures aloft forecast as transmitted over facsimile. Model at the bottom shows how information is plotted around each station. (TT = temperatures in degrees Celsius; DD = direction to nearest 10°; FFF = wind speed in knots.) The complete facsimile transmission included forecasts for eight levels.*

*Interpretation of Winds and Temperatures-Aloft Forecast*    In the first line "FD WBC 190545," "FD" indicates a winds-aloft forecast. "WBC" indicates that the winds-aloft forecast is prepared at the National Meteorological Center through the use of digital computers. (Since all winds-aloft forecasts are now prepared by computers in the National Meteorological Center, the coding WBC will appear on all FD reports.) In "190545" the first two digits (19) mean the nineteenth day of the month. "0545" indicates the time (24-hour clock) of the report in Greenwich Mean Time (Z). The second line, "BASED ON 190000Z DATA," indicates that the forecast is based on data collected at midnight, Greenwich Mean Time, on the nineteenth day of the month.

The third line "VALID 191200Z FOR USE 0600-1500Z" means that the forecast data is valid at 6 a.m. CST, and the forecast is to be used by pilots between 0600Z and 1500Z or midnight to 9:00 a.m. (CST).

In the fourth line of the report "FT 3000, 6000 . . . .," "FT" represents feet and 3000, 6000, etc." represent the altitudes at which winds and temperatures are forecast. The temperature is never forecast for the 3,000-foot level. The wind forecast for each station at 3,000 feet MSL appears in the column below "3000"; the wind and temperature (if applicable) at 6,000 ft. MSL appear in the column below "6000 FT" and so on.

The first reporting station is Dallas, Texas, (DAL). The group of figures "1625" appear in the "3000" column opposite DAL. The first pair of digits of this group when multiplied by 10 represents the true wind direction (the same result is obtained by adding a zero to these two digits). The second pair of digits represents the wind speed in knots. Applying these rules on the group of figures, the wind direction at 3,000 ft. above sea level (MSL) at Dallas, Texas, is forecast to be from 160° (true) and the wind speed is forecast to be 25 knots. The figure group "1827+10" is in the column headed by "6000 FT" for Dallas. Applying the rules to this grouping, the wind direction at 6,000 ft. above sea level at Dallas is forecast to be from 180° (true), wind speed is forecast to be 27 knots, and the temperature is forecast to be +10°C. The temperature at 18,000 ft. at Dallas is forecast to be −12°C.

The first reported level for Abilene, Texas (ABI), is 6,000 ft. The elevation at this location is more than 1,500 ft. and less than 4,500 ft., so the first forecast wind level would be 6,000 ft. Note that temperature forecasts are not included with the 3,000-foot level.

When the wind speed reaches 100 knots or more, a special rule must be applied to the four-digit grouping to find wind direction and speed. Since a private pilot will not normally fly at altitudes where such wind speeds will be encountered, the rule will not be covered in this text. The group of figures "9900" indicates a light and variable wind. Note that a light and variable wind is forecast for the Houston area at 3,000 and 6,000 ft.

*Interpolation for Intermediate Winds and Temperatures*   To obtain the wind direction and speed at an altitude intermediate to those given in the winds-aloft forecast, you must interpolate. For example, the forecast wind direction, wind speed, and temperature at 7,500 ft. at Dallas are 195° (true) 30 knots, and 8°C. We find these values by first finding the value of the wind direction and speed and temperature forecast at 6,000 and 9,000 ft.

| Level | Wind Direction | Wind Speed | Temperature |
|-------|----------------|------------|-------------|
| 6,000 | 180° | 27 | +10 |
| 7,500 | ? | ? | ? |
| 9,000 | 210° | 33 | +06 |

Since 7,500 ft. is halfway between 6,000 ft. and 9,000 ft., we assume that the wind direction and wind speed are halfway between the respective values at 6,000 ft. and 9,000 ft. 195° is halfway between 180° and 210° and 30 knots is halfway between 27 and 33 knots.

## Aviation Weather Reports

Changes in weather frequently are so rapid that conditions at the time of flight are likely to be quite different from those shown on weather maps issued several hours previously. The very latest information is available in reports distributed by teletypewriter. Three types of reports are available—hourly sequence and special surface reports, pilot reports (PIREPS), and radar reports. Radar reports generally are summarized in plain language and are readily understood. This chapter discusses in detail surface aviation weather reports and pilot reports.

*Surface Aviation Weather Reports*   A pilot must become familiar with a few symbols and abbreviations in order to read the sequences. Facility in reading these reports can be acquired in a surprisingly short time, and the reward is well worth the effort. Teletype sequence reports are given below the panels in figures 46, 47, and 49.

The table on pages 63 and 64 present a typical sequence report, with an explanation for interpreting all sequences (also, see fig. 54). It will be noted that the information is in four groups, which might be broadly classified as:

1. Identification.                     3. Instrumental observations.
2. Visual observations.            4. Remarks.

*Examples of Aviation Weather (Sequence) Reports*
   Θ29 SA29Ø821ØØ
   SAT 19⊕E4Ø⊕15TRW‑‑ 1Ø6/77/71/15Ø9/987/TBØ7
      T N MOVG NE OCNL LTGCCCG
   JCT 5Ø⊕15+ Ø94/86/66/1912/987
   AUS E3Ø⊕8Ø⊕1Ø 122/86/7Ø/1916/99Ø/TCU ALQDS RB3ØE45
   ACT S M1Ø⊕4H 138/76/7Ø/1312/995
   COT S A17⊕15 113/85/74/16Ø8/987 BLDUPS DSNT E

*Plain Language Interpretation*   The plain language interpretation of the SAT (San Antonio, Texas) Aviation Weather Report is as follows: Scattered clouds at 1,900 ft. with the ceiling estimated to be 4,000 ft., broken clouds, visibility 15 statute miles, thunderstorm, very light rainshowers, barometric pressure 1010.6 millibars, temperature 77° F., dewpoint 71° F., surface wind from 150° (true) at 9 knots, altimeter setting 29.87; thunder began 7 minutes past the preceding hour (2:07 p.m. CST in this case), thunderstorm north moving to the northeast with occasional lightning cloud to cloud and cloud to ground.

The plain language interpretation of the ACT (Waco, Texas) is as follows: This is a special report as indicated by the "S" which means that a significant change in the weather has occurred during the preceding hour (or since the last report). Measured ceiling of 1,000 ft. overcast, visibility 4 miles in haze, pressure 1013.8 millibars, temperature 76° F., dewpoint 70° F., surface wind from 130° (true) at 12 knots, altimeter setting 29.95.

In the COT (Cotulla, Texas) report, the "A17⊕" means that the ceiling is 1,700 ft., broken clouds, and was obtained by an aircraft.

Of special importance sometimes, is the "remarks" portion of Aviation Weather Reports. There may be important information here that would not show up elsewhere in the report, as illustrated by the following examples:
   ACT S E25⊕8Ø⊕1Ø 112/86/71/1514/987/SWLG CU ALQDS
   AUS E2Ø⊕8Ø⊕1Ø 122/86/7Ø/1916/99Ø/TCU ALQDS
   COT E35⊕1ØØ⊕15 Ø84/9Ø/71/161Ø/979/FEW CB TCU ALQDS.

The first report "remarks" section indicates there are "swelling cumulus clouds in all quadrants" around the station. The "S" following station identification indicates this is a "special report" probably issued because of a lowering ceiling.

The second report "remarks" section indicates there are "towering cumulus clouds in all quadrants." You should interpret this to mean that these towering cumulus clouds could soon develop into thunderstorms.

The third report "remarks" section indicates there are a few "cumulonimbus clouds and towering cumulus clouds in all quadrants." At this station, some of the towering cumulus have already developed into thunderstorms.

Although the three reports are from three different stations, they could well represent three consecutive reports from the same station—starting out with "swelling cumulus" which develop into "towering cumulus" which in turn develop into "cumulonimbus" and thunderstorms. If your destination happened to be one of the above stations, you can see the importance of the "remarks" section. By the time you arrive, the area may be covered or surrounded by thunderstorms. Nowhere else in the reports is danger indicated since ceilings and visibilities are well above VFR basic minimums.

**Pilot Reports (PIREPS)** Surface weather reports spot sample the weather, and frequently weather between reporting stations will differ from that shown by the spot reports. Also, the surface observer cannot observe cloud tops, cloud conditions above an overcast, turbulence, or icing. Pilot reports are the only source of these observations, and a pilot must rely heavily on these reports when available. It behooves all pilots to report weather in flight to aid his fellow flyers. Some pilot-reported information is included in the remarks section of the hourly Aviation Weather report and some in individual pilot reports. Periodically, pilot reports are summarized into a single report called the pilot report summary.

**Example of Pilot Weather Report Summary**
```
    SAT UB Ø81835Z
    GDP SMOOTH 85 PA28
    2Ø NNE CRP-3 NNE ALI 25⊕SCTD RW
    24 NNE CRP LN TSTMS NW-SE CIG 3 HND VSBY 1/4
    JCT-SAT 4Ø⊕6Ø
    3ØE SAT RW MDT TURBC
    INK ALMOST SLD ⊕ BECOMES THEN ⊕ 25 W MAF TOPS 5Ø
    ⊕ INK TO ELP
```

**Plain Language Interpretation** This pilot report summary (UB) was filed from San Antonio, Texas, (SAT) on the 8th day of the month (08) at 1835 GMT (12:35 CST).

Guadalupe Pass (GDP) was smooth at 8,500 ft. MSL reported by a PA28 (Piper Cherokee).

Twenty miles north-northeast of Corpus Christi to a point 3 miles north-northeast of Alice, a broken layer of clouds with bases at 2,500 MSL, and rainshowers.

Twenty-four miles north-northeast of Corpus Christi, a line of thunderstorms extends northwest-southeast, with ceilings of 300 ft. and visibility ¼ mile.

From Junction to San Antonio, an overcast layer of clouds with bases at 4,000 ft. MSL and tops at 6,000 ft. MSL.

Thirty miles east of San Antonio, rainshowers with moderate turbulence.

Over Wink, there is an almost solid overcast with tops at 5,000 ft. MSL becoming clear 25 miles west of Midland.

Clear from Wink to El Paso.

## Weather Maps

The National Weather Service prepares a multitude of weather charts, some of them specifically for aviation. You can easily learn to interpret and use a few of them in determining weather significant to your proposed flights. We have already discussed the winds and temperatures aloft forecast chart and, to some extent, the surface chart. This discussion includes more detailed use of the surface chart and use of the weather depiction chart, the radar summary chart, and the surface and low-level significant weather prognostic charts.

*Surface Chart* Figure 56 is a section of a facsimile surface weather map. You already have learned (Chapter 7) to use isobars in determining surface and low-level winds. You also can identify fronts and high and low pressure centers. By comparing this chart with others to be discussed, you can associate weather patterns with these systems and estimate movements of weather patterns definitely associated with these systems.

*Weather Depiction Chart* The weather depiction chart (fig. 57) portrays graphically areas of low ceiling and restricted visibility, areas of marginal ceilings, and areas of good ceilings and visibilities. The chart covers the conterminous 48 states and southern Canada. Figure 58 shows symbols used in plotting and analyzing the chart.

*Plotted Data* Data plotted on the chart includes:

1. Sky coverage.

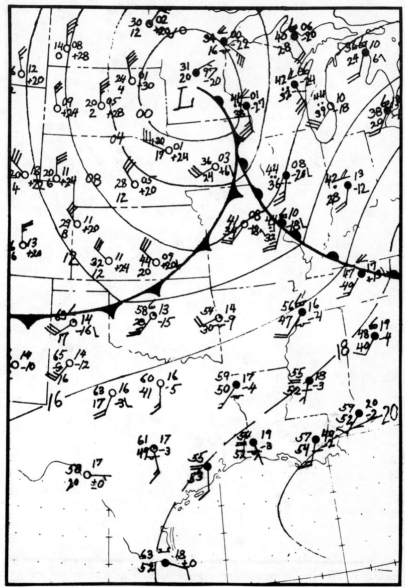

Figure 56. *Section of a surface weather map as transmitted on facsimile.*

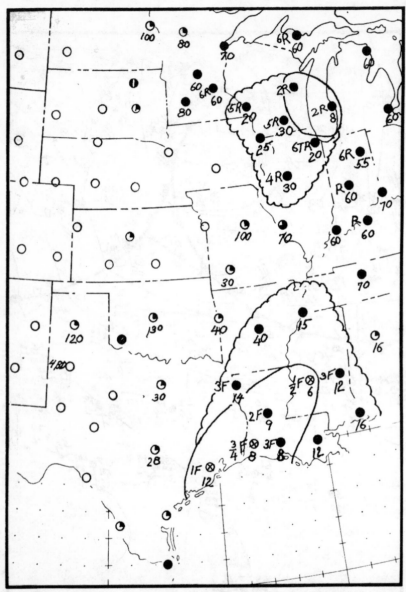

Figure 57. Section of a weather depiction chart as transmitted on facsimile. Compare with figure 56, a surface chart for the same area and approximate time.

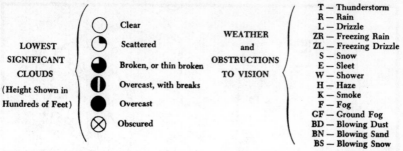

Figure 58. *Symbols used in preparing the weather depiction chart. Note how these symbols are used in figure 57. Cloud cover is shown in station circle; cloud height in hundreds of feet, below the circle; and visibility and weather to the left of the circle.*

2. Visibility (when 6 miles or less).
3. Weather and obstructions to vision.
4. Ceiling height or, if there is no ceiling, the height of the lowest layer of scattered clouds.

***Analyzed Data***   Analysis of the plotted data consists of:

Solid lines enclosing areas where ceilings are below 1,000 ft. and/or visibilities are below 3 miles. These enclosed areas may be shaded red by the local weather station.

Scalloped lines enclosing areas where ceilings are below 5,000 ft. but not below 1,000 ft. and visibilities are greater than 3 miles. These areas may be shaded in blue locally.

Weather depiction charts are prepared every 3 hours beginning with data observed at 0100 Greenwich Mean Time (7:00 p.m. CST).

Designed to give the pilot a "plan view" of a weather situation, the weather depiction chart is used most effectively in conjunction with the surface weather chart which often indicates the causes of cloud formations and/or restrictions to visibility.

Figure 57 is a section of a facsimile weather depiction chart for the same area and approximate time as the surface map in fig. 56. Compare the two charts noting the area of marginal and poor weather extending northward from northern Illinois. This weather no doubt is the result of overrunning associated with the warm and occluded fronts, and you would expect this weather to move with the frontal system. But what about the extensive area of low ceilings and restricted visibilities extending northward from the Gulf of Mexico into Arkansas and western

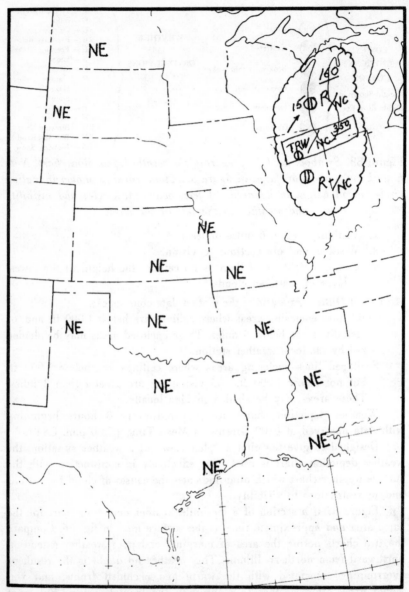

Figure 59. *Section of a radar summary chart as transmitted on facsimile. Compare with surface and weather depiction charts in figures 56 and 57 for the same area and approximate time.*

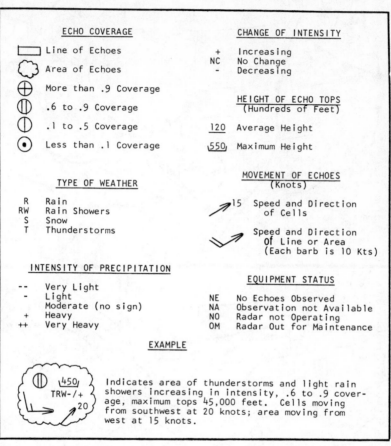

Figure 60. *Symbols used on radar summary chart. Note how these are used in figure 59.*

Tennessee? To determine its movement and expected changes, you would need to refer to forecasts and prognostic charts. Note especially the absence of weather along the cold front. The cold front is dry, and the worst you would expect with it is some turbulence as you fly through the frontal zone. However, you must be alert for more hazardous weather developing along the front if it moves into the area where moist air is moving in from the Gulf of Mexico.

***Radar Summary Chart*** Weather radar generally observes precipita-

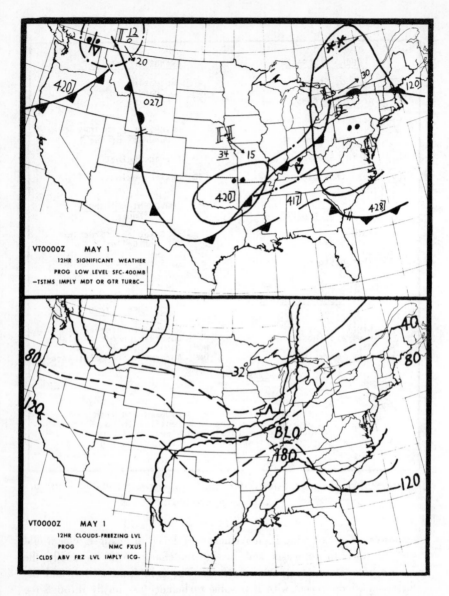

Figure 61. *Twelve- and 24-hour surface and significant weather prognostic*

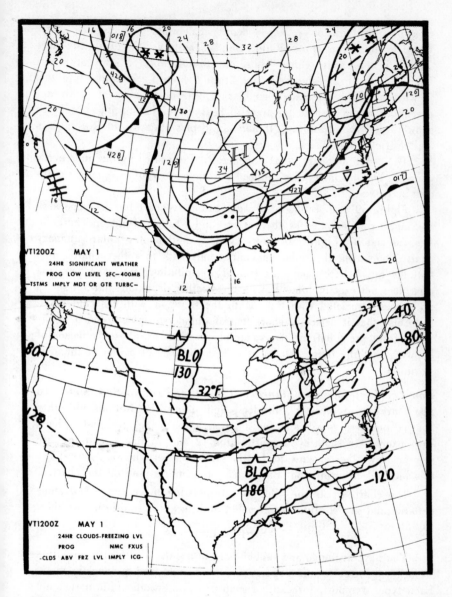

*charts. Facsimile transmission is a four-panel chart as shown here.*

tion only; it does not ordinarily detect small water droplets such as are found in fog and nonprecipitating clouds. The larger the drops, the more intense is the radar return. Thus, one would expect a stronger return from thunderstorms and hail than from lighter precipitation, and this is what happens. The radar summary chart shows areas of significant precipitation and accentuates areas of heavy precipitation associated with showers and thunderstorms. It *will not* depict all areas of low ceilings and restricted visibilities.

The radar summary chart is generally transmitted by facsimile every 3 hours, but the interval is reduced during periods of especially significant activity.

Figure 59 is a section of a radar summary chart for the same area and approximate times as the surface and weather depiction charts in figs. 56 and 57. Figure 60 shows symbols used on the radar summary chart. Comparing the radar summary chart with the other charts, note that the radar detects only the frontal precipitation; and even here, the area does not exactly coincide with the weather depiction chart. It shows no echoes associated with the fog to the south or with the cold front. Note also that it detects a short line of thunderstorms embedded in the warm front precipitation. The radar observations are the only means of knowing that the thunderstorm at Chicago is part of a line of thunderstorms.

***Low-Level Surface and Significant Weather Prognostic Charts*** To assist aviation forecasters, briefers, and pilots, the National Weather Service prepares specifically for aviation a four-panel prognostic chart. Two panels are surface prognostics for 12 and 24 hours, and two are significant weather prognostics for the same time periods. Figure 61 shows this facsimile transmission. Figure 62 lists symbols used on the chart.

The chart assists the pilot in extrapolating movements of weather patterns and in detecting development and decay of significant weather.

## Summary

You have available and should learn to use the wealth of information in printed forecasts and reports and in current and prognostic maps. Each type of report, forecast, or map provides specific information not always available from other sources. Before each flight, glean enough from this wealth of information to determine feasibility, route, and safety of your flight.

Collecting data, plotting it on a chart, and transmitting the chart

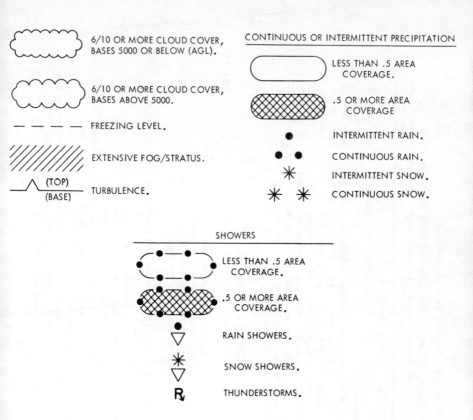

Figure 62. *Symbols used on surface and significant weather prognostic charts. These are used on the charts shown in figure 61.*

takes time. When using a chart of actual weather, remember that depicted weather occurred from 1 to 5 hours earlier. Forecasts and prognostic charts, of course, bridge this time gap. However, forecasts are not always accurate in all details. In the interest of safety, you should always check a few current sequence reports and PIREPs against forecasts and charts to determine if weather is moving and developing as forecast. If possible, use the services of a briefer who can help you interpret weather pertinent to your flight planning. Refer to Chapter 35 for more detailed information concerning weather briefings.

## Interpretation of Weather Reports Sent by Teletype.

DCA 2121ØØZ 15ØE3Ø⊕ 11/2VTRW·BD 152/68/6Ø/2918G3Ø/996/DRK NW VSBY 1V2

### GROUP I. DCA 2121ØØZ

| SYMBOL | ITEM | INTERPRETATION | TRANSLATION |
|---|---|---|---|
| DCA | Station identification. | Indicated by call letters. Call letters and all abbreviations are available at weather offices. | Washington, D. C. |
| 2121ØØZ | Date and Greenwich time. | The first two digits indicate the day of the month; the next four digits give the time (on the 24-hour clock) in Greenwich time. To convert to local time *subtract* 5 hours for eastern standard time, 6 hours for central, 7 hours for mountain, and 8 hours for Pacific. Regular sequences are sent each hour on the hour. When crucial changes occur between reporting times, a special report may be sent. In this case the date-time data will follow the station identification symbol, and the letter "S", followed by a numeral, will be added. | 21st day of the month, 4:00 p. m. eastern standard time. |

### GROUP II. 15 ⊕ E3Ø ⊕ 11/2VTRW·BD

| SYMBOL | ITEM | INTERPRETATION | TRANSLATION |
|---|---|---|---|
| 15Ø | Sky cover | Figures represent hundreds of feet (15 = 1,500 ft.). Symbol indicates amount of cover: ○ = clear; ◐ = scattered; ◑ = broken; ⊕ = overcast. The letter "X" will be used instead of these symbols whenever fog, dust, smoke, or precipitation obscure the sky. If clouds are at varying levels, two or more sets of figures and symbols are entered in ascending order of height. | Scattered clouds at 1,500 ft. |
| E3Ø⊕ | Ceiling | The ceiling figure will always be preceded by one of the following letters: E = estimated; M = measured; W = indefinite; B = balloon; R = radar; A = reported by aircraft. If the ceiling is below 3,000 ft. and is variable, the ceiling symbol will be followed by the letter "V", and in the remarks the range of height will be indicated. | Ceiling estimated 3,000 ft. |
| 11/2V | Visibility | Figures represent miles and fractions of miles. Followed by "V" if less than 3 miles and variable. If the visibility is 6 miles or less, the reason is always given under "Precipitation" or "Obstructon." | Visibility 1½ miles, variable. |
| TRW | Precipitation, thunderstorm, or tornado. | R = Rain; L = drizzLe; E = slEet; A = hAil; S = Snow; W = shoWers; T = Thunderstorm; Z = freeZing. Sometimes followed by + meaning heavy, or by − meaning light. Item omitted if there is no precipitation. Tornado is spelled out. | Thunderstorm; light rain shower. |

110

Interpretation of Weather Reports Sent by Teletype—Continued

| Symbol | Item | Interpretation | Translation |
|---|---|---|---|
| BD | Obstructions to vision. | F = Fog; H = Haze; D = Dust; N = saNd; K = smoKe (sometimes the above letters are preceded by G = ground; I = ice; B = blowing). (See fig. 54.) | Blowing dust. |

## GROUP III.  152/68/60/2918G30/996

Most of the items in this group are separated by diagonal lines (/).

| Symbol | Item | Interpretation | Translation |
|---|---|---|---|
| 152/ | Pressure | Stated in millibars using same system as on the weather map (omitting initial "9" or "10"). | Pressure 1015.2 millibars. |
| 68/ | Temperature | In degrees Fahrenheit | Temperature 68° F. |
| 60/ | Dew point | In degrees Fahrenheit | Dew point 60° F. |
| 2918G30/ | Wind | The wind group consists of at least 4 digits. These 4 digits are interpreted in the same way as in winds-aloft forecasts. The first pair of digits shows the wind direction to the nearest 10 degrees in relation to true north. The second pair of digits represents the wind speed in knots. The symbol "G" following the wind speed indicates gusts. The peak speed of gusts (in knots) follows the "G" symbol, or follows a "Q" symbol when squalls are reported. A calm wind is indicated by 0000. Wind shifts are indicated in remarks by the contraction "WSHFT" followed by the local time of the wind shift. | Wind 290° true, 18 knots; gusts to 30 knots. |
| 996/ | Altimeter setting. | Barometric pressure in inches for the setting of altimeters on aircraft. Given in three figures with the initial 2 or 3 omitted. A number beginning with 5 or higher presupposes an inital 2; a number beginning with 4 or lower presupposes an initial 3. (993 = 29.93, 002 = 30.02, etc.). | Altimeter setting at 29.96 inches. |

## GROUP IV.  DRK NW VSBY 1V2

| Symbol | Item | Interpretation | Translation |
|---|---|---|---|
| DRK NW VSBY 1V2 | Remarks | Any additional remarks are given in teletype symbols and in abbreviations of English words. Any items which are normally sent, but for some reason are missing from the transmission, are represented by the letter "M." | Dark overcast to the northwest. Visibility variable 1 to 2 miles. |

# SECTION III — NAVIGATION

## 12.  Navigation Aids

Every pilot takes pride in his ability to navigate with precision. It is a source of real satisfaction to plan and execute a flight which proceeds directly to the destination, arriving safely according to a predetermined plan with no worry or loss of time because of poor navigating technique.

Lack of skill in navigation may lead to unpleasant and sometimes dangerous situations in which changes of weather, approaching darkness, or shortage of fuel may force the pilot to attempt a landing under hazardous conditions.

Navigation used to be considered a difficult art shrouded in the mysteries of higher mathematics and requiring a combination of skill, intuition, and luck. To a certain extent that was true, but many improvements in instruments, aeronautical charts, pilot techniques, and navigation aids have enabled pilots in recent years to plan their flights with confidence and to reach their destinations according to plan. The prime requirement for success in navigation is a knowledge of a few simple facts and the ability to exercise good judgment based upon those facts.

Our discussion of navigation is limited primarily to the needs of the private pilot without instrument rating. As he gains more experience in flying, he will wish to study the subject in greater detail, but our primary purpose here is to furnish information of practical value in flying under visual flight rules (VFR).

To navigate successfully, a pilot must know his approximate position at all times or be able to determine it whenever he wishes. Position may be determined by:

1. Pilotage (by reference to visible landmarks).
2. Dead reckoning (by computing direction and distance from a known position).
3. Radio navigation (by use of radio aids).
4. Celestial navigation (by reference to the sun, moon, or other celestial bodies).

The basic form of navigation for the inexperienced pilot is pilotage, and it should be mastered first. An understanding of the principles of dead reckoning, however, will enable him to make necessary calculations of flight time and fuel consumption. The ever-increasing use of radio equipment in private planes makes it highly desirable for the pilot to have a thorough knowledge of the use of radio for navigation and communications. Celestial navigation is of little value to the private pilot and is not explained in this handbook.

*Airways*    A significant part of the work of the Federal Aviation Administration is the development and operation of Federal Airways—a vast network of thousands of miles of air highways covering the entire United States, connecting all the principal cities, which is rapidly being extended. While a pilot on a VFR flight is not required to follow the airways, he frequently will find them convenient because they are equipped with various aids and have been established specifically to promote his convenience and safety.

*Airway Aids*    Along the airways, radio navigation aids are appropriately spaced to provide navigation guidance and air-ground communications facilities. Weather reporting service is available through hourly weather broadcasts or at the pilot's request. The Federal Aviation Administration operates many additional facilities and services to assist pilots and to direct the flow of traffic along the airways—such as air route traffic control centers, Flight Service Stations, airport traffic control towers, radar facilities, and instrument approach and landing systems. Some of these facilities and services are discussed more fully in later chapters.

*Aeronautical Charts*    Aeronautical charts for use in the United States are published by the National Ocean Survey. The types of charts of greatest interest to private pilots are:

1. Sectional Aeronautical Charts (scale: about 8 statute miles per inch) —fairly complete detail, primarily for use in pilotage, most widely used by private pilots. These charts are identified by the names of principal cities or geographical features (fig. 63). Complete set of charts consists of 37 sheets.

2. Local Aeronautical Charts (scale: about 4 statute miles per inch) — large scale, primarily for use on VFR flights in highly congested areas, more topographical detail than any other chart. The charts are identified by the names of cities, such as Atlanta Local.

3. Aeronautical Planning Charts (scale: about 80 statute miles per inch)—designed for planning long flights, selected key points may be transferred to more detailed local charts for actual flight use.

4. World Aeronautical Charts (scale: about 16 statute miles per inch) —supplies, on a smaller scale, most of the information appearing on sectional charts. Consists of 11 charts identified by letters and numbers, such as CG-19.

A free index of these and other charts, listing their prices with instructions for ordering, is available upon request from:

Distribution Division (C-44)
National Ocean Survey
Washington, D. C. 20325

Figure 63 shows a map of the conterminous United States upon which is superimposed a key identifying the Sectional Charts and indicating the area covered by each.

It is vitally important that pilots check the publication date on each aeronautical chart to be used on any flight. *Obsolete charts should be discarded and replaced by new editions, ordinarily published every 6 months.* (The Airman's Information Manual contains a list of the dates of the latest edition of each chart.) This is extremely important because critical revisions in aeronautical information are occurring constantly. These include changes in radio frequencies, construction of new obstructions, temporary closing of certain runways and airports, and other temporary and permanent hazards to flight. To make sure your sectional aeronautical chart is up to date, refer to the Sectional Chart Bulletin in the *Airman's Information Manual* (AIM), Part 3. This Bulletin provides the VFR pilot with the essential information necessary to update and maintain his chart. It lists the major changes in aeronautical information that have occurred since the last publication date of each sectional chart. Specifically, it contains the following:

1. Changes to controlled airspace and special use airspace that present hazardous conditions or impose restrictions on the pilot.
2. Major changes to airports and radio navigational facilities.

When a sectional chart is republished, the corrections will be removed from AIM and begin again for the new chart. See Chapter 27 for further information.

To help make sure that the latest charts are used, regularly revised lists entitled "Dates of Latest Prints" are published and are available from the same source as the charts.

# 13.  Chart Reading

### Sectional Aeronautical Charts

While studying this chapter use a Dallas-Ft. Worth Sectional Chart . This is the type of sectional chart most recently issued by the National Ocean Survey. All of the 87 old-type sectional charts have now been converted to 37 of the new-type charts (see fig 63). Hence, discussions here deal with the new chart only. The major change between the old and the new sectional chart is that the old type contained a chart on one side only, while the new type contains a chart on both sides. The pilot should have little difficulty in reading these aeronautical charts. In many respects, they are similar to automobile road maps. The chart name or title appears on one side of each chart. On this same side there also appears various aeronautical symbols as well as information concerning terrain and contour elevations. By referring to these symbols, one may identify aeronautical, topographical, and obstruction symbols (such as radio and television towers). Many landmarks easily recognizable from the air, such as stadiums, race tracks, pumping stations, and refineries, are identified by brief descriptions besides small black squares marking their exact locations. Oil fields are shown by small circles, water tanks and oil tanks are shown by small black circles and labeled accordingly. Many of the items are exaggerated on the chart in order to be seen easily.

Remember, however, that the information on aeronautical charts may be as old as 6 months, depending on the date published. Check the date on the chart to make sure you are using the latest available.

***Relief***    The elevation of land surface, *relief*, is shown on aeronautical charts by brown contour lines drawn at 250-foot intervals. These areas are emphasized by various tints, as indicated in the color legend appearing on each chart.

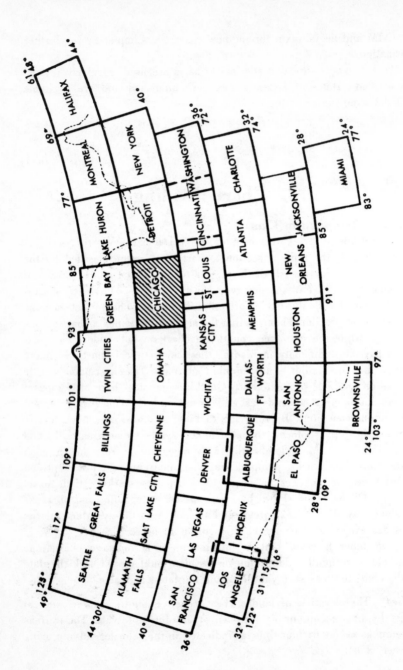

Figure 63. Index of sectional charts.

The manner in which contours express elevation, form, and degree of slope is shown in figure 64. The sketch in the upper part of the figure represents a river valley lying between two hills. In the foreground is the sea, with a bay that is partly enclosed by a hooked sandbar. On each side of the valley is a terrace into which small streams have cut narrow gullies. The hill on the right has a rounded summit and gently sloping spurs separated by ravines. The spurs are cut off sharply at their lower ends by a sea cliff. The hill at the left terminates abruptly at the valley in a steep and almost vertical bluff, from which it slopes gradually away and forms an inclined tableland traversed by a few shallow gullies. Each of these features is represented directly beneath its position in the sketch by contour lines. In figure 64 the contours represent successive differences in elevation of 20 feet—that is, the contour interval is 20 feet. A small

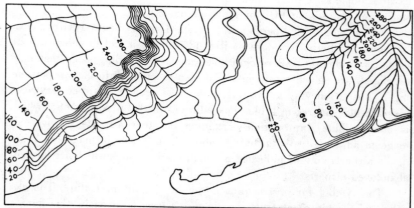

Figure 64. *Altitude, form, and slope of terrain as indicated by contour lines and numerals (U.S. Geological Survey).*

117

interval was used to better illustrate the terrain features that may be visualized through contours.

***Aeronautical Data***  The aeronautical information on the new-type sectional charts is for the most part self-explanatory. Information concerning very high frequency (VHF) radio facilities such as tower frequencies, omnidirectional radio ranges (VOR), and other VHF communications frequencies is shown in dark blue. Likewise, a narrow band of blue tint is used to indicate the center lines of Victor Airways (VOR civil airways between omnirange stations). Low frequency—medium frequency (LF/MF) radio facilities are shown in magenta (purplish shade of red); a narrow band of magenta tint is used to indicate LF/MF airways; and LF/MF frequencies are shown in magenta.

In most instances, FAA radio range stations identify themselves by broadcasting their call signs in International Morse Code. VOR stations use three-letter identifiers, whereas LF/MF range stations may use three-letter identifiers or two-letter identifiers. The two-letter identification is normally used only in areas where a VOR facility and an LF/MF range facility use the same name. For example, the Anchorage, Alaska, VOR facility is identified by the letters ANC (.– –. –.–.) and the Anchorage LF/MF range facility is identified by the letters AC (.– –.–.). Therefore, both identifiers (two-letter for the LF/MF; three-letter for the VOR) and the Morse codes for both, appear on the aeronautical charts; LF/MF in magenta and VOR in blue. (NOTE: The Anchorage facilities are used as an example since there is only one LF range left in the 48 conterminous states, and there is no VOR by the same name.)

All airports having permanent-type, hard-surfaced runways are shown by runway patterns for more positive identification and to enhance their value as landmarks. All recognizable runways including some that may be closed, are shown to aid in visual identification. Information pertaining to airports having an airport traffic area or FSS advisory service is given in blue figures in a blue box adjacent to the airport symbol which is also in blue. Information pertaining to other airports is given in magenta adjacent to the airport symbol which is also in magenta. Abandoned airports may be indicated by small black squares which are labeled, abandoned airports.

The symbol for obstructions is another important feature. The elevation of the top of obstructions above sea level is given in blue figures (with parentheses) beside the obstruction symbol. Immediately below this set of figures is another set of lighter blue figures enclosed in parentheses which represents the height of the top of the obstruction above ground level. Obstructions which extend less than 1,000 ft. above the terrain are shown by one symbol and those obstructions that extend 1,000 ft. or higher above ground level are indicated by a different symbol (see sectional chart). Specific elevations of certain high points in terrain are shown on charts by dots accompanied by black figures indicating the number of feet above sea level.

An explanation for most symbols used on aeronautical charts appears in the margin of the chart. Additional information appears at the bottom of the chart.

*Airport and Air Navigation Lighting and Marking Aids* On sectional charts, lighting aids are shown by a blue star or dot along with certain other symbols and coded information. For the most part, the lighting aids represented on sectional charts pertain to rotating or flashing lights. The color or color combination displayed by a particular beacon and/or its auxiliary lights tells whether the beacon is indicating a landing place, landmark, point of the Federal Airways, or hazard. Coded flashes of the auxiliary lights, if employed, further identify the beacon site. A detailed description of airport and air navigation lighting aids can be found in AIM.

In the same section of the AIM, airport marking aids are also presented. Pilots should study and understand this very important information.

# 14. Measurement of Direction

The equator is an imaginary circle equidistant from the poles of the earth. Circles parallel to the equator (lines running east and west), *parallels of latitude,* enable us to measure distance in degrees of latitude north or south of the equator. Consequently, the angular distance from the equator to the pole (one-fourth of a circle) is 90°. The 48 conterminous states of the United States lie between 25° and 49° N. latitude. The arrows in figure 65 labeled "LATITUDE" point to lines of latitude.

Meridians of longitude are drawn from the North Pole to the South Pole and are at right angles to the equator. The meridian passing through Greenwich, England, the "Prime Meridian," is used as the zero line from which measurements are made in degrees east and west to 180°. The 48 conterminous states of the United States lie between 67° and 125° W.

longitude. The arrows in figure 65 labeled "LONGITUDE" point to lines of longitude.

Any specific geographical point can thus be located by reference to its longitude and latitude. Washington, D.C., is approximately 39° N. latitude, 77° W. longitude. Chicago is approximately 42° N. latitude, 88° W. longitude (fig. 65).

The meridians are also useful for designating time belts. A day is defined as the time required for the earth to make one complete revolution of 360°. Since the day is divided into 24 hours, the earth revolves at the rate of 15° an hour. Noon is the time when the sun lies directly above a meridian; to the west of that meridian is forenoon, to the east is afternoon.

Figure 65. *Meridians and parallels—the basis of measuring time, distance, and direction.*

The standard practice is to establish a time belt for each 15° of longitude, which makes a difference of exactly 1 hour between each belt. In the United States there are four such belts—Eastern (75°), Central (90°), Mountain (105°), and Pacific (120°). The dividing lines are somewhat irregular because communities near the boundaries often find it more convenient to use time designations of neighboring communities or trade centers.

Figure 66 shows the time zones in the United States. When the sun is directly above the 90th meridian, it is noon Central Standard Time. At the same time it will be 1 p.m. Eastern Standard Time, 11 a.m. Mountain Standard Time, and 10 a.m. Pacific Standard Time. When "daylight saving" time is in effect (generally between the last Sunday in April and the last Sunday in October) the sun is directly above the 75th meridian at noon, Central Daylight Time.

These time zone differences must be taken into account during long flights east—especially one that must be completed before dark. Remember, you may be losing an hour when flying from one time zone to another, or, for that matter, when flying from the western edge to the eastern edge of the same time zone. Check the time of sunset at your point of destination and take this into account when you plan an east-

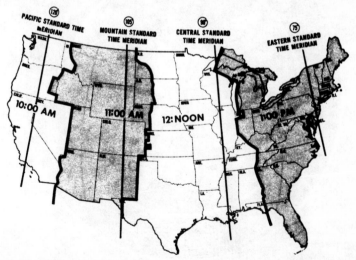

Figure 66. *When the sun is directly above the meridian, the time at points on that meridian is noon. This is the basis on which time zones are established.*

bound flight, if the flight must be completed during daylight. Times of sunset can normally be obtained from a FSS or National Weather Service Station.

In most aviation operations, time is expressed in terms of the 24-hour clock. Air traffic control instructions, weather reports and broadcasts, and estimated times of arrival are all based on this system. For example: 9 a.m. Central Standard Time is expressed as 0900C; 1 p.m. Mountain Standard Time is 1300M; 10 p.m. Eastern Standard Time 2200E. These times will often be abbreviated as 09C, 13M, and 22E, respectively.

**Measurement of Courses**  By using the meridians, direction from one point to another can be indicated in terms of degrees measured in a clockwise direction from true north. Thus, to indicate a course to be followed in flight, the pilot will draw a line on the chart from the point of departure to the destination and measure the angle which this line

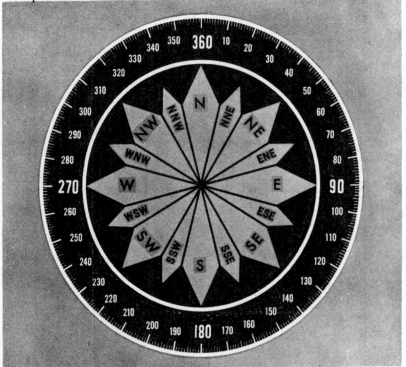

Figure 67. *The compass rose enables the pilot to determine direction in terms of points of the compass and degrees of arc.*

makes with a meridian. Direction is expressed in terms of degrees, as shown by the compass rose in figure 67.

Because meridians converge toward the poles, course measurement should be taken at a *meridian near the midpoint* of the course rather than at the point of departure. The course thus measured on the chart is known as the *true course*, because it represents a direction measured by reference to a meridian or true north. It is the direction of *intended* flight as measured in degrees clockwise from *true north*. As shown in figure 68, the direction from *A* to *B* would be a true course of 065°, whereas the return trip (sometimes called the reciprocal) would be a true course of 245°.

The direction in which the nose of the airplane points during a flight when measured in degrees clockwise from true north, is the *true heading*. Usually it is necessary to head the plane in a direction slightly different from the true course to offset the effect of wind; consequently, the true heading generally does not correspond with the true course. This will be discussed more fully in subsequent chapters; *in this chapter we shall assume no-wind conditions, under which heading and course would coincide.* Thus, for a true course of 065° the true heading would be 065°. However, if we wished to fly by the compass, we should make corrections for magnetic variation and for compass deviation.

***Variation*** Variation is the angle between true north and **magnetic** north at any given place. It is expressed as *east variation* or *west varia-*

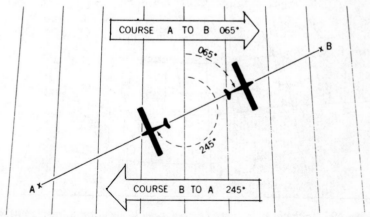

Figure 68. *Courses are determined by reference to meridians on aeronautical charts.*

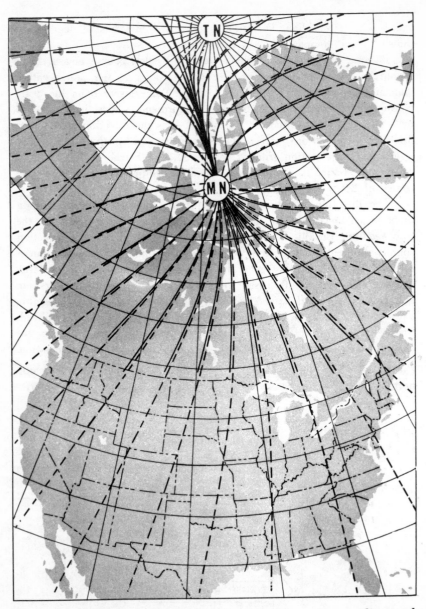

Figure 69. *Magnetic meridians (dotted rules), geographic meridians and parallels are solid black, variation is the angle between a magnetic and geographic meridian.*

*tion* depending upon whether magnetic north (MN) is to the east or west of true north (TN), respectively.

The north magnetic pole is located close to latitude 71° N., longitude 96° W.—about 1,300 miles from the geographic or true north pole, as indicated in figure 69. If the earth were uniformly magnetized, the compass needle would point toward the magnetic pole, in which case the variation between true north (as shown by the geographical meridians) and magnetic north (as shown by the magnetic meridians) could be measured at any intersection of the meridians.

Actually, the earth is not uniformly magnetized. In the United States the needle usually points in the general direction of the magnetic pole but it may vary in certain geographical localities by many degrees. Consequently, the exact amount of variation at thousands of selected locations in the United States has been carefully determined by the National Ocean Survey. The amount and the direction of variation, which change slightly from time to time, are shown on most aeronautical charts as broken red lines, *called isogonic lines*, which connect points of equal magnetic variation. (The line connecting points at which there is no variation between true north and magnetic north is the *agonic line*.) An isogonic chart is shown in figure 70. Minor bends and turns in the isogonic and agonic lines probably are caused by unusual geological conditions that affect the magnetic forces in certain areas.

From this it can be readily seen that on the west coast of the United States the compass needle will point to the east of true north, on the east coast it will point to the west of true north. On a line running roughly through Lake Michigan, the Appalachian Mountains and off the coast of Florida, magnetic north and true north coincide (compare figs. 70 and 71).

Because courses are measured by geographical meridians which point toward true north, and are flown by reference to the compass which points along the magnetic meridian (in the general direction of magnetic north), the true direction must be converted into magnetic direction for the purpose of flight. This conversion is made by adding or subtracting the variation indicated by the nearest isogonic line on the chart. The true heading, when corrected for variation, is known as *magnetic heading*.

At Providence, R. I., the variation is shown as "14° W." This means that magnetic north is 14° west of true north. If we wished to fly a true heading of north, we would have to add these 14° and fly a magnetic heading of 014°. The same correction for variation must be applied to the true heading to obtain any magnetic heading at Providence, or at any point close to the isogonic line "14° W." Thus, to fly east, we would use a magnetic heading of 090° + 14° = 104°. To fly south, the magnetic heading would be 180° + 14° = 194°. To fly west, it would be 270° + 14° = 284°. To fly a true heading of 060°, we would use a magnetic heading of 060° + 14° = 074° (fig. 72).

Now suppose we are in Denver, Colo., where the isogonic line shows the variation to be "14° E." This means that magnetic north is 14° to the east of true north. Therefore, to fly a true heading of north, we would have to subtract these 14° and fly a magnetic heading of 346° (360° − 14°). Again the 14° would be subtracted from the appropriate true heading to obtain the magnetic heading at any point close to the isogonic line "14° E." Thus, to fly east we would use a magnetic heading of 076° (090° − 14°). To fly south the magnetic heading would be 166° (180° − 14°). To fly west it would be 256° (270° − 14°). To fly a true heading of 060°, we would use a magnetic heading of 060° − 14° = 046° (fig. 72).

To summarize: To convert TRUE (measured from the meridians

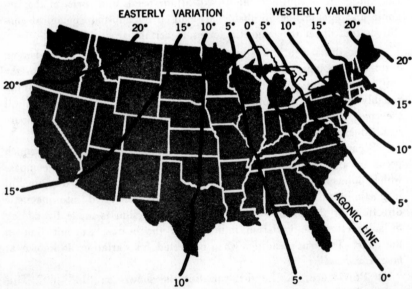

Figure 70. *A typical isogonic chart. The black lines are isogonic lines which connect geographical points with identical magnetic variation.*

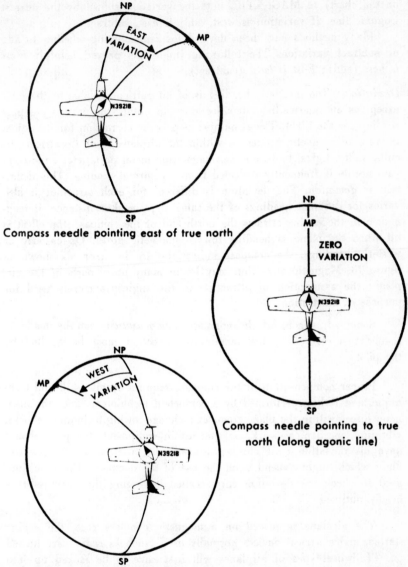

Compass needle pointing east of true north

Compass needle pointing to true north (along agonic line)

Compass needle pointing west of true north

Figure 71. *In an area of west variation a compass needle points west of true north; in an area of zero variation it points to true north; in an area of east variation it points east of true north.*

127

on the chart) to MAGNETIC, note the variation shown by the nearest isogonic line. If variation is west, add; if east, subtract.

Many methods have been devised for remembering whether to add or subtract variation. The following jingle has proved helpful: *West is best* (add); *East is least* (subtract).

**Deviation** The magnetic heading is of no particular value to the pilot except as an intermediate step necessary to obtain the correct compass reading for the flight. The remaining step is the correction for deviation. Because of magnetic influences within the airplane itself (electrical circuits, radio, lights, tools, engine, magnetized metal parts, etc.), the compass needle is frequently deflected from its normal reading. This deflection is *deviation*. The deviation is different for each airplane; it also varies for different headings of the same airplane. For instance, if magnetism in the engine attracts the north end of the compass, the effect is nil when the plane is heading toward magnetic north. On easterly or westerly headings, the compass indications are in error, as shown in figure 73. Magnetic attraction may lie in many other parts of the airplane; the assumption of attraction in the engine is merely used for purpose of illustration.

Some adjustment of the compass, *compensation,* can be made to reduce this error, but the remaining correction must be applied by the pilot.

Proper compensation of the compass requires special skill and technique, and is best performed by a competent technician. Since the magnetic forces within the plane frequently change, owing to landing shocks, vibration, mechanical work, or changes in equipment, the pilot should have his deviation card checked occasionally, particularly before any flight which might depend upon the use of the compass. The procedure used to check the deviation card (called "swinging the compass") is briefly outlined.

The airplane is placed on a magnetic compass rose, the engine started, and electrical devices normally used (such as radio) are turned on. (Tailwheel-types of airplanes will first have to be jacked up into flying position.) The plane is aligned with magnetic north indicated on the compass rose and the reading shown on the compass is recorded. The plane is rotated through each 30° and each reading is recorded. If the airplane is to be flown at night, the lights are turned on and any

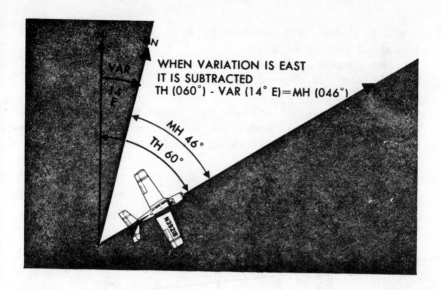

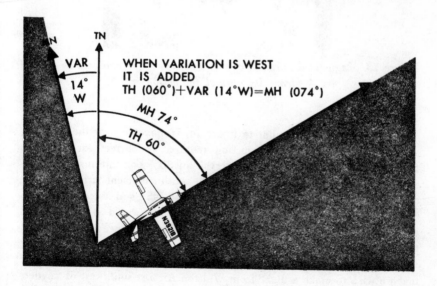

Figure 72. *The relationship between true heading, magnetic heading, and variation in areas of east and west variation.*

significant changes in the readings are noted. If so, additional entries are made for use at night.

As a practical method of roughly checking the accuracy of the compass, the pilot may compare the compass reading with known runway headings.

On the compass card the letters, N, E, S, and W, are used for north, east, south, and west. The final zero is omitted from the degree markings so that figures may be larger and more easily seen.

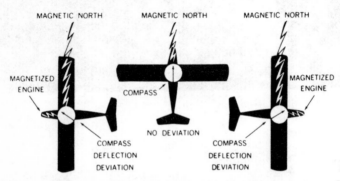

Figure 73. *Magnetized portions of the plane cause the compass to deviate from its normal indication.*

A deviation card, similar to figure 74, is mounted near the compass, showing the addition or subtraction required to correct for deviation on various headings, usually at intervals of 30°. For intermediate readings, the pilot can interpolate mentally with sufficient accuracy. For example, if the pilot wanted the correction for 195° and noted the correction for 180° to be 0° and for 210° to be +2°, he would assume that the correction for 195° would be +1°. *The magnetic heading, when corrected for deviation, is known as compass heading.*

To illustrate the application of the compass corrections, assume that we wish to make a flight from Winston Airport southwest of Snyder, Texas (32° 42′ N. Latitude; 100° 57′ W. Longitude), direct to Mineral Wells Airport southeast of Mineral Wells, Texas (32° 47′ N. Latitude; 98° 03′ W. Longitude). *A line should be drawn on the Dallas-Ft. Worth chart from the center of the Winston Airport to the center of the Mineral*

| FOR (MAGNETIC) ........ | N | 30 | 60 | E | 120 | 150 |
|---|---|---|---|---|---|---|
| STEER (COMPASS) ........ | 0 | 28 | 57 | 86 | 117 | 148 |
| FOR (MAGNETIC) ........ | S | 210 | 240 | W | 300 | 330 |
| STEER (COMPASS) .......... | 180 | 212 | 243 | 274 | 303 | 332 |

Figure 74. *Compass deviation card.*

*Wells Airport.* The mid-meridian for this course is at 99° 30′ Longitude. Measuring the direction of the course line at this meridian with a protractor gives us a true course (TC) of 088°. If there were no wind, our true heading (TH) would be the same as our true course, or 088°. Magnetic variation over comparatively short distances is obtained from the iso-gonic line on the navigation chart nearest the mid-point of the planned route. If the flight distance and direction is such that a number of isogonic lines will be crossed, then the number of degrees of variation added or subtracted must be recomputed as appropriate to allow for significant changes in variation. Variation (VAR) for this course is shown by the mid-isogonic line as 10° E. as shown in fig. 75. Subtracting 10° from 088° gives us a magnetic heading (MH) of 078°. Checking the deviation card for our airplane, we find the instructions "for E (090°) steer 086°," which tell us to subtract 4° from the magnetic heading, making our compass heading (CH) read 078° − 4°, or 074°. We should now be able to take off from Winston Airport and fly direct to Mineral Wells Airport (assuming no wind) with our magnetic compass reading 074°. Figure 75 shows the relationship between true heading, magnetic heading, and compass heading in this particular problem. Of course, the lines depicting true north (TN), magnetic north (MN), and compass north (CN) might fall in any order depending upon the direction of variation and deviation.

The magnetic compass is a thoroughly reliable instrument upon which the pilot may depend if he is aware of its idiosyncracies. When the airplane is banked in a turn, the compass is tilted from the horizontal plane and will give an incorrect reading. This is often called the north-erly turning error. When the speed of the airplane is increasing or de-creasing the compass is subject to an acceleration error. But when the airplane is in steady straight-and-level flight, the pilot may be quite sure that if his judgment disagrees with the compass reading, the error lies in judgment and not in the compass. Frequently, a pilot suffers the

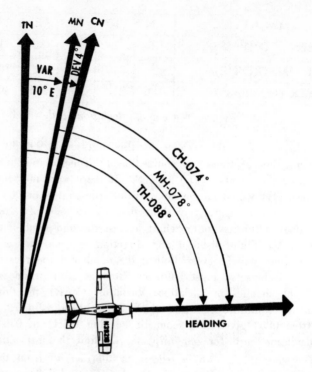

**Figure 75.** *Relationship between true, magnetic, and compass heading for a particular instance.*

illusion that the compass is stuck. This, of course, is possible, but not probable. A simple test is to make a 90° turn using some line on the ground as a point of reference and resume level flight. If the compass then shows a change of 90° in the reading, the pilot may return to his original course with the assurance that his compass is not seriously in error. The magnetic compass will be more fully covered in the section on instruments.

# 15. Basic Calculations

In Chapter 14 we determined how to measure the true course on the aeronautical chart and how to make corrections for variation and deviation, but one important factor has not been considered—wind effect.

***Effect of Wind*** As we learned in our study of the atmosphere, wind is a term used to indicate that a body of air is moving over the surface of the earth in a definite direction. When we say that the wind is blowing from the north at 25 m.p.h., we simply mean that air is moving southward over the earth's surface at the rate of 25 miles in 1 hour.

Under these conditions, any inert object wholly free from contact with the earth will be carried 25 miles southward in 1 hour. This effect becomes apparent when we observe clouds, dust, toy balloons, etc., blown along by the wind. Obviously, an airplane flying within the moving mass of air will be affected in exactly the same way. However, the airplane moves through the air at the same time that the air is moving over the ground. Consequently, at the end of 1 hour of flight, the airplane will be in a position which results from a combination of these two motions: the movement of the air mass in reference to the ground, and the forward movement of the airplane through the air mass.

Actually, these two motions are independent. So far as the airplane's flight through the air is concerned, it makes no difference whether the air is moving or is stationary. A pilot flying in a 70-mile gale would be totally unaware of any wind (except for possible turbulence) unless he looked at the ground. In reference to the ground, however, the airplane would appear to fly faster with a tailwind or slower with a headwind, or to drift right or left with a crosswind.

As shown in figure 76, an airplane flying eastward at an airspeed of 120 m.p.h. in still air, will have a ground speed exactly the same— 120 m.p.h. If the mass of air is moving eastward at 20 m.p.h., the speed of the airplane (airspeed) will not be affected, but the progress of the plane as measured over the ground will be 120 plus 20, or a ground speed of 140 m.p.h. On the other hand, if the mass of air is moving westward at 20 m.p.h., the speed of the airplane still remains the same, but ground speed becomes 120 minus 20 or 100 m.p.h.

If the plane is heading eastward at 120 m.p.h., and the air mass moving southward at 20 m.p.h., the plane at the end of 1 hour will be 120 miles east of its point of departure (due to its progress through the air) and 20 miles south (due to the motion of the air) (fig. 77). Under these circumstances the airspeed remains 120 m.p.h., but the ground speed is determined by combining the movement of the airplane with the movement of the air mass. Ground speed can be measured as the distance from the point of departure to the position of the airplane at the end of 1 hour. The ground speed can be computed in flight by

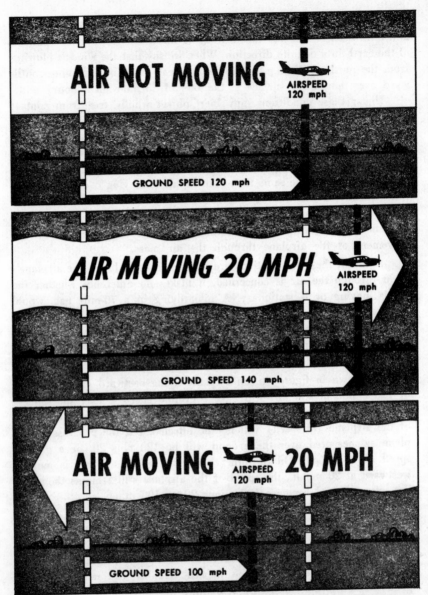

Figure 76. *Motion of the air affects the speed with which airplanes move over the earth's surface. Airspeed, the rate at which a plane moves through the air, is not affected by air motion.*

noting the time required to fly between two points a known distance apart (such as two checkpoints on the course). It also can be determined before flight by constructing a wind triangle, which will be explained in Chapter 16.

The direction in which the plane is pointing as it flies is *heading*. Its actual path over the ground, a combination of the motion of the airplane and the motion of the air, is *track*. The angle between the heading and the track is *drift angle*. If the airplane is headed down the course line with the wind blowing from the left, the track will not coincide with the desired course. The wind will drift the airplane to the right, so the track will fall to the right of the desired course (fig. 78).

By anticipating the amount of drift, the pilot can counteract the effect of the wind, thereby making the track of the airplane coincide with the desired course. If the mass of air is moving across the course from the left, the airplane will drift to the right, and a correction must be made by heading the airplane sufficiently to the left to offset this drift. To state it another way, if the wind is from the left the correction will be made by turning the airplane to the left—correct into the wind. This is the wind correction angle and is expressed in terms of degrees right or left of the true course (fig. 79).

To summarize:

COURSE is the direction toward the destination, as measured on the chart.

HEADING is the direction in which the nose of the airplane points during flight.

TRACK is the actual path made over the ground in flight. (If proper correction has been made for the wind, track and course will be identical.)

DRIFT ANGLE is the angle between heading and track.

WIND CORRECTION ANGLE is correction applied to the course to establish a heading that will make track coincide with course.

AIRSPEED is the rate of the plane's progress through the air.

GROUND SPEED is the rate of the plane's progress over the ground.


*Calculating Time, Speed, Distance, and Fuel Consumption* Before attempting a cross-country flight, a pilot will need to know how to make common calculations for time, speed, and distance, and the amount of fuel required. These are all matters of simple arithmetic, which should present no difficulty.

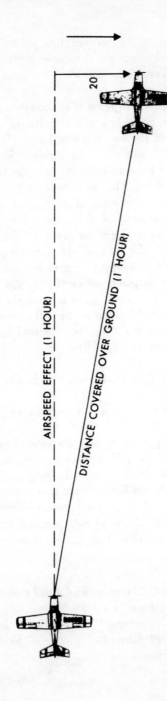

Figure 77. *Airplane flight path resulting from its airspeed and direction, and the wind speed and duration.*

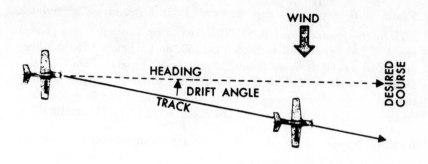

Figure 78. *Effects of wind drift on maintaining desired course.*

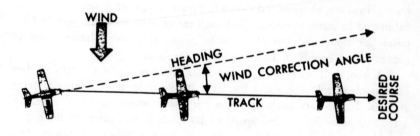

Figure 79. *Establishing a wind correction angle that will counteract wind drift and maintain the desired course.*

**Converting Minutes to Equivalent Hours** Because speed is expressed in miles per hour, it frequently is necessary to convert minutes into equivalent hours when solving speed, time, and distance problems. To convert minutes to hours, divide by 60 (60 minutes = 1 hour). Thus, 30 minutes equals $\frac{30}{60}$ = 0.5 hour. To convert hours to minutes, multiply by 60. Thus, 0.75 hour equals 0.75 × 60 = 45 minutes.

***Time***   $T = \dfrac{D}{GS}$.   To find the time (T) in flight, divide the distance (D) by the ground speed (GS). The time to fly 210 miles at a ground speed of 140 m.p.h. is 210 divided by 140, or 1.5 hours. (The 0.5 hour multiplied by 60 minutes equals 30 minutes.) Answer: 1:30.

***Distance***   $D = GS \times T$.   To find the distance flown in a given time, multiply ground speed by time. The distance flown in 1 hour and 45 minutes at a ground speed of 120 m.p.h. is 120 × 1.75, or 210 miles.

***Ground Speed***   $GS = \dfrac{D}{T}$.   To find the ground speed, divide the distance flown by the time required. If an airplane flies 270 miles in 3 hours, the ground speed is 270 divided by 3 = 90 m.p.h.

***Converting Knots to Miles Per Hour***   Another important conversion is changing knots to miles per hour. Air carriers and the military services use knots rather than miles per hour when reporting speeds. The National Weather Service reports both surface winds and winds aloft in knots. However, airspeed indicators in personal-type airplanes are normally calibrated in miles per hour (although many are now calibrated in both miles per hour and knots). Private pilots, therefore, should learn to convert wind speeds in knots to miles per hour.

A knot is 1 nautical mile per hour. Because there are 6,076.1 feet in a nautical mile and 5,280 feet in a statute mile, the conversion factor is 1.15. To convert knots to miles per hour, simply multiply knots by 1.15. For example: a wind speed of 20 knots is equivalent to 23 m.p.h.

Most computers used in navigation have a means of making this conversion simply by reading the scale. Another quick method of conversion is to use the scales of nautical miles and statute miles at the bottom of aeronautical charts.

***Fuel Consumption***   Airplane fuel consumption rate is computed in gallons per hour.

Consequently, to determine the fuel required for a given flight, you must know the time required. Time in flight multiplied by rate of consumption gives the quantity of fuel required. For example, a flight of 400 miles at a ground speed of 100 m.p.h. requires 4 hours. If the plane consumes 5 gallons an hour, the total consumption will be 4 × 5, or 20 gallons.

The rate of fuel consumption depends on many factors: the condition of the engine, the pitch and speed of propeller rotation, the richness of the mixture, and particularly the percentage of horsepower used for flight at cruising speed. Ordinarily, the pilot will know the approximate rate from cruise performance charts, from his own experience, or from the experience of someone familiar with the plane. In addition to the amount of fuel required for his trip, he should always allow enough reserve for *at least* an additional 45 minutes of flight.

# 16. The Wind Triangle

The wind triangle is a simple graphic explanation of the effect of wind upon flight. It gives the pilot essential information about ground speed, heading, and time for any flight. It is used by all pilots, from the novice to the most experienced navigator, and applies to the simplest kind of cross-country flight as well as the most complicated instrument flight. The seasoned pilot becomes so familiar with the fundamental principles that he can usually make rough estimates adequate for visual flight without actually drawing the diagrams. *The beginning student, however, needs to develop skill in constructing these diagrams as an aid to his complete understanding of wind effect.* Either consciously or unconsciously, every good pilot thinks of his flight in terms of the wind triangle.

If you wish to fly a course to the east, with a wind blowing from northeast, you know you must head the plane somewhat to the north of east to counteract drift. This you can represent by a diagram as shown in figure 80. Each line represents direction and speed. The long dotted line shows the direction the plane is heading, and its length represents the airspeed for 1 hour. The short dotted line at the right shows the wind direction, and its length represents the wind velocity for 1 hour. The solid line shows the direction of the track, or the path of the airplane as measured over the ground, and its length represents the distance traveled in 1 hour, or the ground speed.

In actual practice, do not draw the triangle illustrated in figure 80; instead, construct a similar triangle as shown by the solid lines in figure 81.

Take a typical problem. Suppose you wish to fly from E to P. Draw a line on the chart connecting the two points, measure its direction (see Chapter 14) with a protractor, or plotter, and find the true course to be due east (090°). You then learn from the National Weather

Figures 80 and 81 show how to construct the wind triangle with a protractor or ruler.

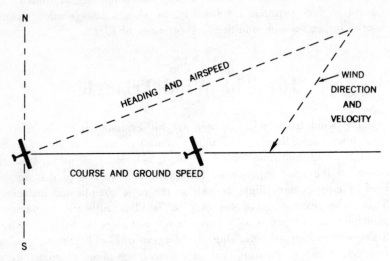

Figure 80. *Principle of the wind triangle.*

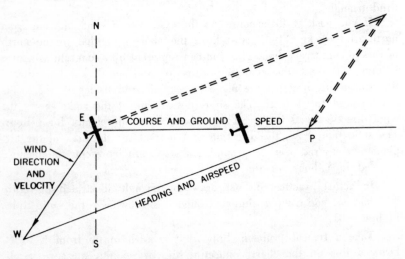

Figure 81. *The wind triangle as it is drawn in navigation practice. Double lines show the triangle as drawn in figure 80.*

Service that the weather is favorable and the wind at the altitude you intend to fly is 35 knots from the northeast (045°). Since the National Weather Service reports the windspeed in knots, convert that speed to approximately 40 m.p.h. You know that your normal airspeed is 120 m.p.h.

Now on a plain sheet of paper draw a vertical line representing north and south. (The various steps are shown in fig. 82).

Place the protractor with the base resting on this line and the curved edge facing east. At the center point of the base, make a dot labeled "E" (point of departure), and at the curved edge, make a dot at 90° (indicating the direction of your course) and another at 45° (indicating wind direction).

With the ruler draw the true course line from E extending it somewhat beyond the dot at 90°, and labeling it "TC 090°."

Next, align the ruler with E and the dot at 45°, and draw the wind arrow from E, not toward 045°, but in the direction the wind is blowing, making it 40 units long, to correspond with the wind velocity of 40 m.p.h. Identify this line as the wind line by placing the letter "W" at the end to show the wind direction. Finally, measure 120 units on the ruler to represent the airspeed, making a dot on the ruler at this point. The units used may be of any convenient scale or value, but once selected, the same scale must be used for each of the linear measurements involved. Then place the ruler so that the end is on the arrowhead (W) and the 120-mile dot intercepts the true course line. Draw the line and label it "AS 120." The point "P," placed at the intersection, represents the position of the plane at the end of 1 hour.

The diagram is now complete.

The distance flown in 1 hour (ground speed) is measured as the number of units on the true course line (88 m.p.h.).

The true heading necessary to offset drift is indicated by the direction of the airspeed line which can be determined in one of two ways:

1. By placing the straight side of the protractor along the north-south line, with its center point at the intersection of the airspeed line and north-south line, read the true heading directly in degrees (076°) (fig. 83).

2. By placing the straight side of the protractor along the true course line, with its center at P, read the angle between the true course and the airspeed line. This is the wind correction angle (WCA) which must be applied to the true course to obtain the true heading. If the wind blows from the right of true

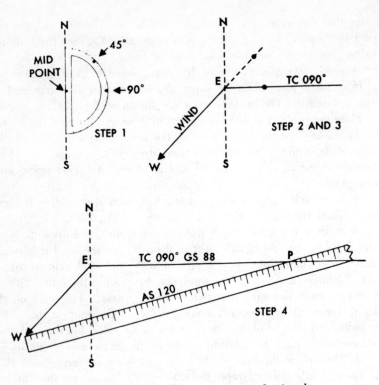

Figure 82. *Steps in drawing the wind triangle.*

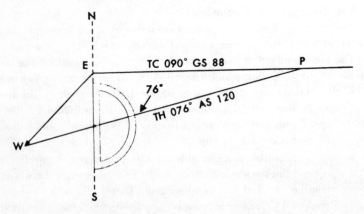

Figure 83. *Finding true heading by direct measurement.*

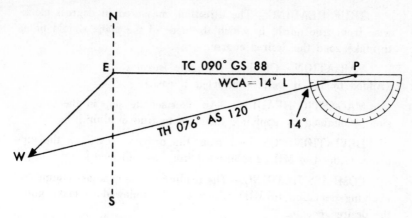

Figure 84. *Finding true heading by the wind correction angle.*

course, the angle will be added; if from the left, it will be subtracted. In the example given, the WCA is 14° and the wind is from the left; therefore, subtract 14° from true course of 090°, making the true heading 076° (fig. 84).

After obtaining the true heading, apply the correction for magnetic variation to obtain magnetic heading, and the correction for compass deviation to obtain a compass heading which enables you to fly directly to your destination by dead reckoning.

***Distance Time and Fuel*** Find the distance to your destination by measuring the length of the course line drawn on the aeronautical chart (*using the appropriate scale at the bottom of the chart*). This scale is approximately 8 miles to an inch for sectional charts. If the distance measures 220 miles, divide by the ground speed of 88 m.p.h., which gives you 2.5 hours (or 2:30) as the time required. If fuel consumption is 8 gallons an hour, you will use 8 × 2.5 or about 20 gallons. Briefly summarized, the steps in obtaining flight information are as follows:

TRUE COURSE.—Direction of the line connecting two desired points, drawn on the chart and measured clockwise in degrees from true north on the mid-meridian.

WIND CORRECTION ANGLE.—Determined from wind triangle. (Added to TC if the wind is from the right; subtracted if wind is from the left.)

**TRUE HEADING.**—The direction, measured in degrees clockwise from true north, in which the nose of the plane should point to make good the desired course.

**VARIATION.**—Obtained from the isogonic line on the chart. (Added to TH if west; subtracted if east.)

**MAGNETIC HEADING.**—An intermediate step in the conversion. (Obtained by applying variation to true heading.)

**DEVIATION.**—Obtained from the deviation card on the airplane. (Added to MH or subtracted from, as indicated.)

**COMPASS HEADING.**—The reading on the compass (found by applying deviation to MH) which will be followed to make good the desired course.

**TOTAL DISTANCE.**—Obtained by measuring the length of the TC line on the chart (using the scale at the bottom of the chart).

**GROUND SPEED.**—Obtained by measuring the length of the TC line on the wind triangle (using the scale employed for drawing the diagram).

**TIME FOR FLIGHT.**—Total distance divided by ground speed.

**FUEL RATE.**—Predetermined gallons per hour used at cruising speed.

*NOTE: Additional fuel for 45 minutes of flight should be added as a safety measure.*

A useful combination Planning Sheet and Flight Log form is shown in figure 85.

**Data for Return Trip**  The true course for the return trip will be the reciprocal of the outbound course. This can be measured on the chart, or found more easily by adding 180° to the outbound course (090° + 180° = 270°), if the outbound course is less than 180°. If the outbound course is greater than 180°, the 180° should be subtracted instead of added. For example, if the outbound course is 200°, the reciprocal will be 200° − 180° = 020°. The wind correction angle will be the same number of degrees as for the outbound course, but since the wind will be on the opposite side (right) of the plane, in the above example, the correction will have to be added to the true course instead of subtracted (270° + 14° = 284°). Thus, the true heading for the return trip will be 284°.

# PILOT'S PLANNING SHEET

PLANE IDENTIFICATION

DATE

| CRUISING AIRSPEED | TC | WIND | | TH | VAR W+ L- | WCA R+ L- | MH | DEV | CH | TOTAL MILES | GS | TOTAL TIME | FUEL RATE | TOTAL FUEL |
|---|---|---|---|---|---|---|---|---|---|---|---|---|---|---|
| | | MPH | FROM | | | | | | | | | | | |
| From: | | | | | | | | | | | | | | |
| To: | | | | | | | | | | | | | | |
| From: | | | | | | | | | | | | | | |
| To: | | | | | | | | | | | | | | |

## VISUAL FLIGHT LOG

| TIME OF DEPARTURE | RADIO FREQUENCIES | | DISTANCE | | ELAPSED TIME | | CLOCK TIME | | GS | | CH | | REMARKS |
|---|---|---|---|---|---|---|---|---|---|---|---|---|---|
| POINT OF DEPARTURE | TOWER | RANGE | POINT TO POINT | CUMULATIVE | ESTIMATED | ACTUAL | ESTIMATED | ACTUAL | ESTIMATED | ACTUAL | ESTIMATED | ACTUAL | BRACKETS, WEATHER, ETC. |
| CHECKPOINTS | | | | | | | | | | | | | |
| 1. | | | | | | | | | | | | | |
| 2. | | | | | | | | | | | | | |
| 3. | | | | | | | | | | | | | |
| 4. | | | | | | | | | | | | | |
| 5. | | | | | | | | | | | | | |
| DESTINATION | | | | | | | | | | | | | |
| 6. | | | | | | | | | | | | | |

The Pilot's Planning Sheet provides space for entering dead-reckoning data.

The Visual Flight Log may be prepared in advance by entering the selected checkpoints, together with the following data: Distance between checkpoints, and cumulative distance; estimated time between checkpoints; clock or cumulative time; groundspeed and Compass Heading.

As the flight progresses, the actual time, groundspeed and Compass Heading should be filled in, thus completing the log.

Figure 85. Pilot's planning sheet and visual flight log.

145

To find the ground speed, construct a new wind triangle. Instead of drawing another complete diagram, however, consider the point E on the previous diagram as the starting point for the return trip and extend the true course line in the direction opposite to the outbound course. The wind line is then in the proper relationship and does not need to be redrawn. The airspeed line (120 units long) can be drawn from the point of the wind arrow (W) to intersect the return-trip true course line, as indicated in figure 86. The distance measured on this course line from the north-south line to the intersection gives the ground speed for the return trip (147 m.p.h.).

Figure 87 shows the various steps for constructing the wind triangle and measuring the true heading and the wind correction angle for the problem in which the true course is 110°, the wind is 20 m.p.h. from the southwest (225°), and the airspeed is 100 m.p.h. Notice that the true heading line has to be extended to insersect the north-south line to measure the true heading directly.

Before attempting to use a computer, you should understand the relationships involved by constructing other wind triangles for various airspeeds, winds, and true courses. Practice on the following problems:

***Exercise No. 1*** By constructing a wind triangle, find the wind correction angle (WCA), true heading (TH), and ground speed (GS) for each of the following conditions:

| | WIND | | True | True |
|---|---|---|---|---|
| | Direction (degrees) | Speed (m.p.h.) | Course (degrees) | Airspeed (m.p.h.) |
| 1. _____ | 135 | 30 | 240 | 120 |
| 2. _____ | 215 | 20 | 260 | 130 |
| 3. _____ | 050 | 33 | 260 | 150 |
| 4. _____ | 330 | 45 | 350 | 150 |
| 5. _____ | 300 | 45 | 100 | 150 |
| 6. _____ | 220 | 30 | 130 | 150 |

*Note: See appendix II for correct answers.*

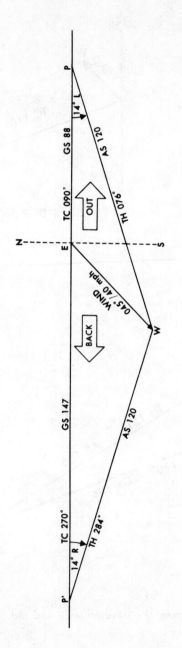

Figure 86. Computations for a round-trip flight.

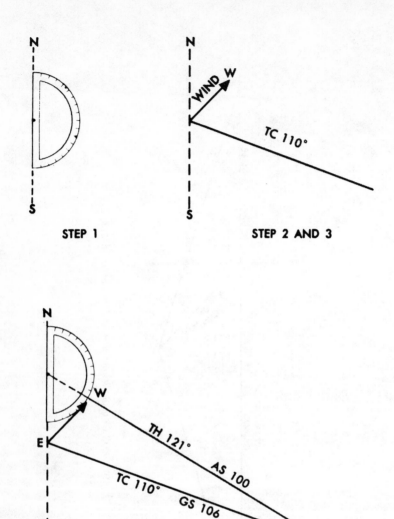

STEP 1

STEP 2 AND 3

Figure 87. *Steps in constructing the wind triangle and the various measurements*

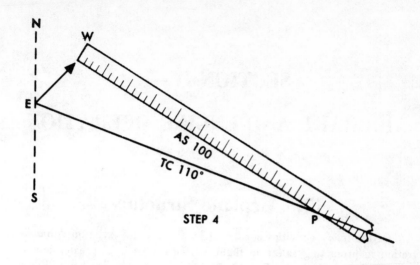

STEP 4

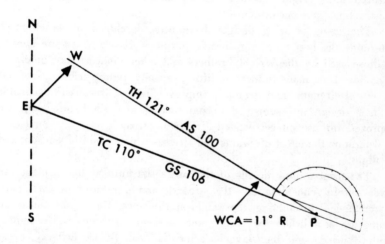

*for a true course of 110°; wind 20 m.p.h. from 225°; airspeed 100 m.p.h.*

# SECTION IV—

# AIRCRAFT AND ENGINE OPERATION

## 17. Airplane Structure

Of the many activities conducted by the Federal Aviation Administration in promoting safety in flight, perhaps none is of greater importance to pilots than certificates of airworthiness for airplanes. Every airplane certificated under the Standard classification has been manufactured under rigid specifications of design, materials, workmanship, construction, and performance.

Thousands of wing designs have been developed in an effort to determine the best types for specific purposes. Basically, all are similar to those used by the Wright brothers and other pioneers, but modifications have been made to increase lifting capacity, reduce friction, increase structural strength, and generally improve flight characteristics. Airfoils of new design are subjected to painstaking analysis before they are approved for use on certificated airplanes. Strength tests are conducted to determine the effect of strains and stresses which might be encountered in flight.

The most minute details of the entire structure of the airplane are given careful consideration—the strength and durability of each part, the method of assembling, the weight and balance. Maximums and minimums are established for performance—takeoff distance, rate of climb, landing speed, spin recovery characteristics, etc. Before delivery, every new airplane has been subjected to a thorough inspection and has been flight-tested. The Standard classification gives adequate assurance that the airplane will not be subject to structural failure *if* properly maintained and flown within the limitations clearly specified. However, the airplane is not safe if abused, improperly maintained, or flown without regard to its limitations.

The goal of airplane design and construction is to obtain maximum efficiency, combined with adequate strength. Excess strength requires excess weight and therefore lowers the efficiency of the airplane by reducing its speed and the amount of useful load it can carry.

The required structural strength is based on the airplane's use. An airplane which is to be used only for normal flying is not expected to be subjected to the excessive strains of acrobatic maneuvers and therefore will not need to be as strong as an airplane intended for acrobatic flight or other special purposes involving severe in-flight stresses.

To permit utmost efficiency of construction without sacrificing safety, FAA has established several categories, with minimum strength requirements for each. Information about limitations of each airplane is made available to the pilot through markings on instruments, placards on instrument panels, operating limitations attached to airworthiness certificates, or airplane flight manuals carried in the airplane.

Airplane strength is measured basically by the total load which the wings are capable of carrying without permanent damage. The load imposed upon the wings depends very largely upon the type of flight in which the airplane is engaged. The wing must support not only the weight of the airplane but also the additional loads imposed during maneuvers such as turns and pullouts from dives. Rough air (turbulence) also imposes additional loads. This has been discussed in Chapter 3.

***Categories of Airplanes***   Airplanes in categories of interest to the private pilot will withstand the limit-load factors shown in the table which follows. The limit loads should not be exceeded in actual operation even though a safety factor of 50 percent above limit loads is incorporated in the strength of the airplane.

| Category | Positive limit load |
|---|---|
| Normal (nonacrobatic) | 3.8 times gross weight. |
| Utility (normal operations and limited acrobatic maneuvers) | 4.4 times gross weight. |
| Acrobatic | 6.0 times gross weight. |

*Note: The negative limit-load factors shall be not less than −0.4 times the positive load factor for the N and U categories, and shall be not less than −0.5 times the positive load factor for the A category.*

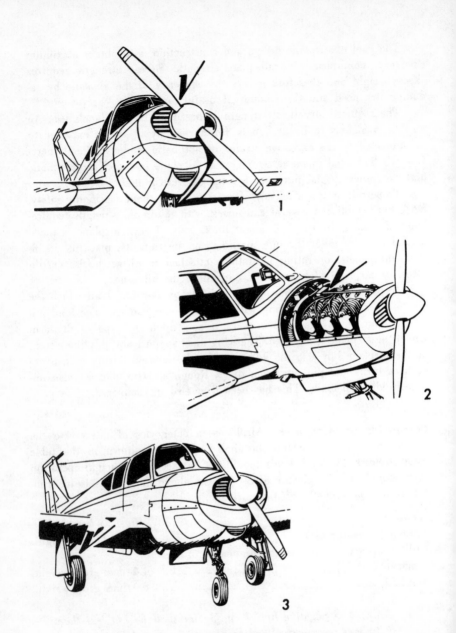

Figure 88. *Preflight inspection should include at least: (1) propell*
*and controls; (6) weig*

4

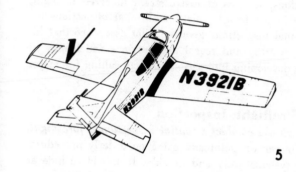

5

6

*2) engine; (3) landing gear; (4) wings and fuselage; (5) control surfaces*
*f baggage and passengers.*

153

**Maintenance** If an airplane is to remain safe for flight, it must be properly maintained. FAA regulations require that an aircraft shall not be flown unless within the preceding 12 calendar months it has been given an annual inspection conducted by authorized personnel. (NOTE: A period of 12 calendar months extends from any day within any month to the end of the last day of the same month of the following year.) When an airplane is to be used to carry passengers for hire or for flight instruction for hire, it must also have had a 100-hour inspection (that is, inspected in accordance with the FAA regulations, within each 100 hours). The private pilot is prohibited by the regulations from carrying passengers for hire (except in certain special cases) or giving flight instruction for hire.

Any unusual conditions, such as excessive strain incurred in flight, hard landings, or abuse in the hangar, make additional inspections advisable. Frequent additional inspections give the pilot assurance that his airplane is thoroughly airworthy and reveal malfunctions which may be remedied quickly before developing into serious defects calling for major repairs.

## Preflight Inspection

*A careful pilot will always conduct a routine inspection before flight.* By always beginning at a certain point and using an orderly procedure, the check can be made systematically and quickly. It should include at least the following items some of which are shown in figure 88.

**Cockpit** Battery (or master) and ignition switches should be checked in the OFF position. The landing gear position selector (if retractable-gear type) should be checked in the DOWN position.

### Powerplant

*Propeller.*—Check for nicks and cracks, tightness of hub, safetying of nuts.

*Engine.*—Check for tightness and safetying of all parts (including cowling). Check for security of all fuel lines and oil lines and look for fuel and oil leaks. Check exhaust manifolds for tightness and absence of cracks or holes (a cracked or broken exhaust manifold is a fire and carbon monoxide hazard).

Many light aircraft cabins are warmed by air that has been circulated around the engine exhaust pipes. A defect in the exhaust pipes or cabin heating system may allow carbon monoxide (CO) to enter the cockpit or cabin. The danger is greatest during the winter months and any time the temperature is such that use of the cabin heating system becomes necessary and windows and vents are closed. But there is danger at other times, too, for carbon monoxide may enter the cabin through openings in the firewall and around fairings in the area of the exhaust system.

CO is the product of incomplete combustion of carbonaceous material. It is found in varying amounts in the smoke and fumes from burning aircraft engine fuels and lubricants. The gas itself is colorless, odorless, and tasteless but is usually mixed with other gases and fumes which can be detected by sight or smell.

When CO is taken into the lungs, it combines with hemoglobin, the oxygen carrying agent in blood. The affinity of the hemoglobin for CO is so much greater than for oxygen that oxygen starvation results. Oxygen starvation of the brain reduces a person's ability to reason and make decisions. Exposure to even very small amounts of CO over a period of several hours will reduce a pilot's ability to operate an airplane safely. Long exposure to low CO concentrations is as hazardous as short exposure to relatively high concentrations.

Susceptibility to CO poisoning increases with altitude. As altitude increases, air pressure decreases and the body has difficulty getting enough oxygen. Add CO, which further deprives the body of oxygen, and the situation can become critical. Inhalation of tobacco smoke also introduces CO into the body in significant quantities.

Early symptoms of CO poisoning are feelings of sluggishness, being too warm, and tightness across the forehead. The early symptoms may be followed by more intense feelings such as headache, throbbing of pressure in the temples, and ringing in the ears. These in turn may be followed by severe headache, general weakness, dizziness, and gradual dimming of vision. Large accumulations of CO in the body result in loss of muscular power, vomiting, convulsions, and coma. Finally, there is a gradual weakening of the pulse, a slowing of the respiratory rate, and . . . death!

*NOTE: For additional information on carbon monoxide and other medical facts pertinent to safety of flight, see AIM, Part 1.*

*Fuel and Oil.*—Check supply visually—do not rely on gauges. Drain into a container a substantial amount of fuel from the fuel strainer (gascolator) and fuel tank, and check for contamination. See that fuel and oil caps are fastened securely to avoid fuel or oil syphonage, which may result in fire or fuel or oil starvation. Be sure fuel and oil vents are open and properly aligned; this will insure proper pressure in the fuel or oil tanks, maintaining steady fuel and oil flow.

*Landing Gear* Check tires for cuts, cracks, and proper inflation. Check struts and fittings for safetying and evidence of cracks, bends, or wear. Lubrication should be adequate but not excessive. Check brake assemblies and look for possible hydraulic leaks.

*Wing, Fuselage, and Tail Surfaces* Check covering for holes, wrinkles, wear, or rot. Wrinkles may indicate internal damage. Check control cables for tension. Check fittings and cables for wear and safetying. Check ailerons, rudder, and elevator for tightness and freedom of movement. Check to see that all surfaces are free from mud, snow, ice, or frost.

*Pitot-Static System.*—Check to see that the static vents are open and that the pitot tube is unobstruced. Obstructions will result in unreliable readings on the airspeed indicator and other pitot-static instruments.

*Controls* Check controls for proper movement. Set stabilizer or elevator trim tab for takeoff position.

Check the loading to be sure it does not exceed limitations as given in the FAA-approved Airplane Flight Manual. Be sure that the maximum weight allowance in the baggage compartment is NOT exceeded. This may produce a tail- or nose-heavy airplane that has very undesirable flight characteristics and is dangerous.

NOTE: The Airplane Flight Manual should be checked for further items of importance to be considered during the preflight inspection.

# 18. Engine Operation

Knowing a few general principles of engine operation will help you obtain dependable and efficient service and avoid engine failure. In this short chapter, it is impractical to discuss in detail the various types of engines and the finer points of operation which you, as a pilot, will learn only through experience. You will have access to the manufacturer's instruction manual, you will be familiar with the operating limitations for the airplane, and you will be able to get specific advice from your flight instructor.

## How an Engine Operates

Most airplane engines operate upon the same principle as automobile engines. As shown in figure 89, the mechanism consists of a cylinder,

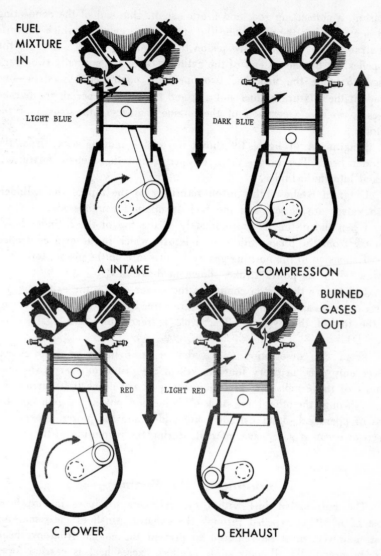

Figure 89. *Four strokes of the piston product: (A) Fuel mixture (light blue) is drawn into cylinder by downward stroke. (B) Mixture (darker blue) is compressed by upward stroke. (C) Spark ignites mixture (red), forcing piston downward and producing power that turns propeller. (D) Burned gases (light red) pushed out of cylinder by upward stroke.*

a piston, a connecting rod, and a crankshaft. One end of the connecting rod is attached to the piston and the other to a crankshaft which converts the straight-line motion of the piston to a rotary motion which turns the propeller. At the closed end of the cylinder there are normally two spark plugs, to ignite the fuel, and two openings, controlled by valves—one to admit the mixture of fuel and air, and the other to permit the burned gases to escape. Operation of the engine requires four strokes of the piston:

Diagram A of figure 89 shows the piston moving away from the cylinder head. The intake valve is opened and the fuel-air mixture is sucked into the cylinder.

Diagram B shows the piston returning to the top of the cylinder. Both valves are closed, and the fuel-air mixture compressed.

When the piston is approximately at the top of the cylinder head, a spark from the plugs ignites the mixture, which burns at a controlled rate. Expansion of the burning gas exerts pressure on the piston, forcing it downward in the power stroke, shown in diagram C.

Just before the piston completes the power stroke, the exhaust valve starts to open, and the burned gases are forced out as the piston returns to the top of the cylinder. The cycle is ready to begin again (diagram D).

From this description notice that a one-cylinder engine delivers power only once in every four strokes of the piston or every two revolutions of the crankshaft. The momentum of the crankshaft carries the piston through the other three strokes. To increase power and gain smoothness of operation, other cylinders are added and the power strokes are timed to occur at successive intervals during the revolution of the crankshaft.

## Cooling of the Engine

The burning of fuel within the cylinders produces intense heat, most of which is expelled through the exhaust. Much of the remaining heat, however, must be removed to prevent the engine from overheating. In practically all automobile engines, excess heat is carried away by water circulating around the cylinder walls. Most airplane engines are air-cooled. They are built with fins projecting from the cylinder walls so that heat will be carried away by air flowing past the fins.

When an engine is operating on the ground, very little air flows past the cylinders (particularly if the engine is closely cowled) and overheating is likely to occur. Overheating may also occur during a prolonged climb, because the engine is usually developing high power at relatively slow air speed.

Operating the engine at a higher temperature than it was designed for will cause loss of power, excessive oil consumption, and detonation. It will also lead to serious permanent injury, scoring the cylinder walls, damaging the pistons and rings, burning and warping the valves.

For engines with a cylinder-head temperature gauge, the proper operating temperature can readily be determined. Many light engines, however, do not have such a gauge, and the pilot must rely on the oil-temperature gauge to indicate engine temperature.

Oil, used primarily to lubricate the moving parts of the engine, also helps reduce engine temperature by removing some of the heat from the cylinders. The pilot should keep a constant check on oil gauges because a variation beyond normal limits indicates engine trouble which calls for an immediate adjustment or landing to prevent serious damage. Using the kind of oil specified by the engine manufacturer will prevent the expensive repairs that inevitably result from improper lubrication.

## Proper Fuel is Essential

The engine must have the proper fuel to operate satisfactorily. Automobile gasoline should not be used because gums and other harmful substances may form in the engine. In addition, automobile gasoline has a much higher vapor pressure than aviation fuel and may produce *vapor-lock,* a vaporization of gasoline in the fuel lines which prevents the flow of fuel to the carburetor.

Aviation gasoline is classified by *octane ratings* and *performance number* power ratings. The proper fuel rating for the engine, as specified by the manufacturer, is always found in the operating limitations and is usually placarded at the fuel filler opening. Using aviation gasoline of a rating higher than specified does not improve engine operation and may sometimes be harmful. *Using aviation gasoline of a lower rating is* definitely *harmful under any circumstances* because it may cause loss of power, excessive heat, burned spark plugs, burned and stuck valves, high oil consumption, and detonation.

*Use of Mixture Control*   The fuel-air mixture in most engines can be changed by adjusting the *mixture control* in the cockpit. The mixture control will normally have a red knob (an indication to use caution). This control enables the pilot to adjust the ratio of the fuel-to-air mixture that goes into the cylinders. This ratio of fuel to air is the most important single factor affecting the power output of an engine.

If the fuel-air mixture is too lean (too little fuel for the amount of air—in terms of weight), rough engine operation, sudden "cutting out" or "back-firing," detonation, overheating, or an appreciable loss of engine power may occur. Lean mixtures must be especially avoided when an engine is operating near its maximum output (such as on take-offs, climbs, and go-arounds). At altitudes of less than 5,000 ft. MSL an excessively lean mixture may cause serious overheating and loss of power.

If the fuel-air mixture is too rich (too much fuel for the amount of air—in terms of weight), rough engine operation and an appreciable loss of engine power may also occur.

Carburetors are normally calibrated for sea-level operation, which means that the correct mixture of fuel and air will be obtained at sea level with the mixture control in the "full rich" position. As altitude increases, the air density decreases, which means that a cubic foot of air will not weigh as much as it would at a lower altitude. This means that as the flight altitude increases, the weight of air entering the carburetor will decrease, although the volume remains the same. The amount of fuel entering the carburetor depends on the volume of air and not the weight of air. Therefore, as the flight altitude increases, the amount of fuel entering the carburetor will remain approximately the same for any given throttle setting if the position of the mixture control remains unchanged. Since the same amount (weight) of fuel is entering the carburetor, but a lesser amount (weight) of air, the fuel-air mixture becomes richer as altitude increases.

We have already discussed the effects of too rich a mixture. To maintain the correct fuel-air ratio, the pilot must be able to adjust the amount of fuel mixed with the incoming air as his altitude increases. To do this the pilot uses the mixture control in the cockpit, which is connected to the carburetor by mechanical linkage.

*Follow the manufacturer's recommendations on leaning the fuel mixture for the particular airplane.*

**Detonation**   Detonation, which is easily detected in an automobile engine by a "pinging" sound, may not be heard in an airplane engine because of other noises. When the engine is operating normally, the spark plug ignites the fuel at the proper instant, and the fuel burns and expands rapidly, exerting an even pressure on the piston. Detonation occurs if the fuel explodes instead of burning evenly. The resulting shock causes loss of power and frequently leads to serious engine trouble. As already stated, detonation may be produced by overheating, low-grade fuel, or too lean a mixture. It may also be caused by opening the throttle abruptly when the engine is running at slow speed. To prevent detonation, therefore, the pilot should use the correct grade of fuel, maintain a sufficiently rich mixture, open the throttle smoothly, and keep the temperature of the engine within recommended operating limits.

*Refueling Procedure* Static electricity, formed by the friction of air passing over the surfaces of an airplane in flight and by the flow of fuel through the hose and nozzle, creates a fire hazard during refueling. To guard against the possibility of a spark igniting fuel fumes, a ground wire should be attached to the aircraft before the cap is removed from the tank. The refueling nozzle should be grounded to the aircraft before refueling is begun and throughout the refueling process. The fuel truck should also be grounded to the aircraft and the ground.

When fueling from drums or cans, proper bonding and grounding connections are extremely important, since there is an ever-present danger of static discharge and fuel vapor explosion. Nylon, dacron, or wool clothing are especially prone to accumulate and discharge static electricity from the person to the funnel or nozzle. Drums should be placed near grounding posts and the following sequence of connections observed:

1. Drum to ground.
2. Ground to aircraft.
3. Drum to aircraft.
4. Nozzle to aircraft before the aircraft tank cover is opened.
5. When disconnecting reverse the order—4, 3, 2, 1.

The passage of fuel through a chamois increases the charge of static electricity and the danger of sparks. The aircraft must be properly grounded and the nozzle, chamois filter, and funnel *bonded* to the aircraft. If a can is used, it should be connected to either the grounding post or the funnel. Under no circumstances should a plastic bucket or similar nonconductive container be used in this operation.

## Fuel Contamination

Water and dirt contamination of fuel systems is potentially dangerous; the pilot must prevent contamination or eliminate contamination that has occurred. Of the many accidents attributed to powerplant failure from fuel contamination, most have been traced directly to:

1. Inadequate preflight inspection by the pilot.
2. Servicing of aircraft with improperly filtered fuel from small tanks or drums.
3. Storing aircraft with partially filled fuel tanks.
4. Lack of proper maintenance.

Each of these factors may result in fuel contamination.

**Preventive Measures for Contaminated Fuel** What can the pilot do to help prevent water from contaminating the fuel? As one preventive measure, he should have the fuel tanks completely filled after each flight, or at least after the last flight of the day. This will prevent moisture condensation within the tank since no air space will be left. Suppose the pilot knows that on his next flight, to be made the next day, he will not be able to carry a full fuel load because of the weight of his passengers and baggage. If this situation arises and he chooses to refuel with only the amount he can carry on his next flight, he must realize that he is adding to the risk of having his fuel contaminated by moisture condensation within the tank. If his flight is cancelled the next day for some reason, then each additional day may add to the amount of moisture condensation within the tanks.

A second preventive measure the pilot can take is *not* to refuel from cans and drums. This practice introduces a major likelihood of fuel contamination.

As has been pointed out, the practice of using a funnel and chamois skin when refueling from cans or drums is hazardous under any conditions, and one that should be discouraged. It is not approved by the FAA. It is recognized, of course, that in remote areas or in emergencies, there may be no alternative to refueling from sources with inadequate anticontamination systems, and a chamois skin and funnel may be the only possible means of filtering fuel. If such is the case, it is imperative that the precautions listed under *Refueling Procedures* be observed.

In addition, it should be clearly understood that the use of a chamois will not always assure decontaminated fuel. Worn out chamois will not filter water; neither will a new, clean chamois that is already water-wet or damp. Most imitation chamois skins will not filter water. There are many filters available that are more effective than the old chamois and funnel system.

**Elimination Measures for Contaminated Fuel** What can the pilot do to eliminate water present in the fuel system of his aircraft? First of all, he should always assume that his fuel *is* contaminated with water, and take the necessary steps to eliminate it during his preflight inspection. He should drain a substantial amount of fuel from the fuel strainer (gascolator) quick drain and, if possible, from each fuel tank sump into a transparent container and check for dirt and water. Water will sink to the bottom of the sample. Water, being heavier than gasoline, seeks the lowest levels in the fuel system. However, experiments have shown that when the fuel strainer is being drained, water in the tank may not appear until all the fuel has been drained from the lines leading to the tank. This would indicate that the water is staying in the tank itself and not forcing the fuel out of the fuel lines leading to the fuel strainer. Therefore, drain enough fuel from the fuel strainer to be sure that fuel is being obtained from the tank itself. This amount will depend on the length of fuel line from the tank to the drain. If water is found in the first sample, drain further samples until no trace appears.

Experiments have also shown that water still remained in the fuel tanks after the drainage from the fuel strainer had ceased to show any trace of water. This residual water could be removed only by draining the fuel tank sumps. Aircraft owners should have quick-drain valves installed in aircraft fuel tanks if not already installed.

## Ignition System

The function of the ignition system is to provide a spark to ignite the fuel-air mixture in the cylinder. The magneto ignition system is used on most modern aircraft engines. Magnetos are self-contained units supplying ignition current without using an external current supply. However, the magneto has to be actuated and the engine started. The aircraft battery furnishes electrical power to operate the starter system; the starter system actuates the rotating element of the magneto; and the magneto then furnishes the spark to each cylinder to start the engine. After the engine starts, the starter system is disengaged, and the battery no longer has any part in the actual operation of the engine. If the battery (or master) switch were turned OFF, the engine would continue to run. However, this should not be done, since battery power is necessary at low engine r.p.m. to operate other electrical equipment (radio, lights, etc.) and, when the generator or alternator is operating, the battery will be storing up a charge, if not already fully charged.

Most modern engines have a dual ignition system—that is, two magnetos to supply the electric current to the dual spark plugs contained in each combustion chamber. One magneto system supplies the current to one set of plugs; the second magneto system supplies the current to the other set of plugs. That is why the ignition switch has four positions: OFF, L, R, and BOTH. With the switch in the "L" or "R" position, only one magneto is supplying current and only one set of spark plugs is firing. With the switch in the BOTH position, both magnetos are supplying current and both sets of spark plugs are firing. The main advantages of the dual system are:

    1. Increased safety. In case one system fails, the engine may be operated on the other until a landing is safely made.

NOTE: That is why it is extremely important for each magneto to be checked for proper operation during the preflight check. This should be done in accordance with the manufacturer's recommendations in the *Airplane Flight Manual.*

    2. Improved burning and combustion of the mixture, and consequently improved performance.

## Carburetor Icing

Carburetor icing is a frequent cause of engine failure. The vaporization of fuel, combined with the expansion of air as it passes through the carburetor, causes a sudden cooling of the mixture. The temperature of the air passing through the carburetor may drop as much as 60° F. within a fraction of a second. Water vapor in the air is "squeezed out" by this cooling, and, if the temperature in the carburetor reaches 32° F. or below, the moisture will be deposited as frost or ice inside the carburetor passages. Even a slight accumulation of this deposit will reduce power and may lead to complete engine failure, particularly when the throttle is partly or fully closed (fig. 90).

***Conditions Favorable for Carburetor Icing*** On dry days, or when the temperature is well below freezing, the moisture in the air is not generally enough to cause trouble. But if the temperature is between 20° F. and 70° F., with visible moisture or high humidity, the pilot should be constantly on the alert for carburetor ice. During low or closed throttle settings, an engine is particularly susceptible to carburetor icing.

***Indications of Carburetor Icing*** For airplanes with fixed-pitch propellers, the first indication of carburetor icing is loss of r.p.m. For airplanes with controllable pitch (constant-speed) propellers, the first indi-

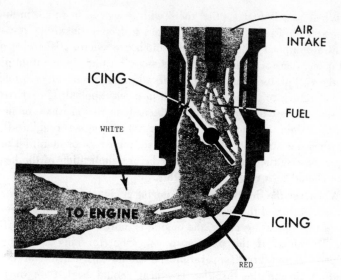

AIR
INTAKE

ICING

FUEL

WHITE

TO ENGINE

ICING

RED

Figure 90. *Formation of ice (white) in the fuel intake system may reduce or block fuel flow (red) to the engine.*

cation is usually a drop in manifold pressure. In both cases, a roughness in engine operation may develop later. There will be no reduction in r.p.m. in airplanes with constant-speed propellers since propeller pitch is automatically adjusted to compensate for the loss of power, thus maintaining constant r.p.m.

*Use of Carburetor Heat* The carburetor heater is an anti-icing device that preheats the air before it reaches the carburetor. This preheating can be used to melt any ice or snow entering the intake, to melt ice that forms in the carburetor passages (provided the accumulation is not too great), and to keep the fuel mixture above the freezing point to prevent formation of carburetor ice.

When conditions are favorable for carburetor icing, the pilot should make the proper checks to see if any is present. When he notes indications of icing, he should immediately apply carburetor heat. In either case the procedure is the same. When initially applying carburetor heat, use the full-on position. It should be left in this position until the pilot is certain no ice is present or, if ice was present, that it has all been removed. If ice is present, applying partial heat or leaving heat on for an insufficient time may aggravate the situation.

When heat is first applied there will be a drop in r.p.m. in airplanes equipped with fixed-pitch propellers and a drop in manifold pressure in airplanes equipped with controllable-pitch propellers. If there is no carburetor ice, there will be no further change in r.p.m. or manifold pressure until the carburetor heat is turned off, when the r.p.m. or manifold pressure will return to the reading before heat was applied. If carburetor ice is present, there will normally be an immediate rise in r.p.m. or manifold pressure (often accompanied by intermittent engine roughness); and then, when the carburetor heat is removed, the r.p.m. or manifold pressure will rise to a setting greater than that before application of the heat. The engine should also run more smoothly.

Whenever the throttle is closed during flight, the engine cools rapidly and vaporization of the fuel is less complete than if the engine were warm. Also, in this operating mode, the engine is more susceptible to carburetor icing. Therefore, if the pilot suspects carburetor-icing conditions and anticipates closed-throttle operation, he should turn carburetor heat full-on before closing the throttle. The heat should be left on during the closed-throttle operation. The heat will help in better fuel vaporization and carburetor ice prevention. Periodically, however, the throttle should be opened smoothly for a few seconds to keep the engine warm, otherwise the carburetor heater may not provide enough heat to prevent icing.

Use of carburetor heat tends to reduce the output of the engine and also to increase the operating temperature. Therefore, the heat should not be used when full power is required (as during takeoff) or during normal engine operation except to check for the presence of, or to remove, carburetor ice. In extreme cases of carburetor icing, after the ice has been removed it may be necessary to apply just enough carburetor heat to prevent further ice formation. *However, this must be done with caution. Check the manufacturer's recommendations on the use of carburetor heat for the airplane you fly.*

The carburetor heat should be checked for proper operation during the preflight check. Follow the manufacturer's recommendations in making this check.

**Fuel Injection**   Fuel injectors have replaced carburetors in some airplanes. In the fuel injection system, the fuel is normally injected into the system either directly into the cylinders or just ahead of the intake valve; whereas, in the carburetor, the fuel enters the airstream at the throttle valve. The fuel injection system is generally considered to be less susceptible to icing than the carburetor system, though impact icing of the air intake is possible in either system. This, however, is not the same as the icing which occurs in carburetors when lowered pressure and fuel vaporization lowers the temperature of the fuel/air mixture to the point where any water vapor or moisture present will freeze to form ice or frost inside the carburetor.

There are several types of fuel injection systems in use today, and though there are variations in design, the operational methods are generally similar. Most designs include an engine-driven fuel pump, a fuel/air control unit, fuel distributor, and discharge nozzles for each cylinder. Technically speaking, most of these so called "continuous-flow" systems are not true fuel injection, since fuel is neither injected directly into the cylinder itself, nor timed to the engine.

Some of the advantages of fuel injection are:

    a. Reduction in evaporative icing.
    b. Better fuel flow.
    c. Faster throttle response.
    d. Precise control of mixture.
    e. Better fuel distribution.
    f. Easier cold weather starts.

Disadvantages are usually associated with:

    a. Difficulty in starting a hot engine.
    b. Vapor locks during ground operations on hot days.
    c. Problems associated with restarting an engine that quits because of fuel starvation.

## Idling Procedure

Whenever the throttle is closed during flight, the engine cools rapidly and vaporization of fuel is less complete. Furthermore, the airflow through the carburetor system under such conditions is not sufficiently rapid to assure a uniform mixture of fuel and air. Consequently, the engine may stop because it is receiving too lean a mixture (starving) or too rich a mixture (loading up). A sudden opening or closing of the throttle may aggravate this condition, and the engine may cough once or twice, sputter, and stop.

Three precautions should be taken to prevent the engine from stopping while idling. First, make sure that the ground-idling speed is properly adjusted (about 550 to 660 r.p.m. minimum for most light engines).

Second, do not open or close the throttle abruptly. Third, keep the engine warm during glides by frequently opening the throttle for a few seconds.

## Starting the Engine

Before starting the engine, move the airplane to a position clear of other aircraft, where the propeller will not stir up gravel or dust to cause damage to the propeller or property, or cause personal annoyance or injury. The wheels should be held firmly, either by adequate parking brakes or blocks in front of the wheels.

*Engines Equipped With a Starter*    The pilot should be familiar with the Owner's Manual or other sources of recommended procedures for starting his particular engine. There are not only differences in procedures applicable to starting engines equipped with conventional carburetors and those equipped with fuel injections, but also between different systems of either carburetion or fuel injection. If the engine has a starter, the pilot should make sure no one is in front of the propeller. He should always check to be sure the area is clear, call "clear," and wait for a response before engaging the starter. The engine should not be cranked with the starter for long periods of time. Continuous cranking beyond 30 seconds duration may damage the starter. In addition, the starter motor should be allowed to cool at least 1 to 2 minutes between cranking periods. If the engine refuses to start under normal circumstances after a reasonable number of attempts, the possibility of problems with ignition or fuel flow should be investigated.

As soon as the engine starts, advance the throttle to obtain recommended warmup r.p.m. and *check the oil pressure gauge immediately.* Unless the gauge indicates oil pressure within a few seconds, stop the engine and determine what is causing the lack of oil pressure. If oil is not circulating properly, the engine can be seriously damaged in a short time.

The engine must reach normal operating temperature before it will run smoothly and dependably. Temperature is indicated by the cylinder-head temperature gauge. If the airplane is not equipped with this gauge you must depend on the oil-temperature gauge. Remember, in this case, that oil warms very slowly in cold weather.

Just before takeoff check engine operation thoroughly—including each magneto separately. Check for proper operation of carburetor heat at magneto-checking r.p.m. *Follow the manufacturer's recommendations when performing all checks.* Use a check list—do not rely on memory.

To enable the pilot to check operation quickly and easily, engine instruments are marked in much the same way as the airspeed indicator. A red line indicates maximum or minimum limits and a green arc indicates normal operating range.

***Engines Not Equipped With a Starter*** If the airplane has no self-starter, the person who is to turn the propeller calls "Gas on, switch off, throttle closed, brakes on." The pilot will check these items and repeat the phrase. The switch and throttle must not be touched again until the person swinging the prop calls "contact." The pilot will repeat "contact" and *then* turn on the switch—never turn on the switch and then call "contact."

If you are swinging the prop yourself, a few simple precautions will help you avoid accidents.

When touching a propeller, always assume that the switch is on, even though the pilot may confirm your statement "Switch off." The switches on many engine installations operate on the principle of short-circuiting the current. If the switch is faulty, as sometimes happens, it can be in off position and still permit the current to flow to the spark plugs just as if it were on.

Be sure the ground is firm. Slippery grass, mud, grease, or loose gravel might cause you to slip and fall into or under the propeller.

Never allow any portion of your body to get in the way of the propeller. This applies even though the engine is not being cranked; occasionally, a hot engine will backfire after shutdown and the propeller has almost stopped rotating.

Stand close enough to the propeller to be able to step away as it is pulled down. If you stand too far away from the propeller, you must lean forward to reach it. This throws you off balance and you may fall into the blades as the engine starts. Stepping away after cranking is a safeguard in case the brakes give way.

In swinging the prop, always move the blade downward by pushing with the palms of the hands. If you push the blade upward, or grip it tightly with your fingers, backfiring may break your fingers or draw your body into the path of the blades.

If you are to remove blocks from in front of the wheels, remember that the propeller, when revolving, is almost invisible. Cases are on record in which people, intending to remove the blocks, attempted to walk directly through the propeller.

Unsupervised "hand propping" of an airplane should not be attempted by the inexperienced, and regardless of the experience level, it should never be attempted by anyone without taking adequate safety measures. Nonpilot passengers, uninformed or without experience in airplane starting procedures, should never be required to handle throttle, brakes, etc., or to remain in the airplane. The airplane should be as securely chocked or tied down as possible. Great care should be exercised in setting the throttle. In some cases, it may be well to consider the procedure of turning the fuel selector valve to "off" after properly priming the engine and prior to actually attempting the hand start. Even with the fuel off, the engine will usually run after it starts for a period of time sufficient to permit returning the fuel selector valve to the "on" position *after* the engine starts.

### Relationship Between Manifold Pressure and Propeller R.P.M.

An airplane equipped with a fixed-pitch propeller has only a throttle power control. In this case, the setting of the throttle controls the propeller r.p.m. and engine r.p.m.

An airplane equipped with a controllable-pitch, constant-speed propeller has two power controls—a throttle and a propeller control. The throttle controls the power output of the engine which is registered on the manifold pressure gauge. The propeller controls the r.p.m. of the propeller (and also the r.p.m. of the engine), which is registered on the tachometer. As throttle setting (manifold pressure) is increased, the pitch angle of the propeller blades is automatically increased through the action of the propeller governor system. The increase in propeller pitch increases the load on the propeller so that the r.p.m. remains constant. As throttle setting (manifold pressure) is decreased, the pitch angle of the propeller blades is automatically decreased. The decrease in propeller pitch decreases the load on the propeller so that the r.p.m. remains constant.

For any given propeller r.p.m., there is a manifold pressure that should not be exceeded. If an excessive amount of manifold pressure is carried for a given r.p.m., the maximum allowable pressure within the engine cylinders could be exceeded, placing undue stress on them. If repeated too frequently, this undue stress could weaken the cylinder components and eventually cause engine structural failure.

What can the pilot do to avoid conditions that would possibly over-stress the cylinders? First, be constantly aware of the tachometer indication (propeller r.p.m.), especially when increasing the throttle setting (manifold pressure). Know and conform to the manufacturer's recommendations for power settings of a particular engine to maintain the proper relationship between manifold pressure and propeller r.p.m. Remember, *the combination to avoid is a high throttle setting (manifold pressure indication) and a low propeller r.p.m. (tachometer indication)*.

When both manifold pressure and propeller r.p.m. need to be changed, the pilot can further help avoid overstress by making power adjustments in the proper order. When power settings are being decreased, reduce manifold pressure before r.p.m. When power settings are being increased, reverse the order—increase propeller r.p.m. first, then manifold pressure. *If propeller r.p.m. is reduced before manifold pressure, manifold pressure will automatically increase and possibly exceed manufacturer's tolerances.*

Summarizing: In an airplane equipped with a controllable-pitch (constant-speed) propeller, the throttle controls the manifold pressure and the propeller control controls the propeller r.p.m. Avoid high manifold pressure settings with low propeller r.p.m. When decreasing power, first decrease manifold pressure, then propeller r.p.m.; when increasing power, first increase r.p.m., then manifold pressure. The preceding is a standard procedure for most situations, but with unsupercharged engines it is sometimes modified to take advantage of auxiliary fuel metering devices in the carburetor. These devices function at full throttle settings, providing additional fuel flow. This additional fuel helps to cool the engine during takeoff and full-power climbs where engine overheating may be a problem. In such instances, a modest reduction in r.p.m. is possible without overstressing the engine, even though the throttle is in the full-power position. If in doubt, the Owner's Handbook, Approved Operations Manual, or manufacturers recommendations should be followed.

# SECTION V — FLIGHT INSTRUMENTS

## 19. The Pitot-Static System Flight Instruments

The pitot-static system (fig. 91) is a source of pressure for operations of the

(1.) Altimeter;

(2.) vertical-speed indicator; and

(3.) airspeed indicator.

The pitot tube is mounted so there is minimum disturbance of the air due to the motion of the airplane. For this reason its location will vary on different types of aircraft. Static vents are generally located flush with the fuselage—one on either side.

Both the pitot-tube opening and the static-vent openings should be checked during the preflight inspection to see that they are not clogged. If clogged, call for a mechanic to clean them out. Clogged or partially clogged openings may cause inaccurate instrument readings. Do not blow into these openings. This can damage any of the three instruments.

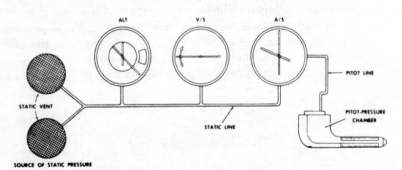

Figure 91. *Pitot-static system with instruments operated from it.*

# The Altimeter

The altimeter (fig. 92) measures the height of the aircraft above a given level. Since it is the only instrument that gives altitude information, the altimeter is one of the most important instruments in the aircraft. To use his altimeter effectively, the pilot must thoroughly understand its principle of operation and the effect of barometric pressure and temperature on the altimeter.

***Principle of Operation*** Air is more dense at the surface of the earth than aloft. As altitude increases, the atmospheric pressure decreases. This difference in pressure at various levels causes the altimeter to indicate changes in altitude. The pressure altimeter is simply a barometer that measures the pressure of the atmosphere, and presents an altitude indication to the pilot in feet. This indicated altitude is

Figure 92. *Sensitive altimeter. The instrument is adjusted by the knob (lower left) so the current altimeter setting (30.34 here) appears in the window to the right.*

correct, however, only if the sea level barometric pressure is 29.92" Hg (inches of mercury), sea level free air temperature is +15° C. (59° F.), and temperature and pressure decrease at a standard rate with increase in altitude. These conditions are requisite to a standard atmosphere, and without appropriate corrections, it is only under standard atmospheric conditions that this type of altimeter is accurate.

***Effect of Nonstandard Pressure and Temperature***  Atmospheric pressure and temperature vary continuously. Rarely is the pressure at sea level 29.92 inches of mercury or the temperature exactly 59° Fahrenheit (standard sea level conditions). If no means were provided for adjusting altimeters to nonstandard pressure, flight could be very hazardous.

On a warm day the expanded air is lighter in weight per unit volume than on a cold day, and the pressure levels are raised. For example, the pressure level where the altimeter indicates 10,000 ft. will be HIGHER on a warm day than under standard conditions. On a cold day the reverse is true, and the 10,000-foot level would be LOWER. The adjustment made by the pilot to compensate for nonstandard pressures does not compensate for nonstandard temperatures. Therefore, if terrain or obstacle clearance is a factor in the selection of a cruising altitude, particularly at higher altitudes, remember to anticipate that COLDER-THAN-STANDARD TEMPERATURE will place the aircraft LOWER than the altimeter indicates. See VFR Exam-O-Gram No. 9 in Appendix I.

***Setting the Altimeter***  Most altimeters are equipped with an altimeter setting window (sometimes referred to as the Kollsman window) which gives the pilot a way to adjust his altimeter for the atmospheric pressure variations discussed previously. FAA regulations provide the following concerning altimeter settings:

The cruising altitude of an aircraft below 18,000 ft. MSL shall be maintained by reference to an altimeter *that is set to the current reported altimeter setting of a station along the route of flight and within 100 nautical miles of the aircraft.* If there is no such station, the current reported altimeter setting of an appropriate available station shall be used—and provided further that, in an aircraft having no radio, the *altimeter shall be set to the elevation of departure or an appropriate altimeter setting available before departure.*

Many pilots confidently expect that the current altimeter setting will compensate for irregularities in atmospheric pressure at all altitudes. Unfortunately, this is not always true. Remember that the altimeter setting broadcast by ground stations is the *station pressure corrected to mean sea level.* The altimeter setting does not account for distortion at higher levels, particularly the effect of nonstandard temperature.

However, it should be pointed out that if each pilot in a given area were to use the same altimeter setting, each altimeter would be equally affected by temperature pressure variation errors, making it possible to maintain desired altitude separation between aircraft.

When flying over high mountainous terrain, remember that certain atmospheric conditions could cause your altimeter to indicate an altitude of 1,000 ft., or more, HIGHER than you actually are. Allow yourself a generous margin of altitude—not only for possible altimeter error, but also for possible downdrafts which are particularly prevalent if high winds are encountered.

As an illustration of the use of the altimeter setting system, we will follow a flight from Love Field, Dallas, Texas, to Abilene Municipal Airport, Abilene, Texas, via the Mineral Wells VOR. Before takeoff from Love Field, Dallas, Texas, the pilot receives a current altimeter setting of 29.85 from the control tower. He applies this setting to the altimeter setting window of his altimeter. He then compares the indication of his altimeter with the known field elevation of 485 ft. If his altimeter is perfectly calibrated, the altimeter should indicate the field elevation of 485 ft. (However, since most altimeters are not perfectly calibrated, an indication of plus or minus 50 ft. is generally considered acceptable. If an altimeter indication is off more than 50 ft. the instrument should be recalibrated by an instrument technician.)

When the pilot is over the Mineral Wells VOR, he makes a position report to the Mineral Wells FAA Flight Service Station. He receives a current altimeter setting of 29.94, which he applies to the altimeter setting window of his altimeter. Before entering the traffic pattern at Abilene Municipal Airport, he receives a new altimeter setting of 29.69 along with other landing instructions from the Abilene tower. Since he desires to fly the traffic pattern at approximately 800 ft. above terrain—the field elevation at Abilene is 1,778 ft.—he maintains an indicated altitude of approximately 2,600 ft. Upon landing, his altimeter should indicate the field elevation at Abilene Municipal (1,778 ft.)

Let's assume that the pilot neglected to adjust his altimeter at Abilene to the current setting. His traffic patern would have been approximately 250 ft. below the proper traffic pattern altitude, and his altimeter would have indicated approximately 250 ft., more than the field elevation upon landing.

Actual setting ----------------------- 29.94
Proper setting ----------------------- 29.69

.25
(1 inch equals)
approximately
1,000 ft.)

.25 x 1,000 ft. = 250 ft.

*The importance of properly setting and reading the altimeter cannot be overemphasized.*

## Altimeters and Altimetry

*Altitude* Knowing the aircraft's altitude is vitally important to the pilot for several reasons. He must be sure that he is flying high enough to clear the highest terrain or obstruction along his intended route; this is especially important when visibility is poor. To keep above mountain peaks, the pilot must note the altitude of the aircraft and elevation of the surrounding terrain at all times. To reduce the potential of a midair collision, the pilot must be sure he is flying the correct altitudes in accordance with air traffic rules (on flights conducted at more than 3,000 ft. above the surface). Often he will fly a certain altitude to take advantage of favorable winds and weather conditions. Also, a knowledge of the altitude is necessary to calculate true airspeeds. (See Exam-O-Gram No. 9, appendix I.)

*Types of Altitude* Altitude is vertical distance above some point or level used as a reference. There may be as many kinds of altitude as there are reference levels from which to measure. However, pilots are usually concerned with five types of altitudes:

ABSOLUTE ALTITUDE—The altitude of an aircraft above the surface of the terrain over which it is flying.

INDICATED ALTITUDE—That altitude read directly from the altimeter (uncorrected) after it is set to the current altimeter setting.

PRESSURE ALTITUDE—The altitude read from the altimeter when the altimeter setting window is adjusted to 29.92. (Used for computer solutions for density altitude, true altitude, true airspeed, etc.)

TRUE ALTITUDE—The true height of the aircraft above sea level— the actual altitude. (Often expressed in this manner: "10,900 ft.

MSL.") Airport, terrain, and obstacle elevations found on charts and maps are true altitudes.

DENSITY ALTITUDE—This altitude is pressure altitude corrected for nonstandard temperature variations. (An important altitude, since it is directly related to the aircraft's takeoff and climb performance.)

## Vertical Speed Indicator

The vertical speed indicator (fig. 93) shows whether the aircraft is climbing, descending, or in level flight. The rate of climb or descent is indicated in feet per minute. If properly calibrated, this indicator will register zero in level flight.

*Principal of Operation*    Before he can use this instrument properly, the pilot must understand one important fact. When the aircraft enters a climb or descent, or levels off, there is a short interval before the instrument gives the correct rate indication. This lag is a result of the time necessary for pressure changes to take place inside the instrument. If pitch changes are small and are made slowly, the indication on the instrument will be a very close representation of the correct rate at any given instant. When a rapid pitch change, or a large pitch change or a combination of the two is made, the instrument may lag far behind the correct indication (*Note*: A vertical speed indicator is now available

Figure 93. *Vertical speed indicator.*

which does not have this lag and gives a correct, instantaneous indication of the rate of climb or descent.)

*Using the Vertical Speed Indicator*  If a pilot understands the lag in this instrument and overcomes the tendency to "chase the needle," the vertical speed indicator can be an aid to smooth precision flying. For example, during straight-and-level flight, small changes in altitude are detected almost instantly by this instrument. Therefore, the vertical speed indicator can be an invaluable aid in maintaining level flight when used with the altimeter.

## The Airspeed Indicator

The airspeed indicator (fig. 94) is a sensitive, differential pressure gauge which measures and shows promptly the difference between (1)

Figure 94. *Airspeed indicator.*

pitot, or impact pressure, and (2) static pressure, the undisturbed atmospheric pressure at flight level. These two pressures will be equal when the aircraft is parked on the ground in calm air. When the aircraft moves through the air, the pressure on the pitot line becomes greater than the pressure in the static lines. This difference in pressure is registered by the airspeed pointer on the face of the instrument, which is calibrated to give the pilot his airspeed in miles per hour, or knots, or both.

***Kinds of Airspeed*** There are three kinds of airspeeds that the private pilot should understand: (1) indicated airspeed; (2) calibrated airspeed; and (3) true airspeed.

***Indicated Airspeed*** The direct instrument reading the pilot obtains from the airspeed indicator, uncorrected for variations in atmospheric density, installation error, and instrument error.

***Calibrated Airspeed*** Calibrated airspeed (CAS) is indicated airspeed corrected for installation error and instrument error. Although aircraft and instrument manufacturers attempt to keep airspeed errors to a minimum, it is not possible to entirely eliminate these errors throughout the airspeed operating range. At certain airspeeds and with certain flap settings, the installation error and instrument error may amount to several miles per hour. This error is generally greatest in the low airspeed range. In the cruising and high airspeed range, indicated airspeed and calibrated airspeed are normally approximately the same.

Airspeed limitations such as those found on the color-coded face of the airspeed indicator, on placards in the cockpit, or in the Airplane Flight Manual or owner's handbook, are usually calibrated airspeeds (sometimes referred to as TIAS—True Indicated Airspeed). Therefore, it may be important for the pilot to refer to the airspeed calibration chart to allow for possible airspeed errors. The airspeed calibration chart may be posted near the airspeed indicator, or it may be included in the Airplane Flight Manual or owners handbook.

The airspeed indicator should be calibrated periodically to make sure it is working properly. Leaks may develop in the tubing, or moisture may collect. Vibrations may destroy the sensitivity of the diaphragm. The instrument may be ruined by blowing into the pitot tube. Dirt, dust, ice, or snow collecting at the mouth of the tube may obstruct air passage and prevent correct indications.

***True Airspeed*** The airspeed indicator registers true airspeed under standard sea level conditions—that is, when the pressure is 29.92 and the temperature is 15° C. Because air density decreases with an increase in altitude, the airplane has to fly faster at higher altitudes to cause the same pressure difference between pitot impact pressure and static pressure. Thus, for a given true airspeed, indicated airspeed decreases as altitude increases.

To put it another way, for a given indicated airspeed, true airspeed increases with an increase in altitude. A pilot can find his true airspeed by two methods.

The first method, which is more accurate, involves using a computer (see Chapter 30). In this method, the calibrated airspeed is corrected for temperature and pressure by the airspeed correction scale on the computer.

Approximate true airspeed can be computed by a second "rule of thumb" method. This is done by adding to the indicated airspeed 2% of the indicated airspeed for each 1,000 ft. of altitude.

*Sample Problem:*
  *Given:*
    IAS _____ 140 m.p.h.
    Altitude _____ 6,000 ft.
  *Find:* True Airspeed (TAS)
*Solution:*
  2% × 6 = 12% (.12)
  140 × .12 = 16.8
  140 + 16.8 = 156.8 m.p.h. (TAS)

**The Airspeed Indicator Markings**  Airplanes of 12,500 lbs. or less manufactured after 1945 and certificated by FAA are required to have airspeed indicators that conform to a standard color-coded marking system. This system of color-coded markings, pictured in figure 95, enables the pilot to determine at a glance certain airspeed limitations which are of vital importance to the safe operation of his aircraft. For example, if during the execution of a maneuver, the pilot notes that his airspeed needle is in the yellow arc and is rapidly approaching the red line, he should react immediately and take necessary corrective action to reduce his airspeed. Of course, at high airspeeds it is essential for the pilot to use smooth control pressures to avoid severe stresses upon the aircraft structure.

The private pilot should understand the airspeed limitations indicated by the color-coded marking system of the airspeed indicator. (See also Exam-O-Gram No. 45, appendix I.)

FLAP OPERATING RANGE (the white arc).

POWER-OFF STALLING SPEED WITH THE WING FLAPS AND LANDING GEAR IN THE LANDING POSITION (the lower airspeed limit of the white arc).

MAXIMUM FLAPS EXTENDED SPEED (the upper airspeed limit of the white arc). This is the highest airspeed at which the pilot should extend full flaps. If flaps are operated at higher airspeeds, severe strain or structural failure may result.

NORMAL OPERATING RANGE (the green arc).

POWER-OFF STALLING SPEED WITH THE WING FLAPS AND LANDING GEAR RETRACTED (the lower airspeed limit of the green arc).

MAXIMUM STRUCTURAL CRUISING SPEED (the upper airspeed limit of the green arc). This is the maximum speed for normal operation.

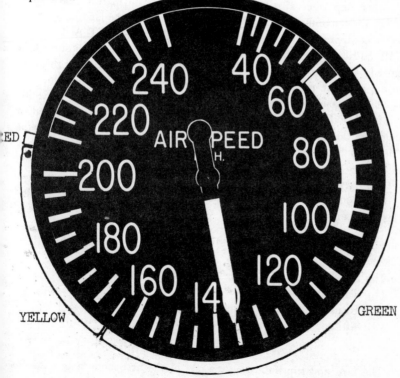

Figure 95. *Airspeed indicator showing color-coded marking system.*

CAUTION RANGE (the yellow arc). The pilot should avoid this area unless in smooth air.

NEVER-EXCEED SPEED (the red line). This is the maximum speed at which the airplane can be operated in smooth air. No pilot should ever exceed this speed intentionally.

***Other Airspeed Limitations*** There are other important airspeed limitations *not* marked on the face of the airspeed indicator. These speeds are generally found on placards in view of the pilot and in the Airplane Flight Manual or owner's handbook.

For example, one of the speeds, a very important one, is the MANEUVERING SPEED. This is the pilot's "rough air" speed and the maximum speed for abrupt maneuvers. If during flight rough air or severe turbulence is encountered, the airspeed should be reduced to maneuvering speed or less, to reduce the stress upon the airplane structure.

Other important airspeeds include LANDING GEAR OPERATING SPEED, the maximum speed for the safe operation of the landing gear for aircraft equipped with retractable landing gear; the BEST ANGLE OF CLIMB SPEED, important when a short field takeoff to clear an obstacle is required; and the BEST RATE OF CLIMB SPEED, the airspeed that will give the pilot the most altitude in a given period of time. The pilot who flies the increasingly popular light twin engine aircraft must know his aircraft's MINIMUM CONTROL SPEED, the minimum flight speed at which the aircraft is satisfactorily controllable when an engine is suddenly made inoperative with the remaining engine at takeoff power. The last two airspeeds are now marked either on the face of the airspeed indicator or on the instrument panel of recently manufactured airplanes.

Description of these airspeed limitations are, through choice, limited to layman language.

# 20. Gyroscopic Flight Instruments

The following flight instruments contain gyrocopes (fig. 96):

(1) Turn and slip indicator.
(2) Heading indicator (directional gyro).
(3) Attitude indicator (artificial horizon or gyro-horizon).

## Turn and Slip Indicator

The turn and slip indicator was one of the first modern instruments used for controlling an aircraft without visual reference to the ground

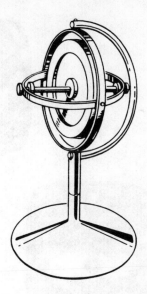

Figure 96. *Model gyroscope.*

or horizon (fig. 97). It is a combination of two instruments, a ball and a turn needle. The ball part of the instrument is actuated by natural forces, while the turn indicator depends upon gyroscopic proprieties for its indications.

Figure 97. *Turn and slip indicator.*

Figure 98. *Indications of the ball in various types of turns.*

***The Ball*** The ball checks the pilot's coordination. It is actually a balance indicator, because it indicates the relationship between the angle of bank and the rate of turn. *It tells the pilot the "quality" of the turn—* whether the aircraft has the correct angle of bank for its rate of turn.

In a coordinated turn, the ball assumes a position between the reference markers (fig. 98, left).

In a skid, the rate of turn is too great for the angle of bank, and the excessive centrifugal force causes the ball to move to the outside of the turn (fig. 98, center). To correct to coordinated flight calls for increasing the bank or decreasing the rate of turn, or a combination of both.

In a slip, the rate of turn is too slow for the angle of bank, and the lack of centrifugal force causes the ball to move to the inside of the turn (fig. 98, right). To correct to coordinated flight requires decreasing the bank or increasing the rate of turn, or a combination of both.

***The Turn Needle*** The turn needle indicates the rate (number of degrees per second) at which the aircraft is turning about its vertical axis. Unlike the attitude indicator (artificial horizon), it does not give a direct indication of the banking attitude of the aircraft. However, for any given airspeed, there is a definite angle of bank necessary to maintain a *coordinated* turn at a given rate. The faster the airspeed, the greater the angle of bank required to obtain a given rate of turn. Thus, the turn needle gives only an *indirect* indication of the aircraft's banking attitude or angle of bank.

Since the turn and slip indicator is one of the most reliable flight instruments used for recovery from unusual attitudes, the pilot should understand and learn to interpret its indications.

***Types of Turn Needles*** There are two types of turn needles—the "2 minute" turn needle and the "4 minute" turn needle. On a 2 minute turn needle, a 360° turn made at a rate indicated by a *one-needle width deflection* would require 2 minutes to complete. In this case, the aircraft would be turning at a rate of 3° per second, which is considered a standard rate turn. With the 4 minute turn needle, a 360° turn made at a rate indicated by a one-needle width deflection would require 4 minutes to complete. In this case, the aircraft is turning at a rate of $1\frac{1}{2}$° per second. A standard rate turn of 3° per second would be indicated on this type of turn needle by a *two-needle width deflection*. You may find a turn-and-slip indicator marked as a "2-minute" turn needle but calibrated so that a two-needle width deflection represents a standard rate of turn of 3° per second.

## The Heading Indicator

The heading indicator (or directional gyro) is fundamentally a mechanical instrument designed to facilitate the use of the magnetic compass. Errors in the magnetic compass are numerous, making straight flight and precision turns to headings difficult to accomplish, particularly in turbulent air. The heading indicator (fig. 99), however, is not affected by the forces that make the magnetic compass difficult to interpret.

Proper use of the heading indicator requires that the pilot be able to adjust the compass card. To do this he pushes in a caging knob (fig. 99) generally located just below the instrument. He then turns this caging knob, thereby rotating the compass card until the desired heading is obtained. It is important to check the indications frequently and reset the heading indicator with the magnetic compass when required.

Check the heading indicator at least every 15 minutes against the magnetic compass. Use great care when reading the magnetic compass.

*Adjust the heading indicator to the magnetic compass indication only when the magnetic compass reading is obtained with the aircraft in wings-level unaccelerated flight.*

The pilot should be familiar with the limits of the heading indicator. The limits of operation vary with the particular design and make of instrument. However, on the type of instrument generally found in light airplanes, the limits for all practical purposes are 55° of pitch and 55° of bank. When either of these attitude limits is exceeded, the instrument "tumbles" or "spills" and no longer gives the correct indication until reset. After the instrument has been spilled, it may be reset with the caging knob.

## The Attitude Indicator

The attitude indicator, or artificial horizon or gyro-horizon, with its miniature aircraft and horizon bar is the one instrument that gives a picture of the attitude of the real aircraft (fig. 100). The relationship of the miniature aircraft to the horizon bar is the same as the relationship of the real aircraft to the actual horizon. This instrument gives an instantaneous indication of even the smallest changes in attitude. It has no lead or lag and is very reliable, if properly maintained.

To aid the pilot in interpreting this instrument's reading, an adjustment knob is provided with which he may move the miniature aircraft upward or downward inside the case. Normally, the miniature aircraft is adjusted so that the wings overlap the horizon bar when the real airplane is in straight-and-level cruising flight.

Figure 99. *Heading indicator.*

Figure 100. *Attitude indicator.*

Some models of attitude indicators are equipped with a caging mechanism. If the instrument is equipped with a caging mechanism, *it should be uncaged only in straight-and-level flight;* otherwise, it will not give proper indications. When uncaging this instrument, uncage it fully; otherwise, it may tumble at lower limits.

The pitch and bank limits depend upon the make and model of the instrument. Limits in the banking plane are usually from 100° to 110°, and the pitch limits are usually from 60° to 70°. If either of these limits is exceeded, the instrument will tumble or spill and will give incorrect indications until reset with the caging mechanism.

Every pilot should be able to interpret the banking scale (fig. 101). Most banking scale indicators move in the opposite direction from that in which the plane is actually banked. This will confuse the pilot if he uses this indicator to determine the direction of bank. This scale should be used only to obtain precision. The relationship of the miniature aircraft to the horizon bar should be used for an indication of the direction of bank of the real aircraft. (An attitude indicator is now available with a banking scale indicator that moves in the same direction as the bank.)

The attitude indicator is a reliable instrument. It is the most realistic flight instrument on the instrument panel. Its indications are very close approximations of the actual attitude of the aircraft itself.

# 21. Magnetic Compass

The magnetic compass (fig. 102) is a simple instrument whose basic component consists of two magnetized steel needles mounted on the float, around which is mounted the compass card. The compass card has letters for cardinal headings, and each 30° interval is represented by a number, the last zero of which is omitted. For example, 30° would appear as a 3 and 300° would appear as 30. Between these numbers, the card is graduated for each 5°.

### Compass Errors

*Variation.* Although the magnetic field of the earth lies roughly north and south, the earth's magnetic poles do not coincide with its geographic poles. Consequently, at most places on the earth's surface, the direction-sensitive steel needles which seek the earth's magnetic field, will not

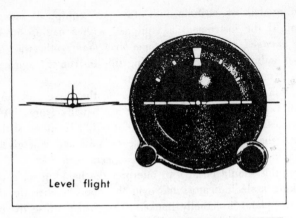

Level flight

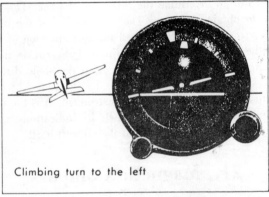

Climbing turn to the left

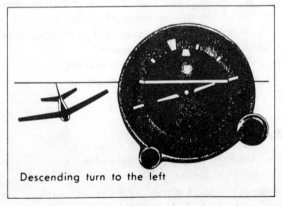

Descending turn to the left

Figure 101. *Various indications on the attitude indicator.*

Figure 102. *Magnetic compass.*

point to True North Pole but to Magnetic North Pole. Furthermore, local magnetic fields from mineral deposits and other conditions distort the earth's magnetic field and cause an additional error in position of the compass' north-seeking magnetized needles with reference to True North. The angular difference between True North and the direction indicated by the magnetic compass—excluding deviation error—is *variation*. Variation is different for different points on the earth's surface and is shown on the charts as broken lines connecting points of equal variation. These lines are *isogonic lines*. The line where the magnetic variation is zero is an *agonic line*. Variation was discussed in Section III.

*Deviation.* Actually, a compass is very rarely influenced solely by the earth's magnetic lines of force. Magnetic disturbances from magnetic fields produced by metals and electrical accessories in an aircraft disturb the compass needles and produce an additional error. The difference between the direction indicated by an undisturbed magnetic compass, and that indicated by a magnetic compass in an aircraft, is *deviation*.

If an aircraft changes heading, the compass' direction-sensitive, magnetized needles will continue to point in about the same direction while the aircraft turns with relation to it. As the aircraft turns, metallic and electrical equipment in the aircraft change their position relative to the steel needles; hence, their influence on the compass needle changes and deviation changes. Thus, deviation depends, in part, on the heading of the aircraft. Although compensating magnets on the compass are adjusted to reduce this deviation on most headings, it is impossible to eliminate this error entirely on all headings. Therefore, a deviation card, installed in the cockpit in view of the pilot, enables him to maintain his desired magnetic headings. Deviation was discussed in Section III.

***Using the Magnetic Compass*** Since the magnetic compass is the only direction-seeking instrument in most aircraft, the pilot must be able to turn his aircraft to a magnetic compass heading and maintain it. Remember these characteristics of the magnetic compass:

(1) If the aircraft is on a northerly heading and a turn is made toward east or west, the indication of the compass lags or indicates a turn in the opposite direction.

(2) If the aircraft is on a southerly heading and a turn is made, the compass needle will indicate a greater amount of turn than is actually made.

(3) If the aircraft is on an east or west heading, no error is apparent while entering a turn to north or south.

(4) If the aircraft is on an east or west heading, an increase in airspeed causes the compass to indicate a turn toward north.

(5) If the aircraft is on an east or west heading, a decrease in airspeed causes the compass to indicate a turn toward south.

(6) If the aircraft is on a north or south heading, no error is apparent while climbing, diving, or changing airspeed.

As you can see, the compass should be read only when the aircraft is flying straight and level at a constant speed. *Reading the compass only under these conditions will reduce errors to the minimum.*

Precision turns to magnetic compass headings are made difficult by these characteristics. If only the magnetic compass is available for making turns to headings, use the following procedure: While in straight-and-level, unaccelerated flight, note the indication on the magnetic compass. Determine the number of degrees you need to turn to reach the desired heading. Then, using reference points on the ground, turn this approximate number of degrees. Recheck the magnetic compass indication when again in straight-and-level, unaccelerated flight. If you have not obtained correct heading, follow the procedure again.

If the pilot thoroughly understands the errors and characteristics of the magnetic compass, that instrument can become his most reliable means of determining heading.

# SECTION VI—AIRCRAFT PERFORMANCE

## 22. Weight and Balance

All airplanes are designed for certain limit loads and balance conditions. Responsibility for making sure that the weight and balance limitations are met before takeoff *rests with the pilot.* Any pilot who takes off in an airplane that is not within the designated limit load and balance condition is not only violating the FAA regulations but inviting disaster.

Three kinds of weight must be considered in the loading of every aircraft. These are empty weight, useful load, and gross weight.

*Empty Weight* The weight of the basic airplane—the structure, the powerplant, and the fixed equipment, all fixed ballast, the unusable fuel supply, undrainable oil, and hydraulic fluid.

*Useful Load (Payload)* The weight of pilot, passengers, baggage, usable fuel, and drainable oil.

*Gross Weight* The empty weight plus the useful load is the gross weight of the airplane at takeoff. When an airplane is carrying the maximum load for which is is certificated, the takeoff weight is called the *maximum allowable gross weight.*

Understand that although your airplane is certificated for a specific maximum gross weight, it will not safely take off with this load under all conditions. For example, conditions that affect takeoff and climb performance—high elevations, high temperatures, and high humidity (high-density altitudes), may require the "off loading" of fuel, passengers, or baggage. (Other factors to consider—runway surface, runway length, the presence of obstacles—will be discussed in Chapter 23.)

In most modern airplanes, the pilot has a loading option. *He must decide the type mission to be flown and load his airplane accordingly.* For example, if all the seats are occupied and maximum baggage is carried, gross weight limitations may require less than full fuel. On the other hand, if the pilot is interested in range, he may elect to carry a full fuel load and carry fewer passengers and less baggage.

**Balance** Not only must the pilot consider the amount of load he carries, he must also determine that the load is arranged to fall within the allowable center of gravity range specified in the airplane weight and balance data. The center of gravity location, often indicated by the letters "c.g.," is the point where an airplane will balance. The allowable range where the c.g. may fall is called the *c.g. range.* The exact location of the range, usually near the forward part of the wing root (fig. 103), is specified for each type of airplane. Obtaining this balance is simply a matter of placing loads so that the average arm of the loaded airplane falls within the c.g. range. *In many modern aircraft, this can be accomplished by using common sense in distributing the load by following placards in the aircraft.* For an increasing number of light aircraft, however, passengers and/or baggage can be loaded in a manner that makes it easier to exceed the center of gravity range. In such instances, considerable care must be exercised if one is to be certain that the aircraft is properly loaded. Currently light aircraft manufacturers provide the data, graphs, charts, and instructions required in computing the weight and balance conditions for specific airplanes at specified gross weights and load placement. Every pilot should be familiar with and understand the use of such materials. Space precludes the individual discussion of each of the several variations in format and method of computation currently in use. In order to become familiar with these variations, pilots should take full advantage of the information which is readily available in owners handbooks or operations manuals.

Many airplanes are certificated in two categories—normal and utility. The normal category applies to normal operations that do not exceed 60° of bank and 30° of pitch. In some aircraft, any weight in the rear seat or baggage compartment automatically precludes any of the maneuvers permitted in the utility category, such as stalls, steep turns, spins, chandelles, and lazy eights. Typically, any such airplane, though operating within *normal* gross weight and c.g. limitations, but exceeding specified weight and c.g. limitations prescribed for its *utility* category, *must* be operated as a normal category airplane. Thus it will be restricted against all maneuvers which exceed 60° of bank and 30° of pitch while in this category. Do not exceed the maximum allowable weight that can be carried in the baggage compartment. In the absence of placards the pilot should refer to the weight and balance data in the Airplane Flight Manual to be sure the load is distributed so the airplane is in proper balance. An airplane loaded outside this range, even

193

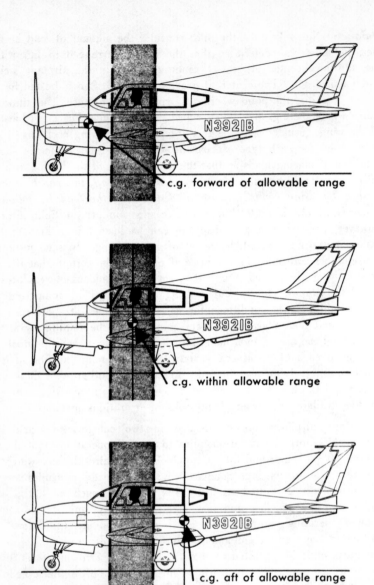

Figure 103. *Before takeoff, be sure the load is distributed correctly to assure proper balance. Flight can be very hazardous if the center of gravity is not within the allowable c.g. range.*

though gross weight limitations are met, may develop very undesirable flight characteristics.

The addition of equipment may have changed the c.g. and empty weight from that listed in the Owner's Manual. Be sure to use the latest weight and balance information in the FAA-Approved Airplane Flight Manual or other permanent aircraft records as appropriate.

Figure 103 (top) shows an airplane loaded forward of the c.g. range. Some of the undesirable characteristics for this airplane would be:

Excessive loads on the nose wheel (tendency to nose over on tail-wheel type airplanes).

Decreased performance.

Higher stalling speeds.

Higher stick forces.

Figure 103 (center) shows an airplane loaded properly.

Figure 103 (bottom) shows an airplane loaded to the rear of the c.g. range.

Some of the undesirable characteristics of this airplane would be:

Decreased static and dynamic longitudinal stability. Under some conditions the airplane may be impossible to control.

Violent stall characteristics.

Very light stick forces (easy to overstress the airplane inadvertently). (Detailed information concerning airplane weight and balance may be found in AC 91-23. Pilot's Weight and Balance Handbook.)

Weight and balance and their relationship to performance is discussed further in Exam-o-Gram No. 13, Appendix I.


*Sample Weight and Balance Problem*   In this sample weight and balance problem for an airplane with a maximum allowable gross weight of 2,650 pounds, the pilot is seeking the answers to two problems: (1) *Is the gross weight within the maximum allowable gross weight?* and (2) *Does the airplane meet balance requirements (is the c.g. within the allowable range)?*

The answer to the first question is relatively simple. Add the weight of items comprising the useful load (pilot, passengers, fuel, oil, and baggage) to the licensed empty weight of the airplane. Then check *total weight* to see that it does not exceed *maximum allowable gross weight*.

The solution to the second question can usually be found by common sense distribution of the load, following the placards in the aircraft or the loading instructions in the weight and balance data.

|  | *Weight* |
|---|---:|
| EMPTY WEIGHT (licensed) | 1,591.0 |
| OIL (10 qts.) at 7.5 lbs. per gallon | 19.0 |
| PILOT AND FRONT SEAT PASSENGER | 347.0 |
| REAR PASSENGERS | 303.0 |
| FUEL (maximum) 55 gal. at 6 lbs. per gallon | 330.0 |
| BAGGAGE | 20.0 |
| Total | 2,610.0 |

Since the maximum allowable gross weight for this airplane is 2,650 pounds and the gross weight falls within this figure, the weight requirements are met with this particular load. Assuming the loading placards or instructions are followed, balance requirements are also met with this load.

# 23.  Aircraft Performance

## Takeoff Performance Data

Far too many takeoff accidents have occurred simply because the pilots involved did not realize the effect of density altitude on airplane performance. This subject was covered in detail in Sections I and II; here it will be discussed only briefly with other factors affecting takeoff distances.

### Factors Affecting takeoff Distances

1. *Pressure Altitude.*—The elevation read from the altimeter when the altimeter setting window (Kollsman window) is adjusted to 29.92. Generally, the higher the pressure altitude, the longer the takeoff distance required.

2. *Temperature.*—While most pilots understand the effects of pressure altitude on airplane performance, many do not realize the extent to which temperature variations can affect performance. Higher than standard temperatures may raise the density altitude of a field by several thousand feet. (Pressure altitude corrected for nonstandard temperature variations is, *density altitude.*)

# TAKE-OFF DATA

TAKE-OFF DISTANCE WITH 20° FLAPS FROM HARD SURFACE RUNWAY.

| GROSS WEIGHT LBS. | HEAD WIND MPH | AT SEA LEVEL & 59°F. | | AT 2500 FT. & 50°F. | | AT 5000 FT. & 41°F. | | AT 7500 FT. & 32°F. | |
|---|---|---|---|---|---|---|---|---|---|
| | | GROUND RUN | TO CLEAR 50' OBSTACLE | GROUND RUN | TO CLEAR 50' OBSTACLE | GROUND RUN | TO CLEAR 50' OBSTACLE | GROUND RUN | TO CLEAR 50' OBSTACLE |
| 2100 | 0 | 335 | 715 | 390 | 810 | 465 | 935 | 560 | 1100 |
| | 15 | 185 | 465 | 225 | 540 | 270 | 625 | 330 | 745 |
| | 30 | 75 | 260 | 95 | 305 | 125 | 365 | 160 | 450 |
| 2400 | 0 | 440 | 895 | 525 | 1040 | 630 | 1210 | 770 | 1465 |
| | 15 | 255 | 600 | 310 | 700 | 380 | 835 | 475 | 1020 |
| | 30 | 115 | 350 | 150 | 420 | 190 | 510 | 245 | 640 |
| 2650 | 0 | 555 | 1080 | 665 | 1260 | 790 | 1500 | 965 | 1835 |
| | 15 | 330 | 735 | 405 | 865 | 490 | 1050 | 655 | 1345 |
| | 30 | 160 | 445 | 205 | 535 | 255 | 665 | 335 | 845 |

Note: Increase distances 10% for each 25°F above standard temperature for particular altitude.

Figure 104. *Takeoff performance data chart.*

3. *Humidity.*—As previously pointed out in Chapter 1, an airplane will require a longer takeoff ground-run when the air is saturated with moisture than under similar conditions in dry air.

4. *Gross Weight.*—Takeoff distances vary with gross weights. Under certain conditions—high density altitude, short runways, etc.—it might become necessary to "off load" part of the useful load to obtain a takeoff margin of safety.

5. *Runway Surface.*—The takeoff performance figures in your Airplane Flight Manual or owner's handbook are generally based on takeoffs from hard-surface runways. Remember that long grass, sand, mud, or deep snow can easily double your takeoff distances.

6. *Headwind Component.*—See takeoff data chart (figure 104) for headwind effect on takeoff distances.

7. *Ground Effect.*—When an airplane is flown at approximately one wing span or less above the surface, the vertical compotent of airflow is restricted and modified, and changes occur in the normal pattern of the flow of the air about the wing and from the wing tips. This change to the vertical component alters the direction of the relative wind in a manner that produces a smaller angle of attack. All this simply means that a wing operating in ground effect with a given angle of attack will generate less induced drag than a wing out of ground effect. Therefore, it is more efficient. While this may be useful in specific situations, it can also trap the unwary into expecting greater climb performance than the airplane is capable of sustaining. In other words, an airplane can take off, and while in ground effect, establish a climb angle and/or rate that cannot be maintained once the airplane reaches an altitude where ground effect can no longer influence performance. Conversely, on a landing, ground effect *may* produce "floating," and result in overshooting, particularly at fast approach speeds.

*Use of Flaps for Takeoff* Some airplanes require the use of partial flaps for best takeoff performance; others no flaps, since the additional drag caused by flaps more than offsets the lift advantage acquired from their use. The pilot should always use the takeoff flap setting recommended in his Airplane Flight Manual or owner's handbook.

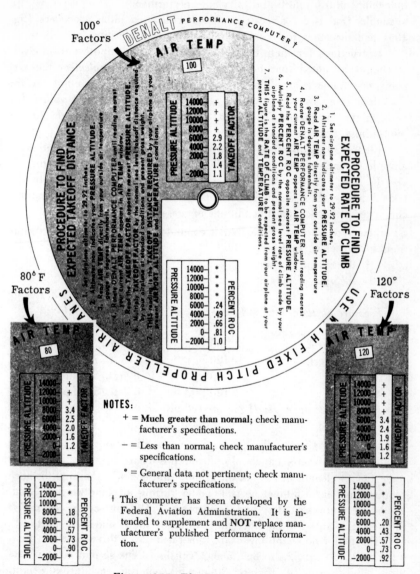

**NOTES:**

+ = **Much greater than normal**; check manufacturer's specifications.

− = Less than normal; check manufacturer's specifications.

° = General data not pertinent; check manufacturer's specifications.

† This computer has been developed by the Federal Aviation Administration. It is intended to supplement and **NOT** replace manufacturer's published performance information.

Figure 105. *The Denault computer.*

199

**The Denalt Computer** This computer was developed by the Federal Aviation Administration to replace the Koch Chart for computing altitude-temperature effects on airplane performance. Two versions are available. One is for aircraft equipped with fixed pitch propellers (fig. 105) and the other for those equipped with variable pitch propellers.

Instructions for their use are printed on the computers themselves. It should be noted that both types of computers *supplement* the airplane manufacturer's published performance data. They *do not replace* this data since they provide only representative or typical values for personal-type airplanes. They can, however, be a valuable aid to the pilot whose airplane has no other takeoff data available.

Figure 105 illustrates the correction factors applicable at pressure altitudes from −2,000 ft. to 14,000 ft. when free air temperature is 80° F., 100° F., and 120° F. These corrections must be made to the takeoff and rate of climb performance data that pertains to operations conducted under standard conditions of pressure and temperature.

*Exercise No. 2* Using the Denalt computer (fig. 105) and the conditions given below, find:

(1) the takeoff distance.

(2) the rate of climb.

| Pressure altitude (ft.) | Temperature (F.) | Takeoff distance & rate of climb (standard pressure & temp.) |
|---|---|---|
| 1. Sea level. | 80° | 715 ft./700 f.p.m. |
| 2. Sea level. | 120° | 715 ft./700 f.p.m. |
| 3. 3,000. | 80° | 875 ft./560 f.p.m. |
| 4. 3,000. | 120° | 875 ft./560 f.p.m. |

*NOTE: See appendix II for correct answers.*

**Takeoff Data Chart** Takeoff data charts are in many Airplane Flight Manuals and owner's handbooks. From this chart the pilot can determine (1) the length of the takeoff ground-run, and (2) the total distance required to clear a 50-foot obstacle under various airplane weights, headwinds, pressure altitudes, and temperatures. Of course, the chart for different airplanes will be different. Figure 104 shows one such chart.

The first column of the chart illustrated gives three possible gross weights (2,100 lbs., 2,400 lbs., and 2,650 lbs.). The second column lists three wind speeds (0, 15, and 30 m.p.h.) opposite each gross weight. The remainder of the chart consists of pairs of columns, each pair having a main heading of a pressure altitude and temperature standard for that altitude (sea level, 59° F.; 2,500 ft., 50° F.; 5,000 ft., 41° F.; and 7,500 ft., 32° F.). The first column of each pair is headed "ground-run": the second "to clear a 50-foot obstacle."

At the bottom of the chart is this note: "Increase distance 10 percent for each 25° F. above standard temperature for particular altitudes."

To determine the takeoff ground run for a given set of conditions, the following procedure should be used:

(1) Locate the computed gross weight in the first column.

(2) Locate the existing headwind in the second column and on the same row as the computed gross weight in (1).

(3) Follow the headwind row out to the first column (headed by "ground-run") of the pair of columns headed by the flight altitude. The number at the intersection of this row and column is the length of the ground-run in feet for the given set of conditions, provided the temperature is standard for the altitude.

(4) Increase the number found in (3) by 10 percent for each 25° F. of temperature above standard (for that altitude). The resulting figure is the length of the ground-run.

The same procedure is followed to find the distance to clear a 50-foot obstacle except that in (3) the headwind row would be followed out to the second column (headed by "to clear a 50-foot obstacle") of the pair of columns headed by the altitude. To find distances based on conditions in between those listed in the chart, you must interpolate.

*Sample Problem.*—What will be the *takeoff ground-run distance* with the following conditions?

Gross weight _____ 2,100 lbs.
Pressure altitude _____ 2,500 ft.
Temperature _____ 75° F.
Headwind _____ 15 m.p.h.

*Solution.*—Applying steps (1), (2), and (3) to the performance chart, we obtain a figure of 225 ft. Since the temperature is 25° above standard, step (4) must also be applied. Ten percent of 225 is 22.5, or approximately 23. Adding 23 to 225 gives a total of 248 ft. for the takeoff ground-run. Putting this in tabular form, we have:

Basic distance exclusive of correction for above       **Ft.**

   standard temperature _____ 225

Correction for above standard temperature (225 × 0.10) ____ 23

Approximate takeoff distance required _____ 248

*Sample Problem.*—What will be the *distance required to takeoff and clear a 50-foot obstacle* with the same airplane and with the following conditions?

Gross weight _____ 2,650 lbs.

Pressure altitude _____ 5,000 ft.

Temperature _____ 91° F.

Headwind _____ Calm

*Solution.*—Following the four-step procedure, except using the "to clear a 50-foot obstacle" column, the solution of this problem gives these results.

Basic distance exclusive of correction for above       **Ft.**

   standard temperature _____ 1,500

Correction for above standard temperature

   (1,500 × 0.20) _____ 300

                                                _____

Approximate distance required to take off and

   clear a 50-foot obstacle _____ 1,800

*Exercise No 3* Find the takeoff ground run distance and the distance necessary to clear a 50-foot obstacle under each of the following sets of conditions.

| Gross weight (lbs.) | Headwind (m.p.h.) | Pressure altitude (ft.) | Temperature (°F.) |
|---|---|---|---|
| 1. 2,100 | 30 | Sea level | 59 |
| 2. 2,650 | Calm | 7,500 | 57 |
| 3. 2,400 | 15 | 2,500 | 50 |
| 4. 2,650 | Calm | Sea level | 109 |
| 5. 2,250 | 15 | 5,000 | 41 |

*NOTE: See appendix II for correct answers.*

# Cruise Performance Data

Cruise performance charts (fig. 106), which are compiled from actual tests, are a valuable aid in planning cross-country flight However,

# CRUISE PERFORMANCE CHART

| Altitude | RPM | M P. | BHP | %BHP | TAS MPH | Gal/Hr. |
|---|---|---|---|---|---|---|
| 2500 | 2450 | 23 | 175 | 76 | 158 | 14.2 |
|  |  | 22 | 166 | 72 | 154 | 13.4 |
|  |  | 21 | 157 | 68 | 151 | 12.7 |
|  |  | 20 | 148 | 63 | 148 | 12.0 |
|  | 2300 | 23 | 164 | 71 | 154 | 13.1 |
|  |  | 22 | 153 | 67 | 149 | 12.2 |
|  |  | 21 | 143 | 62 | 145 | 11.5 |
|  |  | 20 | 135 | 59 | 142 | 11.0 |
|  | 2200 | 23 | 153 | 67 | 149 | 12.1 |
|  |  | 22 | 144 | 63 | 146 | 11.4 |
|  |  | 21 | 135 | 59 | 142 | 10.8 |
|  |  | 20 | 126 | 55 | 138 | 10.2 |
| Maximum Range Settings | 2000 | 20 | 107 | 47 | 126 | 8.7 |
|  |  | 19 | 99 | 43 | 121 | 8.2 |
|  |  | 18 | 89 | 39 | 113 | 7.5 |
|  |  | 17 | 81 | 35 | 105 | 7.0 |
| 5000 | 2450 | 23 | 179 | 78 | 163 | 14.5 |
|  |  | 22 | 169 | 73 | 159 | 13.6 |
|  |  | 21 | 161 | 70 | 156 | 13.0 |
|  |  | 20 | 150 | 65 | 151 | 12.2 |
|  | 2300 | 23 | 167 | 73 | 158 | 13.4 |
|  |  | 22 | 158 | 69 | 155 | 12.6 |
|  |  | 21 | 148 | 64 | 151 | 11.9 |
|  |  | 20 | 139 | 60 | 146 | 11.2 |
|  | 2200 | 23 | 157 | 68 | 155 | 12.4 |
|  |  | 22 | 148 | 64 | 151 | 11.7 |
|  |  | 21 | 138 | 60 | 146 | 11.0 |
|  |  | 20 | 131 | 57 | 143 | 10.5 |
| Maximum Range Settings | 2000 | 19 | 103 | 45 | 126 | 8.5 |
|  |  | 18 | 94 | 41 | 118 | 7.9 |
|  |  | 17 | 86 | 37 | 111 | 7.3 |
|  |  | 16 | 79 | 34 | 103 | 6.8 |
| 7500 | 2450 | 21 | 163 | 71 | 161 | 13.1 |
|  |  | 20 | 153 | 67 | 157 | 12.4 |
|  |  | 19 | 143 | 62 | 152 | 11.7 |
|  |  | 18 | 133 | 58 | 147 | 11.0 |
|  | 2300 | 21 | 151 | 66 | 156 | 12.2 |
|  |  | 20 | 142 | 62 | 151 | 11.6 |
|  |  | 19 | 133 | 58 | 147 | 11.0 |
|  |  | 18 | 125 | 54 | 142 | 10.5 |
|  | 2200 | 21 | 143 | 62 | 152 | 11.4 |
|  |  | 20 | 134 | 58 | 148 | 10.7 |
|  |  | 19 | 126 | 54 | 143 | 10.2 |
|  |  | 18 | 118 | 51 | 138 | 9.7 |
| Maximum Range Settings | 2000 | 19 | 107 | 47 | 131 | 8.7 |
|  |  | 18 | 98 | 43 | 123 | 8.1 |
|  |  | 17 | 90 | 39 | 116 | 7.6 |
|  |  | 16 | 82 | 36 | 107 | 7.0 |

Data based on lean mixture, standard conditions, and maximum gross weight

Figure 106. *A cruise performance chart.*

since the number of variables involved rules out great accuracy, an ample fuel reserve should be provided. Fuel consumption depends largely on altitude, power setting (manifold pressure and propeller r.p.m.), and mixture setting.

This same problem will show how to use the cruise performance chart in figure 106.

*Sample Problem.*—How many flight hours of fuel remain under the following conditions?

Altitude _____ 5,000 ft.
Propeller r.p.m. _____ 2,300 r.p.m.
Manifold pressure (mp) _____ 22″ Hg
Mixture _____ Lean
Fuel remaining _____ 40 gal.

*Solution*—

(1.) Locate the altitude (5,000 ft.) in the altitude column (first column).

(2.) Locate the r.p.m. (2,300) in the r.p.m. column (second column) opposite the altitude (5,000 ft.) just found in (1).

(3.) Locate the manifold pressure (22 inches of mercury) in the MP column (third column) opposite the r.p.m. (2,300) just located in (2).

(4.) Follow this manifold-pressure row out to the column headed by "Gal./Hr.," where the figure 12.6 is read. This is the rate of fuel consumption in gallons per hour.

(5.) Divide fuel remaining (40 gallons) by rate of fuel consumption just found (12.6 gal./hr.). The result is 3.17, the number of flight hours remaining. The 3.17 hours is equivalent to 3 hours and 10 minutes (multiply 0.17 by 60 minutes).

NOTE: The true airspeed (TAS) with this power setting would be 155 m.p.h. (next to last column).

*Sample Problem.*—If in the preceding sample problem, a power setting of 18 inches of manifold pressure and 2,000 r.p.m. were used, how much more flight time would be available?

*Solution*—

(1.) Following the same steps as in the preceding problem (except using the new r.p.m. and MP), a fuel consumption rate of 7.9 gallons per hour is found.

(2.) Dividing the fuel remaining (40 gallons) by 7.9 gives a total remaining flight time of 5.06 hours. When converted, this is equivalent to 5 hours 4 minutes.

(3.) Subtracting 3 hours 10 minutes from 5 hours 4 minutes gives an added flight time (endurance time) of 1 hour 54 minutes.

***Exercise No. 4*** Find the true airspeed (TAS), rate of fuel consumption, and total flight time available under the following conditions:

| | Altitude (ft.) | R.P.M. | Manifold pressure | Fuel available (gals.) |
|---|---|---|---|---|
| 1. | 2,500 | 2,450 | 23 | 55 |
| 2. | 5,000 | 2,200 | 22 | 45 |
| 3. | 7,500 | 2,000 | 16 | 25 |
| 4. | 2,500 | 2,000 | 17 | 25 |
| 5. | 5,000 | 2,300 | 23 | 50 |

*Note: See appendix II for correct answers.*

## Landing Performance Data

Variables similar to those discussed under *Factors Affecting Take-off Distance* also affect landing distances, although generally to a lesser extent. Consult your Airplane Flight Manual or owner's handbook for landing distance data, recommended flap settings, and recommended approach airspeeds.

*Sample Problem.*—With a power-off approach speed of 61 m.p.h. and 40° of flaps, approximately what ground roll will be required under the following conditions? (Refer to fig. 107.)

Elevation ------------------------------------------------------- Sea level
Gross weight ---------------------------------------------------- 2,200 lbs.
Temperature ---------------------------------------------------- 59° F.
Headwind ------------------------------------------------------- Calm

*Solution.*—Approximately 355 ft.

*Sample Problem.*—With power-off approach speed of 66 m.p.h. and 40° of flaps, approximately what total landing distance (including ground roll) would be required to clear a 50-foot obstacle and land under the following conditions?

Elevation ------------------------------------------------------- 2,500 ft.
Gross weight ---------------------------------------------------- 2,600 lbs.
Temperature ---------------------------------------------------- 50° F.
Headwind ------------------------------------------------------- 12 m.p.h.

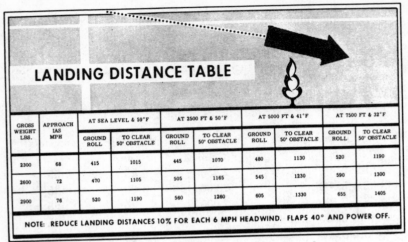

| GROSS WEIGHT LBS. | APPROACH IAS MPH | AT SEA LEVEL & 59°F | | AT 2500 FT & 50°F | | AT 5000 FT & 41°F | | AT 7500 FT & 32°F | |
|---|---|---|---|---|---|---|---|---|---|
| | | GROUND ROLL | TO CLEAR 50' OBSTACLE | GROUND ROLL | TO CLEAR 50' OBSTACLE | GROUND ROLL | TO CLEAR 50' OBSTACLE | GROUND ROLL | TO CLEAR 50' OBSTACLE |
| 2300 | 68 | 415 | 1015 | 445 | 1070 | 480 | 1130 | 520 | 1190 |
| 2600 | 72 | 470 | 1105 | 505 | 1165 | 545 | 1230 | 590 | 1300 |
| 2900 | 76 | 520 | 1190 | 560 | 1260 | 605 | 1330 | 655 | 1405 |

NOTE: REDUCE LANDING DISTANCES 10% FOR EACH 6 MPH HEADWIND. FLAPS 40° AND POWER OFF.

Figure 107. *A landing performance data chart.*

*Solution—*
Basic landing distance before headwind correction ------ 1,030 ft.
Correction for headwind (1,030 × .20) --------------- −206 ft.
Approximate landing distance ---------------------- 824 ft.

Additional information concerning the use of performance charts will be found in VFR Exam-O-Gram No. 33, Appendix I.

# SECTION VII—
# AIRMAN'S INFORMATION MANUAL

## 24. Airman's Information Manual

### Introduction

The *Airman's Information Manual* has been designed as a pilot's operational manual for use primarily within the conterminous United States. It presents, in a four-part document, the information necessary to plan and conduct a flight within the "48 States." Flight information for Alaska, Hawaii, and United States possessions is presented in separate publications.

Although considered as a single document, the AIM (*Airman's Information Manual*) is divided into four parts each of which is presented as an individual booklet which may be purchased separately, or as a complete package. Each part contains a specific category or family of information in a format designed to meet the operational needs of aviation. It consolidates items of similar information and segregates Air Traffic Control procedural information, using a sequence that is arranged for operational use—preflight, departure, enroute, arrival, and landing.

The AIM is intended for cockpit use either collectively or independently by parts. Each of the four parts of AIM is published as loose-leaf pages held together by two staples and three-hole punched to fit a standard three-ring binder. By removing the staples and separating the pages at the fold, you can place them in a three-ring binder and have a loose-leaf book. You may place each part in a separate binder or place them in the same binder, depending on which method best meets your needs. By leaving the staples in, you may use each part as an individual manual since each has a cover.

Each part of AIM is published at varying intervals during the year, depending on the expected frequency of change of information. The various parts and the issuance cycle of each are:

PART 1—Basic Flight Manual and ATC Procedures—issued quarterly.

PART 2—Airport Directory—issued semiannually.

PART 3 & 3A—Operational Data and Notices to Airmen—Part 3 is issued every 28 days; Part 3A is issued every 14 days.

PART 4—Graphic Notices and Supplemental Data—issued semiannually.

The above issuance schedule provides a completely new manual every 6 months. New or amended textual or tabulated material (except in the Airport/Facility Directory) is indicated by a solid dot (•) prefixing the heading, paragraph, or line (see figure 108).

*Part 1—Basic Flight Manual and ATC Procedures* This part is issued quarterly and contains basic fundamentals required to fly in the National Airspace System; adverse factors affecting Safety of Flight; Health and Medical Facts of interest to pilots; ATC information affecting rules, regulations and procedures; a Glossary of Aeronautical Terms: Air Defense Identification Zones (ADIZ); Designated Mountainous Areas: Scatana. and Emergency Procedures.

**AIRMAN'S INFORMATION MANUAL**

DEPARTMENT OF TRANSPORTATION
FEDERAL AVIATION ADMINISTRATION

**PART 1**

**BASIC FLIGHT MANUAL
AND
ATC PROCEDURES**

Annual subscription price $4.00. (Foreign mailing, $1.00 additional.)

## AIRMAN'S INFORMATION MANUAL

# AIRPORT DIRECTORY

# PART 2

**DEPARTMENT OF TRANSPORTATION**
**FEDERAL AVIATION ADMINISTRATION**

***Part 2—Airport Directory*** This part is issued semiannually and contains a Directory of all Airports, Seaplanes Bases, and Heliports in the conterminous United States, Puerto Rico, and the Virgin Islands which are available for transient civil use. It includes all of their facilities and services, except communications, in codified form. Those airports with communications are also listed in Part 3 which reflects their radio facilities. A list of new and permanently closed airports which updates Part 2 is contained in Part 3.

Included, also, is a list of selected Commercial Broadcast Stations of 100 watts or more of power; U.S. Entry and Departure Procedures, including Airports of Entry and Landing Rights Airports; and a listing of Flight Service Station and National Weather Service Telephone Numbers.

Annual subscription price $4.00. (Foreign mailing, $1.00 additional.)

## AIRMAN'S INFORMATION MANUAL

DEPARTMENT OF TRANSPORTATION
FEDERAL AVIATION ADMINISTRATION

# PART 3

### OPERATIONAL DATA
### AND
### NOTICES TO AIRMEN

*Part 3 & 3A—Operational Data and Notices to Airmen* Part 3 is issued every 28 days and contains an Airport/Facility Directory containing a list of all major airports with communications; a tabulation of Air Navigation Radio Aids and their assigned frequencies; Preferred Routes; Standard Instrument Departures (SIDs); Substitute Route Structures; a Sectional Chart Bulletin, which updates Sectional charts cumulatively; Special General and Area Notices; a tabulation of New and Permanently Closed Airports, which updates Part 2, and Area Navigation Routes.

Part 3A is issued every 14 days and contains Notices to Airmen considered essential to the safety of flight as well as supplemental data to Parts 3 and 4.

Annual subscription price $20.00. (Foreign mailing, $5.00 additional.)

210

# AIRMAN'S INFORMATION MANUAL

*Part 4*

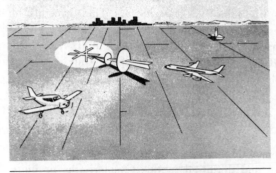

**GRAPHIC NOTICES AND SUPPLEMENTAL DATA**

DEPARTMENT OF TRANSPORTATION
FEDERAL AVIATION ADMINISTRATION

*Part 4—Graphic Notices and Supplemental Data* Part 4 is issued semiannually and contains a list of abbreviations used in the AIM, a tabulation of Parachute Jump Areas; locations of VOR Receiver Check Points (both Ground and Airborne); Special Notice — Area Graphics; and Heavy Wagon and Oil Burner Routes. Future editions will be expanded to include additional Terminal Area Graphics and other data not requiring frequent change.

Annual subscription price $1.50. (Foreign mailing 50 cents additional.)

These publications are available from the Superintendent of Documents, Government Printing Office, Washington, D.C. 20402. Orders may also be placed at any of the following branch bookstores:

GPO Bookstore, Federal Building, Room 1023, 450 Golden Gate Avenue, San Francisco, Calif. 94102.

GPO Bookstore, Federal Office Building, Room 1463 14th Floor, 219 South Dearborn Street, Chicago, Illinois 60604.

GPO Bookstore, Federal Building, 300 N. Los Angeles Street, Los Angeles, California 90012.

GPO Bookstore, Federal Building, Room 135, 601 East 12th Street, Kansas City, Mo. 64106.

GPO Bookstore, Room G25, John F. Kennedy Federal Building, Sudbury St., Boston, Massachusetts 02203.

GPO Bookstore Room 1C46, Federal Bldg.—U.S. Courthouse. 1100 Commerce St., Dallas Texas 75202

GPO Bookstore Room 100, Federal Bldg., 275 Peachtree St. N.E., Atlanta, Georgia 30303.

Orders should be accompanied by check or money order made payable to the Superintendent of Documents.

Beginning with Part 1, the next five chapters of this text will deal separately with Parts 1, 2, 3, 3A, and 4 of AIM. A number of excerpts from each of the parts will be found in these chapters. These excerpts, in the form of numbered figures, are for illustrative purposes only. THEY DO NOT NECESSARILY REFLECT CURRENT DATA AND ARE NOT TO BE USED FOR FLIGHT PLANNING PURPOSES. Only a current edition of AIM is suitable for this.

# 25. Airman's Information Manual - Part 1

## BASIC FLIGHT MANUAL AND ATC PROCEDURES

Selected excerpts from AIM, Part 1, Basic Flight Manual and ATC Procedures, are presented and discussed in this Chapter. One or more excerpts are taken from each family of information pertinent to the VFR pilot. Most of these excerpts, which appear as numbered figures in the text, are largely self-explanatory and no in-depth discussion will be devoted to them. Each excerpt selected is of vital interest to a pilot and should familiarize him with the type and importance of information contained in this part. Remember that this part contains approximately 100 pages of information most of which is of interest to the private pilot and much of which is required knowledge to become a certificated private pilot. Space limitations preclude the inclusion of all of this material.

*Glossary of Aeronautical Terms* An excerpt from this section, shown in figure 108, gives the definition of terms which are consistently misunderstood by pilot applicants; yet, knowledge of each is necessary if FARs are to be compiled with, and safe flight operations are to be conducted. There are other terms in this glossary for which a thorough knowledge is equally important.

*Aeronautical Information and the National Airspace System* This excerpt (figure 109) is self-explanatory and is reproduced here exactly as it appears in AIM.

*Air Navigation Radio Aids* Brief descriptions of the various types of radio aids available for use today are found in this section. Those that are of particular interest and applicability to the private pilot will be discussed in the excerpted examples (figures 110, 111, 112, and 113)

AIRPORT ADVISORY AREA—The area within five statute miles of an uncontrolled airport on which is located a Flight Service Station so depicted on the appropriate Sectional Aeronautical Chart

AIRPORT ADVISORY SERVICE—A service provided by a Flight Service Station to enhance the safety of terminal operations of airports where a station is operating but where there is no control tower.

• MILES—As used in this publication, Miles means nautical miles unless otherwise specified, and means statue miles in conjunction with visibility.

RADAR SERVICE—A term which encompasses one or more of the following services based on the use of radar which can be provided by a controller to a pilot of a radar-identified aircraft.

Radar Separation—Radar spacing of aircraft in accordnace with established minima.

Radar Navigation Guidance—Vectoring aircraft to provide course guidance.

Radar Monitoring—The radar flight following of aircraft, whose primary navigation is being performed by the pilot, to observe and note deviations from its authorized flight path airway, or route. As applied to the monitoring of instrument approaches from the final approach fix to the runway, it also includes the provision of advice on position relative to approach fixes and whenever the aircraft proceeds outside the prescribed safety zones.

VISIBILITY, PREVAILING—The horizontal distance at which targets of known distance are visible over at least half of the horizon. It is normally determined by an observer on or close to the ground viewing buildings or other similar objects during the day and ordinary city lights at night. Under low visibility conditions the observations are usually made at the control tower. Visibility is REPORTED IN MILES AND FRACTIONS OF MILES in the Aviation Weather Report. If a single value does not adequately describe the visibility, additional information is reported in the "Remarks" section of the report.

Figure 108. *Aeronautical terms.*

---

that follow. For more detailed information, consult the appropriate chapter in the Airman's Information Manual.

Figure 110 gives a portion of the information pertaining to *L/MF radio ranges* found in AIM. The low frequency radio ranges are discussed further in Chapter 33.

The utility of *non-directional radio beacons* (figure 111) is not restricted by the line-of-sight limitations enherent to VHF, but their emissions are subject to some of the same disturbances as the low frequency range. Their primary utility for the private pilot is in conjunction with low frequency radio receivers designed to provide Automatic Direction Finding (ADF) or "homing" information. They are still very useful in making so-called ADF instrument approaches at many airports. Additional information on ADF will be found in Chapter 33.

1. Aeronautical information concerning the National Airspace System is disseminated by three methods. The primary method is aeronautical charts. The second method is the Airman's Information Manual (AIM), and the third is the National Notice to Airmen System. These three systems have been designed to supplement and complement each other. The basic difference between these three systems is the frequency of issuance. To the maximum extent possible, aeronautical charts reflect the most current information available at time of printing. The AIM contains static procedural data and data changes known sufficiently in advance to permit publication.

2. Information of a time-critical nature that is required for flight planning and not known sufficiently in advance to permit publication on a chart or in the AIM receives immediate handling through the National Notice to Airmen System.

3. Information distributed by the Notice to Airmen System is categorized into two types—NOTAMs and Airmen Advisories. It is the intent, insofar as possible, to limit to dissemination by NOTAM that time-critical information which would affect a pilot's decision to make a flight; for example, an airport closed, terminal radar out of service, en route navigational aids out of service, etc. Dissemination of information in this category will include that pertaining to all navigational facilities and all IFR airports with approved instrument approach procedures and for those VFR airports which are designated as the destination point on a daily average of two or more general aviation VFR flight plans. All such airports are annotated in Part 2 and Part 3 of this manual by the section symbol "§" and are primarily those airports having an assigned three letter location identifier.

4. Information which is primarily of an advisory or "nice-to-know" nature, plus data on airports not included above, that can be given to the pilot upon request on an "as-needed" basis before departure, while en route, or prior to landing, is classed as an Airmen Advisory and given local distribution via appropriate voice communications, local teletypewriter or telautograph circuits, telephone, etc. Examples of this type are: Men and equipment crossing a runway, snowbanks off the sides of the runways, taxiway closed, etc.

5. Pilots planning a flight should contact the nearest FAA Flight Service Station to obtain current flight information.

Figure 109. *National airspace system.*

---

## LOW/MEDIUM FREQUENCY (L/MF) RADIO RANGE

1. These ranges are classified by their type of antenna. Two types of low-frequency ranges are in use: Loop range (L) and Adcock range (A).

2. It is a popular misconception that loop ranges should not be used for homing. The dual-frequency or "simultaneous" type loop range transmits a nondirectional signal that can be used quite satisfactorily for this purpose.

3. Low-frequency radio range courses are subject to disturbances that result in multiple courses, signal fades and surges over rough country. Pilots flying over unfamiliar routes are cautioned to be on the alert to detect these vagaries, particularly over mountainous terrain.

Figure 110. *Air navigation radio aids.*

## NON-DIRECTIONAL RADIO BEACON (NDB)

1. A low or medium-frequency radio beacon transmits nondirectional signals whereby the pilot of an aircraft equipped with a loop antenna can determine his bearing and "home" on the station. These facilities normally operate in the frequency band of 200 to 415 kHz and transmit a continuous carrier with 1,020-cycle modulation keyed to provide identification except during voice transmission.

2. When a radio beacon is used in conjunction with the Instrument Landing System markers, it is called a Compass Locator.

3. All radio beacons except the compass locators transmit a continuous three-letter identification in code except during voice transmissions.

Figure 111. *Nondirectional radio beacon.*

Currently the *omniranges* are the backbone of the VHF radio air navigation system used by general aviation pilots. Therefore, private pilots should be thoroughly familiar with this system, and all the information pertaining to it. AIM supplies considerably more information about this system than is supplied by figure 112.

## VHF OMNIDIRECTIONAL RANGE (VOR)

1. Omniranges operate within the 108-118 MHz frequency band and have a power output necessary to provide coverage within their assigned operational service volume. The equipment is VHF, thus, it is subject to line-of-sight restriction, and its range varies proportionally to the altitude of the receiving equipment. There is some "spill over," however, and reception at an altitude of 1000 feet is about 40 to 45 miles. This distance increases with altitude.

Figure 112. *VHF omnidirectional range (VOR).*

Though the requirements of FAR 91.25 with respect to *VOR equipment accuracy checks* (figure 113) apply to flight under instrument flight rules, every private pilot should be aware of and concerned with the procedures for determining the accuracy of his VOR receiver.

## VOR RECEIVER CHECK

1. Periodic VOR receiver calibration is most important. If a receiver's Automatic Gain Control or modulation circuit deteriorates, it is possible for it to display acceptable accuracy and sensitivity close in to the VOR or VOT and display out-of-tolerance readings when located at greater distances where weaker signal areas exist. The likelihood of this deterioration varies between receivers, and is generally considered a function of time. The best assurance of having an accurate receiver is periodic calibration. Yearly intervals are recommended at which time an authorized repair facility should recalibrate the receiver to the manufacturer's specifications.

Figure 113. *VOR receiver check.*

Obviously any pilot who expects to rely upon radio as an aid to navigation must be informed as to the type and capabilities of the facility he plans to use. Figure 114 relates to this information.

## CLASS OF VOR/VORTAC/TACAN

VOR, VORTAC, and TACAN aids are classed according to their operational use. There are three classes:

T (Terminal)
L (Low altitude)
H (High altitude)

T class facilities are used to provide service at terminal locations where it is not practical to frequency protect the larger service range of an L class facility. The normal service range for the T, L, and H class aids is included in the following table. Certain operational requirements make it necessary to use some of these aids at greater service ranges than are listed in the table. Extended range is made possible through flight inspection determinations. Some aids also have lesser service range due to location, terrain, frequency protection, etc. Restrictions to service range are listed in Part 3 of this manual.

### VOR/VORTAC/TACAN NAVAIDS
Normal Usable Altitudes and Radius Distances

| Class | Altitudes | Distance (miles) |
|-------|-----------|------------------|
| T | 12,000′ and below | 25 |
| L | Below 18,000′ | 40 |
| H | Below 18,000′ | 40 |
| H | 14,500′ — 17,999′ | 100* |
| H | 18,000′ — FL 450 | 130 |
| H | Above FL 450 | 100 |

* Applicable only within the conterminous U.S.

Figure 114. *Class of VOR/VORTAC/TACAN.*

*VHF/UHF direction finder equipment* can be and has been of inestimable value to the pilot who finds himself in certain types of emergency situations, but before it can be completely effective the pilot must communicate with the appropriate ground station. In addition to the information contained in figure 115, VHF/UHF direction finding is discussed again in Chapter 34 in conjunction with emergency procedures.

216

## VHF/UHF DIRECTION FINDER

1. The VHF/UHF Direction Finder (VHF/UHF/DF) is one of the Common System equipments that helps the pilot without his being aware of its operation. The VHF/UHF/DF is a ground-based radio receiver used by the operator of the ground station where it is located.

2. The equipment consists of a directional antenna system, a VHF and a UHF radio receiver. At a radar-equipped tower or center, the cathode-ray tube indications may be superimposed on the radarscope.

3. The VHF/UHF/DF display indicates the magnetic direction of the aircraft from the station each time the aircraft transmits. Where DF equipment is tied into radar, a strobe of light is flashed from the center of the radarscope in the direction of the transmitting aircraft.

4. DF equipment is of particular value in locating lost aircraft and in helping to identify aircraft on radar.

*Figure 115. VHF/UHF direction finder.*

**Radar** The importance of radar in the National Airspace System is increasing. Even the private pilot should be familiar with its capabilities and limitations. It is particularly important that the aviation community recognize the fact that there are limitations to radar service and that ATC controllers may not always be able to issue traffic advisories concerning aircraft which are not under ATC control and cannot be seen on radar. One of the various types of radar appears in figure 116. A more detailed discussion of radar will be found in this chapter under *Services Available to the Pilot.*

## SURVEILLANCE RADAR

1. Surveillance radars are divided into two general categories: Airport Surveillance Radar and Air Route Surveillance Radar. Airport Surveillance Radar (ASR) is designed to provide relatively short range coverage in the general vicinity of an airport and to serve as an expeditious means of handling terminal area traffic through observation of precise aircraft locations on a radarscope. The ASR can also be used as an instrument approach aid. Air Route Surveillance Radar (ARSR) is a long-range radar system designed primarily to provide a display of aircraft locations over large areas.

2. Surveillance radars scan through 360° of azimuth and present target information on a radar display located in a tower or center. This information is used independently or in conjunction with other navigational aids in the control of air traffic.

*Figure 116. Radar.*

*Airport, Air Navigation Lighting, and Marking Aids* The title of this section indicates the type of information it contains. Most pilots have seen and all should be familiar with the many different types of markings on runways, various colored rotating beacons, visual approach slope indicators (VASI), etc., which are pertinent to the VFR pilots. Figures 117 and 118 illustrate some of the information in this section. Pilots should study and/or review this section carefully. It contains much information which is vital to safe operations at airports, nonetheless, many pilots are not sufficiently familiar with the data provided.

## HAZARDS (RED ALONE)

1. Red flashes only from a rotating beacon or a code beacon mean the presence of an obstruction or obstructions to air navigation or an area on the ground used for purposes hazardous to air navigation. (Reference Advisory Circular No. 70/7460-1, "Obstruction Marking and Lighting," issued by the Federal Aviation Administration.)

2. Steady burning red lights are employed near airports to mark obstructions and are also used to supplement flashing lights in marking en route obstructions.

## MILITARY AIRPORTS

1. Military airport beacons flash alternately white and green, but are differentiated from civil beacons by dual-peaked (two quick) white flashes between the green flashes.

## DAYLIGHT BEACON OPERATION

1. Operation of an airport rotating beacon during the hours of daylight, means that the ground visibility in the control zone is less than three miles and/or the ceiling is less than 1000 feet and that a traffic clearance is required for landings, take-offs, and flight in the traffic pattern.

## LIGHTED TETRAHEDRON AND TRAFFIC INDICATOR

During hours of darkness, flashing lights outlining the tetrahedron or wind tee means that ground visibility is less than 3 miles and/or that the ceiling is less than 1000 feet.

## RIGHT TRAFFIC INDICATOR (AMBER)

A flashing amber light near the center of the segmented circle (or on top of the center of the segmented circle (or on top of the control tower or adjoining building) indicates that a right traffic pattern is in effect at the time.

## VISUAL APPROACH SLOPE INDICATOR (VASI)

1. VASI is designed to provide by visual reference the same information that the glide path unit of an ILS provides electronically. It provides a visual light path within the approach zone, at a fixed plane which an approaching pilot can see and utilize for descent guidance during an approach to a landing. The element of course guidance is obtained from reference to the runway lights.

2. Standard installation of the complete system consists of either 2, 4, or 12 light source units arranged in upwind and downwind light bars. The Visual Glide Slope reference point is midway between the upwind and downwind bars.

3. The following is offered to pilots as yet unfamiliar with the principles and operation of this system and the pilot technique required. The basic principle of the VASI is that of color differentiation between red and white. Each light unit projects a beam of light having a white color in the upper part and a red color in the lower part. The light units are arranged so that the pilot of an aircraft during approach will see the following combination of lights on the upwind and downwind boxes on a 12 light installation:

| | | |
|---|---|---|
| (a) Above glide slope: | white | white |
| | white | white |
| (b) On glide slope: | red | red |
| | white | white |
| (c) Below glide slope: | red | red |
| | red | red |

- 5. In haze or dust conditions or when the approach is made into the sun, the white lights may appear yellowish. This is also true at night when the VASI is operated at a low intensity. Certain atmospheric debris may give the white lights an orange or brownish tint; however, the red lights are not affected and the principle of color differentiation is still applicable.

Figure 117. *Airport lighting.*

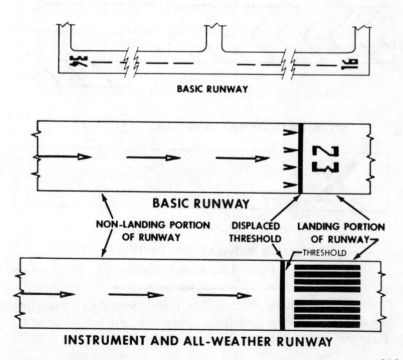

BASIC RUNWAY

BASIC RUNWAY

NON-LANDING PORTION OF RUNWAY     DISPLACED THRESHOLD     LANDING PORTION OF RUNWAY

THRESHOLD

INSTRUMENT AND ALL-WEATHER RUNWAY

1. In the interest of safety, regularity, or efficiency of aircraft operations, the FAA has recommended for the guidance of the public the following airport marking. (Runway numbers and letters are determined from the approach direction. The number is the whole number nearest one-tenth the magnetic azimuth of the centerline of the runway, measured clockwise from the magnetic north.) The letter or letters differentiate between parallel runways:

For two parallel runways "L" "R"

For three parallel runways "L" "C" "R"

a. Basic Runway Marking—markings used for operations under Visual Flight Rules: centerline marking and runway direction numbers.

## RELOCATED THRESHOLD

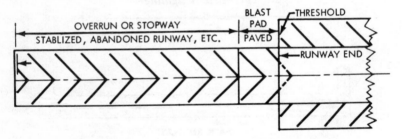

## OVERRUN/STOPWAY AND BLAST PAD AREA

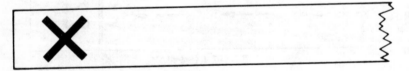

## CLOSED RUNWAY OR TAXIWAY

Figure 118. *Airport marking.*

*The Airspace* This portion of Part 1 deals with the various types of airspace, their location and limits. Applicable weather minimums and operational restrictions are also included.

The operations and needs of airspace users are varied. Because of the nature of some operations, restrictions must be placed upon others for safety reasons. The complexity or density of aircraft movements in other airspace areas may result in additional aircraft and pilot requirements for operation within such airspace. It is of the utmost importance that pilots be familiar with the operational requirements for the various airspace segments. Some of these requirements are depicted in figures 119 and 120.

## CONTINENTAL CONTROL AREA

The continental control area consists of the airspace of the conterminous United States at and above 14,500 feet MSL and Alaska south of lat. 68°00′N, excluding the Alaska peninsula west of long. 160°00′W, but does not include:

1. The airspace less than 1500 feet above the surface of the earth; or

2. Prohibited or restricted areas, other than restricted area military climb corridors, and the restricted areas listed in Subpart D of Part 71 of the FAR's.

## CONTROL AREAS

Control areas consist of the airspace designated as Colored Federal airways, VOR Federal airways, Additional Control Areas, and Control Area Extensions, but do not include the Continental Control Area. Unless otherwise designated, control areas also include the airspace between a segment of a main VOR airway and its associated alternate segments. The vertical extent of the various categories of airspace contained in control areas is defined in FAR Part 71.

## VFR REQUIREMENTS

Rules governing VFR flight have been adopted to assist the pilot in meeting his responsibility to see and avoid other aircraft. Minimum weather conditions and distance from clouds required for VFR flight are contained in these rules. (FAR 91.105.)

## TRANSITION AREAS

1. Controlled airspace extending upward from 700 feet or more above the surface when designated in conjunction with an airport for which an instrument approach procedure has been prescribed; or from 1,200 feet or more above the surface when designated in conjunction with airway route structures or segments. Unless specifically specified otherwise, transition areas terminate at the base of overlying controlled airspace.

2. The designation of transition areas is a means of ensuring that IFR aircraft can remain within controlled airspace for specific operations.

## CONTROL ZONES

1. Controlled airspace which extends upward from the surface and terminates at the base of the continental control area. Control zones that do not underlie the continental control area have no upper limit. A control zone may include one or more airports and

is normally a circular area with a radius of 5 statute miles and any extensions necessary to include instrument departure and arrival paths.

2. Control zones are depicted on charts (for example—on the sectional charts the zone is outlined by a broken blue line).

Figure 119. *Airspace—general.*

---

# SPECIAL USE AIRSPACE

## GENERAL

Special use airspace consists of that airspace wherein activities must be confined because of their nature, or wherein limitations are imposed upon aircraft operations that are not a part of those activities, or both. These areas are depicted on aeronautical charts.

## PROHIBITED AREA

Prohibited areas contain airspace of defined dimensions identified by an area on the surface of the earth within which the flight of aircraft is prohibited. Such areas are established for security or other reasons associated with the national welfare. These areas are published in the Federal Register.

## RESTRICTED AREA

Restricted areas contain airspace identified by an area on the surface of the earth within which the flight of aircraft, while not wholly prohibited, is subject to restrictions. Activities within these areas must be confined because of their nature or limitations imposed upon aircraft operations that are not a part of those activities or both. Restricted areas denote the existence of unusual, often invisible, hazards to aircraft. Penetration of restricted areas without authorization from the using or controlling agency may be extremely hazardous to the aircraft and its occupants. Restricted areas are published in the Federal Register and constitute Part 73 of the Federal Aviation Regulations.

## WARNING AREA

Warning areas is that airspace which may contain hazards to nonparticipating aircraft in international airspace. Warning areas are established beyond the 3 mile limit. Though the activities conducted within warning areas may be as hazardous as those in Restricted areas, Warning areas cannot be legally designated because they are over international waters. Penetration of Warning areas during periods of activity may be hazardous to the aircraft and its occupants. Official descriptions of Warning areas may be obtained on request to the FAA, Washington, D.C.

## INTENSIVE STUDENT JET TRAINING AREA (ISJTA)

Intensive student jet training area is that airspace which contains the intensive training activities of military student jet pilots and in which restrictions are imposed on IFR flight.

222

Information on these training areas may be obtained from any FSS within 100 miles of the area.

## ALERT AREA

Alert areas contain airspace which is depicted on aeronautical charts to inform non-participating pilots of areas that may contain a high volume of pilot training or an unusual type of aerial activity, and pilots should be particularly alert. All activity within an Alert Area should be conducted in accordance with Federal Aviation Regulations, without waiver, and pilots of participating aircraft as well as pilots transiting the area shall be equally responsible for collision avoidance. Information concerning these areas may be obtained upon request to the FAA, Washington, D.C.

# OTHER AIRSPACE AREAS

## AIRPORT TRAFFIC AREAS

1. Unless otherwise specifically designated (FAR Part 93), that airspace with a horizontal radius of five statute miles from the geographical center of any airport at which a control tower is operating, extending from the surface up to, but not including, 3,000 feet above the surface.

2. The rules prescribed for airport traffic areas are established in FAR 91.70, 91.85 and 91.87. They require, in effect, that unless a pilot is landing or taking off from an airport within the airport traffic area, he must avoid the area unless otherwise authorized by ATC. If operating to, from or on the airport served by the control tower, he must also establish and maintain radio communications with the tower. Maximum indicated airspeeds are prescribed. The areas are not depicted on charts. The airport traffic area is illustrated below:

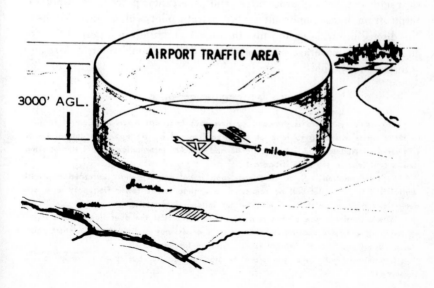

## DISASTER AREA

1. Consists of that airspace below 2,000 feet above the surface within a 5 statute mile radius of an aircraft or train accident, flood, forest fire, earthquake or other disaster of substantial magnitude. The designation of a disaster area is made in a Notice to Airmen.

2. Pilots are not to operate their aircraft within a disaster area unless they are part of the airborne relief activities; they are operating to or from an airport within the area and the operation will not hamper the relief activities; or flight around the area is impracticable because of weather or other reasons and prior notice is given to ATC. (Ref. FAR 91.91)

### • AIRPORT ADVISORY AREA

1. The area within five statute miles of an airport where a control tower is not operating but where a Flight Service Station is located. At such locations, the FSS provides advisory service to arriving and departing aircraft. (See AIRPORT ADVISORIES AT NON TOWER AIRPORTS in Chapter 4.)

2. It is not mandatory that pilots participate in the airport advisory service program, but it is strongly recommended that they do.

Figure 120. *Special use and other airspace.*

---

*Air Traffic Control*  This section of Part 1 concerns itself with the multitude of subjects related to the control of air traffic, such as services available to the pilot, airport operations, ATC clearances, departures, en route and arrival procedures, and emergency procedures. Only excerpts from items important to the private pilot will be included here. No discussion will accompany the material found in figure 121. For more complete coverage of these subjects, pilots should refer to Airman's Information Manual.

### VFR ADVISORY SERVICE

1. VFR advisory service is provided by numerous nonradar Approach Control facilities to those pilots intending to land at an airport served by an approach control tower. This service includes: wind, runway, traffic and NOTAM information, unless this information is contained in the ATIS broadcast.

2. Such information will be furnished upon initial contact with concerned approach control facility. The pilot will be requested to change to the tower frequency at a predetermined time or point, to receive further landing information.

3. Where available, use of this procedure will not hinder the operation of VFR flights by requiring excessive spacing between aircraft or devious routing. Radio contact points will be based on time or distance rather than on landmarks.

4. Compliance with this procedure is not mandatory but pilot participation is encouraged.

# AUTOMATIC TERMINAL INFORMATION SERVICE (ATIS)

Automatic Terminal Information Service (ATIS) is the continuous broadcast of recorded noncontrol information in selected high activity terminal areas. Its purpose is to improve controller effectiveness and to relieve frequency congestion by automating the repetitive transmission of essential but routine information.

Information such as ceiling, visibility, wind, altimeter, instrument approach, and runways in use is continuously broadcast on the voice feature of a TVOR/VOR/VORTAC located on or near the airport, or on a discrete VHF tower frequency. Where VFR arrival aircraft are expected to make initial contact with approach control, this fact and the appropriate frequencies will be broadcast on ATIS. Pilots of aircraft arriving or departing the terminal area can receive the continuous ATIS broadcasts at times when cockpit duties are least pressing and listen to as many repeats as desired. ATIS broadcasts will be updated when there is a significant change in information contained therein.

Sample Broadcast:

"THIS IS WASHINGTON NATIONAL AIRPORT INFORMATION BRAVO. CEILNG MEAS-URED TWO THOUSAND, OVERCAST, VISIBILITY SIX, SMOKE. WIND ONE SIX ZERO DEGREES AT FIVE. ALTIMETER TWO NINER NINER TWO. VOR RUNWAY ONE FIVE AP-PROACH IN USE. LANDING RUNWAY ONE EIGHT. DEPARTURES ON RUNWAY ONE FIVE. NOTAM, GEORGETOWN RADIO BEACON OUT OF SERVICE."

# AIRPORT ADVISORIES AT NONTOWER AIRPORTS

1. Airport Advisory Service-Flight Service Stations (FSS) located at airports where there are no control towers in operation provide advisory information to arriving and departing aircraft. This service is offered for safety purposes; traffic control is not exercised.

2. Airport advisories provide: wind direction and velocity, favored or designated runway, altimeter setting, known traffic (caution: all aircraft in the airport vicinity may not be communicating with the FSS), notices to airmen, airport taxi routes, airport traffic patterns, and instrument approach procedures. These elements are varied so as to best serve the current traffic situation. Some airport managers have specified that under certain wind or other conditions, designated runways are to be used. Pilots using other than the favored or designated runways should advise the FSS immediately.

# RADAR TRAFFIC INFORMATION SERVICE

1. A service provided by radar air traffic control facilities. Pilots receiving this service are advised of any radar target observed on the radar display which may be in such proximity to the position of their aircraft or its intended route of flight that it warrants their attention. This service is not intended to relieve the pilot of his responsibilty for continual vigilance to see and avoid other aircraft.

# TERMINAL RADAR PROGRAMS FOR VFR AIRCRAFT

1. STAGE I SERVICE (Radar Advisory Service for VFR Aircraft)

a. In addition to the use of radar for the control of IFR aircraft, Stage I facilities provide traffic information and limited vectoring to VFR aircraft on a workload permit-ting basis.

b. Vectoring service may be provided when requested by the pilot or with pilot concurrence when suggested by ATC.

c. Pilots of arriving aircraft should contact approach control on the publicized frequency (sectional aeronautical chart/AIM), give their position, altitude, radar beacon code (if transponder equipped), destination, and request traffic information.

d. Approach control will issue wind and runway, except when the pilot states 'HAVE NUMBERS' or this information is contained in the ATIS broadcast. Traffic information is provided on a workload permitting basis. Approach control will specify the time or place at which the pilot is to contact the tower on local control frequency for further landing information. Upon being told to contact the tower, radar service is automatically terminated.

Figure 121. *Air traffic control.*

---

***Radiotelephone Phraseology and Technique*** Only those items deemed most germane to the private pilot in regard to radio communications are depicted in figure 122. More complete coverage will be found in the Airman's Information Manual.

## • CONTACT PROCEDURE

1. Initiate radio communications with a ground facility by using the following format:
   a. Identification of the unit being called.
   b. Identification of the aircraft.
   c. The type of message to follow, when this will be of assistance.
   d. The word 'OVER.'
Example:
   NEW YORK RADIO, MOONEY THREE ONE ONE ONE E, OVER.
2. Reply to callup from a ground facility by using the following format:
   a. Identification of the unit initiating the callup.
   b. Identification of the aircraft.
   c. The word 'OVER.'
Example:
   PITTSBURGH TOWER, CESSNA TWO SIX FOUR FIVE ZEBRA OVER.
      Note.—The word 'OVER' may be omitted if the message obviously requires a reply.
3. Use the same format as for initial callup and reply after communication has been established except, after stating your identification, state the message to be sent or acknowledgment of the message received. The acknowledgment is made with the word 'ROGER' or 'WILCO' and pilots are expected to comply with ATC clearances/instructions when they acknowledge by using either 'ROGER' or 'WILCO.'
   Example:
   APACHE ONE TWO THREE X, ROGER.
4. After contact has been definitely established, it may be continued without further call-up or identification.

# MICROPHONE TECHNIQUE

1. Proper microphone technique is important in radiotelephone communications. Transmissions should be concise and in a normal conversational tone.

   Note.—Identification of Aircraft—Pilots are requested to exercise care that the identification of their aircraft is clearly transmitted in each contact with an ATC facility. Also pilots should be certain that their aircraft are clearly identified in ATC transmissions before taking action on an ATC clearance.

2. When originating a radiotelephone call-up to any air-ground facility, indicate the channel on which reply is expected, if other than normal.

Figure 122. *Radio phraseology and technique.*

---

**Airport Operations** Figures 123 and 124 are excerpts from AIM dealing with airport operations which relate to takeoff and landing information and procedures for tower-controlled and nontower airports.

## TOWER-CONTROLLED AIRPORTS

1. When operating to an airport where traffic control is being exercised by a control tower, pilots are required to maintain two-way radio contact with the tower while operating within the airport traffic area unless the tower authorizes otherwise. Initial call-up should be made about 15 miles from the airport.

2. When necessary, the tower controller will issue clearances or other information for aircraft to generally follow the desired flight path (traffic patterns) when flying in the airport traffic area/control zone, and the proper taxi routes when operating on the ground. If not otherwise authorized or directed by the tower, pilots approaching to land in an airplane must circle the airport to the left, and pilots approaching to land in a helicopter must avoid the flow of fixed wing traffic. However, an appropriate clearance must be received from the tower before landing.

## NON-TOWER AIRPORTS

1. The segmented circle system is designed to provide traffic pattern information at airports without operating control towers. (Refer to AIM, Part 1, for detailed information.)

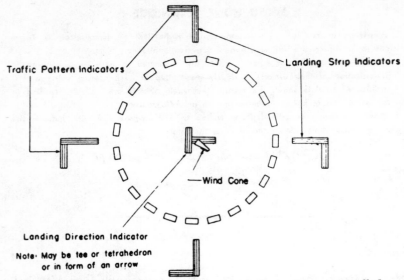

Traffic Pattern Indicators

Landing Strip Indicators

Wind Cone

Landing Direction Indicator

Note: May be tee or tetrahedron
or in form of an arrow

Figure 123. *Airport operations—tower and nontower controlled.*

## USE OF RUNWAYS

Runways are numbered to correspond to their magnetic bearing. Runway 27, for example, has a bearing of 270 degrees. Wind direction issued by the tower is also magnetic.

## • INTERSECTION TAKEOFFS

1. In order to enhance airport capacities, reduce taxiing distances, minimize departure delays, and provide for more efficient movement of air traffic, controllers may initiate intersection takeoffs as well as approve them when the pilot requests. If for ANY reason a pilot prefers to use a different intersection or the full length of the runway or desires to obtain the distance between the intersection and the runway end, HE IS EXPECTED TO INFORM ATC ACCORDINGLY.

Portable traffic control light signals:

| Color and Type of Signal | On the Ground | In Flight |
|---|---|---|
| STEADY GREEN | Cleared for takeoff | Cleared to land |
| FLASHING GREEN | Cleared to taxi | Return for landing (to be followed by steady green at proper time) |
| STEADY RED | Stop | Give way to other aircraft and continue circling |
| FLASHING RED | Taxi clear of landing area (runway) in use | Airport unsafe—do not land |
| FLASHING WHITE | Return to starting point on airport | |
| ALTERNATING RED & GREEN | General Warning Signal—Exercise Extreme Caution | |

Figure 124. *Airport operations—miscellaneous.*

***ATC Clearances and Separations*** Most of this section is more germane to the IFR than to VFR flights. Figure 125, however, deals with information quite important to the private pilot conducting a flight under Visual Flight Rules.

## SPECIAL VFR CLEARANCES

### Special VFR Flight Clearance Procedures (F.A.R. Part 91.107)

• 1. An ATC clearance must be obtained prior to operatin within a control zone when the weather is less than that required for VFR flight (1,000 foot ceiling and 3 miles visibility). Within most control zones, a VFR pilot may request and be given a clearance to conduct special VFR flight to, from, or within the control zone providing such flight will not delay IFR operations. The weather and clearance from cloud requirements for special VFR flight are: 1 mile ground visibility if landing or departing (½ mile for air carriers), 1 mile flight visibility if transiting the control zone, and flight to be conducted clear of clouds. When a control tower is located within the control zone, requests for clearances should be to the tower. If no tower is located within the control zone, a clearance may be obtained from the nearest tower, flight service station or center.

2. It is not necessary to file a complete flight plan with the request for clearance but the pilot should state his intentions in sufficient detail to permit air traffic control to fit his flight into the traffic flow. The clearance will not contain a specific altitude as the pilot must remain clear of clouds. The controller may require the pilot to fly at or below a certain altitude due to other traffic, but the altitude specified will permit flight at or above the minimum safe altitude. In addition, at radar locations, flights may be vectored if necessary for control purposes or on pilot request.

• 3. ATC provides separation between special VFR flights and between them and other IFR flights.

• 4. Within some control zones, the volume of IFR traffic is such that special VFR flight can not be permitted. A list of these control zones is contained in Part III of the AIM.

Figure 125. *Special VFR clearances.*

---

***Preflight.*** The preflight phase of every flight is of the greatest importance. The care exercised by the pilot in familiarizing himself with all available information concerning his flights may well mean the difference between a safe operation and disaster. In fact, FAR 91.5 makes such preflight action mandatory and for all flights not in the vicinity of an airport, the regulation refers to specific items that must be checked. Some of the important points to consider are depicted in figure 126. Additional information relative to weather briefings may be found in Chapter 35.

## GENERAL

1. Every pilot is urged to receive a preflight briefing and to file a flight plan. This briefing would consist of weather, airport, and enroute navaid information. Briefing service may be obtained from a Flight Service Station either by telephone/interphone, by radio when airborne, or by a personal visit to the Station.

2. In addition to the filing of a flight plan, if the flight will traverse or land in one or more foreign countries, it is particularly important that pilots leave a complete itinerary with someone directly concerned, keep that person advised of the flight's progress and inform him, that if serious doubt arises as to the safety of the flight, he should first contact the FSS.

## WEATHER BRIEFING

1. Consult your local flight service station (FSS), combined station/tower (CS/T), or weather bureau airport station (WBAS) for preflight weather briefing. FSS and WBAS personnel are certificated pilot weather briefers; however, since CS/T personnel are not certificated pilot weather briefers, weather briefings they furnish are limited to factual data derived directly from weather sequence and forecast information.

2. When telephoning for information, use the following procedure:

a. Identify yourself as a pilot. (Many persons calling WB stations want information for purposes other than flying.)

b. State your intended route, destination, proposed departure time and estimated time en route.

c. Advise if you intend to fly only VFR.

d. When talking to an FSS, you will be asked your aircraft identification for activity record purposes.

3. You are urged to use the Pilot's Preflight Check List which is on the reverse of the flight plan form. The Check List is a reminder of items you should be aware of before beginning flight. Also provided beneath the Check List is a Flight Log for your use if desired.

# FLIGHT PLAN—VFR

## 1. GENERAL

a. Except for operations in or penetrating a Coastal or Domestic ADIZ or DEWIZ, a flight plan is not required for VFR flight; however, it is strongly recommended that one be filed.

b. To obtain maximum benefits of the flight plan program, flight plans should be filed directly with the nearest flight service station. For your convenience, FSSs provide one-call (telephone/interphone) or one-stop (personal) aeronautical and meteorological briefings while accepting flight plans. Radio may be used to file if no other means are available. Also, some states operate aeronautical communications facilities which will accept and forward flight plans to the FSS for further handling.

c. Pilots are encouraged to give their departure times directly to the flight service station with which the flight plan was filed. This will ensure more efficient flight plan service and permit the FSS to advise you of significant changes in aeronautical facilities or meteorological conditions. The following procedures are in effect: when a VFR flight plan is filed, it will be held until one hour after the proposed departure time and then canceled unless:

1. The actual departure time is received.

2. A revised proposed departure time is received.

3. At a time of filing, the FSS is informed that the proposed departure time will be met, but actual time cannot be given because of inadequate communications.

d. On pilot's request, at a location having an active tower, the aircraft identification will be forwarded to the tower for reporting the actual departure time. This procedure should be avoided at busy airports.

e. Although position reports are not required for VFR flight plans, periodic reports to FAA Flight Service Stations along the route are good practice. Such contacts permit significant information to be passed to the transiting aircraft and also serve to check the progress of the flight should it be necessary for any reason to locate the aircraft or its occupants.

## DEFENSE VFR FLIGHT PLAN

• Detailed ADIZ procedures are found in the emergency section of this chapter. (See FAR 99 and FAR 91.12.)

## CLOSING VFR/DVFR FLIGHT PLANS

VFR and DVFR flight plans must be closed (canceled), or an arrival report filed, within ½ hour (15 minutes for jets) after the estimated time of arrival. To ensure flight plan closure, notify the nearest flight service station. If an FSS is not available, request any air traffic control facility to relay the cancellation to the FSS. If a report is not received within this time, a communications search will be conducted by Federal Aviation Administration facilities. If this search fails to locate your aircraft, a search and rescue center will be advised and an extensive, costly physical search for your aircraft will be initiated.

## 2. CLOSE YOUR FLIGHT PLAN

a. The control tower does not automatically close flight plans since many of the landing aircraft are not operating on flight plans. It remains the responsibility of a pilot to close his own flight plan. This will prevent a needless search.

Figure 126. *Preflight planning.*

---

***Emergency Procedures*** This section of AIM covers the various ways you can declare an emergency in order to obtain assistance, information on crash locator beacons, search and rescue procedures, and rules pertaining to aircraft accidents, incidents, overdue aircraft, and safety investigations. In addition to the information provided in figure 127, emergency radio procedures are discussed in Chapter 34.

## LOCATOR BEACONS

1. Locator Beacons of various types which are independently powered, reliable, and of incalculable value in an emergency have been developed and are gaining wide acceptance as a means of locating downed aircraft and their occupants. These electronic, battery operated beacons are not a fire hazard. They are designed to emit a distinctive downward swept audio tone for homing purposes on 121.5 MHz and/or 243 MHz, preferably on both emergency frequencies. The power source should be capable of providing power for continuous operation from 24 to 48 hours or more at a very wide range of ambient temperatures and can expedite search and rescue operations as well as facilitate accident investigation and analysis.

5. Pilots of aircraft equipped with locator beacons are encouraged to include this information in the REMARKS portion of their flight plans.

Figure 127. *Locator beacons.*

---

***Safety of Flight*** This important chapter in AIM discusses altimetry, important aspects of weather and weather services available to pilots, wake turbulence, medical facts for pilots, and good operating practices. Figures 128, 129, 130, 131, 132, and 133 are typical of the information supplied in this portion of AIM.

1. The accuracy of aircraft altimeters is subject to the following factors: (a) nonstandard temperature of the atmosphere; (b) aircraft static pressure systems (position error); and (c) instrument error. Pilots should disregard the effect of nonstandard atmospheric temperatures except that low temperatures need to be considered for terrain clearance purposes.

Note.—Standard temperature at sea level is 15° C. (59° F.). The temperature gradient from sea level is 2° C. (3.5° F.) per 1000 feet. Pilots should apply corrections for static pressure systems and/or instruments, if appreciable errors exist.

Figure 128. *Altimetry.*

---

*Weather* Much of the information found in this portion of AIM will be covered in detail in Sections II and X of this handbook. AIM includes discussions on weather briefings, transcribed and scheduled weather broadcasts and broadcast weather format, pilot weather reports, turbulence reporting criteria, etc. Because of their importance, the following items (figure 129) are included here as representative of AIM information on weather and its relationship to safety in flight.

## AIRFRAME ICING

The effects of ice accretion on aircraft are cumulative—Thrust is reduced, Drag increases, Lift lessens, Weight increases. The results are an increase in stall speed and a deterioration of aircraft performance. In extreme cases, 2 o 3 inches of ice can form on the leading edge of the airfoil in less than 5 minutes. It takes but $\frac{1}{2}$ inch of ice to reduce the lifting power of some aircraft by 50% and increases the frictional drag by an equal percentage.

A pilot can expect icing when flying in visible precipitation such as rain or cloud droplets, and the temperature is 0 degrees Centigrade or colder. When icing is detected, a pilot should do one of two things, particularly if the aircraft is not equipped with deicing equipment, he should get out of the area of precipitation or go to an altitude where the temperature is above freezing. This "warmer" altitude may not always be a lower altitude. Proper pre-flight action includes obtaining information on the freezing level and the above-freezing levels in precipitation areas. Report icing to ATC/FSS, and if operating IFR, request new routing or altitude if icing will be a hazard. Be sure to give type of aircraft to ATC when reporting icing. Following is a table that describes how to report icing conditions.

## REPORTING OF CLOUD HEIGHTS

1. Ceiling, by definition in Part I Federal Aviation Regulations, and as used in Aviation Weather Reports and Forecasts, is the height above ground (or water) level of the lowest layer of clouds or obscuring phenomenon that is reported as "broken", "overcast", or "obscuration" and not classified as "thin" or "partial". For example, a forecast which reads "CIGS WILL BE GENLY 1 TO 2 THSD FEET" refers to heights above ground level (AGL). On the other hand, a forecast which reads "BRKN TO OVC LYRS AT 8 TO 12 THSD MSL" states that the height is above mean sea level (MSL).

2. Pilots usually report height values above mean sea level, since they determine heights by the altimeter. This is taken in account when disseminating and otherwise applying information received from pilots. ("Ceilings" heights are always above ground level.) In reports disseminated as PIREPS, height references are given the same as received from pilots, that is above mean sea level (MSL or ASL).

Figure 129. *Ceiling and icing.*

---

● **WAKE TURBULENCE**
### GENERAL
EVERY AIRCRAFT GENERATES A WAKE WHILE IN FLIGHT. In the past this turbulence

was attributed to "prop wash." Later studies found this disturbance to be a pair of counter rotating vortices trailing from the wing tips. It was found that the intensity of the vortices increased with the size and weight of the aircraft. As aircraft became larger and heavier, the intensity of the vortices began to pose problems for smaller aircraft. Some of today's jet aircraft, particularly the new jumbo jets, generate roll velocities exceeding the roll control capability of some aircraft. Further, turbulence generated within vortices can damage aircraft components and equipment when encountered at close range. ATC applies procedures designed to preclude wake encounters, but in most VFR situations the pilot sets up his own separation from other aircraft. For his own safety, the pilot must learn to envision the location of the vortex wake generated by large aircraft and adjust his flight path accordingly.

During ground operations, jet engine blast (thrust stream turbulence) can cause damage and upsets if encountered at close range. It is recommended that light aircraft remain at least 200 feet behind a jet operating its engines at idle speed—400 feet behind a taxiing jet—1,000 feet from a jet taking off. Engine thrust velocities generated by large jet aircraft during initial takeoff roll and the drifting of the turbulence in relation to the crosswind component dictate the desirability of lighter aircraft awaiting takeoff to hold well back of the runway edge or taxiway holdline; also, the desirability of aligning the aircraft to face the possible jet engine blast movement. The FAA has established new standards for location of taxiway hold lines at airports served by air carriers as follows:

"Locate all taxiway holding lines such that the distance from the runway structural pavement edge to the taxiway holding line is at least equal to the greater of the following: (1) 100 feet or (2) the wing span of the largest airplane that is expected to use the runway."

Though the following information refers primarily to heavy jets, remember that all aircraft create a wake and that large prop driven aircraft may generate vortices of high intensity.

## VORTEX GENERATION

The circulation and downwash affect of the airflow over the wing causes the air leaving each trailing edge to form a vortex sheet which rolls itself up into a swirling spiral of air aft of the wing tips. After the roll up is completed, the wake consists of two counter rotating vortices.

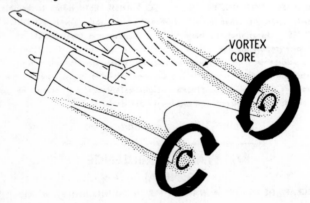

VORTEX CORE

should visualize the location of the vortex trail and use proper avoidance
in a mixed traffic environment. AVOID WAKE ENCOUNTERS BELOW AND
THE GENERATING AIRCRAFT, ESPECIALLY AT LOW ALTITUDE WHERE EVEN A
RY WAKE ENCOUNTER COULD BE HAZARDOUS.

## VORTEX AVOIDANCE PROCEDURES

GENERAL. Under certain conditions airport traffic controllers apply procedures for
ating other aircraft from heavy jets. They will also provide VFR aircraft, which in
ower's opinion may be adversely affected by potential wake turbulence, with the
tion, altitude and direction of flight of the heavy jet. When the tower controller
ises "CAUTION WAKE TURBULENCE," etc., he is following his procedures and warning
u that it may exist. YOU ARE EXPECTED TO ADJUST YOUR OPERATION AND FLIGHT
ATH AS NECESSARY TO PRECLUDE SERIOUS WAKE ENCOUNTERS. Don't hesitate to
equest further information if you believe it will assist you in analyzing the situation.
Remember, even though you have received a clearance to land or takeoff, if you believe
it safer to wait, use a different runway, or in some other way alter your operation, ask
the controller for a revised clearance.

2. The following vortex avoidance procedures are recommended for the various
situations:

a. LANDING BEHIND A HEAVY JET—SAME RUNWAY. Stay at or above the jet's final
approach path—note his touchdown point—land beyond it.

b. LANDING ON A PARALLEL RUNWAY BEHIND A HEAVY JET WHEN THE PARALLEL
RUNWAYS ARE LESS THAN 2500 FEET APART. Note wind for possible vortex drift, request
upwind runway if possible. Stay at or above the jet's final approach flight path—note his
touchdown point—land beyond a point abeam his touchdown point.

c. LANDING BEHIND A HEAVY JET—CROSSING RUNWAY. Cross above the jet's flight
path.

d. LANDING BEHIND A DEPARTING HEAVY JET—SAME RUNWAY. Note jet's rotation
point—land well prior to rotation point.

e. LANDING BEHIND A DEPARTING HEAVY JET—CROSSING RUNWAY. Note jet's
rotation point—if past the intersection—land prior to the intersection. If jet rotates prior
to the intersection avoid flight below the jet's flight path. Abandon the approach unless
landing is assured well before reaching the intersection.

f. DEPARTING BEHIND A HEAVY JET. The tower will withhold clearances for 2 minutes for takeoffs on the same runway, a parallel runway separated by less than 2500 feet,
and any other situation where inflight crossing courses are evident. Pilots should note the
jet's rotation point—climb above the jet's climb path until turning clear of his wake.
Avoid subsequent flight paths which will cross below and behind a heavy jet.

g. INTERSECTION TAKEOFFS—SAME RUNWAY. Towers will withhold takeoff clearance
for 3 minutes behind a large turbojet on the same runway. Be alert to adjacent heavy
jet operations particularly upwind of your runway. Avoid subsequent headings which will
cross below a heavy jet's path closer than 1000 feet.

h. ENROUTE VFR. Avoid flight below and behind a heavy jet's flight path. If you
observe a heavy jet above you on the same track (same or opposite direction) adjust your
position laterally, preferable upwind to the jet.

## VORTEX STRENGTH

1. The strength of a vortex is governed primarily by the weight, speed, and shape of
the wing of the generating aircraft. The basic factor is weight, and the vortex strength
increases with increases in weight and span loading. During a recent test, vortex tangential
velocities were recorded at 150 feet per second or about 90 knots. The greatest vortex
strength occurs when the generating aircraft is HEAVY—CLEAN—SLOW.

2. Induced Roll. A serious wake encounter could result in structural damage. However
the primary hazard is loss of control because of induced roll. Aircraft intentionally flown
directly up the core of a vortex during flight tests tended to roll with that vortex.

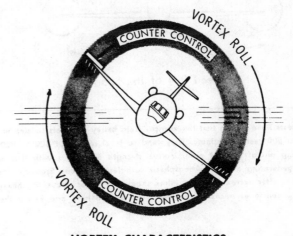

## VORTEX CHARACTERISTICS

Trailing vortex wakes have certain characteristics. Being familiar with these characteristics will assist the pilot in visualizing the location of these vortex wakes.

1. Vortex generation starts with rotation for lift off and ends when the wing unloads
after touchdown.

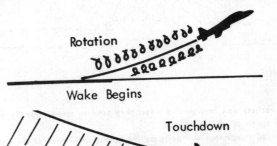

2. The vortex circulation is outward, upward and around the wing tip when viewed from either ahead or behind the aircraft. Tests with heavy aircraft have shown that the diameter of the vortex core ranges from 25 to 50 feet, but the field of influence is larger. The vortices stay close together (about 3/4 of the span) until dissipation. Thus, if persistent vortex turbulence is encountered, a slight lateral change in flight path will usually avoid it.

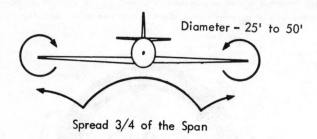

Diameter – 25' to 50'

Spread 3/4 of the Span

3. Flight tests have shown that the vortices from heavy jets start to sink immediately at about 400 to 500 feet per minute. They tend to level off about 800 to 900 feet below the generating aircraft's flight path. Vortex strength diminishes with time and distance behind the generating aircraft. Atmospheric turbulence hastens breakup. Residual choppiness remains after vortex breakup. Pilots should fly at or above the heavy jet's flight path, altering course as necessary to avoid the area behind and below the generating aircraft.

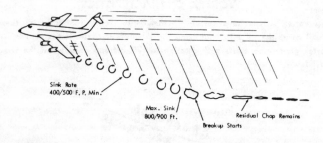

Sink Rate
400/500 F. P. Min.

Max. Sink
800/900 Ft.

Breakup Starts

Residual Chop Remains

4. When the vortices sink into ground effect they tend to move laterally outward over the ground at a speed of about 5 knots.

a. A crosswind component will decrease the lateral movement of the upwind vortex and increase the movement of the downwind vortex. This may result in the upwind vortex remaining in the touchdown zone or hasten the drift of the downwind vortex toward a parallel runway. Similarly, a tail wind condition can move the vortices of a preceding

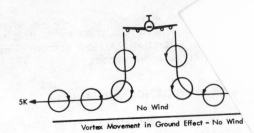

5K

No Wind

Vortex Movement in Ground Effect – No Wind

aircraft into the touchdown zone. Pilots should be alert to heavy aircra... flight path.

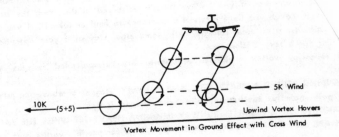

10K    (5+5)

5K Wind

Upwind Vortex Hovers

Vortex Movement in Ground Effect with Cross Wind

Tail Wind

## OPERATIONAL PROBLEM AREAS

1. A wake encounter may not necessarily be hazardous. It can be one or more jolts with varying intensity depending on the direction of the encounter, distance from the generating aircraft and point of vortex encounter. The probability of buffeting and induced roll increases when the encountering aircraft's heading is generally aligned with the vortex trail. Pilots should be particularly alert to calm wind conditions and situations when the vortices:

a. Remain in the touchdown area.

b. Drift downwind to a parallel runway.

c. Sink into the takeoff or landing path of a crossing runway.

d. Sink into the traffic patterns for other airports.

e. Sink into the flight path of VFR flights operating below.

## HELICOPTERS

A hovering helicopter generates a downwash from its main rotor/s similar to the prop blast of a conventional aircraft. In forward flight, this energy is transformed into a pair of trailing vortices similar to wing tip vortices. Pilots of small aircraft and helicopters should avoid both the vortices and the downwash of heavy helicopters.

## PILOT RESPONSIBILITY

Government and industry groups are making concerted efforts to minimize the hazards of trailing vortices. However, the flight disciplines necessary to assure vortex avoidance during VFR operations must be exercised by the pilot. Vortex visualization and avoidance is equal in importance to traffic avoidance.

Figure 130. *Wake turbulence.*

---

# MEDICAL FACTS FOR PILOTS

## GENERAL

Just as your aircraft is required to undergo regular checks and maintenance, you are also required to undergo regular medical examinations to ensure your fitness to fly. The physical standards you are required to meet are minimum standards. You do not have to be a superman to fly. Many defects can be compensated for, as, for example, wearing glasses for visual defects. You may be required to demonstrate by a medical flight test that you can compensate for any other defects of potential significance to flight safety.

Student pilots should visit a Designated Aviation Medical Examiner and determine if they meet the standards before spending much money taking flying instructions.

It should be recalled that humans are essentially earthbound creatures. However if we are aware of certain aeromedical factors, and pay attention to these, we can leave the earth and fly safely. What follows will not be one hard comprehensive lesson in aviation medicine. It will point out the more important factors with which you should be familiar prior to flying.

Modern industry's record in providing reliable equipment is very good. When the pilot enters the aircraft, he becomes an integral part of the man-machine system. He is just as essential to a successful flight as the control surfaces. To ignore the pilot in pre-flight planning would be as senseless as failing to inspect the integrity of the control surfaces or any other vital part of the machine. The pilot himself has the sole responsibility for determining his reliability prior to entering the cockpit for flight.

While piloting an aircraft, an individual should be free of conditions which are harmful to alertness, ability to make correct decisions, and rapid reaction times. Persons with conditions which are apt to produce sudden incapacitation, such as epilepsy, serious heart trouble, uncontrolled diabetes mellitus or diabetes mellitus requiring hypoglycemis agents, and certain other conditions hazardous to flight, cannot be medically certified according to the Federal Aviation Regulations. Conditions such as acute infections, anemias, and peptic ulcers, are temporary disqualifying. Consult your Aviation Medical Examiner when in doubt about any aspect of your health status, just as you would consult a licensed aviation mechanic when in doubt about the engine status. Specific aeromedical factors are herein explained. For additional information on these or other aeromedical flight factors, write to: The Federal Air Surgeon, Federal Aviation Administration, Washington, D.C. 20590.

## FATIGUE

Fatigue generally slows reaction times and causes foolish errors due to inattention. In addition to the most common cause of fatigue, insufficient rest and loss of sleep, the pressures of business, financial worries and family problems, can be important contributing factors. If your fatigue is marked prior to a given flight, don't fly. To prevent fatigue effects during long flights, keep active with respect to making ground checks, radio-navigation position plotting, and remaining mentally active.

## HYPOXIA

Hypoxia in simple terms is a lack of sufficient oxygen to keep the brain and other body tissues functioning properly. Wide individual variation occurs with respect to susceptibility to hypoxia. In addition to progressively insufficient oxygen at higher altitudes, anything interfering with the body's ability to carry oxygen can contribute to hypoxia (anemias, carbon monoxide, and certain drugs). Also, alcohol and various drugs decrease the brain's tolerance to hypoxia.

Your body has no built in alarm system to let you know when you are not getting enough oxygen. It is impossible to predict when or where hypoxia will occur during a given flight, or how it will manifest itself.

A major early symptom of hypoxia is an increased sense of well-being (referred to as euphoria). This progresses to slow reactions, impaired thinking ability, unusual fatigue, and dull headache feeling.

The symptoms are slow but progressive, insidious in onset, and are most marked at altitudes starting above ten thousand feet. Night vision, however, can be impaired starting at altitudes lower than ten thousand feet. Heavy smokers may also experience early symptoms of hypoxia at altitudes lower than is so with nonsmokers.

If you observe the general rule of not flying above ten thousand feet without supplemental oxygen, you will not get into trouble.

## HYPERVENTILATION

Hyperventilation, or over breathing, is a disturbance of respiration that may occur in individuals as a result of emotional tension or anxiety. Under conditions of emotional stress, fright or pain, breathing rate may increase, causing increase lung ventilation, although the carbon dioxide output of the body cells does not increase. As a result, carbon dioxide is "washed out" of the blood. The most common symptoms of hyperventilation are: dizziness; hot and cold sensations; tingling of the hands, legs and feet; tetany; nausea; sleepiness; and finally unconsciousness.

Should symptoms occur which cannot definitely be identified as either hypoxia or hyperventilation, the following steps should be taken:

1. Check your oxygen equipment and put the regulator auto-mix level on 100% oxygen (demand or pressure demand system). Continuous flow-check oxygen supply and flow mechanism.

2. After three or four deep breaths of oxygen, the system should improve markedly, if the condition was hypoxia (recovery from hypoxia is rapid).

3. If the symptoms persist, consciously slow your breathing rate until symptoms clear and then resume normal breathing rate. Breathing can be slowed by breathing into a bag, or talking loud.

## ALCOHOL

Do not fly while under the influence of alcohol. An excellent rule is to allow twenty-four hours between the last drink and takeoff time. Even small amounts of alcohol in the system can adversely affect judgment and decision-making abilities.

Remember that your body metabolizes alcohol at a fixed rate, and no amount of coffee or medication will alter this rate.

By all means, do not fly with a hangover, or a "masked hangover" (symptoms suppressed by aspirin or other medication).

## DRUGS

Self-medication or taking medicine in any form when you are flying can be extremely hazardous. Even simple home or over-the-counter remedies and drugs such as aspirin, antihistamines, cold tablets, cough mixtures, laxatives, tranquilizers and appetite suppressors, may seriously impair the judgment and coordination needed while flying. The safest rule is to take no medicine while flying, except on the advice of your Aviation Medical Examiner. It should also be remembered that the condition for which the drug is required, may of itself be very hazardous to flying, even when the symptoms are suppressed by the drug.

Certain specific drugs which have been associated with aircraft accidents in the recent past are: Antihistamines (widely prescribed for hay fever and other allergies); Tranquilizers (prescribed for nervous conditions, hypertension, and other conditions); Reducing Drugs (amphetamines and other appetite suppressing drugs can produce sensations of well-being which have an adverse affect on judgment); Barbiturates, Nerve tonics or pills (prescribed for digestive and other disorders, barbiturates produce a marked suppression on mental alertness).

## VERTIGO

The word itself is hard to define. To earthbound individuals it usually means dizziness or swimming of the head. To a pilot it means, in simple terms, that he doesn't know which end is up. In fact, vertigo during flight can have very fatal consequences.

On the ground we know which way is up through the combined use of three senses:

1. Vision—We can see where we are in relation to fixed objects.

2. Pressure—Gravitational pull on muscles and joints tells us which way is down.

3. Special Parts In Our Inner Ear—The otoliths tell us which way is down by gravitational pull. It should be noted that accelerations of the body are detected by the fluid in the semi-circular canals of the inner ear, and this tells us when we change position. However, in the absence of a visual reference, such as flying into a cloud or overcast, the accelerations can be confusing, especially since their forces can be misinterpreted as gravitational pulls on the muscles and otoliths. The result is often disorientation and vertigo (or dizziness).

All pilots should have an instructor pilot produce maneuvers which will produce the sensation of vertigo. Once experienced, later unanticipated incidents of vertigo can be overcome. Closing the eyes for a second or two may help, as will watching the flight instruments, believing them, and controlling the airplane in accordance with the information presented on the instruments. All pilots should obtain the minimum training recommeded by the FAA for attitude control of aircraft solely by reference to the gyroscopic instruments.

Pilots are susceptible to experiencing vertigo at night, and in any flight condition when outside visibility is reduced to the point that the horizon is obscured. An additional type of vertigo is known as flicker vertigo. Light, flickering at certain frequencies, from four to twenty times per second, can produce unpleasant and dangerous reactions in some persons. These reactions may include nausea, dizziness, unconsciousness, or even reactions similar to epileptic fit. In a single engine propeller airplane, heading into the sun, the propeller may cut the sun to give this flashing effect, particularly during landings when the engine is throttled back. These undesirable effects may be avoided by not staring directly through the prop for more than a moment, and by making frequent but small changes in RPM. The flickering light traversing helicopter blades has been known to cause this difficulty, as has the bounce-back from rotating beacons on aircraft which have penetrated clouds.

## CARBON MONOXIDE

Carbon monoxide is a colorless, odorless, tasteless product of an internal combustion engine and is always present in exhaust fumes. Even minute quantities of carbon monoxide breathed over a long period of time, may lead to dire consequences.

For biochemical reasons, carbon monoxide has a greater ability to combine with the hemoglobin of the blood than oxygen. Furthermore, once carbon monoxide is absorbed in the blood, it sticks "like glue" to the hemoglobin and actually prevents the oxygen from attaching to the hemoglobin.

Most heaters in light aircraft work by air flowing over the manifold. So if you have to use the heater, be wary if you smell exhaust fumes. The onset of symptoms is insidious, with "blurred thinking," a possible feeling of uneasiness, and subsequent dizziness. Later headache occurs. Immediately shut off the heater, open the air ventilators, descend to lower altitudes, and land at the nearest airfield. Consult an Aviation Medical Examiner. It may take several days to fully recover and clear the body of the carbon monoxide.

## VISION

On the ground, reduced or impaired vision can sometimes be dangerous depending on where you are and what you are doing. In flying it is always dangerous.

On the ground or in the air, a number of factors such as hypoxia, carbon monoxide, alcohol, drugs, fatigue, or even bright sunlight can affect your vision. In the air these effects are critical.

## MIDDLE EAR DISCOMFORT OR PAIN

Certain persons (whether pilots or passengers) have difficulty balancing the air loads on the ear drum while descending. This is particularly troublesome if a head cold or throat inflammation keeps the eustacian tube from opening properly. If this trouble occurs during descent, try swallowing, yawning, or holding the nose and mouth shut and forcibly exhaling. If no relief occurs, climb back up a few thousand feet to relieve the pressure on the outer drum. Then descend again, using these measures. A more gradual descent may be tried, and it may be necessary to go through several climbs and descents to "stair step" down. If a nasal inhaler is available, it may afford relief. If trouble persists several hours after landing, consult your Aviation Medical Examiner.

NOTE.—If you find yourself airborne with a head cold, you may possibly avoid trouble by using an inhaler kept as part of the flight kit.

## PANIC

The development of panic in inexperienced pilots is a process which can get into a vicious circle with itself and lead to unwise and precipitous action. If lost, or in some other predicament, forcibly take stock of yourself, and do not allow panic to mushroom. Panic can be controlled. Remember, Prevent Panic to Think Straight. Fear is a normal protective reaction, and occurs in normal individuals. Fear progression to panic is an abnormal development.

## SCUBA DIVING

You may use your plane to fly to a sea resort or lake for a day's SCUBA diving, and then fly home, all within a few hours' time. This can be dangerous, particularly if you have been diving to depths for any length of time.

Under the increased pressure of the water, excess nitrogen is absorbed into your system. If sufficient time has not elapsed prior to takeoff for your system to rid itself of this excess gas, you may experience the bends at altitude under 10,000 feet where most light planes fly.

Figure 131. *Medical facts for pilots.*

# BIRD HAZARDS

All pilots are requested to contact the nearest FAA Air Route Traffic Control Center, Flight Service Station, or tower (including non-federal) when they observe large flocks of birds and report the: (1) Geographic location (2) Bird Species (if known) (3) Approximate number (4) Altitude (5) Direction of bird flight path.

## Migratory Patterns

The birds considered of greatest potential hazard to aircraft because of large size, abundance, or habits of flying in dense flocks are the whistling swans, Canada geese, snow geese, blue geese, white-fronted geese, mallards, pintails, gulls, vultures, starlings, and blackbirds. Birds of these species are considered particularly hazardous during spring and fall migration and when they are concentrated in wintering areas. At some airports, large flocks of sandpipers, horned larks, tree swallows, longspurs, white pelicans, sandhill cranes, or other species could be a problem at certain seasons.

Unfortunately, we do not have complete data for the United States concerning the migration paths of all of these species, or the exact times of migration, or the altitudes at which these birds fly, or the effects of weather on migration patterns. However, available data are summarized below for birds of six of these species—whistling swans, Canada geese, snow geese, mallards, pintails, and double-crested cormorants.

Since migrating waterfowl tend to dive when closely approached by aircraft, pilots are warned not to fly directly under migrating flocks of swans, geese or ducks.

Figure 132. *Bird hazards.*

---

# GOOD OPERATING PRACTICES

It should be remembered that adherence to air traffic rules does not eliminate the need for good judgment on the part of the pilot. Compliance with the following Good Operating Practices will greatly enhance the safety of every flight.

## Alertness

Be alert at all times, especially when the weather is good. Most pilots pay attention to business when they are operating in full IFR weather conditions, but strangely, air collisions almost invariably have occurred under ideal weather conditions. Unlimited visibility appears to encourage a sense of security which is not at all justified. Considerable information of value may be obtained by listening to advisories being issued in the terminal area, even though controller workload may prevent a pilot from obtaining individual service.

## Judgment in VFR Flight

Use reasonable restraint in exercising the prerogative of VFR flight, especially in terminal areas. The weather minimums and distances from clouds are minimums. Giving yourself a greater margin in specific instances is just good judgment.

Conducting a VFR operation in a Control Zone when the official visibility is 3 or 4 miles is not prohibited, but good judgment would dictate that you keep out of the approach area.

It has always been recognized that precipitation reduces forward visibility. Consequently, although again it may be perfectly legal to cancel your IFR flight plan at any time you can proceed VFR, it is good practice, when precipitation is occurring, to continue IFR operation into a terminal area until you are reasonably close to your destination.

In conducting simulated instrument flights, be sure that the weather is good enough to compensate for the restricted visibility of the safety pilot and your greater concentration on your flight instruments. Give yourself a little greater margin when your flight plan lies in or near a busy airway or close to an airport.

## USE OF CLEARING PROCEDURES

1. **Before Takeoff.** Prior to taxiing onto a runway or landing area in preparation for takeoff, pilots should scan the approach areas for possible landing traffic, executing appropriate clearing maneuvers to provide him a clear view of the approach areas.

2. **Climbs and Descents.** During climbs and descents in flight conditions which permit visual detection of other traffic, pilots should execute gentle banks, left and right, at a frequency which permits contnuous visual scanning of the airspace about them.

3. **Straight and level.** Sustained periods of straight and level flight in conditions which permit visual detection of other traffic should be broken at intervals with appropriate procedures to provide effective visual scanning.

4. **Traffic pattern.** Entries into traffic patterns while descending create specific collision hazards and should be avoided. Where turns are made in a traffic pattern, entry should be on to the downwind leg at the midway point, unless otherwise instructed by the airport air traffic control or when the published traffic pattern indicates otherwise.

5. **Traffic at VOR sites.** All operators should emphasize the need for sustained cockpit vigilance in the vicinity of VORs and airway intersections due to the convergence of traffic.

6. **Training operations.** Operators of pilot training programs are urged to adopt the following practices:

a. Pilots undergoing flight instruction at all levels should be requested to verbalize clearing procedures (call out, "clear" left, right, above or below) to instill and sustain the habit of vigilance during maneuvering.

b. High-wing airplane, momentarily raise the wing in the direction of the intended turn and look.

c. Low-wing airplane, momentarily lower the wing in the direction of the intended turn and look.

d. Appropriate clearing procedures should precede the execution of all turns including chandelles, lazy eights, stalls, slow flight, climbs, straight and level, spins and other combination maneuvers.

**Giving Way**

If you think another aircraft is too close to you, give way instead of waiting for the other pilot to respect the right-of-way to which you may be entitled. It is a lot safer to pursue the right-of-way angle after you have completed your flight.

Figure 133. *Good operating practices.*

---

# 26. Airman's Information Manual - Part 2

## AIRPORT DIRECTORY

This part lists all airports, seaplane bases, and heliports which are available for transient civil use in the conterminous United States, Puerto Rico, and the Virgin Islands. The states and territories are listed alphabetically and the airports in each are listed alphabetically according to the name of the town at which they are located. Note the information indicated by the arrow in figure 134, "ADDISON See DALLAS." This means that the codified information for Addison airport will be found under Dallas, the name of the town near which this airport is located. All of the facilities and services (*except communications*) for each airport are contained in this part of AIM in codified form.

Figure 135 is the airport legend which is used to interpret the codified information contained in Part 2. The codified information for most airports will not contain all of the items shown in the airport legend; however, by the location and format of this codified information, it can easily be interpreted through the use of the airport legend and the legends for the various coded symbols.

The arrows in figure 136 show that NOTAM service is available (arrow No. 1), the city name (Dallas—arrow No. 2) at which the airport is located, the name of the airport (Redbird—arrow No. 3), and the location of the airport in nautical miles (to the nearest mile) and

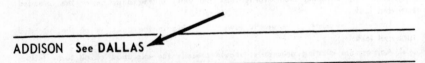

ADDISON  See **DALLAS**

Figure 134. *Airport directory—Addison airport.*

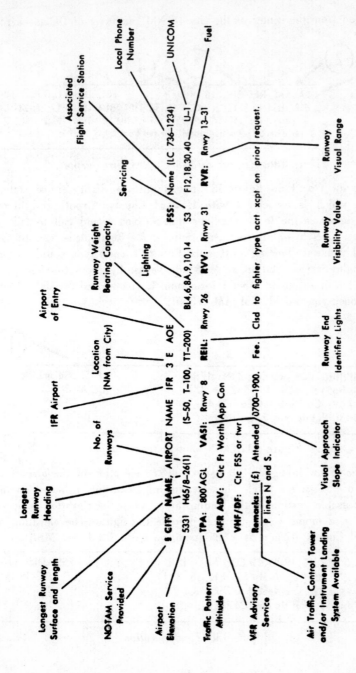

Figure 135. *Airport directory legend.*

direction from the center of the city (6 NM southwest of Dallas—arrow No. 4).

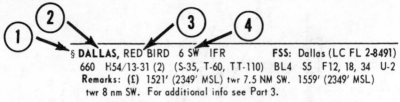

§ **DALLAS,** RED BIRD  6 SW   IFR          **FSS:** Dallas (LC FL 2-8491)
660  H54/13-31 (2)  (S-35, T-60, TT-110)  BL4  S5  F12, 18, 34  U-2
**Remarks:** (£) 1521′ (2349′ MSL) twr 7.5 NM SW. 1559′ (2349′ MSL)
twr 8 nm SW. For additional info see Part 3.

Figure 136. *Airport directory—Red Bird airport.*

Arrow No. 1 in figure 137 points out the flight service station (FSS) which is associated with Howard County Airport and arrow No. 2 indicates the local telephone number you would call to talk to FSS personnel to obtain weather briefings, file flight plans, etc. In this case, if you were landing at Howard County Airport, you could contact the Flight Service Station at Midland, Texas, by radio to close your flight plan or to obtain other information. If you wanted to talk to them by phone, you would dial AM 3-3601.

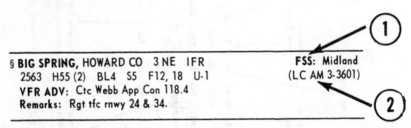

§ **BIG SPRING,** HOWARD CO  3 NE   IFR          **FSS:** Midland
2563  H55 (2)  BL4  S5  F12, 18  U-1          (LC AM 3-3601)
**VFR ADV:** Ctc Webb App Con 118.4
**Remarks:** Rgt tfc rnwy 24 & 34.

Figure 137. *FSS name/phone number.*

The arrow in figure 138 points out the elevation of the airport in feet above mean sea level. The elevation of an airport is based on the highest usable portion of the landing area. When the elevation is below sea level, a minus (−) sign will precede the figure. The elevation of Howard County Airport is 2,563 ft. above mean sea level (MSL).

§ **BIG SPRING,** HOWARD CO  3 NE   IFR          **FSS:** Midland
2563  H55 (2)  BL4  S5  F12, 18  U-1          (LC AM 3-3601)
**VFR ADV:** Ctc Webb App Con 118.4
**Remarks:** Rgt tfc rnwy 24 & 34.

Figure 138. *Field elevation.*

The arrow in figure 139 points to runway information. "H55 (2)." "H" indicates that the runway is hard surfaced; "55" represents the longest runway to the nearest 100 ft. using 70 as the division point; and the number in parentheses "(2)," indicates the total number of runways available. However, *only hard surfaced runways* are counted at airfields with *both* hard surfaced and sod runways. If the runway length does not have an "H" in front of it, the runway surface is sod, clay, etc.

---

§ BIG SPRING, HOWARD CO   3 NE   IFR                    FSS: Midland
  2563   H55 (2)   BL4   S5   F12, 18   U-1              (LC AM 3-3601)
VFR ADV: Ctc Webb App Con 118.4
Remarks: Rgt tfc rnwy 24 & 34.

---

Figure 139. *Runway length.*

Howard County Airport has two hard surfaced runways, the longest of which is 5,500 ft. to the nearest hundred feet. Actually it is between 5,470 ft. and 5,570 ft.

The arrow in figure 140 points to airport lighting information "BL4." To interpret this coded information, you need to refer to the lighting code in the Airport Directory legend (figure 141). "B" indicates that there is a rotating beacon at the airport; "L4" indicates that field lighting consists of low intensity runway lights. If there is an asterisk (*) preceding an element in the lighting information, it means that element operates only on prior request. For example "B*L4" indicates that airport runway lights will be turned on by prior request only (phone call, telegram, or letter). When the asterisk is not shown, the lights are in operation or available sunset to sunrise or by request (radio call). "L" by itself indicates temporary lighting such as flares, smudge pots, lanterns.

---

§ BIG SPRING, HOWARD CO   3 NE   IFR                    FSS: Midland
  2563   H55 (2)   BL4   S5   F12, 18   U-1              (LC AM 3-3601)
VFR ADV: Ctc Webb App Con 118.4
Remarks: Rgt tfc rnwy 24 & 34.

---

Figure 140. *Field lighting.*

# LIGHTING

**B: Rotating Light** (Rotating beacon). (Green and white, split-beam and other types.) Omission of **B** indicates rotating light is either not available or not operating standard hours (sunset-sunrise).

NOTE.—Code lights are not codified, and are carried in Remarks.

**L: Field Lighting** (when code **L4–7** is indicated, lighting **4, 5, 6, 7** is available). An asterisk (*) preceding an element indicates that it operates on prior request only (by phone call, telegram or letter). Where the asterisk is not shown, the lights are in operation or available sunset to sunrise or by request (radio call). **L** by itself indicates temporary lighting, such as flares, smudge pots, lanterns.

**1**—Portable runway lights (electrical)
**2**—Airport Boundary
**3**—Runway Floods
**4**—Low Intensity Runway
**5**—Medium Intensity Runway
**6**—High Intensity Runway
**7**—Instrument Approach (neon)
**8A, B, or C**—High Intensity Instrument Approach

Figure 141. *Field lighting legend.*

Howard County airport has a rotating beacon and low intensity runway lights that are in operation or available from sunset to sunrise or by request (radio call).

The arrow in figure 142 points to aircraft servicing information. When the coded information "S5" is referenced to the servicing excerpt (figure 143) from the Airport Directory legend, you can readily see what services are available. At Howard County Airport, storage facilities, major airframe repairs and major powerplant repairs are all available.

In figure 144, the arrow points to aircraft fuel information "F12, 18." You should know the type of fuel your airplane uses, and when planning any cross-country flights, should check this coded information at airports where you plan to land to determine that your type of fuel is available. By comparing the coded fuel information "F12, 18" with the "fuel"

§ **BIG SPRING,** HOWARD CO 3 NE IFR      **FSS:** Midland
  2563 H55 (2) BL4 S5 F12, 18 U-1      (LC AM 3-3601)
**VFR ADV:** Ctc Webb App Con 118.4
**Remarks:** Rgt tfc rnwy 24 & 34.

Figure 142. *Airport services.*

## SERVICING

**S1:** Storage.

**S2:** Storage, minor airframe repairs.

**S3:** Storage, minor airframe and minor powerplant repairs.

**S4:** Storage, major airframe and minor powerplant repairs.

**S5:** Storage, major airframe and major powerplant repairs.

Figure 143. *Airport service legend.*

legend excerpt (figure 145) from the Airport Directory, you note that Howard County airport has fuel available only in the grades of 80/87 and 100/130. (Note: Color coding is also used to identify grades of fuel. Red, blue, green, purple, and straw colored fuels are used to identify grades 80/87, 91/98, 100/130, 115/145, and jet fuels, respectively. If a fuel rating is 100 or above, it is referred to as a "performance rating" rather than an octane rating.)

§ **BIG SPRING,** HOWARD CO 3 NE IFR      **FSS:** Midland
  2563 H55 (2) BL4 S5 F12, 18 U-1      (LC AM 3-3601)
**VFR ADV:** Ctc Webb App Con 118.4
**Remarks:** Rgt tfc rnwy 24 & 34.

Figure 144. *Fuel.*

In figure 146, the arrow points to UNICOM information. By relating this information "U-1" to the excerpt from the Airport Directory legend,

# FUEL

| Code | Grade |
|------|-------|
| F12 | 80/87 |
| F15 | 91/98 |
| F18 | 100/130 |
| F22 | 115/145 |
| F30 | Kerosene, freeze point $-40°F$ |
| F34 | Kerosene, freeze point $-58°F$ |
| F40 | Wide-cut gasoline, freeze point $-60°F$ |
| F45 | Wide-cut gasoline without icing inhibitor, freeze point $-60°F$ |

Figure 145. *Fuel legend.*

---

§ **BIG SPRING,** HOWARD CO  3 NE  IFR
2563  H55 (2)  BL4  S5  F12, 18  U-1
**VFR ADV:** Ctc Webb App Con 118.4
**Remarks:** Rgt tfc rnwy 24 & 34.

**FSS:** Midland
(LC AM 3-3601)

Figure 146. *Unicom.*

## UNICOM

A private aeronautical advisory communications facility operated for purposes other than air traffic control, transmits and receives on one of the following frequencies:

U1—122.8 MHz for Landing Areas (except heliports) without an ATC Tower or FSS;

U2—123.0 MHz for Landing Areas (except heliports) with an ATC Tower or FSS;

U3—123.05 MHz for heliports.

Figure 147. *Unicom legend.*

figure 147, you note that UNICOM is available at Howard County Airport on a frequency of 122.8 MHz. This is the standard frequency for UNICOMS located at airports without a control tower or FSS.

The arrow in figure 148 points to VFR Advisory Service information. This is the place you would check to see if there is a facility you can call to obtain advisory service on VFR flights. If you are going into Howard County Airport, you could contact Webb Approach Control on the frequency 118.4 MHz, advise them of your position, and that you intend to land at Howard County airport. Webb Approach Control will give you wind, traffic, and NOTAM information, and if you were landing at the airport with a control tower with which Webb Approach Control is associated, they would also give you runway information.

---

§ **BIG SPRING**, HOWARD CO   3 NE   IFR          **FSS:** Midland
  2563   H55 (2)   BL4   S5   F12, 18   U-1          (LC AM 3-3601)
**VFR ADV:** Ctc Webb App Con 118.4
**Remarks:** Rgt tfc rnwy 24 & 34.

---

Figure 148. *VFR advisory service.*

In figure 149 the arrow points to "VHF/DF" information. VHF/DF stands for very high frequency direction finder. When the designation VHF/DF appears in the airport directory information, it indicates that very high frequency direction finder equipment is available at the Mc-Allen Flight Service Station which is located on Miller International airport. To use this service, contact the McAllen FSS on standard FSS frequencies. See Section IX, Chapter 34, for information concerning when and how VHF/DF can be used.

---

§ **McALLEN**, MILLER INTL   2 S   IFR   AOE       **FSS:** McAllen on Fld
  106   H62/13-31 (3)   BL4, 11   S5   F18, 30   U-2   **REIL:** Rnwy 13
**VHF/DF:** Ctc FSS
**Remarks:** (£) For additional info see Part 3.

---

Figure 149. *VHF direction finder.*

The arrow in figure 150 points to the "Remarks" section of the airport directory information for a specific airport, in this case, Dallas Red Bird. This section includes information concerning:

  1. An air traffic control tower and/or an instrument landing system associated with the airport. This will be indicated by the symbol £ appearing after the word "Remarks" and generally followed by the phrase "For additional information see Part 3" (of the AIM).

  2. Landing fees charged by the airport.

3. Runways for which right-hand traffic is used.

4. Operational items affecting the status and usability of the airport, traffic patterns, and departure procedures.

5. The more dangerous obstructions.

---

§ **DALLAS**, RED BIRD  6 SW   IFR          **FSS:** Dallas (LC FL 2-8491)
  660  H54/13-31 (2)  (S-35, T-60, TT-110)  BL4   S5   F12, 18, 34   U-2
  Remarks: (£) 1521' (2349  MSL) twr 7.5 NM SW. 1559' (2349' MSL)
  twr 8 nm SW. For additional info see Part 3.

---

Figure 150. *Airport directory remarks.*

The "Remarks" section for Dallas Red Bird airport (Dallas, Texas) indicates; (1) that a control tower and/or an instrument landing system is associated with the airport, (2) that there are obstruction hazards in the form of towers near the airport, and (3) that additional information appears in Part 3.

Part 2 of AIM also contains a list of commercial broadcast stations for pilots who wish to use them with their radio compass (ADF), as well as information pertaining to telephone numbers and the information provided by Flight Service Stations and National Weather Service Offices.

# 27.  Airman's Information Manual-Part 3

## OPERATIONAL DATA

The sections of Part 3 of the Airman's Information Manual that are probably used most by private pilots are the Airport/Facility Directory, which includes air navigation radio aids and their assigned frequencies; the Sectional Chart Bulletin, which updates sectional charts cumulatively; Special Notices – General; and New and Permanently closed Airports. Discussions and typical examples of these sections follow.

### Airport/Facility Directory

The Airport/Facility Directory contains a tabulated listing of all major airports, heliports, and seaplane bases in the conterminous United States that have terminal navaids and communications facilities (control towers) available at the airport, as well as, all enroute navaids (VOR, radio beacons, etc.). States and territories are listed alphabetically; the airports in each are listed alphabetically by the town at which they are located just as in AIM, Part 2, Airport Directory; and the en route navaids are listed alphabetically by name of the navaids and integrated with the airports.

Figure 151 shows the legend used in interpreting the information for each airport listed in the Airport/Facility Directory. Essentially, this information (and the legend) is divided into three parts — *airport information, communications facilities information,* and *terminal navaids information.* The *airport information* is contained in the first part, down through the first "Remarks." *Communications facilities information* is contained in the second part beginning with the "Tower" line and extending down to but not including the first navaid, "ILS," "BVORTAC," or "NDB," whichever comes first. *Termial navaids information* is contained in the third part, beginning with the first navaid ("ILS," "VOR," or "NDB") and extending through the last "Remarks."

The legend for the airport information portion of the tabulated data for each airport is essentially the same as that for Part 2, Airport Directory of AIM, except that much more is generally available at the airports listed in Part 3 — such as VASI (Visual Approach Slope Indicator), ATIS (Automatic Terminal Information Service), etc.

The availability of VASI at an airport may be shown in two different ways or, in most cases, it is shown in both ways. Arrows 1 and 2 in figure 152 show these two ways. Arrow #1 points to number "10" in the airport lighting information, figure 153. This means that a VASI is available at Dallas, Love Field, Dallas, Texas. Arrow #2 points to "VASI: Rnwy 13R and 31R." This means that the VASI is available when making an approach to runway "13 Right and 31 Right."

Arrow #3 indicates that oxygen for high and low pressure systems is available. High and low pressure replacement bottles are also available.

Arrow #4 indicates that NOTAM service is provided.

Arrows #5 through #7 point out *communications facilities information.* Arrow #5 indicates control tower frequency. Love Field Tower transmits and receives on 118.7 MHz and 124.3 MHz, but can only receive on 122.5 MHz. Arrow #6 points out ground control frequency information. Love Field Ground Control transmits and receives on 121.9 MHz. and 121.65 MHz.

Arrow #7 points to "ATIS" which stands for Automatic Terminal

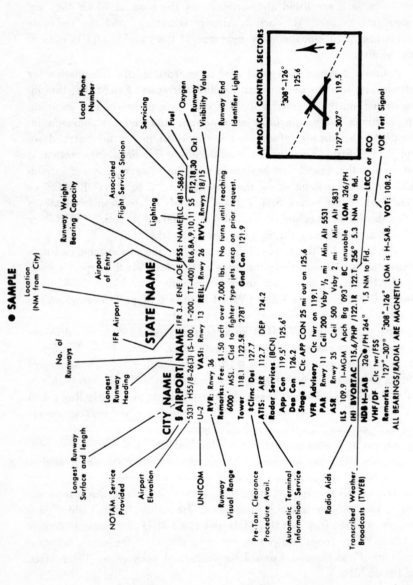

Figure 151. Airport/facility directory legend.

256

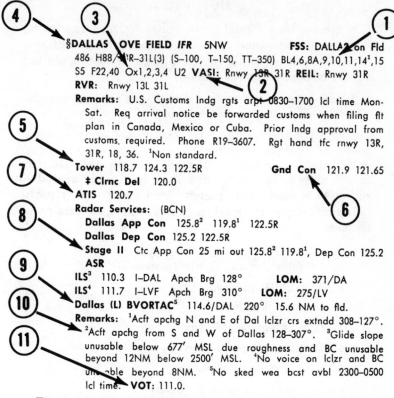

§**DALLAS LOVE FIELD** *IFR* 5NW                              **FSS:** DALLAS on Fld
486 H88/R–31L(3) (S–100, T–150, TT–350) BL4,6,8A,9,10,11,14[1],15
S5 F22,40 Ox1,2,3,4 U2 **VASI:** Rnwy 13R 31R **REIL:** Rnwy 31R
**RVR:** Rnwy 13L 31L
**Remarks:**  U.S. Customs lndg rgts arpt 0830–1700 lcl time Mon-
   Sat.  Req arrival notice be forwarded customs when filing flt
   plan in Canada, Mexico or Cuba.  Prior lndg approval from
   customs. required.  Phone R19–3607.  Rgt hand tfc rnwy 13R,
   31R, 18, 36.  [1]Non standard.
**Tower** 118.7 124.3 122.5R                      **Gnd Con** 121.9 121.65
   ‡ **Clrnc Del**  120.0
**ATIS**  120.7
**Radar Services:**  (BCN)
   **Dallas App Con** 125.8[2] 119.8[1] 122.5R
   **Dallas Dep Con** 125.2 122.5R
   **Stage II**  Ctc App Con 25 mi out 125.8[2] 119.8[1], Dep Con 125.2
   **ASR**
**ILS**[3] 110.3 I–DAL Apch Brg 128°          **LOM:** 371/DA
**ILS**[4] 111.7 I–LVF Apch Brg 310°  **LOM:** 275/LV
**Dallas (L) BVORTAC**[5] 114.6/DAL 220° 15.6 NM to fld.
**Remarks:**  [1]Acft apchg N and E of Dal lclzr crs extndd 308–127°.
   [2]Acft apchg from S and W of Dallas 128–307°.  [3]Glide slope
   unusable below 677′ MSL due roughness and BC unusable
   beyond 12NM below 2500′ MSL.  [4]No voice on lclzr and BC
   unusable beyond 8NM.  [5]No sked wea bcst avbl 2300–0500
   lcl time.  **VOT:** 111.0.

Figure 152. *Airport/facility directory legend—Love Field.*

Information Service and is the continuous broadcast of recorded noncontrol information in selected high activity terminal areas. Its purpose
is to improve air traffic controller effectiveness and to relieve frequency
congestion by automating the repetitive transmission of essential but
routine information. Information such as ceiling, visibility, wind, altimeter, and runways in use is continuously broadcast on the voice feature
of a VOR located on or near the airport, or on a special VHF tower
frequency. Pilots of aircraft departing from or arriving at the terminal
area can receive the continuous ATIS broadcasts at times when cockpit
duties are least pressing and listen to as many repeats as desired. Pilots
departing from or arriving at the Love Field area can receive the ATIS

# LIGHTING

**B: Rotating Light** (Rotating beacon). (Green and white, split-beam and other types.) Omission of **B** indicates rotating light is either not available or not operating standard hours (sunset-sunrise).

NOTE.—Code lights are not codified, and are carried in Remarks.

**L: Field Lighting.** An asterisk (*) preceding an element indicates that it operates on prior request only (by phone call, telegram or letter). Where the asterisk is not shown, the lights are in operation or available sunset to sunrise or by request (radio call). **L** by itself indicates temporary lighting, such as flares, smudge pots, lanterns.

1—Portable runway lights (electrical)

2—Airport Boundary

3—Runway Floods

4—Low Intensity Runway

5—Medium Intensity Runway

6—High Intensity Runway

7—Instrument Approach (neon)

7A—Medium Intensity Approach Lights (MALS)

**8A, B, or C**—High Intensity Instrument Approach (ALS)

9—Sequence Flashing Lights (SFL)

10—Visual Approach Slope Indicator (VASI)

11—Runway end identifier lights (threshold strobe) (REIL)

12—Short approach light systems (SALS)

13—Runway alignment lights (RAIL)

14—Runway centerline

15—Touchdown zone

Figure 153. *Field lighting legend.*

broadcast on 120.7 MHz. See Chapter 25 for an example of an ATIS broadcast.

At the time he requests taxi information, the pilot should advise ground control (or tower, if appropriate) that he has received ATIS information.

Arrow #8 points to information which indicates that Radar Advisory and Sequencing Service (see also figure 121) is available to VFA aircraft and lists the facility to contact and the frequency on which to contact them if you desire information relative to other air traffic in the area. In the case of Dallas' Love Field, you would contact Love Field Approach Control on 125.8 MHz or 119.8 MHz when 25 nautical miles from the airport. Approach Control will give you traffic information for proper sequencing with other VFR and IFR traffic en route to the airport, and will specify when you should contact the control tower for landing. Upon being told to contact the tower, radar service is terminated. Compliance with this procedure is not mandatory, but pilot participation is encouraged.

Arrows #9 through #11 point out terminal navaids information. Arrow #9 points to information which indicates that Dallas VORTAC is located 15.6 nautical miles from the airport on a bearing of 220°; and has a frequency of 114.6 MHz and an identification of DAL.

Arrow #10 points to "Remarks" which state that all aircraft approaching from north and east of the extended localizer course should contact Approach Control on 119.8 MHz; those approaching from south or west of the Dallas VORTAC 128-307° radial should contact approach control on 125.8 MHz. The VOR test facility (VOT) frequency is 111.0 MHz (arrow No. 11).

As noted previously, the Airport/Facility Directory also includes en route air navigation radio aids. These aids are integrated alphabetically with the airports. Figure 154 shows an excerpt from the Airport/Facility Directory which includes some en route radio aids.

Figure 155 is an excerpt from the legend which is used to interpret radio aids information relating to the class designations and operational limitations of the radio aids appearing in figure 154.

For example, arrow #1 (figure 154) points to "Benbrook (L) VOR 108.8/BEO." Benbrook is the name of the radio aid; "(L)" indicates that the facility is normally usable at up to a distance of 40 miles; and "VOR" indicates that it is a "VHF navigational facility—omnidirectional course only." That is, the facility operates on VHF (very high frequency)

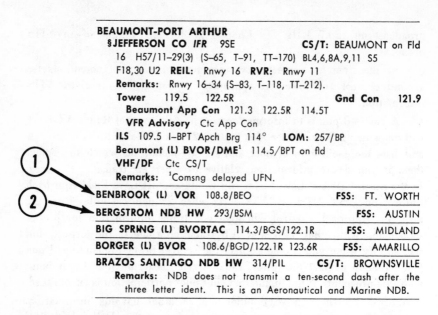

**BEAUMONT-PORT ARTHUR**
§**JEFFERSON CO** *IFR* 9SE  **CS/T:** BEAUMONT on Fld
16 H57/11–29(3) (S–65, T–91, TT–170) BL4,6,8A,9,11 S5
F18,30 U2 **REIL:** Rnwy 16 **RVR:** Rnwy 11
**Remarks:** Rnwy 16–34 (S–83, T–118, TT–212).
**Tower** 119.5 122.5R  **Gnd Con** 121.9
 **Beaumont App Con** 121.3 122.5R 114.5T
 **VFR Advisory** Ctc App Con
**ILS** 109.5 I–BPT Apch Brg 114° **LOM:** 257/BP
**Beaumont (L) BVOR/DME**[1] 114.5/BPT on fld
**VHF/DF** Ctc CS/T
**Remarks:** [1]Comsng delayed UFN.

**BENBROOK (L) VOR** 108.8/BEO  **FSS:** FT. WORTH

**BERGSTROM NDB HW** 293/BSM  **FSS:** AUSTIN

**BIG SPRING (L) BVORTAC** 114.3/BGS/122.1R  **FSS:** MIDLAND

**BORGER (L) BVOR** 108.6/BGD/122.1R 123.6R  **FSS:** AMARILLO

**BRAZOS SANTIAGO NDB HW** 314/PIL  **CS/T:** BROWNSVILLE
 **Remarks:** NDB does not transmit a ten-second dash after the
 three letter ident. This is an Aeronautical and Marine NDB.

Figure 154. *Airport/facility directory radio navigation aids.*

and gives course information from any direction. It operates on a frequency of 108.8 MHz and its identification is BEO (- ... . ---).

Arrow #2 in figure 154 points to "Bergstrom NDB HW 293/BSM." Bergstrom is the name of the facility; "NDB" indicates that the facility is a nondirectional beacon; the legend in figure 155 reveals that "HW" means that this facility is a homing beacon of 50 watts to less than 2,000 watts in power, and without voice facilities: "293/BSM" indicates that the facility operates on a frequency of 293 kHz with morse code identification of BSM (. . - ... . - -).

***Sectional Chart Bulletin.*** This bulletin provides a tabulation of the major changes in aeronautical information since the last publication date of each Sectional Aeronautical Chart. By referring to this tabulation, the VFR pilot can update his chart to include all current and essential data. When a new edition of the Sectional Aeronautical Chart is republished, the corrective tabulation will be removed from the bulletin. Figure 156 represents an excerpt from this bulletin.

***Special Notices – General.*** Special Notices of a general nature or universal application are grouped together under General Notices. The month

# RADIO CLASS DESIGNATIONS

Identification of VOR/VORTAC/TACAN Stations by Class (Operational Limitations):

### Normal Usable Altitudes and Radius Distances

| Class | Altitudes | Distance (miles) |
|-------|-----------|------------------|
| T | 12,000' and below | 25 |
| L | Below 18,000' | 40 |
| H | Below 18,000' | 40 |
| H | 14,500' — 17,999' | 100* |
| H | 18,000' — FL 450 | 130 |
| H | Above FL 450 | 100 |

*Applicable only within the contiguous 48 States.

H=High    L=Low    T=Terminal

NOTE: An H facility is capable of providing L and T service volume and an L facility additionally provides T service volume.

The term VOR is, operationally, a general term covering the VHF omnidirectional bearing type of facility without regard to the fact that the power, the frequency-protected service volume, the equipment configuration, and operational requirements may vary between facilities at different locations.

AB _____ Automatic Weather Broadcast (also shown with ● following frequency).

B _____ Scheduled Broadcast Station (broadcasts weather at 15 minutes after the hour.

DME _____ UHF standard (TACAN compatible) distance measuring equipment.

H _____ Non-directional radio beacon (homing), power 50 watts to less than 2,000 watts.

TACAN _____ UHF navigational facility—omnidirectional course and distance information.

VOR _____ VHF navigational facility—omnidirectional, course only.

VOR/DME __ Collocated VOR navigational facility and UHF standard distance measuring equipment.

VORTAC ___ Collocated VOR and TACAN navigational facilities.

W _____ Without voice facilities on range frequency.

Z _____ VHF station location marker at a LF range station.

Figure 155. *Radio class designation.*

# •ATLANTA

## 3rd Edition, October 16, 1969

Correct airway designation V–56 to V–56S via 098°M Augusta VORTAC and Columbia VORTAC 238°M. Change Atlanta RBn name to Bruce ident to BRU 33°-38'43''N, 84°18'41''W. Restore UNICOM Robbins arpt 33°58'N, 86°23'W. Add UNICOM Centerville arpt 35°-50'N, 87°27'W. Add UNICOM Wilson arpt 32°42'N, 83°39'W. Add obstn 902' MSL (361' AGL) 34°47'38''N, 87°37'29''W. Add obstn 850' MSL (270' AGL') 34°37'-53''N, 86°40'17''W. Delete Rutherford arpt 35°21'N, 81°55'W. Add obstn 1135' MSL (200' AGL) 35°09'50''N, 86°34'18''W. Change Spartanburg RBn name to Fairmont ident to FRT 34°54'08''N, 81°59'06''W. Delete

Figure 156. *Sectional chart bulletin.*

and year the notice is initially inserted into the manual is provided at the conclusion of each Special Notice. Figure 157 depicts excerpts from this section.

## • OPERATION IN PROXIMITY TO HEAVY JET AIRCRAFT

1. Recent tests indicate the previously issued precautionary measures regarding operation in proximity to B747/C5A aircraft were somewhat excessive as to the separation required and insufficient as to the scope of application.

2. These studies show that "heavy jet" aircraft, i.e., those capable of takeoff weights of 300,000 pounds or more, generate greater wake turbulence, both on the ground and in the air. Aircraft in the aviation fleet currently defined as "heavy jets" are Boeing 747, C5A, DC–8–60 Series, Intercontinental DC–8, series 30, 40 and 50, Intercontinental B707, VC–10, IL–62, C–141, B–52, EC–135, VC–137.

3. Pilots should:

a. Review material in AIM Part 1 and Advisory Circular 90–23B pertaining to wake turbulence.

b. Avoid flight within five miles behind a heavy jet when operating at the same altitude or within less than 1,000 feet below.

c. Use extreme caution when taxiing behind a heavy jet. Static test data indicate that the area of concern is within 750 feet behind the tail of the heavy jet aircraft.

d. When operating in the same environment as a heavy jet and being provided radar sequencing/vectors, pilots can expect to be vectored at least five miles behind the heavy jet. Pilots not being provided the radar sequencing/vectors are expected to maintain adequate spacing to ensure that wake turbulence problems are not encountered.

4. Additionally, test data indicate potential wake turbulence problems may exist when parallel runways separated by less than 3,500 feet are being used by any four engine jet aircraft. Pilots should be aware that there is a likelihood that, under crosswind conditions, the wake turbulence created by these operations on one runway will drift across and affect operations on the other runway. Pilots should exercise caution when such conditions exist.

## HEAVY TRAFFIC AROUND MILITARY FIELDS

Pilots are advised to exercise vigilance when in close proximity to most military airports. These airports may have jet aircraft traffic patterns extending up to 2500 feet above the surface. In addition, they may have an unusually heavy concentration of jet aircraft operating within a 25 nautical mile radius and from the surface to all altitudes. This precautionary note also applies to the larger civil airports.

Figure 157. *Special notices.*

*New and Permanently Closed Airports.* This section also includes information on Heliports and Seaplane Bases. Listings are by state. Newly activated airports are listed separately from those that have been abandoned or permanently closed. Figure 158 illustrates both types of information.

## A Checklist for Maintaining Currency of Sectional Charts

1. *Check the latest Sectional Chart Bulletin* (published every 28 days) for any additions, depletions, or revisions for the appropriate sectional chart. Note particularly any airspace restrictions or hazards and airport or radio frequency changes as they apply to your intended flight.
2. *Check the latest NOTAMS* (published every 14 days) for more recent changes to information listed above. Remember, NOTAMS will normally be your only source of information for temporary changes.
3. *Check the Airport Directory* (published every 6 months) for information concerning the airports you intend to use. Although the revision

cycle is approximately the same as that for Sectional Charts, the Directory may have a later publication date.

4. *Check the Airport/Facility Directory* (published every 28 days) for information concerning major airports and navaids you intend to use. Pay particular attention to communication and navaid frequencies for possible changes.

# 28. Airman's Information Manual-Part 3A

## NOTICES TO AIRMEN

Part 3A. Notices to Airmen, is issued every 14 days and is primarily designed to supplement Part 3 of AIM. NOTAMS contain much information that may well affect your flight. A newly constructed television tower that extends as much as 1,500 ft. above the ground in the vicinity of your destination airport may not appear on your chart. Your intended destination airport may be temporarily closed because of construction, flooding, heavy accumulation of snow, or other conditions. Certain runways may be closed or certain areas of the airport may be unsafe for taxiing. There may be other hazards not normally expected. Perhaps, the control tower has changed its transmitting frequency. Some of the air navigation radio aids you plan to use on your flight may be temporarily out of commission or may have had recent frequency changes.

*Permanent and Temporary Data*  The information in NOTAMS falls into two general categories, permanent and temporary. Data considered permanent is preceded by a check mark ( √ ) and is usually cited only once; however, it will be transferred to the next revision of the Sectional Chart Bulletin (figure 156) and carried there until a new Sectional Chart is published. You should note such changes on your charts and other records. Temporary data is normally carried twice unless resubmitted.

NOTAMS are presented alphabetically by states and by cities or localities within states.

*New or Revised Data*  New or revised data is indicated by underlining the first line of the affected item. The new information is not necessarily limited to the underlined portion, which is used only to attract attention to the new insert.

# NEW AND PERMANENTLY CLOSED AIRPORTS

*(Including Heliports and Seaplane Bases)*

## New Airports

The following new airports have been activated and will be included in the next Airport Directory effective March 1970.

| City, Airport Name<br>Distance & Direction from City | Associated<br>FSS |
|---|---|
| **ALABAMA** | |
| Ashford, Wright Fld 5 SE | Dothan |
| Mobile, Brookley Fld 3 S | Mobile |
| **ARIZONA** | |
| Buckeye, Pierce 2 W | Phoenix |

| City, Airport Name<br>Distance & Direction from City | Associated<br>FSS |
|---|---|
| **ILLINOIS** | |
| Auburn, Ross McNaught 5SW | |
| Earlville, Schmidt Fld 2E | Joliet |
| Gibson City Muni 5 ENE | Champaign |
| Havana, Murray Johnson 5S | Peoria |
| New Lenox, Howell 3.5 S | Joliet |
| Springfield, Holiday Inn East Heliport adj SE | Vandalia |

## Closed and Abandoned Airports

The following airports have been abandoned (a) or permanently closed to public use (c) and should be deleted from charts and records:

● **Alabama**
Foley, Chisenhall 1.5 S (c)
Russellville, Wood Dearing 3 E (a)

**Arizona**
● Hereford, Thompson Intl 1 SE (c)
● Inscription House Trading Post 1 N (c)
Quartzsite Arpt 0.4 SW (a)

**Illinois**
Canton, Ingersoll Fld 2.8 NW (a)
Chicago Heights, Wings Fld 4 SW (c)
Hopedale, Land L 4 S (a)
Olney, Ulrich 2 E (a)
Rushville, Flying Club 2.5 NE (a)
Sublette, Truckenbrod Lndg Area 3.5 ENE (a)
Valmeyer, Jacobs 2 NW (n)

Figure 158. *New and permanently closed airports.*

**Sample NOTAM** Figure 159 shows an excerpt from the NOTAM section for Texas. The plain language interpretation of the San Antonio International Airport tabulation (designated by an arrow) is as follows:
Runways 12 right and 30 left are closed due to construction until approximately March 1970. The approach light system for runway 12 right is out of service.


SAN ANTONIO, SAN ANTONIO INTL ARPT: Rnwy 12R–30L clsd for constr until aprxly March 1970. ALS 12R inop.

Figure 159. *NOTAMS.*


# 29. Airman's Information Manual - Part 4

## GRAPHIC NOTICES AND SUPPLEMENTAL DATA

Selected excerpts from Part 4 of AIM are presented and discussed in this chapter.

**Parachute Jumping Areas** Part 4 of AIM lists all *reported* parachute jumping sites in the United States. Unless the listing indicates to the contrary, all activities are conducted during daylight hours under VFR conditions. All times are local and altitudes MSL, unless otherwise specified. Figure 160 represents an excerpt from this section.

**VOR Receiver Check Points** The use of VOR airborne and ground check points which are listed in Part 4 of AIM is explained in Part 1 (see figure 113). In figure 161, VOR receiver check point information for the state of Arizona is in the following order:

Facility name (plus airport name, if needed);
bearing in degrees magnetic from VOR;
location of the check point (distance in nautical miles);
and altitude in feet MSL, if any.

|  | DISTANCE AND RADIAL | MAXIMUM | |
| LOCATION | FROM NEAREST VOR/VORTAC | ALTITUDE | REMARKS |
|---|---|---|---|
| **ALABAMA** | | | |
| Bayou La Batre, Ray Arpt | 12 NM; 217° Brookley | 12,500 | |
| Fort Rucker, Cairns AAF | 5.8 NM; 059° Cairns VOR | 14,500 | Weekends on fld |
| Gadsden | | 12,500 | |
| Harvest | 9 NM; 297° Huntsville | 13,500 | |
| Moundville | 18 NM; 192° Tuscaloosa | 12,500 | |
| Warrior | 11 NM; 350° Birmingham | 12,500 | |

Figure 160. *Parachute jumping areas.*

# ARIZONA

## Airborne—

**Gila Bend:** 191°; 5.5; over apch end of rnwy 35 of Gila Bend Aux. Fld; 2000'.

**Prescott:** 124°; 5.0 NM over approach end rnwy 30; 7000'.

**Tucson:** 258°; 6 NM; main rnwy intersection; 4000'.

**Winslow:** 107°; 5.0 NM; over approach end rnwy 29; 6000'.

**Yuma** (MCAS/Yuma Intl): 166°; 6.5 mi centerline rnwy 17–35; 1500'.

## Ground—

**Douglas** (Bisbee-Douglas Intl): 160°; int of SW ramp and txwy T–2.

**Flagstaff** (Muni Arpt): 158°; 0.5 NM—txwy entrance to T-hangars midfield.

**Kingman** (Muni): 222°; center of runup area west of apch end of rnwy 03.

Figure 161. *VOR receiver check points.*

*Restrictions to En route Navigation Aids* These restrictions are listed in AIM until canceled by the station concerned. Restricted areas are defined in degrees from magnetic north. Figure 162 is an excerpt from this section.

# TEXAS

AUSTIN VORTAC: VOR portion unusable 260–320° beyond 35 mi below 3,500′ MSL.

EL PASO VORTAC: DME portion unusable 265–300° beyond 30 mi below 9,200′ MSL.

HOUSTON VORTAC: DME portion unusable 085–210° beyond 35 mi below 2,500′ MSL.

SALT FLAT VORTAC: Unusable 031–049° beyond 30 NM below 15,000′ MSL.

*Figure 162. Restrictions to navigation aids.*

*Oil Burner Routes* Both the USAF and the U.S. Navy conduct low level navigation/bombing training flights in jet aircraft in both VFR and IFR weather conditions over certain specified routes. These routes and information pertaining to them are found in Part 4. In addition, Flight Service Stations have, in booklet form, the narrative descriptions as well as the charts for these routes. This booklet, revised every 28 days, is also available on a subscription basis from Distribution Division (C-44), National Ocean Survey, Washington, D.C. 20325. Write to them for further information. Figure 163 is representative of this material as found in AIM.

## KANSAS/OKLAHOMA/TEXAS
# DODGE CITY OB–65
### Effective 29 January 1970 thru 22 July 1970

Aircraft shall cross the Dodge City, Kansas, VORTAC (Garden City, Kansas VORTAC 086/34 NM DMS Fix) at FL 230 or as assigned by ARTC; then at FL 230 or assigned altitude direct to 37°46'N, 100°13'W, then descend direct so as to cross 37°28'N, 101°00'W at FL 180; then descend direct so as to cross 37°22'N, 101°15' W at 14,000' MSL; then at 14,000' MSL direct to 37°16'N, 101°30'W; then descend direct so as to cross 37°04'N, 102°00'W at 5,300' MSL; then turn left and descend so as to cross 36°53'N,

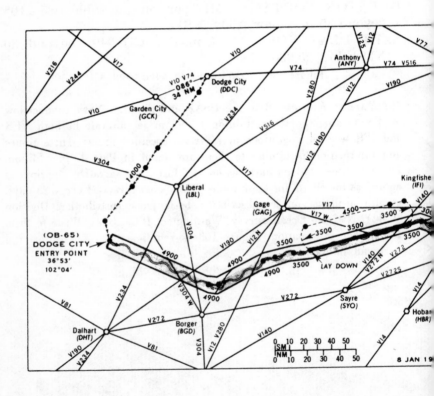

102°04'W (low level entry point) at 4,900' MSL; then at 4,900' MSL direct to 36°02'30"N, 101°09'30"W; then at 4,900' MSL turn left to 36°00'N, 101°02'30"W; then at 4,900' MSL direct to 36°00'N, 100°25'W; then at 4,900' MSL direct to 35°58'N, 100°16'W, then descend direct so as to cross 35°55'N, 100°01'W at 3,500' MSL; then at 3,500' MSL direct to 35°52'30"N, 99°49'W.

Lay Down—After passing 35°52'30"N, 99°49'W, aircraft shall maintain 3,500' MSL through the first bomb run corridor (on centerline from 35°52'30"N, 99°49'W to 35°37'N, 98°34'30"W). After exiting the first bomb run corridor at 35°37'N, 98°34'30"W, aircraft shall maintain 3,500' MSL direct to 35°35'N, 98°25'W; then turn right and descend so as to cross 35°30'N, 98°19'W at 3,000' MSL; then at 3,000' MSL direct to 34°46'N. . . .

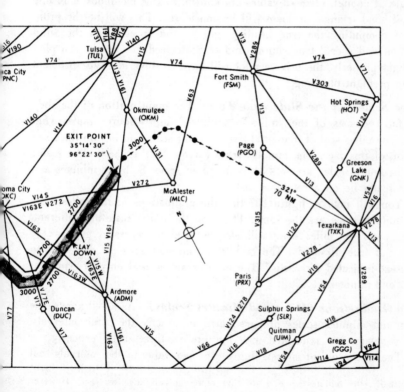

# SECTION VIII — FLIGHT COMPUTER
## 30. Slide Rule Face

The computer illustrated and discussed in this handbook has two sides—the slide rule or calculator face (fig. 165) and the wind face, fig. (166). The slide rule face is used to solve problems involving times, distance, fuel consumption, speed, and nautical-to-statute-mile conversions. The wind face is used to compute certain values associated with the wind triangle, if enough of these values are known. In this handbook only one type of wind triangle problem will be considered. This will be the problem of computing the true heading and ground speed when the wind direction and speed, true course, and true airspeed are known. To plan his flight properly, the private pilot will have to solve this type problem during preflight planning.

***Three Scales on the Slide Rule Face*** The main portion of the slide rule face consists of the "miles," "minutes," and "hours" scales (fig. 164). The miles scale (arrow #1) is the outer scale and lies on the fixed portion of this face. The minutes scale (arrow #2) is the middle scale; and the hours scale (arrow #3) is the inner scale. Both the minutes and hours scales lie on a rotatable disk.

You will note in figure 167 that the graduations of the miles scale and minutes scale are the same. Those on the hours scale are different.

The outer, or miles scale will also be used to represent gallons (of fuel) and true airspeeds. The middle, or minutes scale is also used to represent indicated airspeeds.[1] The hours scale is used only to represent hours and minutes.

***Scale Graduations (Miles and Minutes Scales)*** As noted above, the miles and minutes scales are graduated in exactly the same intervals. Two problems are associated with interpreting these scales properly.

The first problem is assigning the proper value to the intervals that

---

[1] Actually, the minutes scale is used to represent calibrated airspeed. However, since indicated and calibrated airspeeds are approximately the same in the cruising airspeed range, only indicated airspeeds will be used in the flight computer discussion.

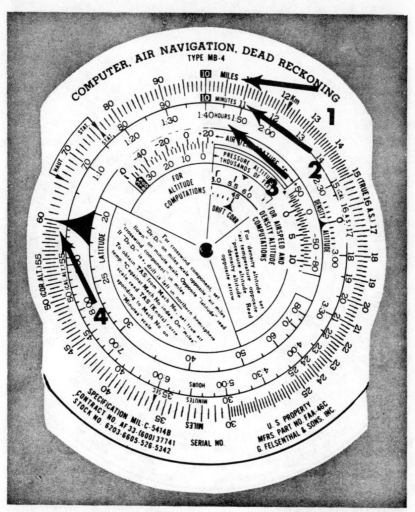

Figure 164. *Three scales and speed index. Arrow #1, miles scale; arrow #2, minutes scale; arrow #3, hours scale; arrow #4, speed index.*

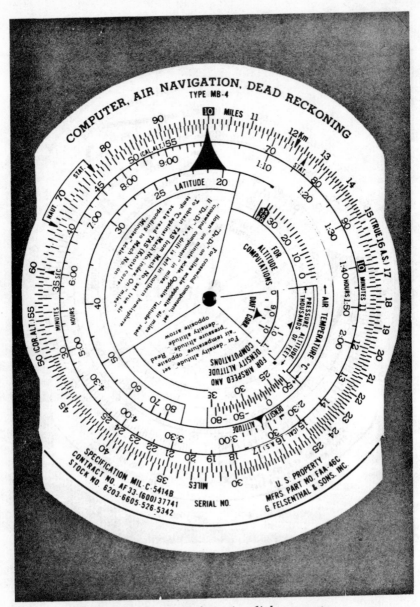

Figure 165. *Slide rule face of a flight computer.*

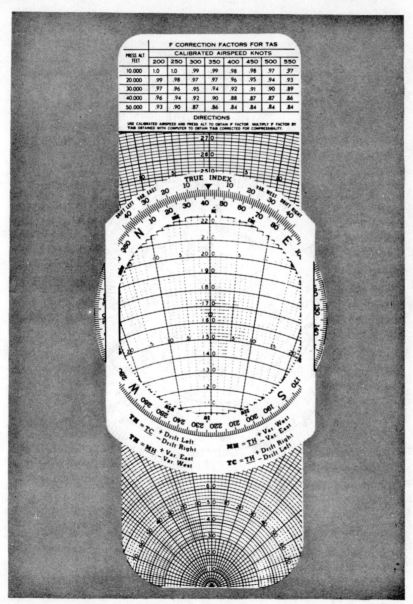

Figure 166. *Wind face of a flight computer.*

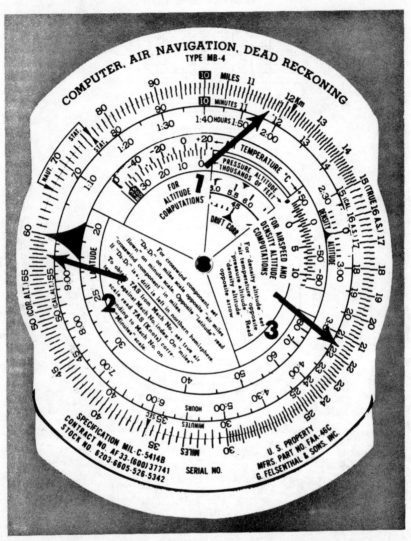

Figure 167. *Assigning values to the graduation of the scales.*

are numbered. The numbered intervals begin with 10 and end with 90. Between 10 and 25, each unit interval is numbered (10, 11, 12, etc.). Between 25 and 60, each 5-unit interval is numbered (25, 30, 35, etc.). Between 60 and 90, each 10-unit interval is numbered (60, 70, etc.). We will choose 60 to illustrate the first problem. This particular mark on the scale could represent 0.6, 6, 60, 600, etc. In the case of calculations made by the private pilot, it will usually indicate 6, 60, or 600.

The second problem is assigning the correct values to the subintervals. By subintervals we mean the graduations that lie between the numbered intervals. These will represent different values. Each subinterval between the numbered intervals from 10 to 15 represent one-tenth (.1) of the larger unit; between 15 and 30, each small subinterval represents two-tenths (.2) of a unit. The large intervals between 25 and 30 represent a unit (26, 27, 28, and 29). Between 30 and 60, each large subinterval represents a unit (31, 32, etc.) and each smaller subinterval five-tenths (.5) of a unit. Between 60 and 100 each subinterval represents one unit. Common sense must be used to determine what values to assign to the subintervals.

We will now take some examples and see how to assign values at various intervals on the scale. The *first step* should be to assign a value to the two numbered intervals on either side of the desired interval (unless the desired interval is numbered). The *second step* is to assign the proper value to the subintervals. To assign the proper value to the subintervals, we must first count the number of subintervals between the numbered intervals.

Now we are ready for examples. For the first example refer to arrow #1, figure 167. We will assign 11 and 12 to the two numbered intervals on either side of our desired interval (indicated by the arrow). There are 10 small subintervals between these two numbered intervals, so each one would have the value of one-tenth (.1). The arrow then points to a value of 11.7. If we assign 110 and 120 to the two numbered intervals, each subinterval has a value of one and the arrow would represent a value of 117.

A second example is indicated by arrow #2. First, we will assign the values 55 and 60 to the two numbered intervals. There are five large subintervals, each of which would have a value of one. Each of these intervals is further divided into two small subintervals having a value of five-tenths (0.5). The graduation indicated by arrow #2 then represents a value of 57.5. If 550 and 600 are assigned to the two numbered intervals, each subinterval has a value of 10 (large interval) and 5 (small interval), respectively, and the graduation represented by arrow #2 has a value of 575. If 5.5 and 6.0 are assigned to the numbered intervals, then by the same reasoning as above, the value of the graduation is 5.75.

A third example is illustrated by arrow #3. If 21 and 22 are assigned to the numbered intervals, each subinterval has a value of two-tenths and the arrow points to 21.6. If 210 and 220 are assigned, each subinterval is equal to two and the arrow points to 216.

*Scale Graduations (Hours Scale)* Between 1 hour and 2 hours on the hours scale, each 10-minute interval is numbered with subintervals for each 5 minutes. Between 2 hours and 5 hours, each half-hour interval is numbered with subintervals for each 10 minutes. Between 5 hours and 10 hours, each hourly interval is numbered with subintervals for each 10 minutes.

*Speed Index* The *Speed Index* is the large black arrow, or triangle-shaped symbol, located at the 60-minute or 1-hour position on the minutes scale (fig. 164, arrow #4). This index enables the operator to locate speeds much more rapidly and easily in time-and-distance problems.

## Time, Speed, and Distance Problems

In Chapter 15, we learned the relationship of time, ground speed, and distance and solved some problems by using arithmetic. We are now ready to solve these same types of problems on the slide rule face of the computer. If we know any two of the three quantities (time, ground speed, or distance), we can find the third quantity.

*Determining the Amount of Time for a Flight* In his preflight planning the pilot will compute his estimated ground speed for a flight based on the forecast winds aloft and his proposed true course as measured on the chart. After computing the ground speed, he will use it, along with the distance to be flown, to determine the total time for the flight.

Now the computer solution:

*Sample Problem.*—If a pilot maintains a ground speed of 140 m.p.h.. how long will it take him to fly 210 miles? (See fig. 168.)

*Solution—*
Given: Ground speed _____ 140 m.p.h.
 Distance to fly _____ 210 miles

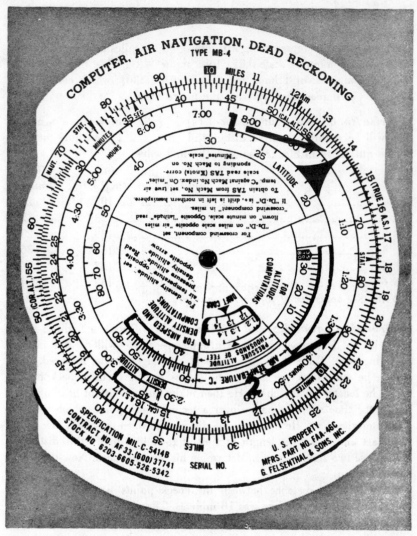

Figure 168. *Finding total flight time when ground speed and distance are known.*

Find: Time of flight.

(1.) Rotate the minutes scale until the speed index falls under 14 on the "miles" scale (fig. 168, arrow #1). The 14 represents 140 m.p.h.

(2.) Under 21 (representing 210 miles) on the miles scale, read 90 on the minutes scale (fig. 168, arrow #2). This represents 90 minutes, or 1 hour and 30 minutes (1:30), which could have been read directly from the hours scale.

*Exercise No. 5* If a ground speed of (a) _____ is maintained, how much time will be required to fly a distance of (b) _____? Substitute the following quantities in blanks (a) and (b) and solve:

|     | *(a)* | *(b)* |
|-----|-------|-------|
|     | *(m.p.h.)* | *(miles)* |
| 1. | 107 | 250 |
| 2. | 123 | 320 |
| 3. | 139 | 205 |
| 4. | 152 | 365 |
| 5. | 157 | 68 |
| 6. | 135 | 43 |

*Note: See appendix II for correct answers.*

**Determining Ground Speed During Flight**   During a flight, a pilot will wish to determine his actual ground speed. He will do this in the following way: Once he is on course at cruising altitude, airspeed, and power, he will check the time as he passes over a certain check point, which he locates on the chart. He then maintains a constant heading and checks the time when he passes over a second check point, which he also locates on the chart. He measures the distance between the check points on the chart and notes the length of time it took him to fly this distance. With these two figures, he can determine his ground speed. Now the computer solution:

Suppose the distance between the check points was 25 miles and the time to fly this distance was 10 minutes. Thus, our problem is:

*Sample Problem.*—If he flew 25 miles in 10 minutes, how many miles will he fly in 1 hour?

*Solution—*

Given: Distance flown _____ 25 miles

Time flown _____ 10 minutes

Find: Ground speed.

(1.) Rotate the minutes scale until the 10 on this scale appears directly under the 25 on the miles scale (fig. 169, arrow #1).

(2.) On the miles scale, opposite the speed index, read 15, which represents the ground speed of 150 m.p.h. (fig. 169, arrow #2).

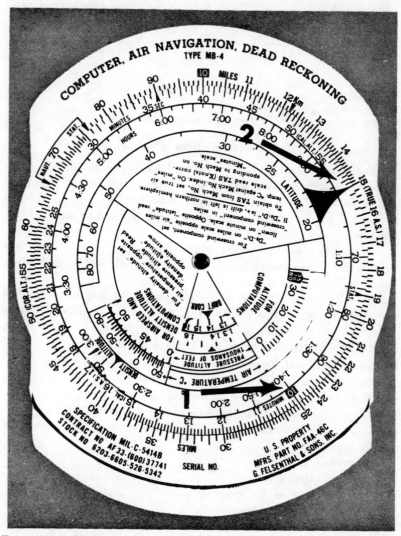

Figure 169. *Finding ground speed when flight time and distance flown are given.*

***Exercise No. 6*** If an airplane flies (a) _____ miles in (b) _____ minutes, what is its ground speed? Substitute the following quantities in blanks (a) and (b) and solve:

|     | (a) (miles) | (b) (minutes) |
| --- | --- | --- |
| 1. _____ | 30 | 12 |
| 2. _____ | 10 | 5 |
| 3. _____ | 13 | 8 |
| 4. _____ | 27 | 15 |
| 5. _____ | 32 | 16 |
| 6. _____ | 27 | 10.5 |

*Note: See appendix II for correct answers.*

## Fuel Consumption Problems

Fuel consumption problems may also be solved on the slide rule face of the computer in the same way as time, distance, and ground speed problems were solved. The miles, or outer scale will be used to represent gallons and gallons per hour; the minutes scale will still be used to represent time.

One of the most important items a pilot should consider on any flight is: Do I have enough fuel to complete the flight with enough left in reserve to fly at least 45 minutes? A pilot should know the amount of usable fuel on board before taking off. He should also know the fuel consumption rate (gallons per hour) of the airplane he plans to fly for the altitude, power setting, and mixture setting at which he plans to fly. This information is available in the Airplane Flight Manual.

***Determining Total Flight Time Available*** One kind of fuel consumption problem a private pilot will have to solve is determining the total flight time available based on the fuel load.

*Sample Problem.*—If an airplane carries 60 gallons of usable fuel and the rate of fuel consumption is 12 gallons per hour, how much flight time is available?

*Solution—*

    Given: Usable fuel _____60 gallons

            Rate of fuel consumption _____12 g.p.h.

    Find: Total flight time available.

(1) Rotate the minutes scale until the speed index falls under 12 on the miles scale (fig. 170, arrow #1). In this case 12 represents gallons and not miles.

(2) Under 60 on the miles scale, read 30 on the minutes scale. In this case, 30 represents 300 minutes, or 5 hours, which could have been read directly from the hours scale (fig. 170, arrow #2). Five hours is the total flight time available.

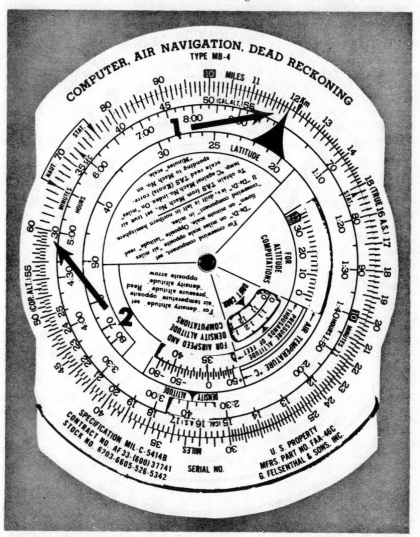

Figure 170. *Finding total available flight time when amount of fuel and rate of fuel consumption are known.*

**Exercise No. 7** If an airplane carries (a) ____ gallons of usable fuel and the rate of fuel consumption is (b) ____ gallons per hour, what is the total flight time available? Substitute the following quantities in blanks (a) and (b) and solve:

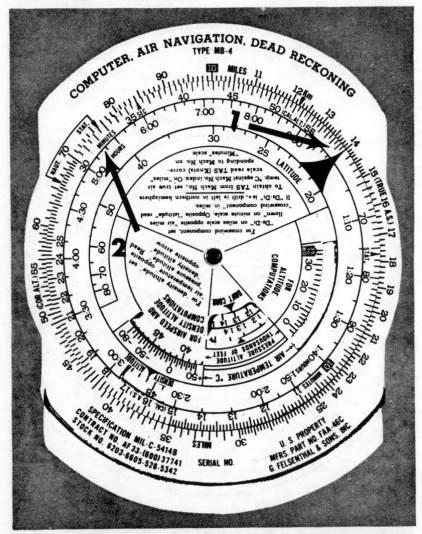

Figure 171. *Estimating amount of fuel to be used when estimated time en route and fuel consumption rate are known.*

|   | (a)<br>(gals.) | (b)<br>(g.p.h.) |
|---|---|---|
| 1. _____ | 36 | 9 |
| 2. _____ | 45 | 8.5 |
| 3. _____ | 37 | 7 |
| 4. _____ | 55 | 13 |
| 5. _____ | 18 | 6.3 |

*Note: See appendix II for correct answers.*

***Determining Total Fuel to be Used on a Flight***  A second type of fuel consumption problem a private pilot should be able to solve is determining how much fuel will be used during a flight.

*Sample Problem.*—How much fuel will be used during a flight of 5 hours and 20 minutes if the rate of fuel consumption is 14 gallons per hour?

*Solution—*

Given:  Time of flight _____5:20 (320 minutes)
Rate of fuel consumption _____14 g.p.h.

Find:  Total fuel used.

(1)  Rotate the minutes scale until the speed index falls under 14 on the miles scale (fig. 171, arrow #1).

(2)  Opposite 32 (representing 320 minutes) on the minutes scale, read 75 on the miles scale (fig. 171, arrow #2). Here 75 represents 75 gallons—the amount to be used on the flight.

The pilot must compare the above computed figure with the amount of usable fuel aboard so that he can determine his refueling points.

***Exercise No. 8***  How much fuel will be used during a flight of (a) _____ if the rate of fuel consumption is (b) _____ gallons per hour. Substitute the following quantities in blanks (a) and (b) and solve:

|   | (a)<br>(time) | (b)<br>(g.p.h.) |
|---|---|---|
| 1. _____ | 3 hours _____ | 7 |
| 2. _____ | 3 hrs 30 min _____ | 11 |
| 3. _____ | 2 hrs 20 min _____ | 9.5 |
| 4. _____ | 4 hrs 15 min _____ | 10.3 |
| 5. _____ | 5 hrs 10 min _____ | 13.7 |

*Note: See appendix II for correct answers.*

# True Airspeed Problems

To compute correctly his ground speed and heading, a pilot must know his true airspeed. To compute his TAS (true airspeed), he must know the pressure altitude at which he will be flying, the temperature in degrees Centigrade at this altitude, and his IAS (indicated airspeed).

The pilot will not know the pressure altitude during his preflight planning. In this case, he can use his proposed indicated cruising altitude. This introduces a slight error, but an insignificant one for the private pilot's use of airspeed readings. Once he reaches his cruising altitude, he can check the pressure altitude if he desires.

The pilot will not know the actual temperature at his proposed cruising altitude during his preflight planning. In this case, he can use the forecast temperature given in the winds-aloft forecast. After arriving at his cruising altitude, he can check his outside air temperature gauge for the actual temperature.

***Determining True Airspeed*** Knowing the altitude, temperature, and IAS, TAS may be determined on the computer in the sector labeled FOR AIRSPEED AND DENSITY ALTITUDE COMPUTATIONS (fig. 172, arrow #1). It is determined in the following way:

(1) Locate the proper free air temperature on the small scale labeled AIR TEMPERATURE °C (arrow #3).

(2) Rotate the disk, setting this temperature opposite the proper pressure altitude in the window marked PRESSURE ALTITUDE THOUSANDS OF FEET (arrow #2). (If the pressure altitude reading is not available, use indicated altitude.)

(3) On the minutes scale, locate the number corresponding to the indicated airspeed. For example, 13 if the airspeed is 130.

(4) Opposite the IAS on the minutes scale, read the TAS on the miles scale.

*Sample Problem.*—What is the TAS of an airplane flying at an IAS of 120 m.p.h. at an altitude of 5,500 ft. with an outside air temperature of + 10° C.?

*Solution*—

Given: Altitude _____ 5,500 ft.

Air temperature _____ + 10° C.

IAS _____ 120 m.p.h.

Find: TAS

(1) Locate + 10° on the small scale marked AIR TEMPERATURE °C. (fig. 173, arrow #1).

(2) Rotate the disk until 5,500 is located directly under + 10 (fig. 173, arrow #1).

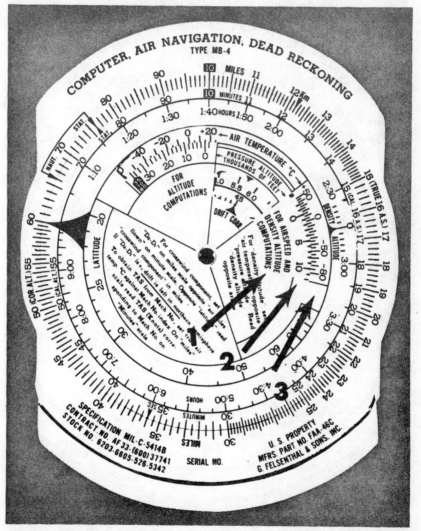

Figure 172. *Sector of computer used for true airspeed computations.*

(3)  Opposite 12 (representing 120 m.p.h.) on the minutes scale, read 132 on the miles scale, which represents a TAS of 132 m.p.h. (fig. 173, arrow #2).

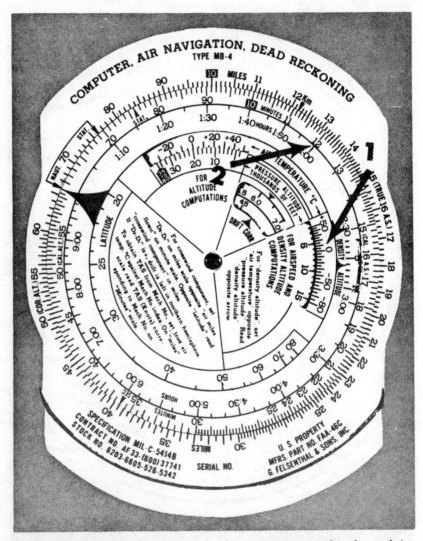

Figure 173. *Finding true airspeed when temperature, altitude, and indicated airspeed are known.*

Two mistakes are frequently made in this computation: One is using the wrong window. Be sure to use the window labeled FOR AIRSPEED AND DENSITY ALTITUDE COMPUTATIONS, and *not* the window labeled FOR ALTITUDE COMPUTATIONS. The second mistake is forgetting that the temperature scale is reversed—the plus temperatures are on the left and the minus temperatures are on the right.

***Exercise No. 9*** Find the TAS when the following pressure altitudes, temperatures, and IAS are given.

| | | Altitude (ft.) | Temperature (°C.) | IAS (m.p.h.) |
|---|---|---|---|---|
| 1. | ------------------------ | 5,000 | 0 | 120 |
| 2. | ------------------------ | 4,000 | − 10 | 145 |
| 3. | ------------------------ | 4,000 | + 10 | 145 |
| 4. | ------------------------ | 7,500 | + 10 | 145 |
| 5. | ------------------------ | 6,500 | − 15 | 150 |

*Note: See appendix II for correct answers.*

***Converting Knots to Miles per Hour*** Since the winds-aloft forecasts give the wind speed in knots, a private pilot must be able to convert knots to statute miles per hour to determine accurately his correct heading and ground speed. Since "knots" actually means "nautical miles per hour," our problem is converting nautical miles to statute miles. Computer solution of this conversion follows.

The conversion sector of the computer is shown in figure 174. The left arrow is labeled "naut." for nautical miles; the right arrow is labeled "stat." for statute miles.

*Sample Problem.*—Suppose we determine from the winds-aloft forecast that the wind speed at our proposed cruising altitude is 33 knots. What is the wind speed in miles per hour?

*Solution*—
(1) Rotate the minutes scale until 33 appears under the arrow labeled "naut." (fig. 174, arrow #1).
(2) On the minutes scale under the arrow labeled "stat." read 38 (arrow #2). This indicates that 33 nautical miles is equivalent to 38 statute miles, or 33 knots = 38 m.p.h.

***Exercise No. 10*** If the following wind speeds are given in knots, find the speed in statute miles per hour.

1. 20 knots        4. 40 knots
2. 16 knots        5. 47 knots
3. 26 knots

*Note: See appendix II for correct answers.*

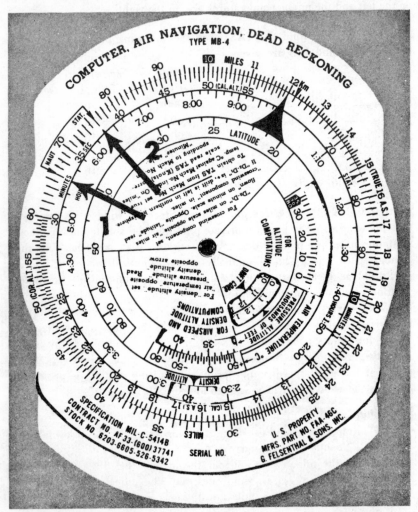

Figure 174. *Converting knots to miles per hour (33 knots equals 38 m.p.h.).*

# 31. Wind Face

The wind face of the computer consists of a movable disk and a sliding grid. The outer rim of the movable disk (indicated by "compass rose" in figure 175) is graduated in degrees from 0° to 360°. The center portion of the movable disk is made from a piece of frosted plastic on which pencil marks may be made.

*Sliding Grid*   The sliding grid (fig. 175) consists of two sets of printed lines and slides up and down through the movable disk. The horizontal lines are arcs of concentric circles whose center is at the very bottom of the sliding grid. These circles, "speed circles," are equidistant, and each one represents 2 miles per hour. At each 10-mile interval, heavier "speed circle" lines appear and are numbered for easy reference. They are used for all measurements of speeds for the wind triangle—wind speed, ground speed, and true airspeed.

The second set of lines is a series of converging straight lines which meet at the center of the concentric circles (bottom of the grid). The center line of this series is the "true course" line,—it will always represent the *true course* in our discussion.[1] The other lines in this set are "true heading" lines, since they will show the number of degrees by which the *true heading* differs from the *true course*. In other words, the true heading lines represent degrees to either side of the center or true course line. Below the 150 speed circle, each line represents 2° and heavy lines appear and are numbered for each 10° interval. Above the 150 speed circle, each line represents 1° and heavy lines appear and are numbered for each 5° interval.

The sliding grid has two sides—a high-speed side and a low-speed side. The private pilot should use only the low-speed side, the only side used throughout this discussion. This side will give greater accuracy because the graduations of the scale are finer.

*Compass Rose (or Azimuth Scale)*   As noted above, the outer rim of the movable disk is graduated in degrees from 0° to 360°. It is indi-

---

[1] There are several correct methods of solving wind vector problems on the computer. The final answer is the same if the correct procedures are used, no matter which method is followed. The system used in this discussion was selected because:

(1) Only the most common type of wind vector problem will be solved in this handbook—that of finding the true heading and ground speed when the wind direction, wind speed, true course, and true airspeed are known.

(2) Using this method requires no juggling of the computer.

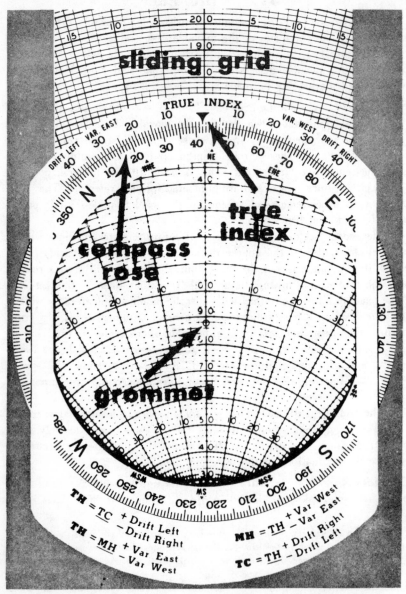

Figure 175. *Important parts of the flight computer wind face.*

cated by the "compass rose" in figure 175. The four cardinal points of the compass, north, east, south, and west, are prominently indicated by N, E, S, and W. The compass rose, or azimuth scale, may be used to set any desired angular direction measured from true north.

The center portion of the compass rose is made from a piece of frosted plastic on which pencil marks may be made and erased. At the center of the compass rose is a small black circle, the grommet (fig. 175). The ground speed will be read under the grommet.

*True Index*   Just above and adjacent to the upper portion of the compass rose or azimuth scale is a fixed scale. Each line on this fixed scale represents 1°. At the middle of this fixed scale is a small black triangle with the apex pointing downward (fig. 175). This small black triangle is the true index. It lies directly above the center line of the sliding grid.

In wind triangle problems, the wind direction and true course will be positioned directly below the true index at various stages of solution.

## Wind Triangle Representation

The various terms associated with a wind triangle were defined and discussed in the section on navigation. Before solving a wind triangle problem on the computer, we will review each term briefly and discuss its relationship or representation on the computer.

*Wind Direction*   The wind direction is that direction *from* which the wind is blowing and is measured in degrees clockwise from true north.

In solving wind triangle problems on the computer, the wind direction will be placed directly below the true index by rotating the compass rose.

*Wind Speed*   The wind speed is the rate of movement of the mass of air over the ground and is given in knots in weather reports and control tower instructions. Before the wind sped is represented on the computer, the speed in knots should be converted to miles per hour as previously shown.

The wind speed is represented on the computer by moving upward from the grommet along the center line of the grid a distance equivalent to the wind speed and making a pencil mark—either a small dot or small cross. In our discussion this pencil mark will be called the wind dot.

*True Course*   True course is the direction of a proposed flight path as drawn on the chart measured in degrees clockwise from true north at the mid-meridian.

The true course is always represented by the center line of the grid. In solving wind triangle problems, place the true course directly below the true index by rotating the compass rose.

***True Airspeed*** The true airspeed of an airplane is its rate of progress through the air. In wind triangle solutions, always place the true airspeed speed circle under the dot.

***Wind Correction Angle*** The wind correction angle is the correction that must be applied to the true course to establish the true heading that enables an airplane to make good a proposed true course. The angle is measured in degrees to the left or right.

The wind correction angle is represented on the computer as the number of degrees, left or right, from the true course line (center line of the grid) to the wind dot.

***True Heading*** True Heading is the actual heading of the airplane in flight, measured in degrees clockwise from true north. It is determined in wind triangle problem solutions by applying the wind correction angle to the true course.

***Ground Speed*** The ground speed of an airplane is its rate of progress over the ground. In wind triangle problem solutions, the ground speed is read under the grommet.

***Wind Triangle Representation*** Figure 176 shows the wind triangle as it should be visualized on the computer, although these lines will not actually be drawn. The following facts, closely related to our discussion, should be noted about this wind triangle:

(1.) The *wind dot* is the point of intersection of the wind line (W) and the true heading-true airspeed line (TH-TAS). Notice that the wind arrow points toward the grommet. This is the way you should always picture the wind when using the computer (as described in this handbook) because it enables you to visualize the effect the wind is having on your airplane. This is important because you can immediately determine whether the ground speed will be less than or greater than the true airspeed by noting whether you have a headwind or a tailwind. You can also immediately determine whether the true heading will be to the left or right of the true course by noting whether there is a crosswind from the

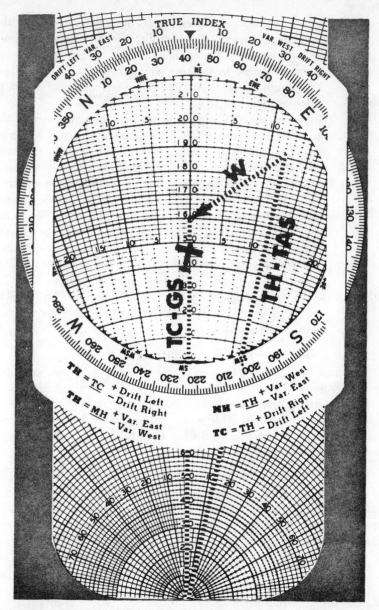

Figure 176. *Wind triangle as it should be visualized in this discussion.*

left or the right. In other words, by merely visualizing the relationship between the wind direction and the course line, you will not make the common mistake of applying the wind correction angle to the true course in the wrong direction. The length of the wind line represents the wind speed in miles per hour.

(2.) The *true course* (TC) is represented by the center line of the grid. The *ground speed* (GS) is represented by the length of the TC-GS line and is read under the grommet. In this case, it is 160 m.p.h.

(3.) The *wind correction angle* is the angle between the true course (TC) line and the true heading line (TH). In the pictured triangle, it is 12° right. The little airplane, which lies on the true course line, has its longitudinal axis displaced to the right of the true course line (into the wind) an amount equal to the wind correction angle. In other words, the longitudinal axis of the airplane is parallel to the true heading line.

(4.) The TAS is represented by the length of the TH/TAS line. The true airspeed circle is placed under the wind dot. In this case, it is 190 m.p.h.

## Solution of a Wind Triangle Problem

We are now ready to solve a wind triangle problem on the computer. The only type of problem we will illustrate in this handbook is the one the private pilot will encounter most often and should solve before taking off on a cross-country flight. This is the problem in which the true course, true airspeed, wind direction, and wind speed are known, and the pilot wants to find true heading and ground speed.

*Sample Problem.*—The pilot measures his true course on the chart and finds it to be 345°. He plans to cruise at a TAS of 140 m.p.h. The winds-aloft forecast gives the wind direction and speed at his proposed cruising altitude as 220° and 33 knots. What is his ground speed and true heading for this flight.

*Solution—*

Given:  Wind _____220°/33 knots

True course (TC) _____345°

True airspeed (TAS) _____ 140 m.p.h.

Find:    Ground speed (GS)

True heading (TH)

| TAS | TC | WIND | | WCA | | TH | GS |
|-----|-----|------|------|-----|-----|----|----|
| | | MPH | FROM | R + | L − | | |
| 140 | 345° | 38 | 220° | ? | ? | ? | |

(1.) Convert the wind from knots to miles per hour, as shown in Chapter 25. By this method, we find that 33 knots is equivalent to 38 m.p.h. The known quantities are entered in a a portion of a flight log.

(2.) Slide the grid through the computer until one of the heavy horizontal lines lies under the center of the grommet. (The 170-mile grid line was chosen for this example.)

(3.) Rotate the compass rose until the wind direction (220°) appears under the true index (fig. 177).

(4.) Measure up from the grommet, along the center line, a length equivalent to 38 miles. (Note—Each horizontal line represents 2 miles.) At this point, place a pencil mark which we will refer to as the wind dot (fig. 177).

(5.) Rotate the compass rose until the true course (345°) appears under the true index (fig. 178).

(6.) Slide the grid through the computer until the TAS (140 m.p.h.) speed line lies directly under the wind dot (fig. 178).

| TAS | TC | WIND | | WCA | | TH | GS |
|-----|-----|------|------|-----|-----|----|----|
| | | MPH | FROM | R + | L − | | |
| 140 | 345° | 38 | 220° | ? | | ? | 159 |

(7.) Read the ground speed (159 m.p.h.) under the grommet.

(8.) Find the wind correction angle by checking the number of degrees between the center line of the grid and the wind dot. In this case, it is 13°. (Note—Below the 150 m.p.h. line, each vertical line is equivalent to 2°; above the 150 m.p.h. line, each vertical line is equivalent to 1°.) Since the wind dot is to the left of the center line, the wind correction angle is 13° left.

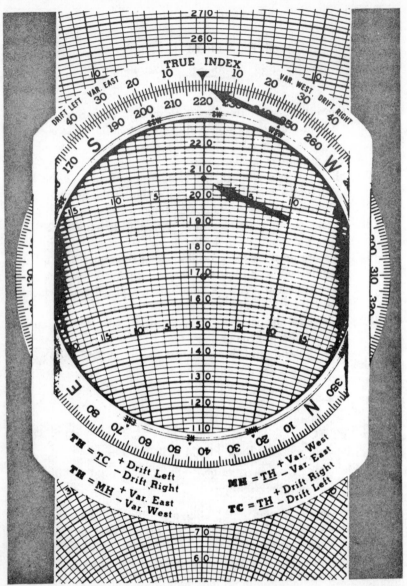

Figure 177. *First step in wind triangle solution—place wind direction under true index and measure up from the grommet (along center line) a length equivalent to the wind speed. Place dot at this point.*

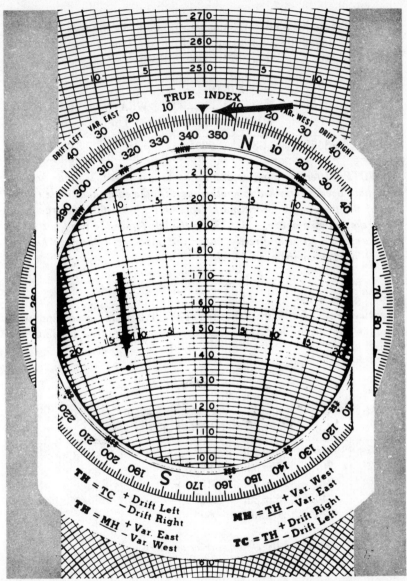

Figure 178. *The next step in wind triangle solution—place true course under true index and adjust sliding grid so the true airspeed circle lies under the wind dot. Then read ground speed and wind correction angle.*

299

(9.) Since the wind correction angle is 13° L, the true heading is found by subtracting 13 from the true course. Thus, the true heading is 332° (345° − 13°).

| TAS | TC | WIND | | WCA | TH | GS |
|-----|-----|------|------|-----------|-----|-----|
| | | MPH | FROM | R+    L− | | |
| 140 | 345° | 38 | 220° | −13° | 332° | 159 |

*NOTE: After the wind correction angle was found, the true heading could have been determined in another way. On the outer fixed scale (either side of the true index), each mark represents 1°. To find the true heading in the example above, count 13° to the left (since the wind correction angle was 13° L) and directly under this mark read the true heading (332°) on the compass rose scale.*

**Exercise No. 11** If the following TAS, TC, wind speed, and wind direction are given, find the wind correction angle, true heading, and ground speed.

| TAS | TC | WIND | | WCA | TH | GS |
|-----|-----|-------|------|-----------|-----|-----|
| | | SPEED | FROM | R+    L− | | |
| 125 | 010° | 35 m.p.h. | 150° | | | |
| 122 | 267° | 42 m.p.h. | 087° | | | |
| 144 | 045° | 15 m.p.h. | 315° | | | |
| 137 | 140° | 36 m.p.h. | 230° | | | |
| 135 | 120° | 20 knots | 060° | | | |

*NOTE: See appendix II for correct answers.*

# SECTION IX —

# RADIO COMMUNICATIONS

## 32. Radio Communications

We have already studied briefly some of the basic principles of navigation. Until recently many pilots relied entirely on pilotage and dead reckoning when making VFR cross-country flights. Even now, some experienced pilots are reluctant to use radio navigation aids and communication facilities because they are not familiar with phraseologies, air traffic control procedures, and the convenience of radio aid in navigation.

However, private pilots can no longer afford to overlook the advantages and safeties made available by the radio. At busy airports throughout the country, arriving and departing air traffic is directed by control towers. Although light-gun signals are sometimes used when small airplanes are not radio-equipped, most airport traffic control instructions are given by radio. For operations of aircraft to, from, or on airports with FAA control towers, aircraft are now required to have both a radio receiver and a transmitter.

On cross-country flights many situations arise which make the use of two-way radio desirable en route. For example, a pilot may wish to obtain information about current weather along his course or the amount of ice or snow on the runways at his destination. Such information may be readily obtained by using the radio to call the nearest FAA Flight Service Station.

***Transcribed Weather Broadcasts*** Equipment is provided at selected FAA flight service stations by which meteorological and Notice to Airmen data is recorded on tapes and broadcast continuously over the low-frequency (200 — 415 kHz) navigational aid (L/MF range or H facility) and VOR.

Broadcasts are made from a series of individual tape recordings. The first three tapes identify the station, give general weather forecast conditions in the area, pilot reports (PIREP), radar reports when available.

and winds aloft data. The remaining tapes contain weather at selected locations within a 400-mile radius of the central point. Changes, as they occur are transcribed onto the tapes.

***Scheduled Weather Broadcasts*** All Flight service stations having voice facilities on radio ranges (VORs) or radio beacons (NDBs) broadcast weather reports and Notice to Airmen information at 15 minutes past each hour from reporting points within approximately 150 miles from the broadcast station.

At each station, the material is scheduled for broadcast, as available, in this order:

(1) Alert Notice announcement.

(2) Hourly Weather Reports.

(3) Weather Advisory. (SIGMETS, AIRMETS, etc.)

(4) Pilot Reports.

(5) Radar Reports.

(6) Notice to Airmen—(NOTAMS, AIRADS-AIRMEN ADVISORIES.)

(7) Alert Notice. (Information concerning overdue aircraft.)

In addition, special weather reports and some Notices to Airmen data are broadcast off-schedule, immediately upon receipt. If you need special forecast service en route, you may obtain it from any Flight Service Station.

The time of observation of weather reports included in a scheduled broadcast is 58 minutes past the hour preceding the broadcast. When the time of observation is otherwise, the observation time is given.

***In-Flight Service*** If your aircraft has two-way radio, you may call any FAA station along your route for any in-flight information or assistance, such as weather reports, special National Weather Service advice (outlined below) to aid in establishing your position or locating an airport. You do not need to be thoroughly familiar with the standard phraseologies and procedures for air/ground communications.

*A brief call to any FAA station, stating your message in your own words, will get immediate attention.*

Personnel at FAA Flight Service Stations are trained to help pilots establish position by: (a) visual reference to terrain features; (b) VHF omnirange indications (triangulation); and (c) low-frequency radio range orientation. (Refer to AIM, Part 3.)

A word of caution relative to the use of aircraft radio transmitters—all pilots should be aware of, and alert to, an operational safety hazard associated with the use of aircraft radio microphones. Sometimes the microphone "button" will stick in the "ON" position. Often the pilot fails to note this condition, but as long as his microphone button (switch) is stuck in the "ON" position he can not receive on the transmitting frequency, and for all practical purposes, neither can the pilots of other aircraft using that frequency. In other words, a microphone button stuck in the "ON" position will either block or seriously interfere with all communications on the particular frequency involved. Pilots should suspect this possibility and therefore check their microphone when unable to obtain a reply to their transmissions. Often it is possible to do this simply by unplugging the microphone. If receiver operation is thereby restored, it is quite likely the problem is a sticking microphone button.

*Pilot Weather Reports (PIREPS)* Whenever 5,000-foot or lower ceilings, 5-mile or lower visibilities, or thunderstorms and related phenomena are reported or forecast, FAA stations are required to solicit and collect PIREPS which describe conditions aloft. Pilots are urged to cooperate and volunteer reports of cloud tops, upper cloud layers, thunderstorms, ice, turbulence, strong winds, and other significant flight condition information. PIREPS should be given directly to FAA stations on normal en route station frequencies.

PIREPS, SIGMETS, and AIRMETS are included at the beginning of scheduled weather broadcasts by FAA stations within 150 nautical miles of the area affected by the potentially hazardous weather. Also, pilots are advised of these reports during preflight briefings by FAA and National Weather Service Stations and in air/ground contacts with FAA stations.

*Weather Broadcast Format* Scheduled *weather broadcasts* (15 minutes past each hour) will begin with the announcement "Aviation Broadcast; Weather." Example:

"AVIATION BROADCAST, WEATHER. OKLAHOMA CITY. OKLAHOMA CITY WILEY POST MEASURED CEILING ONE THOUSAND BROKEN, VISIBILITY TWO, FOG. TEMPERATURE FOUR THREE, DEWPOINT FOUR ONE. WIND ONE NINER ZERO DEGREES AT FOUR. ALTIMETER TWO NINER EIGHT SEVEN." The completed broadcast is ended by saying: "THE TIME IS ONE EIGHT AND ONE QUARTER." Reports for approximately 10 additional stations may follow. The local report is repeated as the last station report. Temperature is not broadcast, for other than the local report, when it is 40° or less or 85° or higher.

When the temperature/dewpoint spread is 5° or less, both the temperature and dewpoint are given. Surface wind direction and speed is given when 10 knots or more (sustained). For this station, wind directions are magnetic; that is, measured from magnetic north rather than true north. The altimeter setting is given for the broadcast stations local report only.

Special weather reports and advisories are broadcast when warranted by significant changes in the weather at a particular station or in a given area.

**Radio Frequencies** To take advantage of the communication and navigation features of the National Airways System, pilots should know something of the radio frequencies assigned for aviation use by the Federal Communications Commission. Aviation frequencies may be checked in the *Airman's Information Manual*, on aeronautical charts, or with the nearest FAA Flight Service Station, tower, or center. Use the most recent revision of the appropriate sections of AIM, rather than aeronautical charts, as the final check on these frequencies (see Chapter 24). Radio frequencies normally of interest to private pilots are:

## AIRCRAFT RECEIVING FREQUENCIES

Low and medium frequencies _____200 to 415 kHz
   (Ranges, towers, beacons, etc.)
Omnirange (VOR) stations _____108.20 through 117.90 MHz
   (Airway track guidance and
   en route communications)
Air traffic control communications _____118.00 through 121.40 MHz
                                   122.20 MHz, 126.70 MHz
Emergency _____121.50 MHz
Airport utility (ground control) _____121.90 MHz, 121.70 MHz
Aeronautical advisory station (UNICOM)__122.80 MHz, 123.00 MHz
   (If the airport has an operating tower, the
   UNICOM frequency is 123.00 MHz. Aero-
   nautical advisory stations that use these
   frequencies are operated by private agen-
   cies such as airport operators.)
   Note: Private aircraft may receive and
   transmit on these frequencies.

# AIRCRAFT TRANSMITTING FREQUENCIES

Private aircraft to towers _____122.40 MHz, 122.50 MHz,
122.60 MHz, and 122.70 MHz

Private or commercial aircraft to FAA
Flight Service Stations __,_____122.2 MHz, 122.3 MHz, 122.6 MHz,
and 123.6 MHz

(Check the *Airman's Information Manual* to
determine additional tower and FSS frequencies.)

Low and medium frequencies are subject to considerable interference from static, whereas the very high frequencies (VHF) give relatively static-free radio communications. VHF reception distances vary with distance from the station and altitude of the aircraft.

Examples of normal VHF reception distances are shown in the following table for aircraft at several altitudes:

| ALTITUDE OF AIRCRAFT<br>*(Above ground station)* | RECEPTION DISTANCE<br>*(Statute miles)* |
|---|---|
| 1,000 ft. | 45 miles |
| 3,000 ft. | 80 miles |
| 5,000 ft. | 100 miles |
| 10,000 ft. | 140 miles |

*NOTE: This table is based on zero elevation of the radio facility. Altitudes and distances shown are theoretical for flat terrain where no physical obstructions intervene.*

**Tuning a Radio Receiver**  An aircraft radio is tuned to the station just as an ordinary home set is tuned. For best reception though, you must recognize certain pecularities of the airplane radio.

Just as when reading other instruments, the pilot should view the frequency indicator from directly in front, preventing an error that might result in no signal or in reception of the wrong station. Another source of error is inaccuracy in frequency calibration, often caused by continued vibration or hard landings. Thus, a station which should be received on 116.40 MHz may appear (on the radio dial) on 116.10 MHz. 116.60 MHz, or at some other frequency. If no signal is received when the set is tuned to a given frequency, turn selector in both directions until the station is tuned in. Then reduce the volume and adjust the frequency control slightly for best reception.

When a station is broadcasting intermittently (a control tower, for example), you may have to ask station personnel for a short or long count (counting from 1 to 5 or from 1 to 10) so that tuning may be completed. At busy locations though, requesting a count is both unnecessary and undesirable because it disrupts normal communications.

Range stations are identified either by code, or by voice recording alternated with code. *It is very important to check this identification to make sure the desired station is being received.*

In recent years an increasing number of aircraft radios )receivers as well as transmitters) are equipped with crystals possessing specific frequency characteristics. This makes it possible to "tune" to an exact frequency simply by selecting the appropriate crystal. This selection is made by rotating a selector to the combination of digits that corresponds to the desired frequency. This eliminates most of the calibration problems cited previously. In most instances, there will also be a capability for single channel "simplex (SCS) communication. That is, non-simultaneous communication between the airplane and the station which utilizes the same frequency for both transmitting and receiving.

***Using an Aircraft Radio Transmitter*** As already indicated, FAA recommends, and good operating practice demands, that pilots use their two-way radios for air/ground communications. To use a transmitter, however, you must obtain two licenses through the Federal Communications Commission (FCC). A radio station license is required for the aircraft transmitter itself, and the pilot must have a restricted radiotelephone operator permit.

When an aircraft has a VHF transmitter, the pilot should be sure he is transmitting on the proper frequency (normally 122.10 MHz for Flight Service Stations, and 122.50 MHz for towers) if his radio equipment is without *simplex* capability.

When he is ready to transmit, the pilot should hold the microphone close to his mouth. After giving thought to what he is going to say, he should speak in a normal tone of voice. Although the message may be phrased in his own words, certain radiotelephone phraseologies are commonly used to reduce the length of transmissions and provide uniformity. The following are a few of these phraseologies:

| *Word or phrase* | *Meaning* |
| --- | --- |
| ACKNOWLEDGE_____ | Let me know that you have received and understand this message. |

| | |
|---|---|
| ROGER_ _ _ _ _ _ _ _ _ _ _ _ _ _ _ _ _ _ _ _ _ | I have received all of your last transmission. (Used to acknowledge receipt; should be used for no other purpose.) |
| AFFIRMATIVE_ _ _ _ _ _ _ _ _ _ _ _ _ _ _ | Yes. |
| NEGATIVE_ _ _ _ _ _ _ _ _ _ _ _ _ _ _ _ _ | That is not correct. |
| I SAY AGAIN_ _ _ _ _ _ _ _ _ _ _ _ _ _ _ _ | *Self-explanatory.* |
| SAY AGAIN_ _ _ _ _ _ _ _ _ _ _ _ _ _ _ _ _ | *Self-explanatory.* |
| STAND BY_ _ _ _ _ _ _ _ _ _ _ _ _ _ _ _ _ | *Self-explanatory.* |
| VERIFY_ _ _ _ _ _ _ _ _ _ _ _ _ _ _ _ _ _ _ | Check with originator. |
| OVER_ _ _ _ _ _ _ _ _ _ _ _ _ _ _ _ _ _ _ _ | My transmission is ended and I expect a response from you. |
| OUT_ _ _ _ _ _ _ _ _ _ _ _ _ _ _ _ _ _ _ _ _ | This conversation is ended; I do not expect a response from you. |
| CORRECTION_ _ _ _ _ _ _ _ _ _ _ _ _ _ _ _ | An error has been made in the transmission (or message indicated). |

Remember, however, that it is not necessary for you to be thoroughly familiar with the standard phraseology and procedures for air/ground communications. A brief call to any FAA station, stating your message in your own words, will receive immediate attention.

*Airport and En Route Communications Procedures*   To illustrate two-way radio communication procedures, we will make an imaginary VFR flight direct from Abilene Municipal Airport, Abilene, Texas, to Love Field, Dallas, Texas.

Follow the flight route on the Dallas-Ft. Worth Sectional Chart which accompanies this handbook.

The pilot should personally check the weather at either a National Weather Service Office or at a Flight Service Station, either by telephone or by visiting the facility. He should then file his VFR flight plan, if weather conditions are satisfactory, with the Abilene Flight Service Station via interphone, telephone, or in person. He will then complete any remaining preparations for the flight.

When ready to taxi he calls the Abilene control tower on the ground control frequency—121.9 MHz. After establishing contact by giving and receiving confirmation of his aircraft identification, he will advise ground control of his position on the airport and request taxi instructions. At some airports it would also be appropriate to advise that you have received ATIS information. Though not mandatory, it is helpful under some conditions if he also gives the type of operation he plans to conduct (VFR or IFR) and his flight plan destination.

Example—

Pilot: ABILENE GROUND CONTROL THIS IS ASTROLARK THREE NINER TWO ONE BRAVO AT HANGAR TWO, READY TO TAXI, VFR FLIGHT TO DALLAS, OVER.

Tower: ASTROLARK THREE NINER TWO ONE BRAVO, CLEARED TO RUNWAY ONE FOUR. WIND ONE THREE ZERO DEGREES AT ONE SIX. ALTIMETER TWO NINER NINER EIGHT. TIME ZERO EIGHT THREE ONE.

Pilot: ASTROLARK THREE NINER TWO ONE BRAVO, ROGER.

After taxiing to run-up position and completing his pretakeoff check list, the pilot changes his radio transmitter and receiver to the appropriate tower frequency and calls the tower.

Pilot: ABILENE TOWER ASTROLARK THREE NINER TWO ONE BRAVO, READY FOR TAKEOFF.

The tower controller determines that there is no conflicting traffic and replies:

Tower: ASTROLARK THREE NINER TWO ONE BRAVO, CLEARED FOR TAKEOFF.

Pilot: ASTROLARK THREE NINER TWO ONE BRAVO, ROGER.

The pilot continues to guard the control tower frequency until leaving the airport traffic area. Then he retunes his VHF communications radio to the appropriate frequency (122.3 MHz) and calls Abilene radio giving his time of takeoff so they can activate his flight plan.

Example—

Pilot: ABILENE RADIO THIS IS ASTROLARK THREE NINER TWO ONE BRAVO, OFF AT ONE ZERO, VFR FLIGHT TO DALLAS. OVER.

Station: Acknowledges the transmission.

While proceeding on his flight, he continues to monitor Abilene radio until within receiving range of Mineral Wells radio, at which time he tunes in Mineral Wells. In the vicinity of Mineral Wells, he contacts

Mineral Wells radio to give a position report. He first establishes contact with them, indicating the frequency on which a reply is expected.

Example—

Pilot: MINERAL WELLS RADIO THIS IS ASTROLARK THREE NINER TWO ONE BRAVO. REPLY ON VOR FREQUENCY. OVER.

Station: ASTROLARK THREE NINER TWO ONE BRAVO. THIS IS MINERAL WELLS RADIO. OVER.

The pilot then proceeds with his message, which usually includes position, time, flight altitude, and VFR flight plan from point of departure to destination.

Pilot: ASTROLARK THREE NINER TWO ONE BRAVO SIX MILES WEST OF MINERAL WELLS ZERO FIVE AT FIVE THOUSAND FIVE HUNDRED ON VFR FLIGHT PLAN ABILENE TO DALLAS. OVER.

Station: Mineral Wells radio acknowledges his position report and will give him the latest weather information (including Dallas weather), NOTAMS, and other information pertinent to his flight.

Pilot: ASTROLARK THREE NINER TWO ONE BRAVO, ROGER, OUT.

While in the vicinity of Fort Worth, the pilot may wish to contact Greater Southwest or Britton radio for further information.

When approximately 25 miles west of Dallas, he calls Dallas approach control on the frequency listed in the current issue of AIM. See fig. 152 for an example.

Pilot: DALLAS APPROACH CONTROL THIS IS ASTROLARK THREE NINER TWO ONE BRAVO TWO FIVE MILES WEST AT THREE THOUSAND. LANDING AT LOVE FIELD. OVER.

Approach control will give him wind and runway information, other traffic in his area, and will advise him at what point to contact the control tower. At the specified point or distance from the airport, the pilot calls the tower.

Example—

Pilot: LOVE TOWER THIS IS ASTROLARK THREE NINER TWO ONE BRAVO, FIVE MILES WEST. REQUEST LANDING INSTRUCTIONS. OVER.

Tower: ASTROLARK THREE NINER TWO ONE BRAVO. FIVE

MILES WEST. CLEARED TO ENTER TRAFFIC PAT-
TERN, RUNWAY THREE SIX, WIND THREE FOUR
ZERO DEGREES AT ONE FIVE. OVER.

Pilot:   ASTROLARK THREE NINER TWO ONE BRAVO.
ROGER.

The pilot then enters the traffic pattern on the downwind leg, and reports to the tower while turning on base leg. After receiving a clearance
to land, he acknowledges and proceeds with his landing. While he is turning off the active runway, the tower instructs him to tune to ground
control frequency for further taxi instructions. After clearing the active
runway, he changes his radio transmitter and receiver to the ground
control frequency, makes a radio check, and acknowledges all taxi instructions. He proceeds to the parking area, continuing to monitor this
frequency until the airplane is parked. If he has not previously closed
his flight plan by radio with the Dallas FSS (or tower), he should go
to the nearest telephone, call the FSS station (or tower), and request
that they close his flight plan from Abilene.

# 33.  Radio Guidance in VFR Flying

In addition to the communications services discussed in the preceding chapter, the National Airways System of the FAA provides several
radio aids to air navigation. For example, the VHF omnirange (VOR)
and the four-course, low-frequency range are particularly useful to VFR
pilots, both for navigation guidance and en route communication. For
assistance mainly to instrument pilots, there are such aids as radar and
instrument landing systems (ILS).

Though new and improved types of electronic equipment are constantly being developed to make flying safer and easier, VORTAC and
VOR are the basic VHF systems currently in use for general aviation radio
navigation. (See fig. 179.) In addition to the bearing information obtained from the omnirange, this system supplies properly equipped airplanes with the distance of the plane from the station. With bearing
and distance known, the pilot can determine his position, eliminating
the need for bearings on two or more stations. Completion of all ground
installations and widespread availability of low-cost equipment for use
in personal planes will bring into fullest use this simplified means of
determining position. However, an airplane equipped with a VOR receiver

Figure 179. *A typical VORTAC station.*

can still use a VORTAC station for bearing information just as it uses a normal VOR station. (NOTE: Throughout this handbook, *VOR* will be used to include both VOR and VORTAC stations.)

In recent years, the VHF omnirange (VOR) has replaced the low-frequency range as the basic radio aid to navigation. Frequencies of omnirange stations are in the VHF band, between 108 and 118 MHz. The word "omni" means *all*, and an omnirange is a VHF radio range that projects courses in all directions from the station, like spokes from the hub of a wheel. Each of these spokes, or *radials*, is denoted by the outbound magnetic direction of the spoke. A *radial* is defined as "a line of magnetic bearing extending from an omnidirectional range (VOR)." In contrast to the situation with low-frequency ranges, which have only four range legs, it is possible to fly to and from omniranges in any direction.

A few of the advantages of flying omniranges are:

(1.) A flight may be made *to* a VOR from any direction, by flying the course to the station.

(2.) A flight may be made to any destination *from* the station by selecting the proper radial. Remember that VOR radials, as shown on charts, are always from the station, never toward.

(3.) When within range of two or more VOR's, a fix may be determined quickly and easily by taking bearings on the stations and determining position on a chart.

(4.) Static-free reception and the elimination of the complex orientation procedures often used by instrument pilots flying low-frequency ranges.

An important fact is that VOR signals, like other VHF transmissions, follow an approximate line-of-sight course. Therefore, reception distance increases with an increase in the flight altitude of an aircraft (fig. 180). A means is usually provided with omnireceivers to indicate when the signal is too weak for satisfactory reception.

In addition to their use in navigation guidance, VOR frequencies are used by FSS personnel for weather broadcasts and other communications.

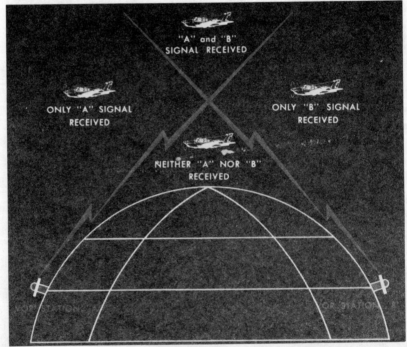

Figure 180. *VHF transmission follows a line-of-sight course.*

VOR stations are assigned three-letter identifications. At some stations these identification letters are broadcast continuously in code. Other stations are identified by a voice recording (example: Dallas VORTAC). alternating with the usual Morse Code identification (DALLAS VORTAC, —.. .— .—.., DALLAS VORTAC, —.. .— .—.., etc.).

*VOR Receivers* VOR receivers are very simple to operate. The desired frequency is selected as previously discussed in Chapter 27. Three basic components are normally used by the pilot in VOR flying (fig. 181). One component is the omnibearing (course) selector, which enables the pilot to select the course he wants to fly. A second component is the "TO-FROM" indicator (also known as the ambiguity meter or sense indicator), which shows him whether the course is TO or FROM the station. The third is a deviation indicator (often called the "LEFT-RIGHT" indicator or vertical needle), which tells him when he is on course, or left, or right of course. Using these three components, the pilot obtains visual indications which give him a variety of information and guidance. The "TO-FROM" indicator and deviation indicator are often combined into a single display as they are in our illustration.

Because accuracy is an important factor in any navigation equipment, pilots should check their VOR receivers periodically to be sure they are functioning properly. Procedures and locations for checking VOR receivers are published by FAA in the *Airman's Information Manual*.

When a pilot wishes to fly directly to a VOR facility, he should:

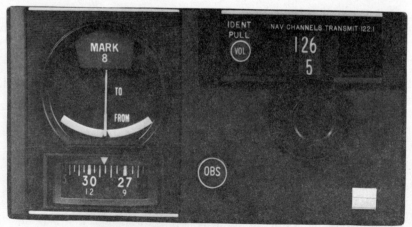

Figure 181. *Typical VOR receiver set.*

(1.) Tune the receiver to the frequency of the VOR and *positively identify the station either by code* or voice recording. (The receiver is properly tuned when there is a positive indication on the TO-FROM indicator. If this indicates neither TO nor FROM or just partially indicates TO or FROM, or there is an oscillation, the signal is unusable.)

(2.) Manually rotate the omnibearing (course) selector until the LEFT-RIGHT needle is centered at the bottom of the dial.

(3.) Check to see that the TO-FROM indicator reads "TO." If it should read "FROM," merely turn the course selector 180° to obtain a "TO" reading, and the LEFT-RIGHT needle is again centered.

(4.) Turn to the approximate heading that will maintain the magnetic course, i.e., the heading on the course selector that will take the airplane directly to the VOR station.

When a pilot wants to fly directly away from a VOR, he should:

(1.) Follow the same procedure in (1.) and (2.) above.

(2.) Check to see that the TO-FROM indicator reads "FROM." If it should read "TO," turn the course selector 180° to obtain a "FROM" reading, and the LEFT-RIGHT needle is again centered.

(3.) Turn to the approximate heading that will maintain the magnetic course, i.e., the reading on the course selector that will take the airplane directly away from the VOR station.

Figure 182 shows various positions of an airplane relative to a VOR station and a desired course line, along with the indications of the VOR receiver components at each position. In referring to figure 182, turn the handbook so you are looking in the direction the airplane is flying.

In position No. 1, the pilot has found (by rotating his omnibearing selector) that his magnetic course TO the station is 030° and has already turned to a magnetic heading of approximately 030°. Note that the omnibearing selector is set on 30 (030°), the TO-FROM indicator reads TO, and the LEFT-RIGHT needle is centered. This indicates that the magnetic course to the station is 030°. If the pilot maintains these indications on his VOR receiver instruments, he will fly directly to the station. When the LEFT-RIGHT needle deviates from the centered position, the pilot should make small corrections in heading to center it again, and in this way he will fly to the station. To get back on course he should make corrections in heading toward the needle.

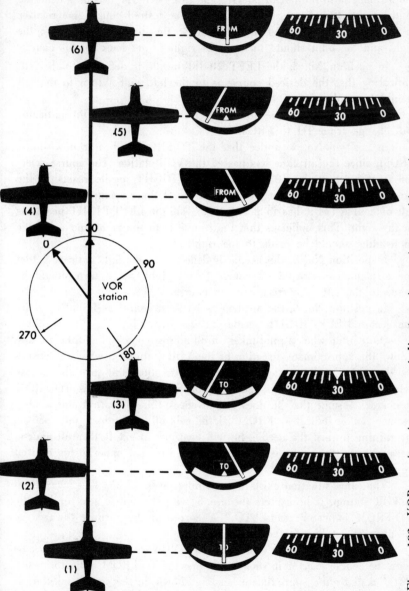

Figure 182. *VOR receiver instrument indications for various positions of an airplane relative to its desired course and the VOR station.*

Position No. 2 in figure 182 shows the component readings when the airplane is to the left of course. The LEFT-RIGHT needle is deflected to the right. It indicates the position of the desired course line relative to the pilot. It is deflected to the right, so the desired course is to the right and the pilot should turn to the right to get back on his course.

In position No. 3, the LEFT-RIGHT needle is deflected to the left, indicating that the desired course is to the left, and a turn to the left should be made.

As the airplane passes over the station, the TO-FROM indicator will change from TO to FROM.

In position No. 4, notice that the TO-FROM indicator now shows FROM, since the airplane has passed the VOR station. The course selector is still set on 30 (030°). The LEFT-RIGHT needle reacts in the same way as during flight TO the station. If the airplane strays to the left of course (as it has in position No. 4), the LEFT-RIGHT needle is to the right. This indicates that the course is to the right and a change in heading should be made to the right.

In position No. 5, the needle is deflected to the left, indicating that the airplane has strayed off course to the right. So, a turn should be made to the left to correct back to course.

In position No. 6, the airplane is back on course as is indicated by the centered LEFT-RIGHT needle.

Quite often when a pilot takes off on a cross-country flight, he already knows the approximate direction of the VOR station on which he wishes to "home in." So he may head in that direction and turn the course selector until the needle is centered but forget to check his TO-FROM indicator. Assume that he does fail to check this indication and further assume that it indicates "FROM." If he gets off course now and corrects by turning toward the needle, he will continue to get farther off course, because now the needle is deflected in the direction opposite his desired course.

The same situation exists when a pilot takes off and flies away from a VOR station, if he centers the needle with the course selector but the TO-FROM indicator reads "TO." A correction by turning toward the needle will get him farther off course.

Summarizing: If you wish to fly to a VOR station, center the needle with the course selector in such a way that the TO-FROM indicator reads, "TO," and fly the approximate heading shown on the course selector. If you wish to fly away from a VOR station, center the needle with the course selector so that the TO-FROM indicator reads "FROM" and again fly the approximate heading shown on the course selector. If you do it this way, you will always correct back to course by turning toward the needle. It may also help you to remember that, whether flying toward or away from the VOR station, your heading and the indication on the course selector should be approximately the same—never 180° out of phase.

***The Low-Frequency Range*** Until the advent of the omnirange (VOR), the low-frequency radio range was the principal air navigation aid in the United States. Though there are no low-frequency ranges now in use in the 48 conterminous states; there are some low-frequency ranges still operating in the State of Alaska. Also many of the old four-course ranges have been converted to L/F nondirectional radio beacons (homers). Therefore, the discussion of low-frequency ranges has been left in this handbook.

The ranges were placed in use at a time when comparatively few airplanes were in operation, and four courses were ample for navigation and air traffic control. Beside the limited number of courses, low-frequency ranges have other limitations, such as poor reception because of static, and complex orientation procedures (mainly of concern to instrument pilots).

Despite these limitations, low-frequency ranges have certain advantages. They operate in the 200 to 400 kHz bank, and a low-frequency receiver is the only equipment needed to receive them. Under normal conditions, the low-frequency range is usable for distances of 50 to 100 miles, and can be received at low altitudes and on the ground.

Like omniranges (VORs), each low-frequency range station is assigned a letter-group identification. Unlike omniranges, however, this identifier may consist of a three-letter or two-letter group. This generally will depend upon whether there is an omnirange station using the same name as the low-frequency station. If an omnirange station and a low-frequency range station located in the same area have the same name, the omnirange generally will be identified by a three-letter group and the low-frequency range generally will be identified by a two-letter group. For example, the Anchorage, Alaska, omnirange is identified by ANC ( .— —. —.— ), and the low-frequency range by AC ( .— —.— ). Low-frequency range signals are interrupted every 30 seconds while the station identification signals are transmitted in code.

Figure 183 represents a typical four-course range. The signals in International Morse Code for A ( .— ) and N ( —. ) are broadcast directionally from special antennas into opposite quadrants. Unless a pilot is flying on or near one of the four courses of the range, he will receive either "dit dah" ( .— ) or "dah dit" ( —. ) signals depending on the quadrant in which the plane is located. When the pilot is flying on a range leg, the A and N signals interlock, giving a monotone or steady on-course hum, popularly known as the beam. Beams (equisignal zones) are wedge-shaped zones approximately 3° wide. On aeronautical charts, the magnetic course to the station is printed on each range leg.

Areas in each quadrant adjacent to range courses are known as bi-signal zones. Here the pilot receives the on-course hum with an A or N in the background, depending on the quadrant in which he is located. In those portions of each of the quadrants remote from the range legs, either an A or N will be received.

Pilots making VFR cross-country flights need not be proficient in complex orientation procedures on low-frequency ranges. They will, however, find these ranges most helpful when used in connection with pilotage.

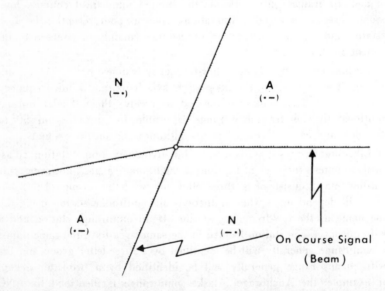

Figure 183. *Quadrants and courses of an LF/MF radio range. (Note: On sectional aeronautical charts, the "N" quadrants are outlined by lines along the range courses.)*

dead reckoning, and VOR flying, for directional guidance to determine position.

*The Automatic Direction Finder* Many personal-type airplanes are equipped with ADF (Automatic Direction Finder) radio sets which operate in the low- and medium-frequency bands. By tuning to low-frequency radio stations such as four-course ranges, nondirectional radio beacons, and commercial broadcast stations, a pilot may use ADF for navigation in cross-country flying. Frequencies of radio aids to navigation are readily obtained from aeronautical charts. Changes since the published date of the latest sectional charts appear in the *Airman's Information Manual.* The sectional chart shows standard broadcasting stations most likely to be used by pilots. Positive identification of the station to which the set is tuned is extremely important.

Probably the most common use of ADF is that of homing by "flying the needle to a station. Another useful practice is to first obtain bearings from two or more radio stations, and then plot radio lines of position on an aeronautical chart to establish position. This is known as plotting a radio fix. Since ADF does not account for wind drift and is susceptible to difficulties from thunderstorms and static, it lacks several of the advantages of VOR. When standard broadcast stations for homing are used, one of the principal disadvantages is the difficulty of positive identification. Nevertheless, pilots who do extensive cross-country flying will do well to make a thorough study of ADF and its uses.

*VFR Flight Using Radio Aids* To illustrate the use of radio aids in cross-country flying, assume that a pilot is making a flight using the Dallas-Ft. Worth Sectional Chart.

He decides to fly from Graham Airport (33° 06′ N.; 98° 33′ W.), Graham, Tex., direct to the Bridgeport VOR, and then fly direct to Majors Field (33° 04′ N.; 96° 04′ W.), Greenville, Tex. Draw these courses on the Dallas-Ft. Worth chart.

With his VOR receiver tuned to the frequency of the Bridgeport VOR (116.5 MHz), he listens carefully for code or voice identification of Bridgeport radio. Next, he turns his course selector (omnibearing selector) until the LEFT-RIGHT (vertical) needle centers at the bottom of the dial and the TO-FROM indicator indicates "TO" the VOR. The course selector should then read 070°, which means his magnetic course to the station is 070°. Keeping the needle centered by making corrections toward the needle to return to course, he flies directly to the station. While he is passing over the station, the LEFT-RIGHT needle may swing sharply back and forth (directly over the station), and the TO-FROM indicator then settles on "FROM," indicating that he is now heading away from the station.

Correction for wind drift and magnetic variation have not been mentioned. Each is automatically compensated for when the pilot makes heading corrections to keep the LEFT-RIGHT needle centered. Since all radials from a VOR are magnetic rather than true bearing, magnetic variation is corrected in the VOR itself Wind drift correction is made automatically by the pilot when he "crabs" the proper amount to keep the needle centered, which enables him to fly a straight-line course to the station.

After he has passed over the Bridgeport VOR, the pilot turns his course selector to 087°, the outbound bearing from the Bridgeport VOR to Majors Field. After making sure the TO-FROM indicator shows "FROM," he simply keeps the LEFT-RIGHT needle centered by turning toward the needle to stay on course.

Before getting out of range of the Bridgeport VOR, he obtains a fix using bearings from the Bridgeport and Greater Southwest VOR's. While tuned to Bridgeport, his LEFT-RIGHT needle is centered indicating that he is on course. Next, he tunes the VOR receiver to the Greater Southwest VOR (110.6 MHz), identifies the station, and turns the course selector until the vertical needle centers and the TO-FROM indicator reads "FROM." From the course selector, he determines that his bearing from the Greater Southwest VOR is 005°. Upon plotting this bearing, he finds that it intersects the bearing from the Bridgeport VOR (the course which he is flying) at a point between a small arm and large arm of Garza-Little Elm Reservoir. This type of fix is most accurate when the cross bearings are approximately 90° apart, as are these two. In situations where more than two VOR's are within reception distance, additional radio bearings may be taken to confirm a fix.

During the latter portion of the flight (assuming he is at a relatively low altitude), he will be out of range of the Bridgeport VOR. However, he will be able to obtain bearings from the Dallas VOR to check progress along his course. For example, suppose he plans to start his letdown over the small lake adjacent to Lake Lavon, 27 miles west of Majors Field. The bearing from Dallas VOR to this point on his course is 032°. To confirm his position, he sets his course selector at 032° with the TO-FROM indicator showing "FROM" the station. Before reaching the point for reducing power for letdown, his vertical needle is to the RIGHT.

320

While approaching this bearing (032° radial), the needle gradually moves toward the LEFT. When the needle becomes centered, he knows that the 032° radial (spoke of the wheel with an outbound magnetic direction of 032°) has been reached, and he double-checks his position by chart reading before beginning the letdown.

He notices from the chart that Majors Field lies on the 076° radial of the Dallas VOR. As an aid in letting him know when he is in the vicinity of the airport, he adjusts the course selector to 076° with the TO-FROM indicator showing "FROM" the station. The vertical needle will be to the RIGHT. When he approaches this radial, the needle gradually moves to the LEFT. When the needle becomes centered, he knows that the 076° radial has been reached and that he should be near the airport.

# 34. Emergency Radio Procedures

We would like to think that getting lost is something that always happens to "other pilots," never to us. Most of this handbook is devoted to information that should be used often and should enable a pilot to complete a flight successfully, confidently, and safely. This chapter is devoted to information to help a pilot complete a flight, but it is information which should seldom have to be used. However, it is information which no pilot should be without in case an emergency does arise and he becomes lost. The chapter explains what *you* must do if you get lost, what can be done *for you, who* can help you, and *how* they will help.

Because of inattention, poor visibility, or unusual wind conditions, a pilot may miss his check point and, as a result, become confused and reach that state of mind in which he thinks he is lost. He can follow a logical procedure to determine his position, locate satisfactory landmarks, and change his course, if necessary. *In no case should the pilot alter his course radically without first determining his position.* Circling aimlessly, doubling back on course, flying on hunches, etc., will only create confusion and make it impossible for him to follow any definite plan.

A recommended procedure is to continue on the established heading, watching prominent landmarks which can be identified on the chart. The pilot sometimes discovers that he has prematurely identified a check point, or has failed to observe one.

He should carefully check the visible landmarks available with his calculated position on the chart. The downwind side of the course should be checked first. If he fails to identify his position within 10 to 15 minutes, he should alter course slightly toward a conspicuous bracket (if available) provided he definitely knows which side of it he is on. He should then follow this bracket in the direction most likely to give him a definite fix. (A bracket is a distinct feature of the terrain which bounds the course on one side and serves as a guide line. Ideal brackets are large rivers, prominent highways, railroads, and mountain ranges. Brackets are desirable on either side of the course. One at right angles to the course at or beyond the destination also is desirable as an end bracket.)

When a landmark is finally recognized, the pilot should accept it with caution and confirm his position by identifying other landmarks before proceeding with assurance. He should then determine the reason for error, and correct his heading to prevent flying off course again.

Because a majority of small airplanes are now equipped with radios, these procedures for determining position are normally combined with the use of radio aids.

Air markers of the type shown in figure 184 often prove a boon

Figure 184. *A typical air marker.*

to pilots. In many instances, pilots who were lost, and low on gas, with radios inoperative, have located their positions from air markers, and have made emergency landings at nearby airports. Each air marker consists of the name of the town painted in large chrome-yellow letters on a dark background; an arrow shows the direction and distance to the nearest airport. These markers usually are painted on rooftops of large buildings conspicuous from the air. However, the number of markers is far too small to be relied upon for navigation.

**Methods of Declaring an Emergency** If the above procedures fail, the lost pilot must call for help and he should not wait too long. In general, private pilots have two ways of declaring an emergency: (1) by transmitting an emergency message, and (2) by flying a triangular pattern.

Ground stations (Flight Service Stations, radar stations, control towers, etc.) have three electronic means of assisting: (1) by receipt of the emergency message transmitted by the pilot; (2) by radar detection of the triangular pattern; and (3) by DF (direction finding) bearings.

**Transmitting Emergency Messages** When a pilot is in doubt about his position, or feels apprehensive for his safety, he should not hesitate to ask for help. That is his first means of declaring an emergency—*to use his radio transmitter and ask for help.* If he is in distress and needs help immediately, he may transmit the word MAYDAY several times before transmitting his message. This should get him immediate attention from all who hear. If he is only uncertain as to his position and wishes to alert ground stations, he may transmit the word PAN several times before transmitting his message. PAN indicates a lesser urgency than MAYDAY, but should get immediate attention

An emergency message may be transmitted on any frequency; however, there are frequencies especially designated for such messages. The emergency frequency most likely available on the airplane radio used by the average private pilot would be the VHF frequency of 121.5 MHz. He should be able to both transmit and receive on this frequency. This would be the best frequency to transmit and receive on during an emergency because almost all control towers, VHF direction finding (DF) stations, radar facilities, and Flight Service Stations guard this frequency. Because of the line-of-sight limitations of VHF, it may not always be possible to establish communications on the standard emergency frequency of 121.5 MHz. In such instances, pilots who find themselves in an emergency phase should use any frequency possible to obtain assistance. Regardless of which type of facility he contacts or frequency he uses, that facility can help him, even if only by alerting other facilities to his difficulty.

**Aid from Flight Service Stations** FAA Flight Service Station personnel are trained to assist pilots in establishing positions by: (a) visual reference to terrain features; (b) VHF omnirange indications (triangulation); and (c) low-frequency radio range orientation. One of these methods should help the pilot locate his position.

**Aid from Radar Stations** Any radar station in the general area of a lost airplane will attempt to locate it on the radar screen. The pilot would be requested to make a series of turns or changes of heading that would enable the radar personnel to distinguish his plane from other airplanes on their screen. Listen carefully and follow their instructions. After positive identification by the radar station, the pilot will be notified of his position. He can then be given a heading to an airport or any point in the radius of coverage of the radar station.

**Aid from DF Stations** A direction-finding station is a ground-based radio receiver capable of indicating the bearing from its antenna to a transmitting airplane. There are HF, VHF, and UHF direction-finding stations. However, only VHF stations will be discussed here since this is the type of radio transmitter most likely to be in the airplane of the average private pilot.

If a pilot is unable to establish communication with a VHF/DF facility, or if there is doubt about whether this service is available, he may ask for the service through any Flight Service Station or tower. His request will be relayed immediately to the appropriate DF facility. The pilot must remember that VHF transmissions follow line of sight; therefore, the higher his altitude, the better his chance of obtaining this service.

This example illustrates the procedure to be followed when using a direction-finding station:

(1.) Pilot calls VHF/DF station: "DALLAS HOMER, THIS IS ASTROLARK THREE NINER TWO ONE BRAVO REQUESTING *EMERGENCY* HOMING. OVER."

(2.) VHF/DF station acknowledges call up: "ASTROLARK THREE NINER TWO ONE BRAVO, THIS IS DALLAS HOMER, TRANSMIT FOR TEN SECONDS. OVER."

(3.) Pilot replies: "DALLAS HOMER, THIS IS ASTROLARK THREE NINER TWO ONE BRAVO" (pilot then holds his transmitter switch down for 10 seconds). This is followed by "ASTROLARK THREE NINER TWO ONE BRAVO. OVER."

(4.) VHF/DF station replies: "ASTROLARK THREE NINER TWO ONE BRAVO, THIS IS DALLAS HOMER, COURSE WITH ZERO WIND, ZERO THREE ZERO DEGREES. OVER."

(5.) Pilot acknewledges: "DALLAS HOMER, THIS IS ASTRO-LARK THREE NINER TWO ONE BRAVO. MY COURSE IS ZERO THREE ZERO DEGREES. OUT."

In order that a close check may be kept on the lost pilot, this procedure will be repeated as many times as necessary to bring him safely to the station.

When the pilot transmits for homing, his transmission must be long enough for the station personnel to rotate their antenna to obtain a bearing on him. The transmission must be steady for them to get a good fix.

The course given the pilot by the DF station is the magnetic course to the station. However, unless the pilot has a good knowledge of wind conditions (which is unlikely, if he is lost), he will probably use the course given to him as a heading. If there is a strong crosswind, the course the station gives him will change each time he transmits for homing.

*Emergency Lost Procedure With Radio Inoperative* What can a pilot do if he becomes lost and his radio is inoperative? His problem is how to let someone know he is lost. Perhaps only his transmitter is out and the receiver still operates. If he could only alert a radar station, personnel at this station could transmit instructions to him, even though he could not acknowledge them. We will divide the problem into two parts: (1) when only the transmitter is inoperative, and (2) when transmitter and receiver are inoperative.

With an inoperative transmitter and an operative receiver, the pilot can fly a triangular pattern to the RIGHT (fig. 185, bottom). He should hold each heading for 2 minutes and make the turns at a rate of approximately $1\frac{1}{2}°$ per second. A minimum of two such patterns should be completed before the original course is resumed. This pattern should be repeated at 20-minute intervals. While flying this pattern, the pilot should have the emergency frequency of 121.5 MHz tuned in on his radio receiver. If his pattern is observed by radar controllers, instructions will be transmitted to him by the radar personnel.

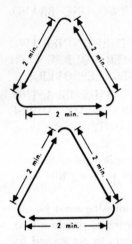

Figure 185. *If you are lost and the airplane radio is not operating properly, fly a triangular pattern. If only the transmitter is inoperative, fly the pattern to the right (bottom). If receiver and transmitter are inoperative, fly the pattern to the left (top).*

If transmitter and receiver are both inoperative, the lost pilot should fly the same triangular pattern to the LEFT (fig. 185, top). If the pattern is observed by radar personnel, an escort airplane will be dispatched, if possible. If a pilot is lost in limited visibility conditions or at night, he may turn on his landing lights and navigation lights to aid the interceptor airplane. When a rescue airplane arrives, the pilot of the lost airplane should follow him.

**The Four C's in an Emergency Situation**   In any emergency situation, you should remember the FOUR C's:

(1.)   *CONFESS* your predicament to any ground station. You should not wait too long. Give search and rescue a chance!

(2.)   *COMMUNICATE* with the ground link station and pass as much of the distress message on the first transmission as possible. They need information for best search and rescue action.

(3.)   *CLIMB* to a higher altitude, if possible, to get better radar and DF (direction finding) detection.

(4.)   *COMPLY*—especially with advice and instructions received.

To the above Four C's might be added a fifth—*CONSERVE* fuel by using an economical or maximum endurance power setting. Such a setting can be determined from the Airplane Flight Manual, but the pilot should be familiar enough with his airplane to approximate the setting.

# SECTION X—FLIGHT PLANNING

## 35. Preflight Planning

What should the private pilot do to prepare himself for a cross-country flight?

FAA regulations state, in part, that before beginning a flight, the pilot-in-command of an aircraft shall familiarize himself with all available information concerning that flight. For flights not in the vicinity of an airport, this must include information on available current weather reports and forecasts, full requirements, alternatives available if the planned flight cannot be completed, and any known traffic delays of which he has been advised by ATC.

Careful preflight planning is extremely important. With adequate planning the pilot can complete his flight with greater confidence, ease and safety. Without it he may become a statistic—figures show *inadequate preflight planning* is a significant cause of fatal accidents.

*Assembling Necessary Materials* The pilot should collect the necessary material well before the flight to be sure nothing is missing. Appropriate current sectional chart and charts of areas adjoining the flight route should be among this material if his route of flight takes him close to the border of a chart. By having this information he will be prepared to circumnavigate weather or locate his position should he become lost. To determine the charts that cover surrounding areas, check the small replica of a map of the U.S. which appears on each of the new sectional charts. This map gives the coverage of each chart and identifies them by name (see pg. 67). For example, the charts surrounding the Dallas-Ft. Worth chart are: Wichita, Kansas City, Memphis, Houston, San Antonio, and Albuquerque.

The latest *AIM* should be among the material. It is available through the Superintendent of Documents, U.S. Government Printing Office, Washington, D.C. 20402. The *Airman's Information Manual* is available on an annual subscription basis (at present $29.50).

Additional equipment should include a computer, plotter, and any other item appropriate to the particular flight—for example, if a night flight, carry a flashlight; if a flight over desert country, carry a supply of water.

*Weather Check* You may wish to check the weather before you continue with other aspects of flight planning to see, first of all, if the flight is feasible and, if it is, which route is best. You should visit the local National Weather Service airport station or the nearest FAA Flight Service Station, if available. A personal visit is best because you will have access to the latest weather maps and charts, area forecasts, terminal forecasts, SIGMETS and AIRMETS, hourly sequence reports, PIREPS, and winds-aloft forecasts, and you will have a weather briefer to interpret the weather for you.

If a visit is impractical, telephone calls are welcomed. Some National Weather Service stations have "restricted" (unlisted) telephone numbers on which *only* aviation weather information is given. These numbers, along with other National Weather Service and FSS numbers, are listed in the AIM, part 2. When telephoning for aviation weather information, identify yourself as a pilot; state your intended route, destination, intended time of takeoff, approximate time en route; and advise if you intend to fly only VFR.

Unfortunately, there are still many general aviation pilots who are inclined to scoff at or ignore aviation weather forecasts and briefings, since the weather information they received has not always proved entirely accurate. Unfortunately, weather forecasting today is not the exact science one would like it to be and there is no question that there is a requirement for greater forecasting accuracy. However, the adequacy or accuracy of the forecasts concerned in more than 1,000 cases was examined in considerable detail and it was determined that in 80% to 85% of those cases, the forecasts adequately depicted the weather conditions with which the pilots would have faced if they had in fact received those forecasts. Accordingly, it is considered that, with those odds, a pilot simply cannot afford to initiate a flight without full knowledge of the available weather data, including the forecasts. Of course, the weatherwise pilot looks upon weather briefings and forecasts as help and advice and not fixed absolutes. *It is almost as bad for a pilot to have blind faith in weather information and forecasts as it is for him to have none at all.* The pilot who understands not only the weather information as given, but appreciates its limitations as well, is the pilot who will be able to make the most effective use of all the weather service available to him. He will always be wary of the marginal weather situation.

Much of the following has been discussed previously in this Handbook in one way or another, but it bears repeating. It is presented here in step-by-step sequence and should be carefully reviewed.

Weather briefings are provided in the interest of assuring that you receive the best available weather information for effective flight planning. Adequate briefings, *properly understood and applied*, are the best bases for determining whether your flight should be executed as planned, postponed, altered, or cancelled. Safety demands your careful consideration of current and forecast weather before you depart on any flight.

## How to Get a Briefing

1. Person to person—Visit the nearest National Weather Service airport station or FAA Flight Service Station.

2. By telephone—Call the nearest National Weather Service airport station or FAA Flight Service Station, or call PATWAS (Pilot Automatic Telephone Answering Service). The telephone numbers of these facilities may be found in the Airman's Information Manual.

3. By radio—Tune to any L/MF (Low/Medium Frequency) "H" Radio Beacon for continuous transcribed weather broadcasts (TWEBS). Tune to any NAVAID with voice broadcast at 15 minutes after each hour for scheduled weather broadcasts. Call the nearest FAA Flight Service Station radio facility.

## Information for the Briefer

1. Your name, type of pilot certificate held, e.g., student, private, commercial, and whether instrument rated.

2. Type of aircraft and aircraft number.

3. Point of departure and destination.

4. Proposed route and flight altitude.

5. Estimated time of departure and arrival plus time needed to reach alternate if required.

6. Whether you wish to go IFR or VFR.

## Items the Weather Briefing Should Contain

1. Weather synopsis (positions and movement of pressure systems, fronts, precipitation areas, etc.).

2. Current weather (at point of departure, en route, including pilot reports, terminal, and alternate if weather is marginal).

3. Forecast weather (at point of departure, en route, terminal, and alternate if required).

4. Alternate routes.

5. Hazardous weather (tornadoes, tropical storms, thunderstorms, hail, turbulence, icing, duststorms, or sandstorms).

6. Forecast winds aloft.

7. A request for pilot reports (help the briefer and fellow pilots by reporting via radio immediately any adverse weather, particularly that which is significantly different from that forecast).

## Recommendations

1. If possible, obtain a complete weather briefing to determine if your flight can be conducted safely. Consider your own skill and experience and the limitations of your equipment, and we repeat, if there is *any* doubt, don't go. Once you have begun your flight, update your weather information frequently.

2. File an appropriate flight plan with FAA.

3. If you are not instrument rated, avoid "VFR On Top" and "Special VFR." Being caught above an undercast when an emergency descent is required (or at destination) is a hazardous position for the VFR pilot. Also, accepting a clearance out of certain airport control zones with no minimum ceiling and 1-mile visibility as permitted with "Special VFR" is an invitation to disaster for a VFR pilot. The weather and/or the terrain within the control zone and beyond may be totally unsuitable for visual flight.

4. Avoid flight through or near thunderstorms. Recent research has proven beyond any doubt that *all* thunderstorms are potentially dangerous and should be given a *wide* berth.

5. Avoid flight through areas of known or forecast severe weather. You may encounter tornadoes, squall lines, hail, and severe or extreme turbulence. Severe or extreme clear air turbulence may be encountered frequently at low and intermediate levels up to 20 miles ahead of squall lines. The "roll cloud" ahead of a squall line is a visible sign of violent

turbulence, but the absence of a roll cloud should not be interpreted as denoting the lack of turbulence.

6. Avoid flight through areas of known or forecast icing conditions unless your aircraft is well equipped with deicing/anti-icing devices. Ice accumulation through areas of freezing precipitation and wet snow can be rapid and heavy. In addition to airframe icing, carburetor icing can occur when visible moisture is present and when moisture is not visible under the right atmospheric conditions (i.e., low temperature, high humidity).

7. Avoid flight at low altitudes over mountainous terrain, particularly near the lee slopes. If the wind velocity near the level of the ridge is in excess of 40 knots and approximately perpendicular to the ridge, mountain wave conditions are likely over and near the lee slopes. If the wind velocity at the level of the ridge exceeds 50 knots, a strong mountain wave is probable with strong up and down drafts and severe or extreme turbulence. The worst turbulence will be encountered in and below the rotor zone which is usually 8 to 10 miles downwind from the ridge. This zone is characterized by the presence of "roll clouds" if sufficient moisture is present. Altocumulus standing lenticular clouds are also visible signs that a mountain wave exists, but their presence is likewise dependent upon moisture. The mountain wave *downdrafts may exceed the climb capability of your aircraft.*

8. Avoid areas of low ceilings and restricted visibility unless you are instrument proficient and have an instrument equipped aircraft, then proceed with caution and have planned alternates.

9. Use caution when landing on runways that are covered by water or slush which cause hydroplaning (aquaplaning), a phenomenon that renders braking and steering ineffective because of the lack of sufficient surface friction. Snow- and ice-covered runways are also hazardous.

10. Use caution when taking off or landing during gusty wind conditions.

11. Avoid taking off or landing too close behind large aircraft. "Wake turbulence" caused by these aircraft can be hazardous.

12. When you have completed your flight, visit or call the National Weather Service airport station or FAA Flight Service Station, if at all possible, and for the benefit of your fellow pilots, discuss the weather that you encountered.

***In-Flight Visibility and the VFR Pilot*** In Section II of this Handbook, basic information relative to the atmosphere and weather behavior was presented. Here in Section X, we emphasize the necessity for proper planning and use of the weather information available, based on a clear understanding of what it can and cannot do. We also outline specific hazards and how to cope with them, but in the final analysis it is the pilot's judgment that is the critical factor. Establish your own personal weather limitations based on a realistic assessment of your limitations and that of your equipment. In nearly every instance, if weather conditions are marginal, or if there is any suspicion of worsening weather, the safest rule is—do not go!

Statistics indicate that on a national basis, over 25 percent of all fatal accidents and over 31 percent of all fatalities result from taking off or continuing into adverse weather with subsequent loss of aircraft control. In other words, cold hard facts indicate that weather-involved accidents continue to account for an unnecessarily high number of fatalities for VFR pilots. A VFR pilot is one who does not have an instrument rating *or* an instrument rated pilot who is not current. It is also a fact that the average pilot who has had no training in instrument flight will lose control of his aircraft in a matter of seconds when he loses outside references.

The inescapable conclusion to the preceding is that VFR pilots must stay out of weather, and to stay out of weather, he must understand the limitations, as well as, the capabilities of present day meteorology. He must neither expect the impossible, nor neglect the attainable. Recent studies of aviation forecasts indicate the following:

1. For up to 12 hours and even beyond, a forecast of *good* weather (ceiling 3,000 ft. or more and visibility 3 miles or greater) is much more likely to be correct than is a forecast of conditions below 1,000 ft. or below 1 mile.

2. However, for 3 to 4 hours in advance, the probability that below VFR conditions will occur is more than 80 percent if *below* VFR is forecast.

3. Forecasts of single reportable values of ceiling or visibility instead of a range of values imply an accuracy that the present forecasting system does not possess beyond the first 2 or 3 hours of the forecast period.

4. Forecasts of poor flying conditions during the first few hours of the forecast period are most reliable when there is a distinct weather system, such as a front, a trough, precipitation, etc., which can be tracked

and forecast, although there is a general tendency to forecast too little bad weather in such circumstances.

5. The weather associated with *fast-moving cold fronts and squall lines* is the most difficult to forecast accurately.

6. Errors in forecasting *the time of* occurrence of bad weather are more prevalent than errors in forecasting whether it will occur or will not occur within *a span* of time.

7. Surface visibility is more difficult to forecast than ceiling height, and snow reduces the visibility forecasting problem to one of *rather wild guesswork*.

Available evidence shows that forecasters CAN predict the following at least 75 percent of the time:

1. The passage of fast-moving cold fronts or squall lines within plus or minus 2 hours, as much as 10 hours in advance.

2. The passage of warm fronts or slow-moving cold fronts within plus or minus 5 hours, up to 12 hours in advance.

3. The rapid lowering of ceiling below 1,000 ft. in prewarm front conditions within plus or minus 200 ft. and within plus or minus 4 hours.

4. The onset of a thunderstorm 1 or 2 hours in advance if radar is available.

5. The time rain or snow will begin within plus or minus 5 hours.

6. Rapid deepening of a low pressure center.

Forecasters CANNOT predict the following with an accuracy which satisfies present aviation operational requirements:

7. The time freezing rain will begin.

8. The location and occurrence of severe or extreme turbulence.

9. The location and occurrence of heavy icing.

10. The location of the occurrence of a tornado.

11. Ceilings of 100 ft. or zero before they exist.

12. The onset of a thunderstorm which has not yet formed.

13. The position of a hurricane center to nearer than 100 miles for more than 12 hours in advance.

14. The occurrence of ice/fog.

These indications of what can and cannot be predicted will vary, depending on the climatology and general weather conditions of the area. In general, rare events are more difficult to predict than common events. Weather conditions which have a pronounced daily variation, such as the occurrence of nighttime radiation fog or of afternoon convective clouds, can be forecast more reliably than conditions which have small daily variation.

Similarly, weather conditions which depend on interaction of wind flow with mountain ranges, coastal areas, or large bodies of water are more reliably forecast than similar weather conditions which are associated with cyclonic storms moving slowly over flat, uniform terrain. In either instance, however, the pilot who plans ahead and keeps informed of what the weather is doing and what it is forecast to do, even if he has to land to do so, is exercising good judgment.

The pilot who predicates his safety for several hours of flying on *one* forecast or briefing may well be gambling with his life.

***Visibility vs. Time*** In order to stay out of clouds, VFR pilots are often forced to go to low altitudes to remain VFR. Even when they are able to remain clear of the clouds, visibility, more often than not, is marginal, and it is here that visibility in a very real sense relates to time as much as to distance. That is, how many seconds ahead can a pilot see with 1 mile visibility? How many seconds does he have to perceive, interpret, act, and obtain aircraft reaction?

***How Fast Can You See*** Cruising at 95 knots, an aircraft travels 160 feet per second. If we relate this to 1 mile visibility, the pilot can see 33 seconds ahead. Matters get worse as speed increases and/or visibility decreases! The pilot can see ahead only 20 seconds if cruising at 154 knots with 1 mile visibility. You may think this is plenty of time to do things such as turning before you reach zero-zero conditions looming ahead, or to miss an obstruction, but is it?

***Reaction Time*** It takes time, very precious time under marginal conditions of visibility, for the eye to see something, for the brain to interpret what the eye sees, for the brain to send a message to your muscles to do something, for the muscles to do it, and finally for the airplane to respond to your muscles. On the average, this all takes from 4 to 5 seconds. Subtract this time from, say, 10 to 20 seconds that a pilot can see ahead, and he will not, at certain speeds and/or angles of bank, miss whatever it is he is trying to miss. At 160 knots with a reaction time of 5 seconds, he will travel 1,400 ft. before anything even begins to happen in the way of evasive action.

***Radius of Turn*** Suppose a pilot must turn away from a range of hills or a mountain, or a low-lying cloud bank. If he is flying at 154 knots, he will have moved in the direction of his obstruction approximately

3,900 ft. by the time he completes a 90° turn (1,400 ft. for reaction time, plus 2,457 ft. for radius of turn). If visibility is less than three-quarters of a mile, he will never make it—without the help of a good headwind. If he has a tailwind and only 1 mile visibility, he may never make it. Even at 95 knots he will use more than one-quarter of a mile. Obviously, the safe thing to do if caught in such restricted visibility, low-altitude conditions is to slow down. *Do not fly faster than you can see* if you have an option.

*The Cockpit Cut-Off Angle and In-Flight Visibility.* All too often, adequate visibility at the surface becomes marginal, or even below minimums at altitude, yet the VFR pilot may continue on his way simply because surface visibilities are reported at values comfortably above minimums. Some method of determining in-flight visibility with reasonable accuracy is, therefore, important. A rule of thumb (figure 186) which will not be equally accurate for all airplanes, but which is usually better than guessing is as follows:

*The approximate visibility in miles will equal the number of thousands of feet above the surface when the surface is just visible over the nose of the airplane.* In other words, at that point where the surface first appears over the nose of the airplane, your slant-range visibility

# RULE OF THUMB
## when surface is just visible over nose of aircraft the forward visibility will be approximately 1 mile for each 1000 feet altitude.

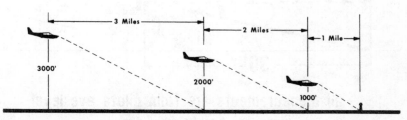

Figure 186. *Rule of thumb.*

will be approximately 2 miles if you are flying at 2,000 ft. *above the surface*. This rule of thumb is based on the cockpit cut-off angle. All airplanes do not have the same cut-off angle, therefore, the rule of thumb will not be equally accurate for all airplanes. As will be subsequently explained, the cockpit cut-off angle for any airplane can be determined rather easily. Once it is determined for a given airplane, it will remain constant as long as the eye level of the pilot is not changed. The steps in determining this cut-off angle on the ground are as follows (see figure 187):

(1.) Adjust the aircraft's ground attitude to correspond as closely as possible to its normal cruise pitch attitude.

(2.) While sitting as you normally would, adjust the pilot's seat to the same position used in flight.

(3.) Measure the vertical distance from eye level and the ground. (Six feet in the example.)

(4.) Look straight out over the nose of the airplane (cockpit cut-off angle) and determine the spot where the surface is first visible.

(5.) Measure the distance from directly under the eye position to the spot established in step 4 (30 ft. in the example).

(6.) At this point you can determine the visibility either by establishing a simple proportion, or by solving for the tangent value using the information in the following table. In either case, the result represents the least slant-range visibility you could have when flying at 1,000 ft. above the ground.

## COMPUTING CUTOFF ANGLE

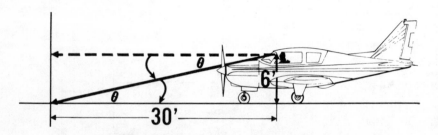

all measurements are from pilots eye level

Figure 187. *Cockpit cut-off angle.*

| Tangent Value | Angle (°) | Approximate Visibility at 1,000' AGL. |
|---|---|---|
| 0.052 | 3 | 19,000 ft. (5,280 ft. = 1 statute mile) |
| .070 | 4 | 14,280 |
| .087 | 5 | 11,500 |
| .105 | 6 | 9,530 |
| .123 | 7 | 8,130 |
| .141 | 8 | 7,090 |
| .158 | 9 | 6,330 |
| .176 | 10 | 5,750 |
| .194 | 11 | 5,150 |
| .213 | 12 | 4,710 |
| .231 | 13 | 4,320 |
| .249 | 14 | 4,010 |
| .268 | 15 | 3,730 |
| .287 | 16 | 3,480 |
| .306 | 17 | 3,270 |
| .325 | 18 | 3,070 |
| .344 | 19 | 2,910 |
| .364 | 20 | 2,750 |

NOTE: At 500 ft. above the ground, visibility in ft. would be approximately half of the 1,000 ft. value.

*Tangent Value Method:* The tangent value (tan θ) is equal to 6 ft. divided by 30 ft. or,

$$\tan \theta = \frac{6}{30}$$
$$\tan \theta = .20$$

Referring to the information in the table and locating the value closest to .2, it is apparent that the cut-off angle is somewhere between 11° and 12°. Accurate interpolation reveals that with this cut-off angle the visibility is 5,000 ft.

*Proportion Method:* Six ft. is to 30 ft. as 1,000 ft. is to "X" ft.

$$\frac{6 \text{ ft.}}{30 \text{ ft.}} = \frac{1,000 \text{ ft.}}{X \text{ ft.}} \text{ or,}$$
$$6X = 30,000 \text{ ft.}$$
$$X = 5,000 \text{ ft.}$$

One must understand that in either case the visibility thus obtained would be the very least one could have from the cockpit to the ground straight ahead. It can, of course, be more than this in respect to slant range, but if you can see the ground at this altitude, it cannot be less. Horizontally or laterally, visibility may be more or significantly less, depending on in-flight weather conditions. However, the visibility to the ground ahead (a primary VFR reference for aircraft control) would, in the example cited, be at least 5,000 ft. If the pilot must descend in order to see the ground over the nose of the airplane, his slant-range visibility is proportionally less. (See Note in table.)

***Using the Aeronautical Chart***  Draw the course to be flown on the sectional chart or charts. The course line should begin at the center of the airport of departure and end at the center of the destination airport. If the route is direct, the course line will consist of a single straight line. If the route is not direct, it will consist of two or more straight line segments—for example, you may choose a route via a VOR station which is off the direct route but which will make navigating easier.

Appropriate check points should be selected along your route and noted in some way. These should be easy-to-locate points such as large towns, large lakes and rivers, or combinations of recognizable points such as towns with an airport, towns with a network of highways and railroads entering and departing, etc. Normally choose only towns indicated by splashes of yellow on the chart. *Do not choose towns represented by a small circle*—these may turn out to be only a half-dozen houses. (In isolated areas, however, towns represented by a small circle can be prominent checkpoints.

You should check along and to either side of your route for alert, warning, restricted, prohibited and intensive student jet training areas, or Air Defense Identification Zones (ADIZ). Each area will have its restrictions printed on the chart either within the area or somewhere near the border, depending on its size. Detailed information concerning ADIZ can be found in Part 1, AIM.

Study the terrain along your route. This is necessary for several reasons. It should be checked to determine the highest and lowest elevations to be encountered so you can choose an appropriate altitude which will conform to FAA regulations. (If you are flying above 3,000 ft. above the terrain, you must conform to the cruising altitude appropriate to the direction of flight.) Check your route for particularly rugged terrain so you can avoid it. Areas where a takeoff or landing will be made should be carefully checked for tall obstructions. Television transmitting towers may extend to altitudes over 1,500 ft. above the surrounding terrain. It is essential for you to be aware of their presence and location. You must know the location of any such obstruction all along your route if the flight will be made at a low altitude.

Make a list of the navigation aids you will use along your route and the frequency on which you can receive each one. Indicate the aids that have voice facilities so you will know on which stations weather broadcasts can be received.

It is important that you utilize the chart legend to determine the meaning of chart symbols or colors that you may not be familiar with. Instructions on plotting direct courses can be found on the chart itself if you need to use both front and back sides.

## Use of the Airman's Information Manual

Make a list of the Flight Service Stations along your route and the frequencies which you can use for transmitting and receiving (in addition to the navigation aid frequencies selected from the chart). Check the correctness of navigation aid frequencies selected from the aeronautical chart. This can be done by checking the Sectional Chart Bulletin, NOTAMS, and the appropriate navigational aid information in Part 3, AIM.

Study available information about each airport at which you intend to land. This should include a study of the following sections: NOTAMS; Airport Directory if the airport has no control tower; and Airport/Facility Directory if the airport has a control tower. Most of the information will be found in the Airport and Airport/Facility Directories. This includes location, elevation, runway and lighting facilities, available services, availability of UNICOM, types of fuel available (use to decide on refueling stops), FSS located on the airport, control tower and ground control frequencies, traffic information, remarks and other pertinent information. The NOTAMS section, issued every 14 days, should be checked for additional information on hazardous conditions or changes that have been made since issuance of the Airport and Airport/Facility Directory sections. Remember that the information in the Airport Directory section may be up to 6 months old and that in the Airport/Facility Directory should be no more than 28 days old.

The Sectional Chart Bulletin subsection should be checked for major changes that have occurred since the last publication date of each sectional chart you plan to use. Remember, your chart may be up to 6 months old.

The published date of the chart appears at the top of the legend side of the chart.

The *Airman's Information Manual* will generally have the latest information pertaining to such matters and should be used in preference to the information on the back of the chart, if there are differences.

*Airplane Flight Manual Data*   Check your Airplane Flight Manual to determine the proper loading of your airplane (weight and balance data). You must know the weight of the usable fuel and drainable oil aboard. the weight of the passengers, the weight of all baggage to be carried, and the empty weight of the airplane to be sure your total weight does not exceed the maximum allowable. You will also have to know the distribution of the load to tell if the resulting center of gravity is within limits. Be sure to use the latest weight and balance information in the FAA-approved Airplane Flight Manual or other permanent aircraft records, as appropriate, to obtain empty weight and empty weight center of gravity information.

Determine the takeoff and landing distances from the appropriate charts, based on the calculated load, elevation of the airport, and temperature; then compare these distances with the amount of runway available. Remember, the heavier the load and the higher the elevation, temperature, or humidity, the longer your takeoff roll and landing roll and the lower your rate of climb will be. (See Exam-O-Gram No. 33, appendix I.)

Check the fuel consumption charts to determine the rate of fuel consumption at your estimated flight altitude and power settings. Calculate your rate of fuel consumption, then compare it with the estimated time for your flight so you can decide upon refueling points along your route.

*Using the Plotter, Computer, etc.*   When you draw your course line on the aeronautical chart, use a protractor (or plotter) to determine your true course. Then determine the magnetic variation from the mid-isogonic line, apply it to your measured true course and obtain your magnetic course. When flying at or above 3,000 ft. above the surface, you must know the magnetic course to decide whether to fly at an even-thousand-plus-five-hundred-feet level or an odd-thousand-plus-five-hundred-feet level. Then measure the length of your course line, *using the distance scale at the bottom of the chart* and NOT the scale on the plotter.

If after a thorough weather check you decide that the flight can be made safely, you should obtain the winds-aloft forecast and choose an altitude, with as favorable winds as possible, that will conform to FAA regulations. Of course, you may wish to sacrifice favorable winds at times in order to fly at an altitude where there is no turbulence. After determining your altitude and the forecast winds at that altitude, use this information and your estimated true airspeed, and measured true course, to compute (on your computer) the true heading and groundspeed. From the computed true heading, determine your compass heading by applying variation (already obtained from the mid-isogonic line on the chart) and deviation (obtained from the compass correction card). From your computed groundspeed and measured course distance, determine the total flight time. Then use the computed total time and your estimated fuel consumption rate to determine the amount of fuel you will consume during the flight.

After making the necessary computations, you are ready to file your flight plan.

*VFR Flight Plan*   An examination of en route accidents shows a striking relationship between the number of accidents by aircraft not on flight plans and those on flight plans. Filing a flight plan is not required by FAA regulations; however, it is good operating practice, since the information contained in the flight plan will be used in search and rescue operations in event of emergency.

Though flight plans can be filed in the air by radio, it is usually best to file a flight plan with the nearest FSS in person or by phone just before departing. After takeoff, contact the FSS by radio and give them your takeoff time so they can activate your flight plan. To avoid congestion of already busy communication channels, use radio for filing flight plans *only* when it is impossible to file any other way.

When a VFR flight plan is filed, it will be held by the FSS until 1 hour after the proposed departure time and then canceled unless:

(1)   The actual departure time is received; or

(2)   A revised proposed departure time is received; or

(3)   At the time of filing, the FSS is informed that the proposed departure time will be met, but actual time cannot be given because of inadequate communication.

The FSS specialist who accepts your flight plan will not inform you of this procedure, however.

Remember, there is every advantage in filing a flight plan; the one thing you must not forget is to *close your flight plan upon arrival.* Do this by telephone with the nearest FSS, if possible, to avoid radio congestion. If there is no FSS near your point of landing, you may close it by radio with the nearest FSS on arriving over your destination.

Figures 188 and 189 show the flight plan form a pilot files with the Flight Service Station. When you file a flight plan by telephone or radio, give the information in the order of the numbered spaces. This enables the FSS specialist to copy the information more efficiently. Most of the spaces are either self-explanatory or nonapplicable to the VFR flight plan (such as item 13). However, some spaces may need explanation.

Item 4 asks for the estimated true airspeed in knots. If you are able to convert your airspeed from miles per hour to knots, there is no problem. If you are not able, then report your airspeed in miles per hour.

Item 6 asks for your proposed departure time in Greenwich Mean Time (indicated by the "Z"). If you are unable to convert local standard time to Greenwich Time, give the time as local standard and the FSS will convert it to Greenwich. To convert local standard time to Greenwich Mean Time, add 5 hours to Eastern Standard Time (EST); add 6 hours to Central Standard Time (CST); add 7 hours to Mountain Standard Time (MST); and add 8 hours to Pacific Standard Time (PST). To convert local daylight time to Greenwich Mean Time, add 4 hours to

FEDERAL AVIATION AGENCY

**FLIGHT PLAN**

*Form Approved.*
*Budget Bureau No. 04-R072.3*

| | | | | |
|---|---|---|---|---|
| 1. TYPE OF FLIGHT PLAN: FVFR / VFR / IFR / DVFR | 2. AIRCRAFT IDENTIFICATION | | | |
| 3. AIRCRAFT TYPE/SPECIAL EQUIPMENT 1/ | 4. TRUE AIRSPEED (KNOTS) | 5. POINT OF DEPARTURE | 6. DEPARTURE TIME: PROPOSED (Z) / ACTUAL (Z) | 7. INITIAL CRUISING ALTITUDE |
| 8. ROUTE OF FLIGHT | | | | |
| 9. DESTINATION (Name of airport and city) | 10. REMARKS | | | |
| 11. ESTIMATED TIME EN ROUTE: HOURS / MINUTES | 12. FUEL ON BOARD: HOURS / MINUTES | 13. ALTERNATE AIRPORT(S) | 14. PILOT'S NAME | |
| 15. PILOT'S ADDRESS AND TELEPHONE NO. OR AIRCRAFT HOME BASE | 16. NO. OF PERSONS ABOARD | 17. COLOR OF AIRCRAFT | 18. FLIGHT WATCH STATIONS | |

CLOSE FLIGHT PLAN UPON ARRIVAL

1/ SPECIAL EQUIPMENT SUFFIX
A—DME & 4096 Code transponder
B—DME & 64 Code transponder
D—DME
L—DME & transponder—no code
T—64 Code transponder
U—4096 Code transponder
X—Transponder—no code

0052-027-8000

FAA Form 7233—1 (4-66) FORMERLY FAA 398

Figure 188. *Flight plan form.*

| SCALE 1:1,000,000 | WORLD AERONAUTICAL CHARTS | Nautical Miles | Statute Miles |

**PILOT'S PREFLIGHT CHECK LIST** — DATE

| WEATHER ADVISORIES | ALTERNATE WEATHER | NOTAMS |
| EN ROUTE WEATHER | FORECASTS | AIRSPACE RESTRICTIONS |
| DESTINATION WEATHER | WINDS ALOFT | MAPS |

**FLIGHT LOG**

| DEPARTURE POINT | VOR | RADIAL | DISTANCE | | TIME | | |
|---|---|---|---|---|---|---|---|
| | IDENT. | TO | LEG | | PT-TO-PT CUMULATIVE | TAKEOFF | GROUND SPEED |
| | FREQ. | FROM | REMAINING | | | | |
| CHECK POINT | | | | | | ETA | |
| | | | | | | ATA | |
| | | | | | | | |
| | | | | | | | |
| | | | | | | | |
| | | | | | | | |
| | | | | | | | |
| | | | | | | | |
| | | | | | | | |
| | | | | | | | |
| DESTINATION | | | | | | | |
| | | | TOTAL | | | | |

POSITION REPORT: FVFR report hourly, IFR as required by ATC

| ACFT. IDENT. | POSITION | TIME | ALT. | IFR/VFR | EST. NEXT FIX | NAME OF SUCCEEDING FIX | PIREPS |

REPORT CONDITIONS ALOFT—
CLOUD TOPS, BASES, LAYERS, VISIBILITY, TURBULENCE, HAZE, ICE, THUNDERSTORMS

SCALE 1:500,000 — SECTIONAL AERONAUTICAL CHARTS — Nautical Miles — Statute Miles

**CLOSE FLIGHT PLAN UPON ARRIVAL**

Figure 189. *Back of flight plan form.*

Eastern Daylight Time (EDT); add 5 hours to Central Daylight Time (CDT); add 6 hours to Mountain Daylight Time (MDT); and add 7 hours to Pacific Daylight Time (PDT).

Item 7 asks for the initial cruising altitude. Normally you can enter "VFR" in this block, since you will choose your own cruising altitude to conform to FAA regulations (on IFR flights, air traffic control designates the cruising altitude).

Item 8 asks for the route of flight. If the flight is to be direct, enter the word "direct"; if not, enter the actual route to be followed such as via certain towns or navigation aids.

Item 12 asks for the fuel on board in hours and minutes. This is determined by dividing the total usable fuel aboard in gallons by your estimated rate of fuel consumption in gallons.

Item 18 can be ignored since Flight Following Service is no longer available.

Figure 189 shows the reverse side of the flight plan. This is used as a check list for—and a place to enter—the information pertinent to your flight. It also contains a measuring scale for both Sectional Aeronautical Charts and World Aeronautical Charts.

Even if you decide not to file a flight plan, make regular position reports to Flight Service Stations to receive altimeter setting, SIGMETS, and advisories to small aircraft. This will also enable search and rescue action to be focused in the proper area in case of an emergency. Remember, the Flight Service Stations are anxious to help you in every way possible. It is only sensible to take advantage of their services.

# APPENDIX I—
# SELECTED EXAM-O-GRAMS

## VFR Exam-O-Gram No. 9
## Altimetry

Your altimeter is a vitally important instrument. You will agree that flight without this instrument would indeed be a haphazard undertaking —yet, HOW WELL DO YOU KNOW YOUR ALTIMETER? Take this short quiz on altimetry; grade yourself by checking the answers and explanations that follow.

1. Check your ability to quickly interpret your altitude by jotting down the readings of the six altimeters pictured. *Allow yourself 1 minute.*

2. FAR requires that you maintain your cruising altitudes (VFR as well as IFR) by reference to your altimeter. What do regulations require concerning the setting (or adjustment) of your altimeter?

3. If you are flying in very cold air (colder than standard temperatures), you should expect your altimeter to read
   (a) *higher* than your actual altitude above sea level.
   (b) *lower* than your actual altitude above sea level.
   (c) *the same* as your actual altitude above sea level.

4. Here are four altitudes with which you should be familiar. Briefly give the meaning of each.
   (1) *Indicated altitude.*
   (2) *Pressure altitude.*
   (3) *Density altitude.*
   (4) *True altitude.*

5. *Assume* that your proposed route crosses mountains with peaks extending to 10,900 feet above sea level. Prior to crossing this range, you adjust the altimeter setting window of your altimeter to the *current altimeter setting* reported by a Flight Service Station located in a valley near the base of this mountain range. If you maintain an indicated altitude of 11,500 feet by your altimeter, *can you be assured of at least 500 feet vertical clearance of these mountain peaks?*

## Answers to Questions on Altimetry

1. (1) 7,500 ft., (2) 7,880 ft., (3) 1,380 ft., (4) 8,800 ft., (5) 12,420 ft., (6) 880 ft.

   If your altimeter is the three-pointer-type sensitive altimeter such as those pictured, an orderly approach to reading your altitude is to first glance at the smallest hand (10,000-ft. hand); next read the middle hand (1,000-ft. hand); and last, read the large hand (100-ft. hand). For the two-pointer altimeter, simply read the small hand first and the large hand next.

2. Your altimeter should be set to the *current reported altimeter setting* of a station along the route of flight (Flight Service Stations, Control Towers, etc.). If your aircraft is not equipped with a radio, you should obtain an altimeter setting prior to departure if one is available, or *you should adjust your altimeter to the elevation of the airport of departure.*

3. If you are flying in cold air, you should expect your altimeter to indicate HIGHER than you actually are. There is an old saying —one well worth remembering—that goes something like this: "WHEN FLYING FROM A HIGH TO A LOW OR HOT TO COLD, *LOOK OUT BELOW!*" In other words, if you are flying from a high pressure area to a low pressure area or into colder air, you had better be careful because you probably aren't as high as you think—assuming, of course, that no compensations are made for these atmospheric conditions.

4. (1) *Indicated altitude*—That altitude read directly from the altimeter (uncorrected).

   (2) *Pressure altitude*—The altitude read from the altimeter when the altimeter setting window is adjusted to 29.92. (This al-

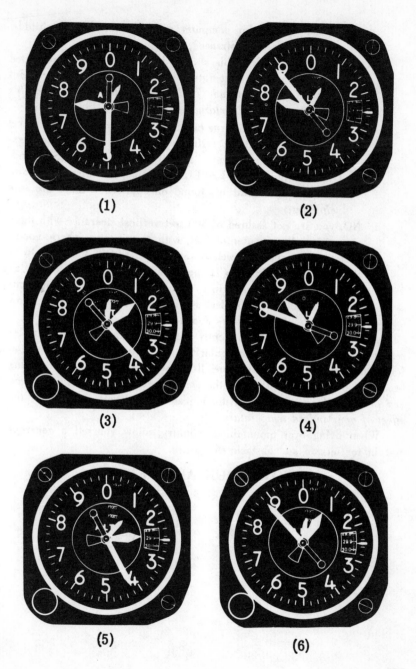

(1)  (2)

(3)  (4)

(5)  (6)

titude is used for computer solutions for density altitude, true altitude, true airspeed, etc.).

(3) *Density altitude*—This altitude is pressure altitude corrected for nonstandard temperature variations. (It is an important altitude as *this altitude is directly related to the aircraft's takeoff and climb performance.*)

(4) *True altitude*—The true height of the aircraft above sea level —the actual altitude. (Often you will see a true altitude expressed in this manner: "10,900 ft. MSL"—the MSL standing for MEAN SEA LEVEL. Remember that airport, terrain, and obstacle elevations found on charts and maps are *true altitudes.*)

5. NO, you are not assured of 500 feet vertical clearance with these mountains. As a matter of fact, with certain atmospheric conditions, you might very well be 500 feet *BELOW* the peaks with this indicated altitude. (To begin with, 500 feet is hardly an adequate separation margin to allow on flights over mountainous terrain—1,500 to 2,000 feet is recommended in order to allow for possible altitude errors and downdrafts.)

A majority of pilots confidently expect that the current altimeter setting will compensate for irregularities in atmospheric pressure. Unfortunately, this is not always true. Remember that the altimeter setting broadcast by ground stations is the *station pressure corrected to Mean Sea Level.* It does not reflect distortion at higher levels, *particularly the effect of nonstandard temperature.*

When flying over mountainous country, allow yourself a generous margin for terrain and obstacle clearances.

## KNOW YOUR ALTIMETER

# VFR Exam-O-Gram No. 13

# Weight and Balance

Loading the family automobile for a trip requires little serious planning. You can C-R-A-M as much luggage into the trunk as you have space, squeeze as many persons into the seats as you have room, and top off the gas tank with no thought given to Gross Weight or Center of Gravity. A similar approach to loading your "flying machine" could result in a serious accident.

WHAT IS EXCESSIVE WEIGHT? Assume that your airplane is a 4-place airplane with a baggage allowance of 120 pounds, a usable fuel capacity of 39 gallons, and an oil supply of 8 quarts. On a hypothetical flight you take on full fuel and oil servicing, toss the suitcases in the baggage compartment, and you and your three passengers eagerly climb aboard. This seems like a reasonable load, but if you had placed each of them on the scales you might have found that you and the passengers average 180 lbs. each (720 lbs.), and the four suitcases, 30 lbs. each (120 lbs.). The usable fuel load weighs 234 lbs. and the oil 15 lbs. Assume, also, that the Weight and Balance Data for the airplane shows an *empty weight* of 1,325 lbs. and a maximum allowable *gross weight* of 2,200 lbs. NOW, add the weight of the useful load to the empty weight and compare the total to the allowable gross weight. (1,089 lbs. + 1,325 lbs. = 2,414 lbs.) . . . *214 lbs. excess!*

WHAT RESTRICTIONS ARE THERE ON WEIGHT AND BALANCE? In many civilian airplanes it is not possible to fill all seats, baggage compartment, and tanks, and still remain within the approved weight and balance limits. If you do not wish to leave a passenger behind (a normal reaction) you must reduce your fuel load and plan on shorter legs en route or cut down on the baggage carried, or both. Frequently, restrictions are placed on rear seat occupancy with maximum baggage allowance aboard. By all means follow *your* airplane's Weight and Balance restrictions. The loading conditions and the empty weight of your particular airplane may differ from those shown in the Owner's Manual, especially if modifications have been made or equipment has been added to the original basic airplane.

### IS CRUISE PERFORMANCE AFFECTED BY AN EXCESS LOAD?

At normal weight, the airplane requires a certain angle of attack to maintain straight-and-level flight at a given airspeed. To sustain a heavier load at that same airspeed, the angle of attack must be greater to provide the increased lift that is necessary. More power must be added to overcome the increased drag which results from the increased angle of attack. Additional power, in turn, burns more fuel, thereby reducing the range of the aircraft.

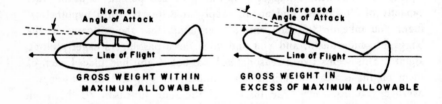

### IS CLIMB PERFORMANCE AFFECTED BY AN EXCESS LOAD?

Time to climb to a given altitude is lengthened, because the angle of attack is greater and the extra thrust required to carry the additional weight limits the rate of climb and may limit the climbing speed, since this depends on the surplus power available. The additional time in climbing at the higher power setting also increases the fuel consumption.

IS "G" FORCE TOLERANCE AFFECTED? Assume that your airplane has a limit-load factor of 3.8 "G's". If the allowable gross weight is not exceeded, this means the wings can safely support 3.8 times the weight of the airplane and its contents. In accelerated flight (pull-ups, turns, turbulent air) the actual load on the wings would be much greater than the normal load, which of course results in much greater stresses in the wing structure. Overloading, therefore, has the effect of decreasing the

"G" load capability of the aircraft and thus could result in the wing being stressed to the point of popped rivets, permanent distortion, or structural failure.

HOW IS AN AIRPLANE BALANCED? An airplane, like a steelyard scale, is in perfect balance when the weight is distributed in such a manner that it remains level when freely suspended. In an airplane, however, as long as the center of gravity lies anywhere *within specified limits*, balance can be maintained in flight. Flight with the c.g. outside of this range results in unsatisfactory or *dangerous flight characteristics*. Loading an airplane then, is simply a matter of distributing the load so that the c.g. falls within the allowable range. This can be accomplished by arranging the load in accordance with the center of gravity envelope provided for each airplane.

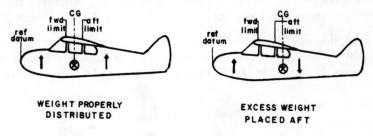

WEIGHT PROPERLY
DISTRIBUTED

EXCESS WEIGHT
PLACED AFT

DOES IMPROPER LOAD DISTRIBUTION AFFECT SAFETY? YES! When loading conditions cause the center of gravity to fall outside allowable limits, stability is adversely affected and erratic control forces may develop. Stalling speed, takeoff distance, and landing speed may be increased to the point of *actual danger*.

Due to the size of many baggage compartments there might be a tendency to fill them to capacity, ignoring the placarded baggage weight limitations. This could produce a center of gravity aft of allowable limits creating a highly dangerous flight condition. The result would be a nose-high altitude which could lead to a stall from which recovery might not be effected due to inadequate elevator control.

## AN AIRPLANE'S BEHAVIOR IN THE AIR
## IS DEPENDENT ON WEIGHT AND BALANCE!

# VFR Pilot Exam-O-Gram No. 22

## Potential Midair Collisions

Analyses of answers to Pilot and Ground Instructor Written Examinations indicate that many applicants do not fully understand several areas in the Regulations and procedures that were devised as safety measures for VFR flying. Two of the areas will be covered in this Exam-O-Gram that seem to give applicants the most difficulty. They concern the Hemispherical Rule for VFR cruising altitudes and Airport Advisory Service at uncontrolled airports.

A pilot who does not keep abreast of and comply with the latest Regulations and procedures could be a source of danger to himself and to others in his vicinity. A Federal Aviation Administration report

*Failure to comply with Regulations and procedures increases the degree of potential mid-air collision hazards!*

indicated that 549 "near mid-air" collisions were *reported* within the United States during calendar year 1962. This compared with 516 reports for 1961 and 470 reports during 1960. It would be reasonable to assume that other "near mid-air" collisions occurred that were not reported.

Could any pilot with considerable flying experience truthfully say that he has never been involved in a "near miss" with other aircraft — or — that he is not seriously concerned about mid-air collisions? It is often so easy to fly for a long period of time with our head in the cockpit while we study charts or change radio frequencies. Finally, something tells us that we should start looking around, and then we suddenly realize how foolish we were to expose ourselves to the potential hazards of a mid-air collision while we were preoccupied.

Most pilots know very well the danger of not properly guarding the airplane from other aircraft while their attention is divided between things inside and outside the cockpit—yet is there a pilot flying today who will not some day break this rule of common sense?

## TO AVOID OR REDUCE THE HAZARD OF TOO MUCH "EYES-INSIDE-THE-COCKPIT" FLYING, WHAT ACTION SHOULD A PILOT TAKE IN VFR CROSS-COUNTRY PREFLIGHT PLANNING?

(a) He should obtain from proper charts all the information pertinent to his route of flight. Information such as: headings, distances, checkpoints, altitudes, etc., should be placed in a flight log format. On the reverse side of the FLIGHT PLAN (FAA Form 7233-1) a flight log is provided for pilots.

(b) All necessary charts should be folded in proper sequence and conveniently located in the cockpit.

(c) The current issue of Airman's Information Manual (AIM) should be referred to with particular attention to NOTAMS and Airport/Facility Directory sections. All radio frequencies to be used on the flight should be written on the flight log for ready reference during the flight.

(d) The AIM Airport Directory or Airport/Facility Directory sections should be consulted to obtain airport data and to review VFR procedures for approaches to busy air terminals. For example: The Airport/Facility Directory section for Nashville Metropolitan Airport states: "Traffic Information—Contact Approach Control on 120.6 . . 25 miles out."

(e) The Airman's Information Manual should be reviewed for additional information under such headings as: Good Operating Practices, Air Navigation Radio Aids, Airport-Air Navigation Lighting and Marking Aids, Weather, Preflight, Departure, Radar Assistance to VFR Aircraft, VFR Cruising Altitudes, Arrival, and Emergency Procedures.

(f) A careful study of the Sectional or World Aeronautical Charts should be made to determine if your route of flight will traverse a Prohibited, Restricted, Alert, or Warning Area.

HOW DOES THE TOWER ASSIST IN PREVENTING MID-AIR COLLISIONS AT A CONTROLLED AIRPORT? Although it is always the direct responsibility of the pilot, when flying in VFR weather conditions, to avoid collision with other aircraft, the information and clearances issued by the controller in the tower are intended to aid pilots to the fullest extent in avoiding collisions. The controller in the tower issues clearances that can be safely followed without collision hazard if reasonable caution is exercised by the pilot. By advising the tower of your position well in advance of entering the control zone (normally a minimum of 15 miles out), you will be able to receive information on other aircraft which might be in your vicinity as well as being assured of a safe and orderly entry into the traffic pattern under the direction of the control tower.

> Note to Student Pilots: To receive additional assistance while operating in areas of concentrated air traffic, a student pilot should identify himself as a student pilot during his initial call to an FAA radio facility (Control Tower, FSS, Approach Control, etc.). For example: "Dayton Tower, this is Fleetwing 1234, Student Pilot, over."

At busy airports an expansion of the normal tower service is made possible through the use of ATIS and/or radar. The availability of these services can be determined by checking the airport/facility directory in Part 3, AIM. By using the frequencies thus obtained, the pilot can receive directions and information much sooner than might be available through tower communications only. Thus the potential for mid-air collision is reduced.

WHY SHOULD A PILOT CHECK THE *SPECIAL NOTICES – AREA* SECTION OF THE AIRMAN'S INFORMATION MANUAL? Before departing on an extensive cross-country flight in unfamiliar country, the pilot should check the *Special Notices – Area* section for such notices as "Terminal Radar Service Areas" and "Terminal Area Notices." For example: Special Air Traffic Rules apply to VFR flights in the Valparaiso, Florida, terminal area because of the high speed special activities conducted in the vicinity of Eglin AFB.

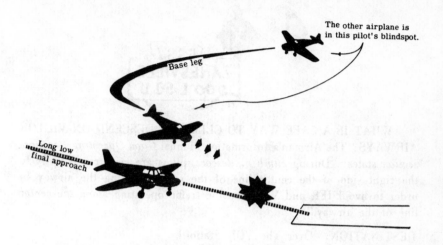

The other airplane is in this pilot's blindspot.

Base leg

Long low final approach

The collision that is about to happen as illustrated can happen at *any* airport. *A number of such accidents have already occurred – LOOK AROUND – DO NOT LET IT HAPPEN TO YOU.*

IS TRAFFIC INFORMATION AVAILABLE AT CERTAIN NON-CONTROLLED AIRPORTS? Yes, at certain noncontrolled airports (no control tower) where FAA Flight Service Stations are operating, there is available to you an *Airport Advisory Service.* Use of this radio service will aid you in avoiding mid-air collisions.

WHAT SERVICE DOES THE AIRPORT ADVISORY SERVICE PROVIDE? The Flight Service Station (FSS) at uncontrolled airports provides airport advisory service to aircraft operating to or from the airport on which the station is located. The airport advisory service provides the following information to aircraft which are in communication with the station: Wind Direction and Velocity; Favored Runway; Altimeter Setting; *Pertinent Known Traffic;* Pertinent Known Field Conditions; Airport Taxi Routes and *Traffic Patterns,* etc.

NOTICE! There may be other aircraft in the vicinity of the airport not in communication with and thus not known by the FSS.

HOW DOES THE PILOT KNOW WHERE TO FIND AIRPORT ADVISORY SERVICE LOCATIONS? The locations are appropriately depicted on the Sectional Charts in this manner:

WHAT IS A SAFE WAY TO CLIMB OR DESCEND ON VICTOR AIRWAYS? The Airman's Information Manual *Good Operating Practices section* states: "During *climb* or *descent*, pilots are encouraged to fly to the right side of the center line of the radial forming the airway in order to avoid IFR and VFR cruising traffic operating along the center line of the airway."

DESTINATION:  Over The VOR Station!

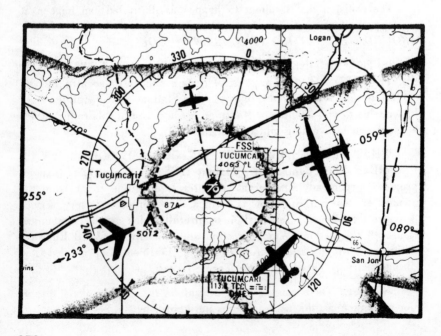

The FAA Near Mid-Air Collision Report for Calendar Year 1962 indicates that 446 (81.24%) of the incidents occurred in clear skies and unrestricted visibility conditions. Of the 549 incidents reported *256 (46.6%) occurred over a VOR facility*, and the aircraft were utilizing VOR as the navigational aid in 89% of the en route incidents. *BE ALERT AT ALL TIMES*: Unlimited visibility appears to encourage a sense of security which is not at all justified.

DOES THE HEMISPHERICAL RULE OF CRUISING ALTITUDES PLAY AN IMPORTANT ROLE IN THE AVOIDANCE OF MID-AIR COLLISIONS? Yes, the rule is specifically designed to provide altitude separation, and applies to *local* as well as *cross-country flights*.

Many Airman Written Examination applicants are incorrectly answering questions pertaining to the Hemispherical Rule for VFR cruising altitudes. When an aircraft is operated in VFR level cruising

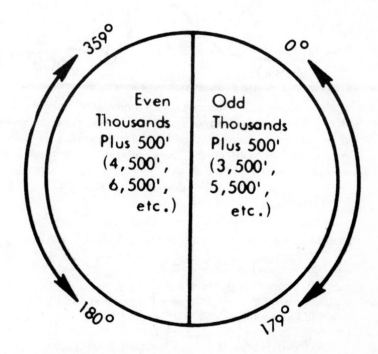

WHEN 3,000' ABOVE THE SURFACE

flight above *3,000 feet above* the surface and below 29,000 feet, the cruising altitudes (shown in the illustration) shall be observed in accordance with the magnetic course being flown. (NOTE: See Airman's Information Manual.)

DO THE VFR CRUISING ALTITUDES APPLY BELOW 3,000 FEET? No, only when you are flying above *3,000 feet* above the surface.

Assume that in the diagram below your flight traverses terrain with the approximate elevations as depicted. You desire to select a *constant*

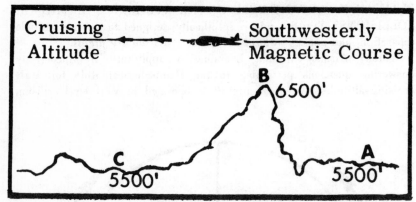

cruising altitude which will conform to VFR cruising altitude requirements and also have sufficient altitude above mountain peaks to avoid downdrafts or extreme turbulence. Altitudes above the surface in mountainous areas should be based on the lowest general terrain (excluding deep crevices or canyons).

|  |  |  |
|---|---|---|
|  | 5,500′ general terrain elev. |  |
| For example: + | 3,000′ above terrain. |  |
|  | 8,500′ effective altitude. |  |

10,500′ correct (even +500′) at points A, B, C.

10,000′ incorrect at points A, B, C.
9,500′ incorrect at points A, B, C.
9,000′ correct at point B; incorrect at points A, C.
8,500′ correct (even +500′) at points A, B, C.

8,000′ correct at A, B, C. ⎫
7,500′ correct at A, B, C. ⎬ less than 3,000′ above surface *but* inadequate
7,000′ correct at A, B, C. ⎭ safety above peaks.

# VFR Exam-O-Gram No. 33
## Use of Performance Charts

A report of an accident was stated in the following words: "Takeoff was attempted on a 1,600-foot strip; the airplane cleared the fences but sank back and struck a ditch." The pilot stated that he failed to consider the effects of the grassy, rough field, the 90° F. temperature, heavy load of fuel and passengers, and the calm wind. COULD THE USE OF THE TAKE-OFF PERFORMANCE CHART FOR HIS AIRCRAFT HAVE PRE-DICTED THE SAD ENDING TO THIS FLIGHT?

WHAT ARE PERFORMANCE CHARTS? They are charts that de-scribe or predict the performance of an aircraft under a given set of conditions or ground rules. They may be in tabular or graph form. *(Because of their importance to safety, all applicants are being tested, and will continue to be tested, on use of performance charts in the written examinations.)*

WHERE DO YOU FIND PERFORMANCE CHARTS? You can find them in the FAA-approved Airplane Flight Manual and the Owner's Manual or Handbook prepared by the manufacturer. In many cases, the FAA-approved Flight Manual must be carried in the aircraft at all times.

ARE THE CONDITIONS OR GROUND RULES UNDER WHICH YOU USE A PARTICULAR TYPE PERFORMANCE CHART ALWAYS THE SAME? No. The particular set of conditions or ground rules, as well as format, will vary with the manufacturer. Although ground rules for their use may be different, the information obtainable is essentially the same—takeoff and landing distance (ground run or roll and to clear a 50-foot obstacle), fuel consumption, rate of climb, true airspeed, etc.

HOW ACCURATE SHOULD YOU CONSIDER THE PREDIC-TIONS OF PERFORMANCE CHARTS? You will be headed in the safe direction if you always consider the performance of the airplane you fly to be less than predicted by the performance charts. The following state-ment is contained in one airplane flight manual: "Flight tests from which the performance data was obtained were flown with a new, clean airplane, correctly rigged and loaded, and with an engine capable of delivering its full rated power." You can expect to do as well only if your airplane, too, is kept in the peak of condition.

IS IT NECESSARY THAT YOU ALWAYS CONSULT PERFORMANCE CHARTS PRIOR TO TAKEOFF OR LANDING? No. Obviously, if you are taking off or landing on a 10,000-foot runway in a light airplane, you need not check the takeoff or landing data charts. But where is the dividing line—6,000? 4,000? 2,000? This depends on a lot of factors which include the equipment you are flying; pilot skill, proficiency, and familiarity with equipment; and the relative values of the three major factors affecting aircraft performance (density altitude, gross weight, and wind) plus the type and condition of the runway.

WHEN SHOULD YOU CHECK YOUR PERFORMANCE CHARTS? Any time there is doubt in your own mind, whether it be due to the length and/or condition of the runway, the high-density altitude, a recognition of your own limitations, or a lack of familiarity with the equipment you are flying—which will be alleviated through the use of performance charts. You should begin an operation with complete confidence in its success. Use everything at your disposal to establish this confidence. Charts do not cover all conditions that might have an effect on performance; but by making adequate allowances to the information obtained, you can ensure a greater margin of safety.

WHAT CAN YOU OBTAIN FROM TAKEOFF PERFORMANCE CHARTS? You can find the predicted length of the takeoff ground run and/or the predicted distance necessary to clear a 50-foot obstacle (which includes the ground roll). For example:

OBSTACLE TAKE-OFF DATA · 15° FLAPS

| Wind Vel. mph | Sea Level | | | 2000 Ft. | | | 4000 Ft. | | | 6000 Ft. | | | 8000 Ft. | | |
|---|---|---|---|---|---|---|---|---|---|---|---|---|---|---|---|
| | Temp. F | Ground Run Ft. | To Clear 50' Obst. Ft. | Temp. F | Ground Run Ft. | To Clear 50' Obst. Ft. | Temp. F | Ground Run Ft. | To Clear 50' Obst. Ft. | Temp. F | Ground Run Ft. | To Clear 50' Obst. Ft. | Temp. F | Ground Run Ft. | To Clear 50' Obst. Ft. |
| 0 | 30 | 785 | 1175 | 20 | 900 | 1310 | 15 | 1060 | 1580 | 10 | 1260 | 1895 | 0 | 1175 | 2305 |
| | 59 | 890 | 1320 | 52 | 1035 | 1535 | 15 | 1215 | 1810 | 38 | 1130 | 2170 | 30 | 1695 | 2735 |
| | 90 | 1005 | 1490 | 80 | 1160 | 1720 | 75 | 1380 | 2065 | 70 | 1610 | 2560 | 60 | 1890 | 3275 |
| 10 | 30 | 620 | 955 | 20 | 715 | 1095 | 15 | 850 | 1300 | 10 | 1015 | 1570 | 0 | 1195 | 1920 |
| | 59 | 705 | 1080 | 52 | 830 | 1260 | 15 | 975 | 1495 | 38 | 1160 | 1810 | 30 | 1380 | 2290 |
| | 90 | 805 | 1220 | 80 | 935 | 1125 | 75 | 1110 | 1715 | 70 | 1335 | 2135 | 60 | 1575 | 2780 |

**CHART 1**    NOTE: Decrease distance approximately 15% for 100 pounds decrease in gross weight.

Chart 1: At an elevation of 4,000 feet, zero wind, 75° F., 15° of flaps, and maximum gross weight (2,300 lbs. for this airplane) the predicted ground run is 1,380 feet and the predicted distance necessary to clear a 50-foot obstacle is 2,065 feet. If the airplane weighed 200 lbs. less than maximum gross weight, these distances would be reduced by 30% and become 966 feet and 1,445 feet, respectively. (See NOTE at bottom of chart.)

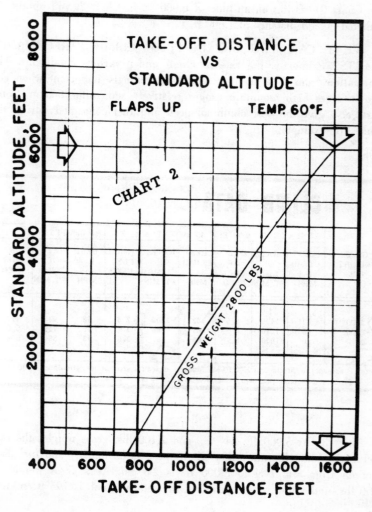

Chart 2: At an elevation of 4,000 ft., 75° F., flaps up, and gross weight of 2,800 lbs., the takeoff distance is 1,600 ft. If you get 1,275 ft., it is because you used the same set of ground rules that you used in Chart 1. Since Chart 2 is based on standard altitude (standard temperature and pressure), you must first convert the elevation (to be completely accurate, the pressure altitude at that elevation) and temperature to a density altitude. A temperature of 75° F. at an elevation (pressure altitude) of 4,000 ft. results in a density altitude of approximately 6,000 ft. (see Chart 9). Using an altitude of 6,000 ft. in Chart 2, you obtain the predicted takeoff distance of 1,600 ft. (75° F. = 24° C.)

WHAT CAN YOU OBTAIN FROM CLIMB PERFORMANCE CHARTS? Primarily, the rate of climb under various conditions. The information from these charts becomes exceedingly important when you have to cross high mountain ranges relatively soon after takeoff. Some charts also give the best climb airspeed and fuel consumed during the climb. For example:

## CLIMB DATA

| GROSS WEIGHT LBS. | AT SEA LEVEL & 59°F. | | | AT 5000 FT. & 41°F. | | | AT 10000 FT. & 23° F. | | |
|---|---|---|---|---|---|---|---|---|---|
| | BEST CLIMB IAS MPH | RATE OF CLIMB FT/MIN | GAL. OF FUEL USED | BEST CLIMB IAS MPH | RATE OF CLIMB FT/MIN | From SL FUEL USED | BEST CLIMB IAS MPH | RATE OF CLIMB FT/MIN | From SL FUEL USED |
| 2100 | 87 | 1470 | 1.5 | 82 | 1200 | 2.8 | 78 | 925 | 4.3 |
| 2400 | 88 | 1210 | 1.5 | 84 | 960 | 3.1 | 80 | 710 | 5.0 |
| 2650 | 90 | 1030 | 1.5 | 86 | 795 | 3.5 | 83 | 560 | 5.9 |

Note: Flaps up, full throttle and 2600 RPM. Mixture leaned for smooth operation above 5000 ft. Fuel used includes warm-up and take-off allowance.

Chart 3: At 5,000 ft., 41° F., and 2,100 lbs. gross weight, the rate of climb is 1,200 ft./min.; best climb speed is 82 m.p.h.; and fuel used to climb from sea level to 5,000 ft. is 2.8 gal. At a gross weight of 2,650 lbs. under the same conditions, the rate of climb is 795 ft./min.

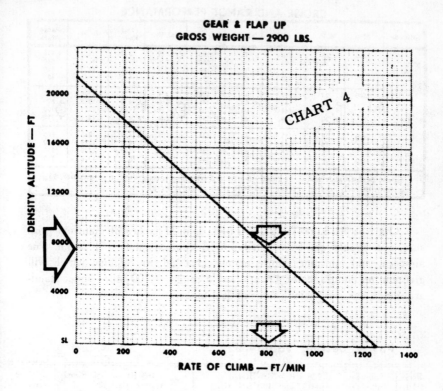

**GEAR & FLAP UP**
**GROSS WEIGHT — 2900 LBS.**

DENSITY ALTITUDE — FT

CHART 4

RATE OF CLIMB — FT/MIN

Chart 4: At 5,000 ft., 86° F., and 2,900 lbs. gross weight, the rate of climb is approximately 810 ft.—not 970 ft. Note that you must first convert the altitude and temperature to a density altitude using the Density Altitude Chart (Chart 9). The density altitude at this altitude and temperature is approximately 7,750 ft. (86° F. = 30° C.)

WHAT CAN YOU OBTAIN FROM CRUISE PERFORMANCE CHARTS? Some of the items you can obtain include recommended power settings at various altitudes, along with percent of brake horsepower at these settings, rate of fuel consumption (gal./hr.), true airspeed, hours of endurance with full tanks, and range in miles under standard conditions and zero wind. Not all of these values are obtainable from all charts. For example:

## CRUISE AND RANGE PERFORMANCE

| Altitude | RPM | M. P. | BHP | %BHP | TAS MPH | Gal/Hr. | End. Hours | Mi/Gal. | Range Miles |
|----------|-----|-------|-----|------|---------|---------|-----------|---------|-------------|
| 5000 | 2450 | 23 | 179 | 78 | 163 | 14.5 | 3.8 | 11.2 | 615 |
|  |  | 22 | 169 | 73 | 159 | 13.6 | 4.0 | 11.7 | 640 |
|  |  | 21 | 161 | 70 | 156 | 13.0 | 4.2 | 12.0 | 660 |
|  |  | 20 | 150 | 65 | 151 | 12.2 | 4.5 | 12.5 | 685 |
|  | 2300 | 23 | 167 | 73 | 158 | 13.4 | 4.1 | 11.8 | 650 |
|  |  | 22 | 158 | 69 | 155 | 12.6 | 4.4 | 12.2 | 675 |
|  |  | 21 | 148 | 64 | 151 | 11.9 | 4.6 | 12.7 | 700 |
|  |  | 20 | 139 | 60 | 146 | 11.2 | 4.9 | 13.1 | 720 |
|  | 2200 | 23 | 157 | 68 | 155 | 12.4 | 4.4 | 12.5 | 685 |
|  |  | 22 | 148 | 64 | 151 | 11.7 | 4.7 | 12.9 | 710 |
|  |  | 21 | 138 | 60 | 146 | 11.0 | 5.0 | 13.3 | 730 |
|  |  | 20 | 131 | 57 | 143 | 10.5 | 5.2 | 13.6 | 750 |

Cruise performance shown is based on standard conditions, zero wind, lean mixture, 55 gallons of fuel, no fuel reserve, and 2650 pounds gross weight.

Chart 5: At 5,000 ft., 2,300 r.p.m., and 21 inches of manifold pressure, you should get 64% rated power, approximately 151 m.p.h. true airspeed, and consume approximately 11.9 gal./hr. of fuel which will give you an endurance of 4.6 hrs. and a range of 700 miles under standard conditions, zero wind, and full fuel tanks.

## Power Setting Table —

| Press. Alt. 1000 Feet | Std. Alt. Temp. °F | 138 HP — 55% Rated Approx. Fuel 10.3 Gal./Hr. RPM AND MAN. PRESS. | | | | 163 HP — 65% Rated Approx. Fuel 12.3 Gal./Hr. RPM AND MAN. PRESS. | | | |
|------|------|------|------|------|------|------|------|------|------|
|  |  | 2100 | 2200 | 2300 | 2400 | 2100 | 2200 | 2300 | 2400 |
| SL | 59 | 21.6 | 20.8 | 20.2 | 19.6 | 24.2 | 23.3 | 22.6 | 22.0 |
| 1 | 55 | 21.4 | 20.6 | 20.0 | 19.3 | 23.9 | 23.0 | 22.4 | 21.8 |
| 2 | 52 | 21.1 | 20.4 | 19.7 | 19.1 | 23.7 | 22.8 | 22.2 | 21.5 |
| 3 | 48 | 20.9 | 20.1 | 19.5 | 18.9 | 23.4 | 22.5 | 21.9 | 21.3 |
| 4 | 45 | 20.6 | 19.9 | 19.3 | 18.7 | 23.1 | 22.3 | 21.7 | 21.0 |
| 5 | 41 | 20.4 | 19.7 | 19.1 | 18.5 | 22.9 | 22.0 | 21.4 | 20.8 |
| 6 | 38 | 20.1 | 19.5 | 18.9 | 18.3 | 22.6 | 21.8 | 21.2 | 20.6 |
| 7 | 34 | 19.9 | 19.2 | 18.6 | 18.0 | 22.3 | 21.5 | 21.0 | 20.4 |
| 9 | 27 | 19.4 | 18.8 | 18.2 | 17.6 | — | 21.3 | 20.7 | 20.1 |
| 8 | 31 | 19.6 | 19.0 | 18.4 | 17.8 | — | — | 20.5 | 19.9 |
| 10 | 23 | 19.1 | 18.6 | 18.0 | 17.4 | — | — | — | 19.6 |

## CHART 6

Chart 6: At 8,000 ft. you can obtain 55% rated power and 10.3 gal./hr. fuel consumption with 2,200 r.p.m. and 19 inches of manifold pressure.

## CRUISE PERFORMANCE

| ALT. | RPM | % BHP | TAS MPH | 58.8 Gal Endurance Hours | 58.8 Gal Range Miles |
|------|-----|-------|---------|--------------------------|----------------------|
| 2500 | 2500 | 75 | 130 | 6.0 | 773 |
|      | 2350 | 63 | 118 | 7.1 | 832 |
|      | 2200 | 53 | 107 | 8.4 | 894 |
| 3500 | 2525 | 75 | 131 | 6.0 | 775 |
|      | 2400 | 65 | 121 | 6.9 | 827 |
|      | 2250 | 55 | 110 | 8.0 | 874 |
| 4500 | 2550 | 75 | 132 | 6.0 | 780 |
|      | 2400 | 63 | 120 | 7.0 | 841 |
|      | 2250 | 53 | 109 | 8.3 | 905 |
| 5500 | 2600 | 77 | 135 | 5.8 | 775 |
|      | 2450 | 65 | 123 | 6.8 | 837 |
|      | 2300 | 55 | 112 | 8.0 | 887 |

## CHART 7

Chart 7: At 5,500 ft. and 2,450 r.p.m., you have 65% rated power, should obtain approximately 123 m.p.h. true airspeed, have an endurance of 6.8 hrs., and a range of 837 miles.

Use cruise performance charts to plan refueling stops. If you learn that your airplane performs differently than predicted by the chart, use this information; especially when performance is worse than predicted by the chart.

## STALL SPEEDS IAS

| CONFIGURATION | 0° | ANGLE OF BANK 20° | 40° | 60° |
|---------------|-----|------|------|------|
| Flaps Up — Power Off | 72 mph | 74 mph | 82 mph | 102 mph |
| Flaps Up — Power On | 69 mph | 71 mph | 79 mph | 98 mph |
| Flaps Down (30°) — Power Off | 64 mph | 66 mph | 73 mph | 91 mph |
| Flaps Down (30°) — Power On | 55 mph | 57 mph | 63 mph | 78 mph |

## CHART 8

**WHAT CAN YOU LEARN FROM STALL SPEED CHARTS?**
Chart 8 is a typical example of a stall speed chart taken from an airplane flight manual. Note and continually be aware of the wide variation in stall speed between straight-and-level flight and various angles of bank. Note that the stall speed in a 60° bank with flaps up and power off (102 m.p.h.) is almost double the stall speed in straight-and-level flight with flaps down and power on (55 m.p.h.). Even with power on in the 60° bank, the stall speed is reduced only 4 m.p.h. to 98 m.p.h. Study this chart and be aware of its significance, especially during traffic patterns and landings. You will find similar charts in any airplane flight manual.

**WHAT CAN YOU OBTAIN FROM LANDING PERFORMANCE CHARTS?** The same type of information that you get from takeoff performance charts—distance required to clear a 50-foot obstacle, length of the ground run, and in some cases, the recommended approach speed on which these figures are based, Landing performance charts will generally be used in the same way as takeoff charts for any given airplane, since each manufacturer usually follows the same format in these two charts. If you can read takeoff charts, you should have no difficulty reading landing charts.

**HOW CAN YOU OBTAIN VALUES FROM PERFORMANCE CHARTS FOR CONDITIONS INTERMEDIATE TO THOSE GIVEN?** By interpolation. For example, in Chart 1 find the ground run required at an elevation 5,000 ft., 72.5°F., zero wind, and maximum gross weight:

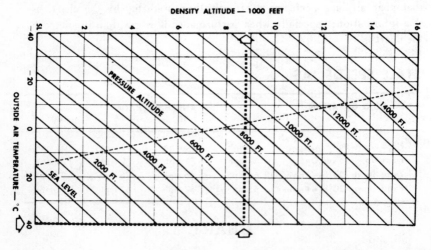

Ground run at 4,000 ft., 75°F., zero wind = 1,380 ft.
Ground run at 5,000 ft., 72.5°F., zero wind =  ? ft.
Ground run at 6,000 ft., 70°F., zero wind = 1,640 ft.

$$1,640 - 1,380 = 260$$
$$\frac{1}{2} \times 260 = 130$$
$$1,380 + 130 = 1,510$$

Since 5,000 ft. is halfway between 4,000 and 6,000 and the temperature is halfway between 75° and 70°, the ground run should be halfway between 1,380 and 1,640, which is 1,510 ft.

Find the distance to clear a 50-foot obstacle at 4,000 ft., 65°F., zero wind, and maximum gross weight:

Distance at 4,000 ft., 45°F., zero wind = 1,810 ft.
Distance at 4,000 ft., 65°F., zero wind =  ? ft.
Distance at 4,000 ft., 75°F., zero wind = 2,065 ft.

$$2,065 - 1,810 = 255$$
$$2/3 \times 255 = 170$$
$$1,810 + 170 = 1,980$$

Since 65° is two-thirds of the way between 45° and 75°, the distance should be two-thirds of the way between 1,810 and 2,065 which is 1,980 ft.

IF INTERPOLATION IS DIFFICULT OR YOU ARE IN DOUBT ABOUT YOUR COMPUTATION, HOW CAN YOU ENSURE BEING ON THE SAFE SIDE? Use a condition more adverse than the one that actually exists—one that you can read directly from the chart without interpolating. Suppose, for example, you were taking off from an airport at an elevation of 5,200 ft. with a 5 m.p.h. headwind, a temperature of 65° F., and maximum gross weight. By using an elevation of 6,000 ft., a zero m.p.h. wind, and 70° F., you can read the takeoff distance directly from Chart 1. The conditions you are using are more adverse than the actual conditions. If the results indicate that takeoff is feasible, then you should have no difficulty taking off under the actual conditions.

Chart 9: Density Altitude Chart. At an elevation of 5,000 ft. (assuming pressure altitude and elevation are identical) and a temperature of 40° C. (104° F.) the density altitude is approximately 8,750 ft.

(NOTE: Charts 1, 3, 5, 6, and 7 are excerpts from charts. Charts 2, 4, 8, and 9 are complete.)

# VFR Pilot Exam-O-Gram No. 45
# Airspeeds and Airspeed Indicator Markings
# (Series 2)

Most FAA written tests contain several test items involving airspeed. Analyses show that many applicants are not knowledgeable concerning airspeeds. The use of performance charts, computation of navigation problems, and filing of flight plans involves the use of true airspeed. However, in various configurations and flight conditions, airplanes are also operated with reference to calibrated airspeed.

WHAT ARE THE DIFFERENT AIRSPEEDS? The four principle airspeeds are defined below.

*Indicated Airspeed* (IAS) is the uncorrected speed read from the airspeed dial. It is the measurement of the difference between impact pressure and atmospheric pressure in the pitot-static system.

*Calibrated Airspeed* (CAS) is indicated airspeed corrected for instrument error and installation error in the pitot-static system. As the aircraft flight attitude or configuration is changed, the airflow in the vicinity of the static inlets may introduce impact pressure into the *static source*, which results in erroneous airspeed indications. The *pitot section* is subject to error at high angles of attack, since the impact pressure entering the system is reduced, when the pitot tube is not parallel to the relative wind. Note in the airspeed correction table the different between indicated and calibrated airspeed in the lower speed ranges. Performance data in aircraft flight manuals is normally based on calibrated airspeed.

| Flaps | IAS | 40 | 50 | 60 | 70 | 80 | 90 | 100 | 110 | 120 | 130 | 140 |
|---|---|---|---|---|---|---|---|---|---|---|---|---|
| Flaps Up | CAS | 55 | 60 | 66 | 72 | 80 | 89 | 98 | 108 | 117 | 127 | 136 |
| Flaps Down | CAS | 52 | 58 | 65 | 73 | 82 | 91 | 101 | — | — | — | — |

*Equivalent Airspeed* (EAS) is calibrated airspeed corrected for compressibility factor. This value is very significant to pilots of high-speed aircraft, but relatively unimportant to pilots operating at speeds below 250 knots at altitudes below 10,000 feet.

*True Airspeed* (TAS) is calibrated airspeed (or equivalent airspeed if applicable) corrected for air density error. TAS is the actual speed of the aircraft through the air mass. Air density error is caused by non-standard pressure and temperature for which the instrument does not automatically compensate. The standard airspeed indicator is calibrated to read correctly only at standard sea level conditions—that is, when the pressure is 29.92 inches Hg and the temperature is 15°C.

HOW IS TRUE AIRSPEED DETERMINED? To find TAS, it is necessary to—(a) work a computer solution, or (b) have in the aircraft an airspeed indicator, similar to the one illustrated, which incorporates

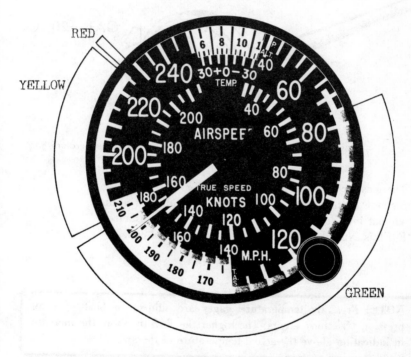

that portion of a computer which is necessary for determining TAS in the cruising speed range. This represents the current trend in the design of flight instruments that reduce pilot workload. In either case, the prerequisites for determining TAS are pressure altitude*, CAS, and outside air temperature.

Example: For a pressure altitude of 6,500 feet, a CAS** of 175 m.p.h., and an outside air temperature (OAT) of +20° C., you would use the instrument as follows: With the adjusting knob, set the pressure altitude (6,500 feet) opposite the OAT (+20°C.). The needle then shows a TAS of 202 m.p.h. while on the inner portion of the dial the needle is registering an IAS of 175 m.p.h. or 152 knots.

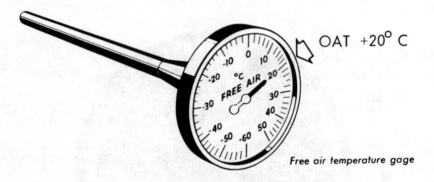

OAT +20° C

Free air temperature gage

*The most accurate method of solving for TAS is by use of pressure altitude. However, you can use indicated altitude without introducing too great an error in most instances.
**For this example the IAS and CAS are assumed equal.

NOTE: Free air temperature gages are subject to heat of compression (friction) errors. The higher the TAS the more the increase in indication above the actual temperature of the air.

DO SOME INSTRUMENTS AUTOMATICALLY REGISTER TRUE AIRSPEED? Yes, more advanced true airspeed indicators contain components which correct for pressure altitude, OAT, and compressability to automatically provide TAS without computations on the part of the pilot.

WHAT ADDITIONAL AIRSPEED INDICATOR MARKINGS ARE REQUIRED IN MULTI-ENGINE AIRPLANES? FAR Part 23, which deals with Airworthiness Standards for airplanes of 12,500 lbs. or less, was amended November 11, 1965, to require the following airspeed markings in multi-engine airplanes: (a) a *blue radial line* to show the best rate of climb speed (V_y) with one-engine-inoperative. (b) a *red radial line* to show (V_mc) the minimum control speed with one-engine-inoperative. Note in the following illustration that these markings for key speeds in multi-engine airplanes are *in addition* to those normally required for other airplanes.

WHICH MULTI-ENGINE AIRPLANES ARE REQUIRED TO HAVE THESE MARKINGS? Only those airplanes which were type certificated under Part 23 on or after November 11, 1965, are required to have these markings. However, airplanes type certificated before that date may also be so marked at the option of the owner.

NOTE: THE COLORED MARKINGS ON AIRSPEED INDICATORS ARE BASED ON *CAS*, NOT *IAS*.

# VRF Pilot Exam-O-Gram* No. 48

## Midair Collisions (Series #3)

Compliance with flight rules prescribed in FAR Part 91 and adherence to good operating practices listed in the Airman's Information Manual, will materially reduce the possibility of pilots becoming involved in midair collisions. General aviation written tests contain test items on FARs that are related to midair collisions. Unfortunately, too many pilots look upon the FARs merely as a disagreeable requirement for passing a written test and do not associate FARs with their everyday flying.

In 1968, 2,230 incidents were reported under the FAA "Near Midair Collision Study Program." Of these, 1,128 were "hazardous" in that the aircraft missed only by chance or after one or both pilots took evasive action. The present phenomenal growth in number of aircraft and hours flown in U.S. civil aviation, is rapidly increasing the midair collision problem.

The National Transportation Safety Board special accident prevention study entitled "Midair Collisions in U.S. Civil Aviation - 1968," lists 38 midair collisions involving 76 aircraft. In preparing this Exam-O-Gram, a study was made of 31 of the general aviation accident reports of midair collisions that occurred in 1968 and 23 reports of midairs which occurred prior to October in 1969.

This Exam-O-Gram attempts to show pictorially, where and how some midairs have occurred, as well as other places where the midair hazard may strike again. All pilots should become aware of and exercise every precaution against, the midair collision potentials at controlled high-density terminal arrival and departure areas. The photographs above show how rapidly a jet on takeoff can become a real hazard to another airplane cruising at 2,000 feet above the ground near a busy airport.

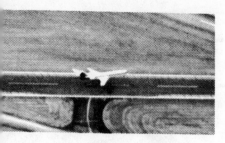

JET ON ROTATION                    15 SECONDS LATER

60 SECONDS AFTER TAKEOFF AND
PASSING THROUGH 2,000' AGL

**WHAT COLLISION PRECAUTIONS SHOULD YOU TAKE FOR CROSS COUNTRY FLIGHTS?** In preflight planning, check the special general and area notices and special graphics notices of AIM and the aeronautical charts to determine if the proposed route passes through a restricted area, oil burner route, intensive student jet training area, etc.

Have any fatal midairs happened as depicted in the following illustration? *The answer is YES!*

Even though the formation of jets is in a steep climb, they are climbing at 365 knots IAS (420 mph).

9,500 ' MSL

## FLYING NEAR A MILITARY AIRFIELD.

### • Heavy Traffic Around Military Fields

Pilots are advised to exercise vigilance when in close proximity to most military airports. These airports may have jet aircraft traffic patterns extending up to 2,500 feet above the surface. In addition, they may have an unusually heavy concentration of jet aircraft operating within a 25 nautical mile radius and from the surface to all altitudes. This precautionary note also applies to the larger civil airports.

NOTE: When turning a high-wing airplane the pilot lowers the wing and thus hides the area into which he is turning. In a low-wing airplane, the cabin roof hides the area into which the pilot is turning—especially in right turns.

Pilots of high-wing and low-wing airplanes can be in each other's blind spots. Collisions of this type have happened most frequently in the traffic patterns at uncontrolled airports. Collisions like this can occur:

(a) on the entry leg of the pattern when the low-wing airplane descends on top of the other airplane; (b) on the downwind leg of the pattern with one of the airplanes flying at an improper pattern altitude—that is, the high-wing airplane climbs or the low-wing airplane descends to return to the desired altitude; (c) on final approach or just before touchdown.

When there is a slower airplane ahead of you in the pattern flying about 100 feet lower than your altitude, it is possible to overtake and never see the slower airplane hidden beneath the nose of your aircraft. Remember, the silhouette of an airplane below the horizon tends to blend with, and be lost in, the surrounding landscape features.

---

*OTHER ACTUAL MIDAIRS*
1—Two solo students· departed on the same cross-country flight and ran together while looking at their charts.
2—One airplane descended on top of a white colored airplane which blended with the snow covered terrain.

---

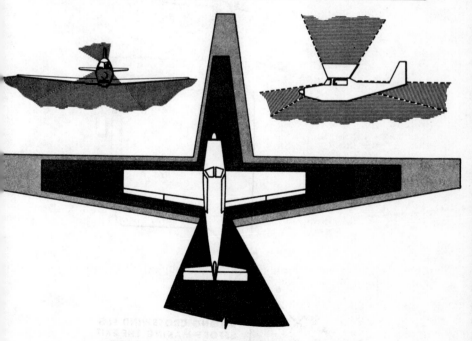

**THE BLIND SPOTS WIDEN AND EXTEND
TO INFINITY AS SHOWN ABOVE**

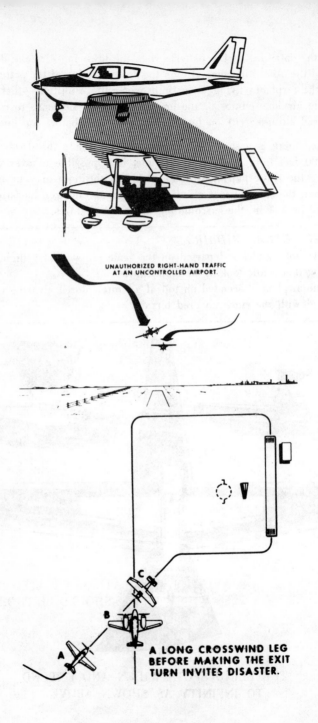

UNAUTHORIZED RIGHT-HAND TRAFFIC
AT AN UNCONTROLLED AIRPORT.

A LONG CROSSWIND LEG
BEFORE MAKING THE EXIT
TURN INVITES DISASTER.

**WHEN HAS THIS TYPE COLLISION OCCURRED?** It usually happens when one pilot is flying the traffic pattern in an unauthorized direction. Of the cases studied, there were three midairs involved with one of the pilots in each incident flying a right hand pattern while a left hand pattern was in use—and still another midair involved a pilot flying a left hand base leg in noncompliance with the published right hand traffic. The use of UNICOM at uncontrolled airports can make flying around them safer. Even though there is no UNICOM station or Flight Service Station in operation at some of these airports, you can alert other pilots of your presence by announcing your position in the pattern on appropriate frequencies. This subject is covered in Part 1 of AIM under "Traffic Advisories at Nontower Airports."

Of the accident reports studied, there were eight midairs elsewhere in the pattern (entry, exit, downwind, etc.). One fatal accident occurred when a student and his instructor in a light aircraft were leaving the pattern and collided with a multi-engine aircraft on the downwind leg (as represented by airplanes *B* and *C*).

This illustration also shows how an airplane making a pattern entry to the downwind leg could collide head-on with another airplane that has flown a *long crosswind leg before making the exit turn*. (See airplanes *A* and *C*).

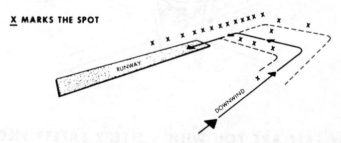

**X MARKS THE SPOT**

APPROXIMATE POSITION OF MID-AIR COLLISIONS THAT OCCURED DURING 1968 IN THE DOWN-WIND, BASE-LEG AND FINAL APPROACH.

SOME FEDERAL AVIATION REGULATIONS RELATED TO MID-AIR COLLISIONS WITH WHICH PILOTS SHOULD BE THOROUGH-LY FAMILIAR AND ADHERE TO, INCLUDE: 91.9, Careless and Reckless Operation; 91.11, Liquor and Drugs; 91.65, Operating Near Other Aircraft; 91.67, Right-of-Way Rules; 91.70, Aircraft Speed; 91.87, Operation at Airports with Operating Control Towers; 91.89, Operation at Airports Without Control Towers; and 61.73, General Limitations.

\* \* \* \* \*

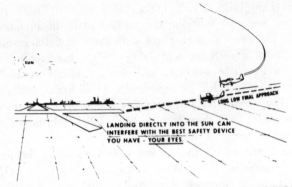

LANDING DIRECTLY INTO THE SUN CAN INTERFERE WITH THE BEST SAFETY DEVICE YOU HAVE - YOUR EYES.

## SITUATIONS CONDUCIVE TO MIDAIR COLLISIONS

Constant vigilance is a *must* when practicing pylon 8's, low level ground track maneuvers like "turns about a point," or "S turns across a road."

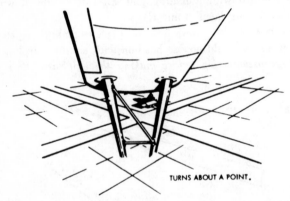

TURNS ABOUT A POINT.

## HOW SAFE ARE YOU WITH A SLEEPY SAFETY PILOT ?

ARE CLEARING PROCEDURES HELPFUL IN REDUCING AIR-CRAFT COLLISION POTENTIAL? Yes, pilots should execute gentle banks, left and right, when climbing or descending, rather than spending long periods of time climbing and descending straight ahead. The AIM good operating procedures state in part: "Appropriate clearing procedures should precede the execution of all turns including chandelles, lazy eights, stalls, slow flight, climbs, straight-and-level, spins, and other combination maneuvers." Personnel of the FAA flight instructor refresher unit, are recommending that trainees of the flight instructor refresher clinics teach the use of clearing turns prior to the execution of certain maneuvers. They suggest: 90° clearing turns, 180° clearing turns, or whatever clearing is deemed necessary to ascertain that the area is clear before performing any maneuver. They also stress that there should be no delay in entering a maneuver upon completion of the clearing turns. This can be accomplished by performing the necessary conditions of flight (reducing airspeed, adding carburetor heat, etc.) while in the clearing turns.

OPERATING FROM AN UNCONTROLLED AIRPORT
ON DIFFERENT RUNWAYS.

CLOSED CURTAINS ARE NICE FOR THE PASSENGERS,
BUT THEY DON'T IMPROVE THE VISIBILITY.

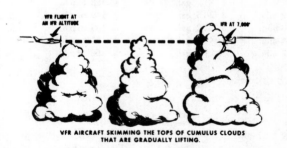

VFR FLIGHT AT
AN VFR ALTITUDE

VFR AT 7,000'

VFR AIRCRAFT SKIMMING THE TOPS OF CUMULUS CLOUDS
THAT ARE GRADUALLY LIFTING.

For several decades military flying schools have taught their pilots to perform at least one 180° clearing turn in each direction before entering such maneuvers as spins, Cuban 8's, Immelmans, etc., where considerable altitude changes are involved.

# APPENDIX II — ANSWERS TO EXERCISES

*Exercise No. 1—*

| WCA | TH | GS (m.p.h.) |
|---|---|---|
| 1. 14° L | 226° | 124 |
| 2. 6° L | 254° | 115 |
| 3. 6° R | 266° | 178 |
| 4. 6° L | 344° | 107 |
| 5. 6° L | 94° | 191 |
| 6. 12° R | 142° | 147 |

*Exercise No. 2—*

| Takeoff distance | Rate of climb |
|---|---|
| 1. 930 ft. | 602 f.p.m. |
| 2. 1,144 ft. | 469 f.p.m. |
| 3. 1,750 ft. | 319 f.p.m. |
| 4. 1,925 ft. | 280 f.p.m. |

*Exercise No. 3—*

| | Ground Run (feet) | To clear 50-foot (feet) |
|---|---|---|
| 1. | 75 | 260 |
| 2. | 1,062 | 2,019 |
| 3. | 310 | 700 |
| 4. | 666 | 1,296 |
| 5. | 325 | 730 |

*Exercise No. 4—*

| TAS | Gal./hr. | Flight Time |
|---|---|---|
| 1. 158 | 14.2 | 3:52 |
| 2. 151 | 11.7 | 3:51 |
| 3. 107 | 7.0 | 3:34 |
| 4. 105 | 7.0 | 3:34 |
| 5. 158 | 13.4 | 3:44 |

*Exercise No. 5—*

1. 2 hrs. 20 min.
2. 2 hrs. 36 min.
3. 1 hr. 28 min.
4. 2 hrs. 24 min.
5. 26 min.
6. 19 min.

*Exercise No. 6—*

1. 150 m.p.h.
2. 120 m.p.h.
3. 98 m.p.h.
4. 108 m.p.h.
5. 120 m.p.h.
6. 154 m.p.h.

*Exercise No. 7—*

1. 4 hrs.
2. 5 hrs. 19 min.
3. 5 hrs. 18 min.
4. 4 hrs. 14 min.
5. 2 hrs. 52 min.

*Exercise No. 8—*

1. 21 gal.
2. 38.5 gal.
3. 22.2 gal.
4. 43.7 gal.
5. 71 gal.

*Exercise No. 9—*

1. 128 m.p.h.
2. 149 m.p.h.
3. 155 m.p.h.
4. 165 m.p.h.
5. 160 m.p.h.

*Exercise No. 10-*

1. 23 m.p.h.
2. 18.4 m.p.h.
3. 30 m.p.h.
4. 46 m.p.h.
5. 54 m.p.h.

*Exercise No. 11—*

| WCA | TH | GS (m.p.h.) |
|---|---|---|
| 1. 10° R | 020° | 150 |
| 2. 0° | 267° | 164 |
| 3. 6° L | 039° | 143 |
| 4. 15° R | 155° | 131 |
| 5. 9° L | 111° | 122 |